Policing a Free Society

Policing a Free Society

Herman Goldstein
University of Wisconsin—Madison

Ballinger Publishing Company • Cambridge, Massachusetts
A Subsidiary of J. B. Lippincott Company

Prepared in part under Grant Number 74NI-99-0037 from the National Institute of Law Enforcement and Criminal Justice, Law Enforcement Assistance Administration, U.S. Department of Justice. Points of view or opinions stated in this document are those of the author and do not necessarily represent the official position or policies of the U.S. Department of Justice.

International Standard Book Number: 0-88410-216-5

Library of Congress Catalog Card Number: 76-13589

Printed in the United States of America

Library of Congress Cataloging in Publication Data

Goldstein, Herman, 1931–
   Policing a free society.

   1. Police. 2. Criminal justice, Administration of. I. Title.
HV7921.G65   363.2   76-13589
ISBN 0-88410-216-5

To my wife, Shulamit
and our children
Mark, David, and Rahel

Contents

✳

Preface

The most critical issues that arise in the policing of our society have not received the attention they require. It is true that public interest in the police and their problems increased dramatically in the past decade and, as a consequence, both the human and the financial resources devoted to working on them have been expanded tremendously. But this new interest and the increased investment of resources have been consumed for the most part in addressing issues and effecting changes that do not get at the problems of central importance in the struggle to improve the quality of police service.

The primary objective of this book, which is addressed to those concerned with improving police service, is to penetrate beyond the matters that have tended to preoccupy both the police and citizens interested in police operations—to thereby direct attention to the fundamental issues that must be faced. My hope is that a work that dwells on these issues and that demonstrates their relationship to the day-to-day problems of policing will promote more intensive consideration of them.

The pressures to deal in an isolated manner with specific problems and proposals for change in the police field are great and have often been misleading. A major goal of this work, therefore, has been to present a comprehensive, integrated framework for viewing the police and their problems. Developed through the course of the book, this framework is intended to facilitate exploration of the major issues that have been identified, to clarify the relationship of these issues to each other, and to provide a basis for critically reexamining some of the more traditional areas in which efforts to improve police operations have been concentrated in the past.

So ambitious an effort draws upon one's total experience with the police and with police problems. In acknowledging the help I have received, therefore,

I wish to make special note of my gratitude to the late O. W. Wilson. Having stimulated my initial interest in policing, "O.W." subsequently arranged for me to participate in a major research project on the police, provided me with a unique opportunity to acquire administrative experience in a large urban police agency, and encouraged me to develop my own critical perspectives of policing from an academic base. I owe much to having been associated with him.

Work on this book was first undertaken as part of the program of research and teaching in law enforcement and criminal justice administration supported by a grant from the Ford Foundation to the University of Wisconsin Law School. This program, now fully integrated into the law school, enabled me to engage in numerous activities that have helped sharpen my understanding of the police and to organize my materials into initial drafts. Summer support from the university's graduate school made it possible for me to examine specific issues in detail. And a grant from the National Institute of Law Enforcement and Criminal Justice provided the time, free from other duties, that was required to complete the drafting of the materials and to prepare them for publication. I appreciate the confidence these institutions have displayed in me and the commitment to the importance of work in this field that their support reflects.

A number of individuals with different areas of expertise and with varying perspectives on police problems reviewed early drafts of some of the chapters. Egon Bittner, David C. Couper, Gary P. Hayes, Robert M. Igleburger, Hervey A. Juris, Otto B. Kreuzer, Henry J. Sandman, Frank A. Schubert, Lawrence M. Sherman, Frank P. Sherwood, and Robert Wasserman all offered helpful comments and suggestions. In addition to reviewing the early drafts, Mark Furstenberg and Thomas J. Sweeney gave many hours of their time to providing a detailed critique of the final draft of the entire manuscript. Frank J. Remington, by his presence on the law school faculty, has been a ready source of encouragement and sound advice. I am deeply grateful to each of these individuals. But since I did not always accept their advice, I rush to assert that I alone, of course, am responsible for whatever errors or omissions may be found in the text.

I was blessed, in preparing the manuscript for publication, with an unusually dedicated team of assistants. As a student researcher in the last stages of the project, G. Stephen Long painstakingly checked numerous sources of information, prepared citations, and compiled the bibliographies. Elizabeth Uhr greatly improved the manuscript with her keen eye and good editorial judgment. And Lucille Hamre made many valuable suggestions as she exercised her usual care and precision in transforming rough copy into cleanly typed drafts.

I owe a special note of thanks to the staff of the law school's Criminal Justice Reference and Information Center. My intensive use of the center throughout this project has impressed me anew with the superb job they have done in building and indexing so comprehensive a collection of materials relating to the police.

H.G.

Madison, Wisconsin
March, 1976

Chapter 1

The Basic Problems

The police, by the very nature of their function, are an anomaly in a free society. They are invested with a great deal of authority under a system of government in which authority is reluctantly granted and, when granted, sharply curtailed. The specific form of their authority—to arrest, to search, to detain, and to use force—is awesome in the degree to which it can be disruptive of freedom, invasive of privacy, and sudden and direct in its impact upon the individual. And this awesome authority, of necessity, is delegated to individuals at the lowest level of the bureaucracy, to be exercised, in most instances without prior review and control.

Yet a democracy is heavily dependent upon its police, despite their anomalous position, to maintain the degree of order that makes a free society possible. It looks to its police to prevent people from preying on one another; to provide a sense of security; to facilitate movement; to resolve conflicts; and to protect the very processes and rights—such as free elections, freedom of speech, and freedom of assembly—on which continuation of a free society depends. The strength of a democracy and the quality of life enjoyed by its citizens are determined in large measure by the ability of the police to discharge their duties.

UNEVEN DEVELOPMENT OF THE POLICE

Important as the responsibilities of the police are in a free society, it is ironic that we as a nation have given so little attention—on a continuing basis and in a positive fashion—to the provisions made for carrying them out. The police function has not been the subject of systematic study until quite recently. Public interest in the inner workings of a police agency—its administration, policies, practices, and the laws under which it operates—has, for the most part, been in response to revelations of police wrongdoing or to a sudden realization that police services provided in the past were not adequate to meet the needs of the present. Several waves of public concern over the police have swept across the entire country, as was the case when the national commission that documented use of the third degree reported its findings in the 1930s.[1] But most spurts of public interest in the police have resulted from local events, such as an exposé of corruption or other wrongdoing. Improvement in police operations, therefore, has come to depend heavily upon local standards and on the ability of local institutions to call police inadequacies to public attention. This accounts, in large measure, for the slow and uneven development of the American police.

While improvements in policing have usually resulted from revelations of wrongdoing or the documentation of inadequacies, it does not follow that public dissatisfaction has always produced change. With monotonous regularity, peaks of interest in the police have been followed—at both the national and local levels —by the appointment of a group of citizens to examine the specific problem that has surfaced and to make recommendations for dealing with it. In the heat of the moment, the appointment of such a group has often, by itself, been sufficient to reduce public anxiety. And with a reduction in public anxiety, public interest begins to fade so that, by the time the study is completed, support to implement its recommendations is lacking.

Where public concern has led to efforts to improve police operations, both police practitioners and citizen study groups have placed a great deal of confidence in a uniform scheme for developing a "perfect" police agency—now commonly referred to as the professional model. This model results from the work of August Vollmer, Bruce Smith, O. W. Wilson, and those police administrators who followed their lead. It is based on the commitment made in the early history of policing in this country to organize police agencies along military lines as well as the commitment made in the early part of this century to insulate police administration from the influence of partisan politics. The professional model stresses operating efficiency, to be achieved by centralized control, clean-cut lines of organization, fuller and more effective use of police personnel, greater mobility, improved training, and increased use of equipment and technology. It also emphasizes the need for integrity and higher education for police personnel. Since the 1950s, Los Angeles has often been cited as the best example of a larger police agency whose organization and operations most fully conform with the model. And it was with the objective of implementing this model that O. W. Wilson himself took on the task in 1960 of reorganizing the Chicago Police Department.

Advances in the professional model during the early 1960s consisted, for the most part, of improvements in police technology. Dazzling developments in radio communications and in the application of the computer to the processing of police data enabled the agencies that were most progressive, according to prevailing standards, to make even further strides toward achieving a higher level of operating efficiency. Records systems were dramatically improved, centralized control of police personnel was tightened, and, as a consequence, the amount of time that elapsed between the receipt of a call for assistance and the arrival of a police officer on the scene was greatly reduced.

Not all agencies, however, adopted the professional model. Reflecting a continuation of the uneven development of the police, many agencies, including some of the largest, had not yet taken the most elementary steps—in the early 1960s—toward upgrading their operations. Some remained mired in local politics. Some were hampered by corruption. And others were so steeped in the traditional methods of operating that they lacked the initiative to make the minimal improvements required to keep up with the times. So as late as 1965 many police departments were not providing any systematic training for their personnel; were sadly lacking in the most basic equipment; were making extremely inefficient use of their manpower; and continued to follow obsolete and cumbersome procedures in their daily operations. These conditions were the target of attack of those committed to police reform in 1965, as the police entered a decade in which unprecedented demands were to be made upon them and as a wave of nationwide interest in their operations led to still another cycle of study and reform.

THE EXPERIENCE OF THE PAST DECADE

New Pressures

Each of the major problems for which the police have traditionally been held responsible has increased significantly in this past decade. The incidence of violent crime has risen sharply and continues to climb. The corresponding increase in the fear of crime has resulted in mounting pressure on the police to provide security—often at the cost of dealing more directly with the crime problem.

The Watts riot in the summer of 1965 signaled the beginning of the large-scale disorders that were to occur in cities throughout the country over the next several years. Urban rioting, while not a new phenomenon, was new for this generation of police personnel. The most immediate challenge, for the police, was to bring the riots under control while minimizing loss of life, injury, and property damage. Additionally, because the riots were a form of protest against a whole range of problems and injustices that plague our society, the police were pressured into examining aspects of their own operations that may have contributed to the widespread discontent of minority groups in urban areas.

Through much of the past decade, demonstrations of various forms against both private interests and government policies have taxed police resources to the maximum degree. The civil-rights marches for integration of public facilities, for fair employment practices, and for open occupancy, in retrospect caused relatively minor problems compared to the subsequent demonstrations, staged primarily by college students, against the war in Vietnam. Some of the most radical groups that emerged in this period of racial and political unrest engaged in terrorist-type activities. Terrorist bombings continue.

With the end of the war, fewer demonstrations have been staged; but those which have occurred, such as over busing as a way of correcting racial imbalance in the public schools, remind us that the most agonizing consequences of rapid social change continue to be the responsibility of the police.

While endeavoring to meet all of these new demands on their time and resources, the police themselves have become subject to much closer scrutiny and to much more frequent challenge than at any time in the past. The charge has often been made that a good deal of the unrest—especially in the depressed areas of large cities—results from police practices of questionable legality and propriety that have evolved over the years. The volume of complaints against individual police officers has skyrocketed, as has the number of civil actions brought against them.[2]

In addition to meeting this criticism from outside, police administrators have had to learn to cope with the increased militancy of their own personnel. Police unions and the assertion by officers—collectively and individually—of newly acquired rights have introduced still another complex and often conflicting element into the array of pressures brought to bear upon police agencies. In some jurisdictions, problems of labor-management relations are so complicated that they have become the chief's predominant concern.

Thus, for most of the decade, the police—especially in the larger cities—have been operating under tremendous pressure in an atmosphere of almost continual crisis. Their concern, of necessity, has often been limited to surviving the summer, the week, or even the day without serious incident. Their success, in the eyes of the public, has depended much more on their response to immediate needs than on their plans for the future.

The Police Response

The quality of the police response to these pressures has varied a great deal between one jurisdiction and another, and often even within the same jurisdiction over a period of time. Officers in some agencies have been careful not to exceed their authority, while ill-trained personnel in other agencies have operated with little regard for the dignity and rights of individual citizens. Some departments have done unusually well in apprehending serious offenders, while others have done poorly. Citizens in many communities have received a rapid, courteous, and helpful response to all requests for police service, while inefficiency, discourtesy, and apathy have been the norm elsewhere. Some police officers in the inner core of a large city have won accolades for the manner in which they have provided assistance in solving the endless array of complicated problems they encounter; others have incurred the wrath of the community by their aggressive behavior. Similar variations were apparent in the police response to demonstrations. Whereas some departments handled the protests of recent years with judgment and restraint, others responded in ways that escalated rather than diminished the level of violence.

Even though the police response varied, generalizations can be made. It has become very clear that the capacity of even the most highly developed and sophisticated agency to cope with violent crimes has been vastly overrated. It is obvious, too, that the aura of omnipotence which the police cultivate and upon which much of their effectiveness depends is of little value in direct and highly visible confrontation with massive demonstrations and civil disorder. Perhaps most important is the realization that even some of the best-staffed agencies lack the kind of understanding, sensitivity, and commitment that is required if they are to deal effectively with the tensions and conflict of social change and political dissent.

Unfortunately, political leaders who made the major decisions involving police personnel in the last ten years were not well informed about the actual capabilities of the police. As a consequence the police were frequently committed to achieving goals that were beyond their ability. They were called upon to "banish" all crime; to prevent looting in the middle of a riot; and to enforce certain laws in the face of massive violation. In the period from 1964 to 1971, for example, local officials, inexperienced in quelling large-scale disturbances and naive about police capabilities, repeatedly committed their police personnel to responding to the requests of equally naive college administrators for assistance in clearing campus buildings or ending some other form of campus disruption. What was surprising was not that the police performance was frequently poor, but rather that the police did as well as they did, given their lack of preparation for the task and the limited capacity of even the best-prepared agencies to handle such conflicts.

Proposals for Improvement

Within a period of just five years (1965-1970), four presidential commissions were appointed to explore problems relating to the police: The President's Commission on Law Enforcement and Administration of Justice, sometimes referred to as the President's Crime Commission (1965); the National Advisory Commission on Civil Disorders (1967); the National Commission on the Causes and Prevention of Violence (1968); and the President's Commission on Campus Unrest (1970).[3] These were followed in 1971 by creation of the National Advisory Commission on Criminal Justice Standards and Goals.[4] Each commission, in the context of dealing with the problem for which it was created, underscored the importance of the police role, documented the need for change, and offered specific agendas for improving police functioning.

At the local level, commissions appointed by governors and mayors in response to increased concern over crime and civil disorders produced additional volumes that replicated and supplemented the studies and recommendations produced by the nationally sponsored groups. Local jurisdictions are now conducting additional studies to determine how the provisions they have made for police service relate to the standards set forth by the most recent national commission.

Many of the specific recommendations for improving the police—especially those made by the President's Crime Commission and the National Advisory Commission on Criminal Justice Standards and Goals—called for more widespread adoption of programs and changes associated with the professional model of policing. These two commissions, in particular, gave added impetus to some specific suggestions, such as the more effective use of police personnel and, most emphatically, the requirement that police officers have some college education. Responding to the racial and political turmoil of the decade, all of the studies went beyond previous proposals for implementing the professional model by recommending that the police develop more humanitarian responses to the problems they were called upon to handle and thereby improve relationships with the community. They advocated programs to facilitate communication between individual officers and the residents of the areas they policed; to recruit more members of minority groups into police service; to eliminate practices that were offensive; and to provide greater help to citizens requesting police assistance. The commissions also began to deal with some of the more basic problems in the police field. They urged the police to view their function in broader terms; to acknowledge the discretion they exercised and subject it to control by a system of policy-making; and to develop methods more satisfactory than the criminal justice system for handling some aspects of the police job.

Implementation and Assessment

In contrast with the studies of prior years, the cycle of concern, study, and proposed reform of this past decade has led to a tremendous surge of activity made possible chiefly by the availability of federal funds, first from the Office of Law Enforcement Assistance, created in 1965, and, since 1968, from the Law Enforcement Assistance Administration (LEAA), created under the Omnibus Crime Control and Safe Streets Act.[5] The planning agencies established under the provisions of the act have greatly multiplied the number of individuals who design and administer programs to improve the criminal justice system, including the police. In addition, LEAA has directly financed many projects and research efforts in an attempt to respond to the needs identified by the various studies as well as those revealed by its own more recent inquiries.[6] And yet, although federal funds, augmented by matching expenditures by state and local governments, have been used for a variety of innovative programs, many of which are described subsequently in this book, the vast bulk of the new resources allocated to the police has been used to enable police agencies to acquire the long-established elements of the professional model, such as communications equipment, computers, vehicles, specialized units, and limited forms of training and education.

As police agencies continue to strive for increased operating efficiency, there is satisfaction in many quarters that this, by itself, is a worthwhile goal. Many of the specific improvements police seek to implement—such as providing a quick response to a citizen's call for assistance—are extremely important. But just as the reports of the several recent commissions reveal a new interest in exploring beyond the standard formulas of reform, an increasing number of people have come to express dissatisfaction with the professional model and its commitment to efficiency as the *ultimate* goal of police reform. They are disappointed with current efforts and uncertain how future resources should be invested.[7]

Among the factors contributing to present doubts is the realization that police agencies that have adopted major elements of the professional model have not been demonstrably more effective in handling the increased demands made upon them. Admittedly, it is difficult to define and measure effectiveness. But broad indicators make it clear, for example, that some of the most "modernized" departments have had even more difficulty than the more traditional departments in handling demonstrations and disturbances. Most analysts of police operations contend that the success of the streamlined departments in preventing crime and apprehending offenders has not been markedly different from that of other agencies.[8] And even where it appears that the professional departments achieve more effective control over their personnel, it is not clear that this always results in an improvement in the quality of police service.

For all its merit, the professional model as applied in some jurisdictions has led to a highly impersonal kind of policing that is ill suited to today's needs. Although individual officers have gained reputations for honesty, intelligence, and efficiency, some of the departments have taken on a rigidity and uniformity in their operations that result in limiting their ability to respond effectively to the needs of the communities they serve. The emphasis that the professional model places upon mechanical improvements, in particular, has created problems. In the absence of other changes, the acquisition of modern equipment and technology has led both the police and the public to assume that some agencies have a potential effectiveness far in excess of their actual capacity.

A second reason for disappointment with recent reforms is that new programs are frequently not solving the problems for which they were devised. This is the view, in particular, of those police administrators who, following the suggestions of some of the commissions, have sought to introduce new values to policing through programs intended to increase the sensitivity of the police to the delicate nature of the police function; to develop a greater appreciation of the need for adherence to legal standards; to improve relations with minority groups; and to achieve more effective control over police conduct.

One often finds that such programs are subverted in the process of being implemented so that the intentions of those initiating them are not realized. Many police agencies, for example, have committed themselves to elaborate police-community relations programs with the avowed purpose of facilitating two-way communication with the community. But these programs have tended to turn into public-relations projects. The new position of police legal advisor was seen by some as a way of injecting a fresh new perspective into the decision-making processes of a police agency. Police agencies, however, have filled these newly created positions with individuals who see their role as defending rather than challenging agency practices and policies. Likewise, the programs to improve recruitment, to strengthen training, and to encourage college study have usually failed to carry out the intentions of those who most vigorously advocated them.

In fact, despite all of the changes that have been made, most of the problems from which the police field has long suffered remain. The need for stronger, more broadly based, and more articulate leadership continues to be critical. The unwillingness of administrators to deal more aggressively and forthrightly with wrongdoing and corruption invites outside controls. The closed character of police agencies and the defensive posture police have assumed continue to stand in the way of meaningful reform. Except for a relatively small number of notable breakthroughs, the police have generally been reluctant to challenge existing practices, to conduct research, and to engage in experimentation. As a consequence the field itself has demonstrated little ability to come up with new and more effective ways for coping with the complex problems it must handle.[9]

WHY IMPROVEMENTS IN THE POLICE HAVE BEEN LIMITED IN THEIR IMPACT

Why have recent efforts not produced more satisfying results? Why are those police agencies that are most advanced, based on prevailing standards, not consistently more effective in delivering quality police service? Why do some of the most modernized agencies suffer internally from some of the same problems experienced by the agencies that have resisted the professional model? And why do new programs so seldom accomplish their objectives?

The answer, I believe, is that we have been preoccupied with building a superstructure without having laid an adequate foundation; that the whole reform movement in policing has been shortsighted in focusing almost exclusively on improving the police establishment (its organization, staffing, equipment, and so on) without having given adequate attention to some serious underlying problems that grow out of the basic arrangements for policing in our society. Paramount among these are the ambiguity surrounding the police function and the numerous conflicts and contradictions inherent in police operations.

Most efforts to improve police functioning have gone forward on the assumption that the prevention of crime and the apprehension of criminals are the primary tasks of the police. But these assumptions have been based more on the mythology surrounding policing than upon an accurate assessment of what it is that police do. The police themselves perpetuate this myth. As a result, individuals are recruited into the field who may possess the characteristics required for dealing with criminals, but not necessarily the abilities that are essential for carrying out the multitude of other police tasks. The training they receive, which in the past has usually been based on the same stereotype of policing, does not provide instruction on how to deal with the incidents police most commonly handle. Many other aspects of police operations and management are affected by the same misconceptions.

The contrast between what the police actually do and the provisions made for staffing and directing the police agency is but one of a jumble of contradictions and conflicts within which the police must work. As one delves more deeply into the various factors that shape police functioning, one finds that laws, public expectations, and the realities of the tasks in which the police are engaged require all kinds of compromises and often place the police in a no-win situation. Consider, for example, the following:

Statutes usually require—and much of the public, in theory, expects—the police to enforce all of the laws all of the time. Yet the public will not tolerate full enforcement of many laws, and the police would be held up to ridicule were they to attempt full enforcement.

The public holds the police responsible for preventing crime and apprehending all criminals, and the police endeavor to live up to this expectation. But the police, omnipotent as they may seem, are in reality extremely limited in their ability to cope with crime.

The police are expected and equipped to act in a coercive authoritarian manner in some situations. The same officers, however, must also be capable of being supportive and friendly in the vast majority of circumstances in which they become involved.

The image that the police seek to project is one of complete neutrality, achieved by uniform objective application of their authority. But the incredible array of circumstances with which they must deal demands all kinds of flexibility in their day-to-day operations.

The police have come to be viewed as capable of handling every emergency. In reality, however, they have neither the authority nor the resources to deal effectively with much of the business that comes their way.

Policing is grounded on the existence of a system of criminal justice that operates with reasonable effectiveness in adjudicating guilt and in imposing sanctions upon those found guilty. But the system as it exists in many communities today—and especially in the large urban areas—is so overcrowded and disorganized that it is capable of neither achieving justice nor administering punishment.

And finally, there is the basic pervasive conflict between crime-fighting and constitutional due process which is inherent in the police function in a free society. The police are expected to deal aggressively with criminal conduct, but must do so in accordance with procedures that prohibit them from engaging in practices which—from the standpoint of poorly informed citizens—appear to be most expeditious and potentially most effective.

If both legal mandates and public expectations are taken literally, and if the reality of the situations that the police confront is recognized, the demands on the police appear so contradictory that the police task is simply unworkable—an impossible mission. A number of police administrators have made modest efforts during the past several years to recognize the broad nature of the police function, to recognize police discretion, and to develop alternatives to the criminal process —all of which have been intended to reach these underlying problems. But the vast majority of the improvements that have been made in the police establishment have had no effect upon these basic dilemmas. On balance, the situation has grown more complex as the demands made upon the police have increased and as the professional model has masked the need for more basic reform.

The many contradictions with which the police must live have had profound effects both on the quality of police service and on the impact of police reforms. The need for compromise—with the law, with administrative directions, with public expectations, and even with one's personal ethics—has become an important, albeit unarticulated, requirement of the police job. The present system places a high value on the officer who is willing to profess that he meets all the demands made upon him while making the accommodations needed to avoid conflicts. Many of the required accommodations are made at the street level, based upon the judgment of line officers, with little guidance and control from officers of superior rank.

This situation makes for some rather unusual working conditions. Specifically, police officers are often required to ignore their oath of office; to ignore much of what is taught in formal training; to bluff or lie, not necessarily out of malevolence, but often out of a desire to be helpful in the face of the irreconcilable demands upon them; to subject themselves to disciplinary actions and civil suits for ignoring the law while following the instructions of their superiors; and to work under a style of supervision that is often more concerned with protecting the organization and supervisory personnel against allegations of wrongdoing than with providing positive guidance to prevent improper behavior in the first place.

The awareness of the need to operate outside the accepted legal framework of their job—a need that is shared to some degree by all officers—is one of the factors that feeds the police subculture: that intricate web of relationships among peers that shapes and perpetuates the pattern of behavior, values, isolation, and secrecy that distinguish the police.[10] Police officers quickly learn that they must improvise, especially when responding to the extraordinary, highly emotional, and often threatening situations that they confront in their peculiar working environment. They not only lean on each other for assistance in handling these incidents; they frequently establish among themselves a consensus on how these situations should be treated. So while one finds great variation in the style of individual officers, the values upon which many police actions are based are those of the police subculture. The police subculture, therefore, emerges as a formidable force—created in part by the impossible character of the police function and in part by the environment in which the police work—that determines the way in which much police business is handled. It is inclined to oppose strongly any proposed changes in policing that are seen as threatening the protective bond between officers. This accounts for much of the resistance expressed by rank-and-file police officers to the proposals made during the past decade for police reform, and it explains, too, why many new programs have been stripped of some of their more important components.

Our failure to concern ourselves sufficiently with the ambiguity in the police function and with the other conflicting pressures brought to bear upon the police has substantially reduced the potential effectiveness of the most common proposals for improving police operations. Beyond this, the continuing need for compromise that these pressures have created makes police officers unusually vulnerable to criticism, pressing them to take shelter in the police subculture. And as they do so, we unwittingly contribute toward strengthening a force that, by its nature, is resistant to change and is in a unique position to subvert those changes that are initiated.

FOCUSING UPON FUNDAMENTAL ISSUES

In order to make the police function more workable, to reduce the conflicting pressures on the police, and to assure that future investments in police improvement will bring a greater return, we must go back to fundamentals. We must rethink widely held assumptions regarding the police function; recognize the discretion inherent in police work; and establish the values basic to policing. To reduce present pressures on the police, we must better align public expectations with an accurate assessment of what the police can do; increase the capacity of the police to carry out their responsibilities more effectively; and improve related systems upon which the police depend. And, finally, we must continually bear in mind that the objective of all police reform is not simply to create a perfected police establishment, but to improve the quality of police service.

Rethinking the Police Function

Thoughtful police administrators have long recognized that their function relating to crime competed with other responsibilities, and that many conflicting demands were made on the typical municipal police agency. But not until recently was this fact documented, openly acknowledged, and discussed. Additional developments have stimulated further interest in the specific nature of the police function: not only in what police do, but in what they ought to do. The desire to provide more intensive and more rational training, for example, has led to studies of the jobs for which individuals are to be trained. The charge that testing procedures for initial entry are racially biased has forced police agencies to better define the job for which applicants are examined. And current speculation about the value of higher education for police personnel will require similar inquiries. Exploration and clarification of the police function are the most basic of the basics that must be undertaken in providing a firm foundation for improving police service.

Recognizing Discretion

Closely related to the narrow crime-fighting concept of the police function is the assumption that police agencies are ministerial, acting in strict accord with legislative provisions. Until recently the broad discretion police actually exercise in carrying out their responsibilities was unrecognized. And to this day legislatures do not appear to be aware of it, courts have only begun to take cognizance of it, and many police administrators continue to deny it.

Much of the reluctance to face up to the fact that police exercise discretion results from misgivings about how this extremely complicated area should be structured and controlled. It is easier to retreat to the simplistic notion that the police have no authority to exercise discretion and live with the duplicity that posture requires. But the cost in doing so is tremendous for those concerned with improving the quality of police service. The endless array of important decisions—most of which are of a discretionary nature—that are made on a daily basis by police administrators, by supervisors, and by line officers are at the very heart of policing. Indeed, they are what policing is all about. It becomes critical, therefore, to recognize the presence and importance of discretion, to provide for its control, and to weigh carefully the implications that the discretionary nature of the police function has for the organization, staffing, and training of police personnel.

A Commitment to Democratic Values

The model of a police agency that has emerged in this country has been a neutral, sterile kind of organization, devoid of a clear commitment to any values other than operating efficiency. It lacks specific standards by which the quality of its end product can be accurately assessed. Absent an effort to build a set of values into policing, those that prevail are the values of the police subculture. This accounts, in large measure, for the radically different judgments made about the quality of police service by police personnel as compared with those made by critics on the outside.

That we have failed to build a set of values into policing is all the more disturbing because of the peculiar nature of the police function in a free society. Under a system of government in which so high a value is placed on individual freedom, an extraordinarily heavy responsibility falls upon those who, for the limited purpose of helping to maintain that society, are authorized to interfere in the lives of citizens and to use force. The police are not only obligated to exercise their limited authority in conformity with the Constitution and legislatively enacted restrictions; they are obligated as well to see to it that others do not infringe on constitutionally guaranteed rights. These requirements introduce into the police function the unique dimension that makes policing in this country such a high calling.

One of the consequences of the current situation is that the police in some communities, especially in the congested areas of large cities, place a higher priority on maintaining order than on operating legally. Constitutional and statutory requirements—such as those that provide limitations on the right to search, provide protection from self-incrimination, and guarantee access to counsel and release on bail—continue to be viewed by many police as technicalities that seriously interfere with "effective law enforcement." Many police officials and much of the public fail to understand the responsibilities of the police in providing equal law enforcement, in assuring due process, in protecting the rights of minorities, in protecting the privacy of the individual, and in protecting the right of political dissent. Most bothersome is the fact that talk about supporting democratic values in the context of police operations has come to be equated, by many police and by some elements of the public, with a soft and permissive attitude toward criminals and toward unruly elements in our society. This situation is exacerbated when the loudest critics of the police, who vociferously defend constitutional rights, fail to acknowledge the complexity of the police task and seem totally unaware of the problems the police must handle on the streets, often under extremely difficult circumstances.

It is a big order to urge that a concern for preserving and extending democratic values be made the ethos of professional police work; that the police be committed—aggressively, overtly, and unashamedly—to creating a system of policing in which this is the foremost goal. Yet such a stance has many positive features. Recognition that the police function is governed by a complicated set of rules and that a high value is attached to conforming with those rules would make the police job more challenging and more rewarding. Activities such as protecting the right of an unpopular speaker to speak or sheltering from attack a person accused of a heinous crime would take on new significance if they were understood as vital to a democratic way of life and, indeed, as best exemplifying the differences between policing a democratic and a totalitarian nation. And the example set by the police in conforming to the law and in acting in an even-handed manner to protect constitutional rights would, in the long run, win greater respect and cooperation from the community.

Such an approach will require that training and education provide officers with a much better understanding of the underlying principles of our system of government and of the ways in which we depend on the police to give meaning to these principles. Likewise, the day-to-day direction of police agencies and the manner in which individual performance is rewarded will have to be revised to elicit greater support for the values inherent in policing a free society. And to support these changes, a much greater effort will have to be made to educate the broader community so that the pressures that have pushed police in the opposite direction are reduced.

Altering Public Expectations

The police are constantly criticized for not meeting goals that cannot possibly be achieved. A newspaper editorial, for example, chides the local police for a rising crime rate. A group of citizens complains that the police have failed to enforce the prohibition against use of marijuana. An investigating commission castigates the police for failing to remove several hecklers from amidst a large and unruly audience. In all these situations the police are seriously limited in what they can do by the laws under which they operate, by tactical considerations, by the lack of adequate personnel, and by factors over which they have no control. Thus, for example, in the case of crime, factors like the birth rate, unemployment, the sense of community that exists in a given neighborhood, and even the weather probably have much more to do with the incidence of crime than do the police.

Yet most view the inability of the police to deal with these problems as a failure. In order to avoid such criticism, the police often attempt the impossible. This may involve taking shortcuts, acting improperly or illegally, or following unwise procedures. Aside from inviting more criticism, such responses perpetuate public expectations that are unrealistic.

The police must ask themselves if presenting a tough, albeit undefined, stance is of such importance that it offsets the cost in not sharing with the community a more precise description of police capabilities. Greater openness regarding their true capacity in handling various aspects of their business would greatly reduce the pressures now brought to bear upon the police. It would increase the willingness of the public to provide the police with additional resources when such a need is demonstrated. And it would increase the likelihood that the public would more aggressively explore alternatives for dealing with some of the problems now relegated to the police—a development which is long overdue.

The situation is so aggravated, at the moment, that the chief of police who is truthful in assessing police potential runs the risk of being replaced by one who is willing to assert the omnipotence of his agency, misleading as this may be. One cannot, therefore, expect to correct present practices overnight. But the need to develop both a more rational form of policing and a more rational response to some of the problems with which the police cope compels a gradual retreat from the position that police administrators have traditionally assumed.

Providing Needed Authority and Resources

Legislatures have commonly given the police responsibilities without considering how these responsibilities are to be carried out. As a consequence, under pressure to perform their assigned tasks, the police use their limited authority for many functions for which it is ill suited. The power to arrest, for example, is used for such varied purposes as safeguarding chronic inebriates, detaining mentally ill persons, and stopping family quarrels. The absence of more appropriate authority—as well as the resources with which to be helpful—leads to public criticism of the police, the frustration of police personnel, and the misuse by the police of that authority which they do have.

Some progress has recently been made toward providing the police with a greater diversity of both authority and resources. Although these efforts raise many complex issues, the experimentation to date nevertheless confirms the value of such steps to relieve pressures on the police and, at the same time, improve the quality of the police response to frequently recurring problems. Further explorations along these lines, however, must face even more realistically the nature of the incidents police are called upon to handle and the environment in which the police work.

As the agency of last resort, the police become involved with the most aggravated behavioral problems that occur in our society. They must deal with earthy matters—the coarse and the unrefined—that are outside the range of situations likely to be experienced by the average citizen. Much of their business involves the unpredictable and the bizarre. Although some items of police business are self-contained, most are interwoven with other problems of social disorganization. An unusually high percentage of the people with whom the police are in frequent contact represent the extremes: the most impoverished, the least educated, the most eccentric, the most conniving, the most pernicious, and the most dangerous.

The laws, resources, and procedures with which the police are equipped must be sufficient and appropriate to enable them, within constitutional limitations and subject to proper review, to deal with unusual problems as well as the more common ones. Otherwise police officers tend to conclude that those who provide them with their authority, resources, and other forms of support are simply unaware of the exceptional situations they must handle. And from this conclusion they may rationalize that since these situations were unanticipated, exceeding their authority in order to deal with them is justified.

It is inimical to our system of government to have a situation in which a government agency or an individual in that agency determines that, when the complexity or threat posed by a specific problem extends beyond a certain threshold, the public interest justifies setting aside the laws under which the agency is required to operate. Adherence to legal standards and especially to due process is most crucial in those cases in which the pressure to suspend these standards is most intense. If the provisions made for police service ignore the range of incidents requiring some form of intervention by the police, the architects of such provisions may unwittingly contribute to a net increase in police misconduct rather than its curtailment.

Improving Related Systems

The police are an integral part of the criminal justice system. What the police do within that system affects the operations of the prosecutor, the courts, and those engaged in corrections. And what each of these agencies does affects the police. Likewise, the police are part of the juvenile justice system, the mental health system, and several other systems designed to deal with specific problems. When these other systems and resources are not adequate, or are not working fairly and efficiently, tremendous pressures build up on the police, distorting their operations.

Of special concern have been the congestion and inordinate delays in the operation of the criminal justice system in many of our larger cities. Staffing is frequently inadequate. Facilities are often deplorable. Procedures tend to be grossly inefficient. And the volume is usually overwhelming. These conditions negate police efforts and detract substantially from whatever deterrent effect the criminal justice system generates.

With the public looking to the police to deal with crime, and with the criminal justice system the principal means by which the police are expected to do so, it should come as no surprise that, when that system breaks down, the police develop a wide range of informal practices and accommodations in order to cope with their work load. To the extent that some of these practices and accommodations are undesirable, the most obvious way to eliminate them is either to restore the capacity of the criminal justice system to handle a larger volume of cases or to provide more appropriate alternatives. The inadequacy of the systems upon which the police so heavily depend is still another factor that contributes to making the present arrangements for policing unworkable. Minimum improvements must be made in related systems before one can expect that improvements in the police establishment will produce the desired results.

Measuring Police Efforts by the Quality of
Service Delivered

Like all bureaucracies, police agencies frequently become so preoccupied with their internal operations that they tend to lose sight of the fact that the ultimate measure of their achievements is the quality of their end product. Even if a police agency has the most modern communication system, vehicle-maintenance program, and computer-based method for distributing and assigning officers— enabling an officer to reach the scene of a call for assistance within minutes—it is of dubious merit if the officer, on showing up, satisfies neither the citizen who summoned aid nor the community's standard of quality service. It is often startling to observe, in looking at a given police agency, the contrast between the highly controlled and seemingly infallible operations at headquarters and the disorganized, ineffective, and at times even offensive actions of police officers on the streets and in the homes of local residents. Police administrators become absorbed in administrative matters to the point that they are sometimes unaware of what is happening on the streets.

Concentrating on the end product of policing—on the actual delivery of services—requires analyzing what the police currently do in responding to the various types of incidents that repeatedly require their attention. For a large percentage of incidents, individual police officers have improvised different responses. Where current responses vary according to the officer handling the case, an effort to institutionalize the best possible response would constitute a major improvement. Where a given department's response is uniform, it is likely that it has been passed on from older officers to the younger ones and has not been critically examined for years. It is imperative that traditional police responses to problems that arise in the community, which have too often been viewed narrowly as crime problems to be dealt with by the criminal law, be carefully evaluated, and that alternative means for handling different categories of problems be explored.

THE NEED FOR A BALANCED PERSPECTIVE

In attempting to direct attention to fundamental issues relating to the basic arrangements for policing in this country, there is a danger of selling short the importance of the provisions made for the police establishment itself: its organization, leadership, staffing, training, education, equipment, and administrative procedures. The intention here is not to relegate these matters to a position of unimportance, but rather to present these needs in proper perspective and to provide a sound foundation upon which decisions related to them can be based.

It should be emphasized, moreover, that efforts to improve the police establishment need not await resolution of all of the issues that have been raised. Given the critical nature of the current situation, work must go forward at all levels. Admittedly, until some of the fundamental problems are dealt with, precise guidance for improvement in specific areas may be lacking. But some progress is realized if those making specific improvements are at least aware of the issues that have been raised.

Thus, for example, efforts must be intensified to provide more effective leadership in the police field. The quality of future leadership will have a major influence upon the ability of the field to address fundamental problems. But the required leadership is quite different from the stereotyped police leadership of the past. Those who head police agencies must recognize the fundamental problems in policing and have the capacity to contribute toward developing satisfactory solutions to them. Likewise, other areas must be reexamined with the objective of deciding how best to develop them in order to maximize their impact on the entire field.

The relationship between fundamental issues and the more traditional areas in which police reform has concentrated is reflected in the organization of this book. By way of emphasizing the importance of addressing basic problems, the greater part of the volume (chapters 2–8) is devoted to exploring a series of fundamental issues that have been seriously neglected and must be addressed if a more solid foundation is to be laid for the future development of the police field. These chapters focus on the police function; the role of the police in dealing with serious crime; the development of alternatives to the criminal process; the need for recognizing and structuring discretion; the political accountability of the police to the public; the control of police-citizen contacts; and the special problem of police corruption.

In chapters 9 through 11 several of the important traditional areas of concern in police reform are examined (the development of new leadership; the process of upgrading personnel; and the use being made of higher education), with the objective of reassessing current efforts in these areas, given the new perspectives developed in the earlier chapters. Chapter 12, the final chapter, explores the process by which change, both in the basic arrangements for policing and in the structure of the police establishment, might best be effected.

NOTES

1. National Commission on Law Observance and Enforcement, *Report on Lawlessness in Law Enforcement* (Washington, D.C.: Government Printing Office, 1931; reprint ed., Montclair, N.J.: Patterson Smith, 1968).

2. See, generally, Wayne W. Schmidt, *Survey of Police Misconduct Litigation 1967–1971* (Evanston, Ill.: Americans for Effective Law Enforcement, Inc., 1974).

3. For the major summary reports filed by these study groups, see President's Commission on Law Enforcement and Administration of Justice, *The Challenge of Crime in a Free Society* (Washington, D.C.: Government Printing Office, 1967); National Advisory Commission on Civil Disorders, *Report of the National Advisory Commission on Civil Disorders* (Washington, D.C.: Government Printing Office, 1968); National Commission on the Causes and Prevention of Violence, *To Establish Justice, To Insure Domestic Tranquility*, Final Report (Washington, D.C.: Government Printing Office, 1969); President's Commission on Campus Unrest, *The Report of the President's Commission on Campus Unrest* (Washington, D.C.: Government Printing Office, 1970).

4. National Advisory Commission on Criminal Justice Standards and Goals, *Police* (Washington, D.C.: Government Printing Office, 1973).

5. The Office of Law Enforcement Assistance was created by the Law Enforcement Assistance Act of 1965, Pub. L. No. 89–197, 79 Stat. 828. LEAA was created by Title I of the Omnibus Crime Control and Safe Streets Act of 1968, 82 Stat. 197 *et seq.* (1968).

6. For the latest summary of LEAA-financed programs, see Law Enforcement Assistance Administration, *Sixth Annual Report of LEAA* (Washington, D.C.: Government Printing Office, 1975). For a summary of the research pro-

gram of LEAA's National Institute of Law Enforcement and Criminal Justice, see Law Enforcement Assistance Administration, *Annual Report of the National Institute of Law Enforcement and Criminal Justice: Fiscal Year 1975* (Washington, D.C.: Government Printing Office, 1976).

7. Patrick V. Murphy, for example, states that "a survey of the past ten years in policing is, overall, discouraging," and similarly labels the outlook for much-needed basic police changes as "discouraging." See Patrick V. Murphy, *A Decade of Urban Police Problems*, Sixteenth Annual Wherrett Lecture on Local Government (Pittsburgh: Institute for Urban Policy and Administration, Graduate School of Public and International Affairs, University of Pittsburgh, 1974).

8. For a contrary view, however, see Thomas A. Reppetto, "The Influence of Police Organizational Style on Crime Control Effectiveness," *Journal of Police Science and Administration* 3 (1975): 274-279. Reppetto compares the operations of a professionalized department and a traditional police agency and tentatively concludes that the differences he found in crime and clearance rates, at least for murder and auto theft, were a result of the organizational style of the agencies. He therefore cautions against abandoning the "doctrines of classical police administration theory."

9. On the occasion of his recent resignation from the position of deputy administrator of LEAA, Charles R. Work is quoted as having stated that "the original notion was that we would be flooded with all these great ideas. And lo and behold, they didn't come at all." He complained that local law enforcement officials were apparently incapable of coming up with new ideas—especially for combating crime. "Local Crime Fight Ideas Called Poor," *Wisconsin State Journal*, 27 November 1975.

10. For an analysis of the full range of factors that contribute to the formation of the police subculture, see William A. Westley, *Violence and the Police* (Cambridge, Mass.: MIT Press, 1970); Jerome H. Skolnick, *Justice Without Trial* (New York: John Wiley and Sons, 1966), pp. 42-70; Michael Banton, *The Policeman in the Community* (New York: Basic Books, 1964); John Van Maanen, "Working the Street: A Developmental View of Police Behavior," in *The Potential for Reform of Criminal Justice*, ed. Herbert Jacob (Beverly Hills, Calif.: Sage Publications, 1974); and Richard N. Harris, *The Police Academy* (New York: John Wiley and Sons, 1973).

Chapter 2

The Police Function

The police function is incredibly complex. The total range of police responsibilities is extraordinarily broad. Many tasks are so entangled that separation appears impossible. And the numerous conflicts among different aspects of the function cannot be easily reconciled. Anyone attempting to construct a workable definition of the police role will typically come away with old images shattered and with a new-found appreciation for the intricacies of police work.

In this chapter some of the major factors that contribute to the complexity of the police role will be identified; some of the efforts that have been made to better understand police functioning will be reviewed: and, in an effort to advance this understanding, a broad conceptual framework for viewing the totality of police operations will be suggested.

POLICE AS PART OF THE CRIMINAL
JUSTICE SYSTEM

Police functioning relies heavily upon and is almost inextricably interrelated with the operations of the criminal justice system—the process of arrest, prosecution, trial, sentencing, imprisonment or probation, and parole. The integral role of the police in processing individuals through the system is obvious. Less recognized is the fact that the system is the principal method available to the police for handling a wide range of diverse situations. For many of these situations the system is clearly inappropriate and, even when appropriate, often awkward in its application. But in the absence of alternatives it is used, and often perverted in its use, in order to get things done. The need to use the criminal justice system, even if it involves only the authority to arrest, understandably confers upon the

21

incidents for which it is used the full panoply of consequences commonly associated with a criminal offense. This causes many problems for the individual affected, for the police, and for the criminal justice system itself. It explains, among other things, the tendency of the police to label a high percentage of their total business criminal.

Police functioning within the criminal justice system is important not only for the use the police make of the system to process alleged criminal offenders; the heavy reliance police place upon the system has made their operations within it almost synonymous, in the public's mind, with police work. That is why, in attempting to analyze the police function, one must look first at the role of the police within the system.

Prior to the 1950s, studies of crime and the criminal justice system tended to look separately at the operations of each of the major agencies in the system: the police, the prosecutor, the courts, and corrections.[1] The interrelationships between the agencies, to the extent that they were examined at all, were viewed primarily in terms of statistical analyses of the cases processed. "Mortality tables" were used to draw attention to points in the system where large numbers of cases "died," with the conclusion that this was often due to the inefficiency of the different agencies in the system. Although the better studies qualified their mortality tables, the use of them gave rise to a widespread notion that, if the criminal justice system were operating at the peak of its efficiency, the same number of cases would be handled at each stage in the system. To this day, crudely produced journalistic analyses of crime and of the workings of the criminal justice system develop mortality tables that reach similar conclusions.

The concept, of course, is a terribly naive one. It ignores the varying legal standards that are applied at different stages in the criminal process; more evidence is needed to convict than to prosecute. It also ignores the fact that prosecutors and judges are expected to bring their own considerations to bear in processing a case, and these differ from the considerations of the police. But most important, it ignores the dynamics of the criminal justice system—the complex factors and pressures that determine how the system actually operates, especially in a large urban community.

Starting with sociologist William Westley's pioneering work in 1951, empirical studies have documented these complexities. Although it received relatively little attention at the time, Westley's doctoral thesis afforded unusual insight into the actual operations of a medium-sized midwestern police department.[2] The American Bar Foundation's study of the administration of criminal justice in the United States, begun in 1955, was the first major effort to record and report actual observations of the daily activities of police officers, prosecutors, judges, and correctional personnel.[3]

The Westley study and the summaries and analyses of the data collected in the American Bar Foundation's study offered a sharp contrast to the image of police functioning and the operations of the criminal justice system that, up to that time, had been conveyed in textbooks, in descriptions of formal legal procedures, and in popularized accounts of police activity. Informal arrangements were found to be more common than was compliance with formally established procedures. The pressures of volume, public pressures, interagency pressures, and the interests and personal predilections of functionaries in the system were found in many instances to have more influence on how the system operated than did the Constitution, state statutes, or city ordinances. Among the most significant findings relating to the police that the American Bar Foundation's survey disclosed were these:

1. Police functioning was heavily affected by and very dependent upon the functioning of the rest of the agencies in the criminal justice system. Likewise, the functioning of these other agencies was heavily influenced by police practices and policies.
2. Arrest, commonly viewed as the first step in the criminal process, had come to be used by the police to achieve a whole range of objectives in addition to that of prosecuting wrongdoers; for example, to investigate, to harass, to punish, and to provide safekeeping.
3. The volume of business handled by the police greatly exceeded the amount of business that was processed through the rest of the criminal justice system.
4. A great variety of informal methods outside the criminal justice system had been adopted by the police to fulfill their formal responsibilities and to dispose of the endless array of situations which the public—rightly or wrongly —expected them to handle.
5. Individual police officers were found to be routinely exercising a great deal of discretion in deciding how to handle the tremendous variety of circumstances with which they were confronted. Specifically, police exercised a great deal of discretion in deciding whether or not to arrest and prosecute in situations in which there was ample evidence that a criminal law had been violated.

With documentation of the actual process by which the system operated, there were few demands that changes be made so as to fit police functioning and the operations of the rest of the system back into the simpler, more rigid mold that served as the basis for the earlier forms of statistical analysis. Rather, the departures from the formal criminal process were of such volume and so gross that they resulted in widespread acknowledgment of the need to face up to them. Each of the deviations from the neat legislatively defined process indicated a complex problem crying for attention.

Although the American Bar Foundation's study made it clear that much police activity took place outside the criminal justice system, its major impact was to draw attention to the interdependence of the agencies in the system, and this resulted in a recognition of the need to view each agency, including the police, as a part of the whole. Because the focus of the study was criminal justice, this was an understandable conclusion. As a consequence it became fashionable in many quarters to talk about the criminal justice system as a *system*.

The concept was strongly reinforced and given widespread publicity in 1967 by the President's Commission on Law Enforcement and Administration of Justice.[4] The commission's studies were themselves based on the need to view the system as a system, and this approach was reflected in many of the recommendations that were made. The urgings of the commission were met, to some degree, by the action of Congress in adopting the Omnibus Crime Control and Safe Streets Act of 1968. Funds were to be made available to a state under this act only if the state adopted a comprehensive plan for improving law enforcement—a provision that was interpreted from the outset as requiring an integrated statewide concern for the operations of the police, the prosecutor, defense counsel, the courts, and correctional agencies. The multitude of criminal justice commissions that now exist at the state and local levels of government charged with developing comprehensive coordinated plans for dealing with crime grew out of the same act, as did the new occupation of criminal justice planner.

Viewing the police as an integral part of the criminal justice system gained widespread acceptance. Textbooks previously devoted to policing were expanded and renamed to cover the total criminal justice system. College programs, previously labeled police science, were retitled as programs in criminal justice administration. In some quarters, there was even talk of educating people as criminal justicers, with the implication that such people would be capable, as generalists, of working interchangeably at various points in the criminal justice system.

EXAMINING THE MULTIPLE FUNCTIONS OF THE POLICE

Time Spent on Tasks Unrelated to Crime

More recent studies of the police have dwelled on the high percentage of police time spent on other than criminal matters, and they thus call into question the value of viewing the police primarily as a part of the criminal justice system. Elaine Cumming, Ian Cumming, and Laura Edell, in their study, found that more than half of the calls made to the police appeared to involve requests for help in personal and interpersonal matters.[5] James Q. Wilson reported, based upon his studies of calls to the police in Syracuse, that only one-tenth of the calls afforded an opportunity for the police to perform what he termed a narrowly defined law enforcement function.[6] Albert J. Reiss reported that the Chicago police categorized as noncriminal 83 percent of the incidents they handled in a 28-day period.[7] And Thomas Bercal concluded that only 16 percent of all calls made to the police in Detroit were crime related.[8]

What do police do with their time if they are not working on matters related to crime? The studies report the large number of hours devoted to handling accidents and illnesses, stray and injured animals, and intoxicated persons; dealing with family disturbances, fights among teen-age gangs, and noisy gatherings; taking reports on damage to property, traffic accidents, missing persons, and lost and found property. They cite the amount of time devoted to administering systems of registration and licensing; to directing traffic; to dealing with complaints of improper parking; to controlling crowds at public events; and to dealing with numerous hazards and municipal service defects that require attention.

The widest array of police services is reported in the congested and depressed areas of the large cities, for here the combination of poverty, unemployment, broken homes, poor education, and other elements of social disorganization results in the police officer often being called upon to serve as surrogate parent or other relative, and to fill in for social workers, housing inspectors, attorneys, physicians, and psychiatrists. It is here, too, that the police most frequently care for those who cannot care for themselves: the destitute, the inebriated, the addicted, the mentally ill, the senile, the alien, the physically disabled, and the very young.

Tremendous significance has been attached to these accounts of police activity because they so directly challenge the stereotype of the police function firmly established in the minds of both the police and the public as consisting primarily of preventing crime and apprehending criminals. This is the image that has been cultivated by the police themselves. It is the image that has been reinforced by most of the popular literature, television serials, and motion pictures of the police. And it is the image that has had a pervasive influence upon the organization, staffing, and operation of police agencies.

Problems in Describing Police Activity

Police themselves have done little to describe the full range and importance of their activities.[9] The typical report of a police agency will bury large volumes of highly significant work in statistical entries that record the number of calls received for service or the number of miscellaneous complaints handled. Numerous incidents are classified in such broad categories as "disturbances," concealing the range and diversity of situations the officer encounters. Police officers who are occasionally requested to fill out job-classification forms as part of a personnel study will consistently sell themselves short by understating the variety and significance of what they do. And persons who have accompanied a police officer during a tour of duty often report, after they have had what they thought was an exceedingly rich exposure to a wide range of challenging police jobs, that the officer apologizes for a slow and uninteresting experience.

The fullest descriptions we have of police work have been compiled by persons outside police agencies.[10] Some of them, cited earlier, relied most heavily upon analyses of calls made to the police for service; others actually observed activity in the field. Although the results of these inquiries provide insights that are gigantic advances over what was previously available, the most ambitious among them is not fully comprehensive in its description of everything a police agency does. By observing a police officer patrol an area where the demand for police service is high, one can gain an understanding of the full range of situations a police officer on patrol is likely to handle. The picture that emerges, however, cannot be said to be typical of patrol work throughout a city, nor does it reveal the services provided by other than patrol officers. Much police work is carried out by specialists, such as detectives, youth officers, and traffic officers. Analysis of calls for services—rather than observation—facilitates quantification for an entire community, but has the disadvantage of ignoring the information that becomes available on responding to a call, information that often changes the character of an incident. Analysis of calls also ignores the vast amount of police work that is self-initiated, both by patrol officers and by the specialists.

Neither analysis of routine telephone calls nor field observation will give a clear picture of the exceptional situations that pose unusual demands on the police. An outbreak of racial violence in a high school, for example, is an increasingly frequent occurrence in large cities. The demonstrations and conflicts of recent years (such as the anti-war marches and the controversy over busing to achieve school integration) not only required the mobilization of large numbers of police for long periods of time; the challenge they posed has had a much greater effect upon the nature of police operations than is suggested by the amount of time devoted to dealing directly with them.

Describing police work by identifying specific tasks can be misleading because substantial portions of police time are formally committed to ambiguous objectives such as preventing crime—a task not easily quantifiable. What the police do (or do not do) to prevent crime must be taken into consideration in attempting to put together a total picture of the police function.

And finally, even if it is possible to get a comprehensive and accurate picture of what the police do in a given community, generalizations beyond this are difficult because police work differs greatly from one jurisdiction to another. Not only do variations in demands made upon the police result from demographic factors—such as the makeup, stability, and density of the population; communities also tend, over a period of time, to develop different styles of policing that, in turn, serve to screen out or reinforce what a community subsequently expects of its police.[11]

Attempts to Explain and Categorize the Different
Tasks of the Police

Increased awareness of the multiplicity of tasks that fall to the police has led to inquiries as to how the police came to perform such a potpourri of services. Police officers and administrators often complain that the public and some government officials view police officers riding about their community as idle, and therefore ideally suited to perform a variety of miscellaneous tasks that require doing. Historians, however, are quick to point out that police had riot-control duties and were performing various service functions for municipal government long before they assumed as much responsibility as they now have for criminal matters.[12]

It is commonly noted that the police are the only agency available seven days a week, twenty-four hours a day to respond to a citizen's need for help—other than to fight a fire or repair a utility malfunction. Another common explanation for the multiplicity of police tasks is that practically all such tasks initially require some investigation, and the police are the agency of government most skilled and best equipped to conduct such preliminary inquiries.[13]

The most sophisticated explanation for the myriad duties assigned to police has been developed by Egon Bittner, who argues that the capacity of the police to use coercive force lends thematic unity to all police activity.

> Whatever the substance of the task at hand, whether it involves protection against an undesired imposition, caring for those who cannot care for themselves, attempting to solve a crime, helping to save a life, abating a nuisance, or settling an explosive dispute, police intervention means above all making use of the capacity and authority to overpower resistance to an attempted solution in the native habitat of the problem.[14]

From this observation Bittner concludes that the training, organization, and staffing of a police agency should be directed toward handling what he refers to as "situational exigencies" with minimum force.[15]

Concern with the multiplicity of police functions has led, too, to some interesting efforts to categorize different aspects of the police role. Michael Banton, for example, observed that the police officer on patrol is primarily a peace officer, not a law officer. Rather than enforce the law, he spends most of his time supervising his beat and responding to calls for assistance.[16] In an effort to break down the peace-keeping responsibilities of the police, Bittner identifies five types of situations in which the police commonly become involved: (1) the regulation of various types of businesses that lend themselves to exploitation for undesirable and illegal purposes; (2) the handling of a wide variety of situations in which the law has in fact been violated, but the officer chooses to dispose of the situation by employing some alternative to invoking the criminal process; (3) intervention in an infinite array of situations—to arbitrate quarrels, to pacify the unruly, and to aid people in trouble; (4) dealing with mass phenomena, such as crowds, where there is the potential for disorder; and (5) caring for those who are less than fully accountable for their actions, such as the young, the alcoholic, and the mentally ill. As to each of these activities, Bittner notes that police functioning is "only in a trivial sense determined by those considerations of legality that determine law enforcement."[17]

In his study of police behavior in eight communities, James Q. Wilson initially separates police functioning into service administration and law administration. He dismisses the former—which he identifies as including the provision of first aid, directing traffic, recovering stolen property, and helping old ladies—as being of less importance because it does not raise questions of legal standards, community objectives, or the interests and opinions of third parties.[18] Dwelling on law administration, Wilson then separates the "order maintenance" functions of the police from their "law enforcement" duties. He uses "order maintenance" to describe police activities in which the police must assess blame, in which the officer is most likely to do something other than make an arrest, and in which substantial discretion is exercised. The order-maintenance function is one in which "subprofessionals, working alone, exercise wide discretion in matters of utmost importance (life and death, honor and dishonor) in an environment that is apprehensive and perhaps hostile." "Law enforcement" is viewed as what an officer does when there is no dispute; when routine steps are taken to make the offender liable to the penalties of the law.[19] The distinctions drawn between these categories are clouded somewhat because, as Wilson acknowledges, arrest is so commonly used in order maintenance and discretion is so commonly exercised in law enforcement.

Police Reactions to Descriptions of Their Work

Since the image the police maintain of themselves as primarily crime fighters is so strongly established, it is not surprising that they are questioning the claims being made about the true nature of their job.

Much of this questioning stems from the different perspectives of those outside and those within police agencies. For example, the contention that police spend little of their time on criminal matters understandably makes no sense to the many officers working in the core of a large city, who commonly race from one serious crime to another. They work in a world of guns and knives, of hostility and distrust, of wholesale violence, and of neighbor preying upon neighbor. They are expected to handle routinely and with little public notice incidents such as a "man with a gun," a stabbing in a bar, or an intrafamily homicide, any one of which, were it to occur in a smaller community, would draw banner headlines. But common as this situation is in the center of large cities, it is the exception in the total picture of policing. Moreover, even in blighted urban areas, the police have been found to spend a lot of time on matters not so directly related to crime, though these matters may seem trivial given the high incidence of serious misconduct. In these areas the police must, in addition to handling serious crime, deal with the fullest range of situations that police are commonly called upon to handle elsewhere—often in their most aggravated form.

Of greater importance for our purposes is the questioning of the recent studies that reflects disagreement with the way activities have been classified. The use of the category "unrelated to crime" creates the impression that a clear line can be drawn between criminal and noncriminal matters, when no such line exists. How the police handle a domestic dispute, for example, may relate very directly to their role in preventing an assault or a homicide, though responding to domestic disputes is often categorized as unrelated to crime. Likewise, many police tend to see their work in dealing with nuisances, controlling crowds, and helping intoxicated persons as crime related because they may have to take criminal action against violators if their primary effort fails.

Still another reason why the police dispute the claim that they spend as much as 80 percent of their time on matters unrelated to crime is that crime, for purposes of this classification, is usually limited to serious crime. Thus, in the breakdowns that have been used, dealing with disorderly drunks, abandoned cars, children playing in the street, shoplifters, soliciting street prostitutes, and motorists who run red lights would generally be classified as noncriminal activity. But because these incidents technically constitute violations of the law, the police and others classify them as part of the law enforcement/criminal responsibilities of the police.

PROBLEMS CREATED BY THE VARIED
MEANINGS OF "CRIME"

Recognition of the wide range of functions performed by the police constitutes in itself a giant step toward better understanding of the true nature of police work. But from the foregoing discussion it should be apparent that the full impact of this new awareness is seriously weakened by the heavy reliance on the term "crime" in describing what the police do. The tendency to use the term to encompass all wrongdoing, however petty, not only accounts for some of the disagreement over the meaning of recent studies; the ambiguity surrounding the term contributes in a more general way to the confusion that hampers efforts to gain a better understanding of the police function.

The police have traditionally been linked to crime in much the same way that doctors have been linked to illness. But in the medical field the relationship is much more specific: illnesses have been categorized; the factors causing them have been isolated; preventive programs have been developed and tested; and the actual capacity of medical personnel to prevent and control specific diseases has been established. In contrast, within the police field and in the community much of the talk relating to crime remains at a very general level, despite the fact that "crime" is no more meaningful a term than "illness."[20] The problem is aggravated because the word is so freely bandied about—by politicians, by policemen, and by the public generally—as if it had uniform meaning.

Operational Consequences

The failure to make meaningful distinctions among different categories of crime has some very direct consequences on the daily operations in police agencies. Police personnel obviously treat offenders differently, based upon the seriousness of the crime they are alleged to have committed, but certain procedural steps are frequently applied uniformly to all persons who come under the legal rubric of having committed a crime. A man accused of indecent exposure will be handcuffed. A shoplifter will be jailed. A businessman who fails to renew the license on his cigarette vending machine will be mugged and fingerprinted. A female traffic violator will be subjected to a complete body search upon being temporarily detained.

Individuals treated this way often plead that they are not "criminals." Called upon to defend their response, the police often explain either that uniform procedures must be applied or, less sympathetically, that the individuals are, in fact, alleged criminals—in a legal sense—and therefore have no basis for complaint. By lumping all crimes together, police can justify any action that, within legal limits, can be used against the most dangerous criminals—regardless of its propriety.

It is, of course, absurd to argue that the police have the same responsibilities regarding a robbery, for example, as they would have regarding disorderly conduct, simply because both are defined by the legislature as criminal offenses. Indeed there is reason to believe that the primary intent of the legislature, in labeling such things as disorderly conduct criminal, was not to abolish all such behavior but rather to convey authority to the police to "do something" when the public interest seems to warrant that something be done. This describes the use commonly made of statutes defining crimes such as disorderly conduct and vagrancy, whatever the intention of the legislature, and accounts for prosecutions under them being challenged with increasing frequency on grounds that the statutes are too vague—that they do not give adequate notice of the conduct that is prohibited.[21]

Another operational consequence of the failure to make meaningful distinctions between different categories of crime is the tendency on the part of police personnel and the public to apply the "good guy-bad guy" dichotomy to all categories of alleged criminals. When a police agency sets out to apprehend individuals who, in the eyes of the community, are alleged to have committed particularly outrageous crimes, their effort takes on some of the characteristics of a hunt. Vast resources are invested. Tenseness and excitement pervade the ranks. All possible avenues are pursued, as officers, with dogged determination and with adrenalin flowing, seek their prey. And throughout the process, the feeling develops—given the focus of public attention on the case—that the very reputation of the agency is at stake. There is nothing wrong with applying this approach to dangerous offenders, assuming the rights of the alleged offender are properly protected. But serious problems do arise if the same dichotomy and the same techniques are applied to other kinds of alleged criminals without regard to the nature of their offenses. In a number of incidents in recent years, for example, police stalked political demonstrators who committed minor offenses in much the same manner as they pursued more serious criminal offenders.

Still another consequence of the broad use of the criminal label is that it makes citizens unwilling to cooperate with the police. Many citizens commit minor offenses that label them as criminals. It is generally assumed that the numbers player and the marijuana smoker will be less than fully supportive of the police because they are afraid their own violations will be detected. Moreover, including them in the broad cateogry of criminal offenders forces them to identify—in varying degrees—with the more serious criminal element.

Crimes of Concern to the Police

The link between the police and crime suggests that the police are concerned with all crime, but this is not the case. There are hundreds of laws on the statute books of the typical state, the violation of which constitutes a criminal offense. The police traditionally are committed to enforcing but a small percentage of them. Everyone expects the police to be concerned with homicide, rape, robbery, and burglary. No one expects them to be concerned with businesses engaged in monopolistic practices, with persons illegally practicing law, or with income tax evaders. As for some other violations, however, the responsibility of the police is less clear.

Who is to handle complaints regarding violations of laws intended to protect the consumer, the failure of landlords to provide heat, wrongdoing on the part of public officials, the refusal of a bar owner to serve black people, or violations of laws intended to protect the environment? Until recently these may have been somewhat academic questions. But now the defrauding of a consumer, the mistreatment of a tenant, and blatant discrimination on the basis of race or sex are viewed as offenses that are similar to many crimes for which the police or the prosecutor have routinely accepted responsibility. It no longer makes any sense, for example, for the police to investigate and prosecute passers of bad checks or shoplifters while ignoring fraudulent practices of merchants. Nor is it sensible for the police to enforce eviction notices but disclaim responsibility for investigating a tenant's complaint of unsanitary and unsafe conditions. So not only are the police not responsible for investigating all crimes, but those which they are expected to handle are not specifically defined and are subject to change in changing times.

A CONCEPTUAL FRAMEWORK FOR VIEWING THE POLICE

The Need for Such a Framework

With new awareness of the wide range of functions that police have, and with increased sensitivity to the problems involved in categorizing police activities as criminal or noncriminal, the inadequacies in using the criminal justice framework as the primary means for viewing police functioning are all the more apparent. Just how misleading the use of the framework can be is illustrated by examining two issues that have been of great interest in the police field.

The exclusionary rule, whereby evidence obtained in violation of a defendant's constitutional rights is inadmissible in a prosecution, remains a subject of great controversy in the police field. When first applied in the 1950s by the United

States Supreme Court to proceedings in the state courts, it was seen as a method for controlling police conduct. The original support for it was based largely upon the assumption that the primary role of the police was to prosecute alleged offenders. The blocking of a prosecution, it was assumed, would result in the police giving greater attention to the legality of their procedures. But since in practice the police have a wide range of diverse objectives, of which prosecution is but one, the potential effectiveness of the exclusionary rule as a control device is limited to that relatively small percentage of police business when the police are intent on prosecution, when the case advances to the point it is subject to judicial review, and when prosecution is dependent on the use of evidence subject to being excluded because of the manner in which it was obtained.

It does not follow from this analysis that the exclusionary rule ought to be abandoned. Strong arguments have been offered in support of it on other grounds. Our new awareness of the diverse nature of the police function, however, makes it abundantly clear that the exclusionary rule is far from an effective way to achieve a comprehensive review of police conduct.

A somewhat similar example is afforded by the many proposals to improve police functioning by decriminalizing certain forms of behavior. The operation of the criminal justice system would be greatly expedited if it were not necessary to process the thousands of persons who, for example, are arrested for being drunk and disorderly. The energies and talents of those functioning within the system could then be applied to more serious criminal activities. From the standpoint of the police, however, this solution is not the panacea it is often made out to be, for the police do not simply process intoxicated persons because drunkenness is criminal. The public expects the police to deal with the nuisances created by intoxicated persons and to provide for their safety—and they will most likely continue to expect the police to do this. Decriminalization of drunkenness will require that some alternative provisions be made for police handling of the many intoxicated persons who might otherwise have been arrested. If careful thought goes into designing such alternatives, police functioning will be improved. Many benefits would flow from the simple fact that the conduct was no longer labeled criminal. But if no provisions are made, or if the provisions that are made do not work effectively, the police will have even less satisfactory means for dealing with intoxicated persons than that which has been crudely carved out of the criminal justice system. (Some of the new programs designed to improve the police response to intoxicated persons are described in chapter 4.) Recognition of the full range of police responsibilities places similar limitations on proposals for decriminalizing other forms of conduct.

To analyze the *totality* of police functioning and the police *as an institution*, it is essential to break through the confining criminal justice framework, for it is now clear that it is not sufficiently comprehensive to encompass all that goes on in the daily operations of a police agency. The bulk of police business, measured in terms of contacts with citizens, takes place *before* invoking the criminal justice system (for example, checking suspicious circumstances, stopping and questioning people, maintaining surveillance), makes use of the system for *purposes other than prosecution* (to provide safekeeping or to investigate), or occurs in its entirety *outside* the system (resolving conflict, handling crowds, protecting demonstrators). This vast volume of activity vitally affects many people. Because it is carried out by the police, it involves the use of varying degrees of authority and coercion, which police officers are commonly assumed to have. And since much of this authority is borrowed from the police role in the criminal process and has a questionable legal basis, police functioning in these areas raises issues that are extremely difficult and complex. In order to gain a better understanding of these issues, we need a conceptual framework for viewing the police function that is sufficiently broad to encompass all that the police do, based on the *realities* of police work.

Viewing the Police as an Agency of Municipal Government Housing a Variety of Functions

We should recognize that a police agency as an institution has a life and an importance of its own—independent of the systems to which it relates and the problems for which it is responsible. A concern with the police as an institution goes beyond any one aspect of its functioning. It focuses attention upon an agency of government in which are housed a variety of responsibilities. And it requires working through the problems that arise when so varied a combination of responsibilities is housed within a single agency.

Viewing the police—first and foremost—simply as an agency of municipal government, elementary as this concept may seem, serves a number of important purposes. It puts to rest the argument that police functioning should be viewed solely within the context of the criminal justice system. It rids us of the notion that the police are a legal institution created with a function strictly defined by statute, and substitutes in its place a more flexible concept of the police as an administrative unit of local government. And it contributes toward challenging the widely held belief that dealing with crime is the sole function of the police; that all other tasks are peripheral or ancillary.

More positively, viewing the police primarily as an agency of municipal government is a way of emphasizing the fact that each community has the opportunity to make its own judgments as to what its police force should do. This seems especially appropriate in the light of recent demands for more decentralized control of police operations.

Implicit in this approach is the belief that most of the noncriminal functions police now perform are not inappropriate tasks if a community concludes that the police agency is the logical administrative unit in which to house them. Many proposals have been made to relieve the police of responsibilities related to such matters as traffic, animals, alcoholics, and domestic disputes, so that they can devote more of their time to dealing with serious crime.[22] In response, however, it has been pointed out that the police role in performing these tasks may, from the public's standpoint, be more important than dealing with some aspects of crime; there is serious question whether making more police time available to combat crime will in fact have an impact upon the amount of crime, given prevailing techniques; many of these tasks are simply not separable; it may be desirable for the police to perform helpful services to offset their punitive functions; and it may be that no private or other government agency can perform these tasks more effectively than can the police.[23]

Separating Methods from Objectives

Much of the difficulty in attempting to dissect the police function stems from the tendency to confuse police objectives with the methods the police employ in achieving them. This is especially true for law enforcement, which is so often viewed as an end in itself rather than a means to an end. Admittedly, statutes frequently define the police job as enforcing the law. In practice, however, the police have a whole range of objectives, and law enforcement is but one of several methods by which they get their job done.

Of course police frequently do set out in search of law violators but, for the most part, police work calls for dealing with specific situations. Often these situations involve behavior that has been prohibited by state statute or local ordinance. Where this is the case, the police may choose to prosecute, or they may choose to deal with the situation in some other manner. If no element of a violation is present, they obviously cannot initiate a prosecution, but they are nevertheless usually expected to take some form of action.

The distinction between objectives and methods can be illustrated by looking at the police role in regulating motor-vehicle traffic. Their basic objective is to facilitate the movement of traffic so that people can get where they want to go with a minimum of congestion, property damage, injury, or death. Enforcing the traffic laws is not a goal in itself, but one of several means for achieving this basic objective. In addition to enforcing the law, the police direct traffic in congested areas; they educate the public in safe driving habits; and they often warn drivers who violate the laws. When they do resort to enforcing the law, department policy or specific circumstances may determine which offenders are charged with an ordinance violation and which with violating a state statute. All these alternatives are methods by which the police accomplish their basic objective of facilitating the flow of traffic.

The distinction becomes much more difficult to make when the police are dealing with serious crime. Indeed some would argue that it is artificial to draw any line in such cases; that the police action, for example, in dealing with the rape problem in a community and in enforcing the law against rape is one and the same. Actually, the function of the police as it relates to a problem such as rape is much broader than enforcing the criminal law; it is to deal with the problem with which the law itself is intended to deal. Ideally a police agency would gain sufficient insights into the rape problem to enable it to develop positive programs for minimizing the number of rapes in the community. Such a program would, of course, include provisions for efficient use of the criminal justice system to prosecute those alleged to be guilty of rape. But it would also provide information for the public on how to avoid rape; a range of services for rape victims; and even perhaps efforts to arrange help for seriously maladjusted individuals who come to police attention. Prosecution, providing information and services, and making referrals are all means to an end. The end or objective, in this illustration, is to deal more effectively with rape as a form of serious criminal conduct.

Separating methods employed by the police from the objectives the police are expected to achieve should not be construed to mean that the methods are outside the police function. The total police function includes the objectives of the police and the methods they employ. But it is essential that the distinction be drawn if we are to understand the realities of police work.

Acknowledging the Multiple Objectives of the Police

If one penetrates beyond the generalizations about what the police do (such as maintain the peace, prevent crime, serve and protect); if one goes beyond the literal descriptions of how police spend their time (such as recovering lost property, locating missing persons, directing traffic, and patrolling); and if one separates out the various means police employ in getting their work done (initiating prosecutions, issuing warnings, providing information), one can begin to see more clearly the objectives to which the police are committed.

An effort was made to do just this as part of the recent American Bar Association project to develop standards for the urban police function.[24] As the original draftsman of the list of objectives produced by that study, I have felt free in altering it somewhat here to read as follows:

1. To prevent and control conduct widely recognized as threatening to life and property (serious crime).
2. To aid individuals who are in danger of physical harm, such as the victim of a criminal attack.
3. To protect constitutional guarantees, such as the right of free speech and assembly.
4. To facilitate the movement of people and vehicles.
5. To assist those who cannot care for themselves: the intoxicated, the addicted, the mentally ill, the physically disabled, the old, and the young.
6. To resolve conflict, whether it be between individuals, groups of individuals, or individuals and their government.
7. To identify problems that have the potential for becoming more serious problems for the individual citizen, for the police, or for government.
8. To create and maintain a feeling of security in the community.[25]

To set out the multiple objectives of the police in this manner has several distinct advantages. Dealing with serious crime is placed in perspective as but one of the objectives of the police. Activities in which the police have always been engaged, but which have often been thought to be peripheral or even improper, are explicitly recognized. This has special implications in assessing operating procedures. Specific patrol practices, for example, may be considered wasteful if measured solely for their value in apprehending persons who have committed serious crimes, but they may be extremely effective in creating a feeling of security in the community and in providing quick assistance to the victim of a crime or accident.

When police objectives are identified, the interrelationship between different aspects of the total police function becomes more apparent. What the police do in attempting to achieve one objective may well affect their capacity to carry out another. The resolution of conflict, for example, may prevent a riot, an assault, or a homicide. Caring more effectively for the intoxicated may reduce the number of persons particularly vulnerable to being robbed. And there is reason to believe that what the police do in identifying and solving minor problems affects the degree of cooperation they receive in dealing with major crimes.

The competition between objectives also becomes apparent. It may surface at the administrative level in the form of a policy question about the distribution of limited police manpower, the priority to be given to calls for police assistance, or the use to be made of the limited time available for training programs. Or it may arise at the operating level in the context of a given incident calling for a quick judgment. For example, what is the primary objective of the police in handling a tense situation on a city street stemming from a speaker attempting to address a hostile audience? Is it to protect the speaker's constitutional right to speak, or to avoid violence, or to resolve the conflict, or to facilitate the movement of disrupted traffic? Often, much to the dismay of the parties involved, it has been the concern for traffic that has dictated police operating procedures.

Whether an agency pursues objectives on its own initiative or only in response to citizen requests is a clear indication of what objectives it considers important. In his study of everyday transactions between citizens and the police, Reiss developed the helpful distinction between reactive and proactive policing. The first describes police activity that is mobilized in response to a citizen's request. The second describes police actions taken on their own initiative.[26] This reactive/proactive dichotomy can be applied with equal value to other aspects of police functioning. Thus, for example, in enforcing laws against gambling, do the police act only upon a citizen complaint, or do they aggressively seek to identify violations? And in dealing with racial strife, do they attempt to prevent tensions from building up, or do they become involved only when conflict erupts?

Separating Methods of Immediate Intervention
from Methods of Disposition

In the vast majority of individual cases handled by the police, their action can be separated into two stages. At the first stage they employ a variety of methods to intervene, heavily influenced by the feeling that "something must be done quickly." Having taken care of the immediate crisis and having acquired additional information, the police then proceed, at a less hurried pace, to the second stage, where they choose from among various alternatives to dispose of the case.

Thus, for example, in responding to a fight they must first separate the combatants, check for the presence of weapons, establish whether any injury has occurred, and acquire information and evidence on the nature of the conflict. They can then decide whether to prefer criminal charges, mediate the situation, or take no further action.

The initial stage may call for very limited intervention as, for example, when the sole purpose is to conduct an investigation in order to establish facts upon which a more far-reaching decision can be based. The intervention, in this instance, might consist of no more than asking a few questions, Or the intervention may be more vigorous and disruptive, such as when police freeze a situation until more information becomes available, order people to disperse or move on, or use some degree of force in dispersing or restraining individuals.

The distinction drawn here between initial police intervention and final disposition does not mean that the two stages are always clearly separable. They sometimes occur together as, for example, when a temporary solution, applied at the moment of crisis, turns out to be an effective final disposition. An order to move on may be all that is required to dispose permanently of an annoying situation.

Acknowledging the Alternative Forms of Immediate Intervention

It is gradually being recognized that the police use a variety of techniques to intervene in a wide range of unpredictable situations calling for a prompt, frequently instantaneous, response. James Q. Wilson, in setting forth his concept of order maintenance, observed that the public expects the police to "put a stop to" certain kinds of behavior. "Though he may use the law to make an arrest, just as often he will do something else, such as tell people to 'knock it off,' 'break it up,' or 'go home and sober up.' "[27] Bittner argues that the application of immediate solutions to problems is a distinguishing feature of most of what the police do. By way of illustration, he points out that while police officers will rarely take action when informed of white-collar crimes (though their primary responsibility is commonly defined as law enforcement), they will spring into action

> to pull a drowning person out of the water, to prevent someone from jumping off the roof of a building, to protect a severely disoriented person from harm, to save people in a burning structure, to disperse a crowd hampering the rescue mission of an ambulance, to take steps to prevent a possible disaster that might result from broken gas lines or water mains, and so on, almost endlessly, and entirely without regard to the substan-

tive nature of the problem, as long as it could be said that it involved *something-that-ought-not-be-happening-and-about-which-someone-had-better-do-something-now!*[28]

It is not simply the availability and readiness of the police that result in their being expected to handle such situations. The police bring with them the kind of authority—real or implied—that must be invoked if such incidents are to be dealt with in a timely and effective manner.

Specifically, the intervention may involve any one of the following actions:

Conducting an investigation.
Stopping and questioning.
Conducting a frisk.
Taking a person into custody for investigation.
Taking a person into protective custody (a person attempting suicide, for
    example).
Issuing an order to desist (as from loud noises, or fighting).
Issuing an order to leave (to a disorderly customer, for instance).
Issuing an order to separate (as in domestic quarrels).
Issuing an order to move on (to a street-corner gathering or streetwalking
    prostitutes, for example).
Issuing an order to freeze a situation pending further investigation (as, for
    example, on discovering a homicide in a tavern).
Using force or threatening to use force.

Although such actions—except for the use of force—may seem less disruptive and invasive than an arrest made with the intention of prosecution, they nevertheless can have a major impact upon the individuals involved. Taken together they give rise to many more complaints about police behavior than police operations within the criminal justice system. Such actions are a major cause of the hostility commonly displayed toward the police.

One must, of course, rush to point out that some of these methods are without clear legal authorization; some, as employed by the police, are patently illegal. Indeed, one of the values in identifying these alternative forms of action is to subject them to more careful scrutiny, with the full expectation that this will result in some current police practices being eliminated, some being modified, and some, although currently illegal but apparently desirable, being legally authorized. Limited forms of authority, if provided, will obviate the need for a more disruptive form of intervention.

Some of the actions described here would, from the legal standpoint, constitute an arrest. In practice, therefore, the police decision to arrest serves two quite distinct functions. It serves the traditional purpose as the initial step in the criminal process. If individuals are to be prosecuted, they must, with some few exceptions, first be arrested by the police. But arrest is also used to achieve an immediate intervention. When used for this limited purpose there is usually no assurance and may be no intent—at the time the arrest is made—that prosecution will follow. This explains why the police so often make an arrest and only subsequently determine the legal basis for the arrest. The limited objective is to deal with an exigency, and to do so by taking temporary custody of the individual. Arrest has come to have meaning and importance as a form of intervention independent of the criminal justice system.

Acknowledging the Alternative Forms of Disposition

In order to dispose of the large volume of diverse cases they handle, the police employ a number of systems in addition to the criminal justice system and a variety of improvised procedures which are rarely acknowledged formally but are generally assumed to be as effective as, if not more effective than, more formal processing. Because we have blinded ourselves over the years to the fact that police do choose from among various forms of disposition, the choice is usually left to individual police officers with minimal guidance from their superiors, and subject to no formal review. These decisions, however, can have a profound effect upon people's lives. Rather than perpetuate the notion that these police actions outside of the criminal justice system are reluctantly and infrequently employed, it is far preferable—especially given their frequency—to recognize them as clear and, if properly used, appropriate alternatives.

What specifically are the different forms of disposition utilized by the police? The criminal justice system is, of course, the most familiar. But contrary to common assumptions its use is not mandated when an offense occurs. There is some support (including statutory provisions) for the notion that police are required to follow a pattern of full enforcement, but this support is being rapidly eroded by overwhelming evidence that selective enforcement is necessary, is often desirable, and in any case is a fact of life.[29]

Whether an individual can be processed through the juvenile justice system rather than the criminal justice system is determined by the age of the alleged offender. But within this limit the police do exercise tremendous discretion in deciding whether to utilize the system at all, or to arrange some other less formal disposition such as referral to a social agency. In contrast to the police role in prosecuting adults, the discretion exercised by the police in processing juveniles has received much more widespread recognition.

A study of hospitalization of the mentally ill in seven states reports that police are involved in approximately one-fourth of all psychiatric hospitalizations.[30] But until recently the authority of the police in most states to take mentally ill persons into custody was not clearly defined. If a police officer thought it was necessary to do so, he would often arrest the person for disorderly conduct. When attempts at suicide were considered criminal, that charge was commonly brought. Gradually, in the course of updating their statutes relating to mental illness, state legislatures have been providing police with specific emergency procedures for detaining and committing for a limited number of hours, pending further review, those believed to be mentally ill.[31]

A very high percentage of people proceeded against by the police (especially traffic violators) are processed under city ordinances. Such processing is commonly lumped together with criminal prosecutions, but it actually differs significantly in that an arrest for an ordinance violation often does not involve taking a person into physical custody; is not, upon conviction, considered a criminal offense productive of a criminal record; and most frequently results in a sentence consisting of no more than a modest fine. A city-ordinance violation obviously carries with it much less onus than the violation of a state statute. In some jurisdictions the police are free to choose between a state charge and a city-ordinance charge when a specific form of behavior is prohibited by both state statute and city ordinance. Sometimes it is a matter of departmental policy (especially where a charge under the ordinance results in the fines remaining with the municipality), but often the choice is left to the discretion of individual officers.

Mediation, referral to other agencies, providing information, and recommending that a person initiate a prosecution on his own are all less formal devices—sometimes employed crudely and sometimes in a sophisticated manner—that the police use in disposing of their business. In the use of each there is obviously some coercive element in the form of an inference that failure of the parties to accept the alternative will result in an arrest and prosecution. How important this coercive element is in accounting for the effectiveness of the police action is a matter of some speculation.[32]

The police are often called upon to arrange temporary custody of people such as small children who are lost or neglected; runaways; intoxicated or addicted persons; mentally ill persons; and those who are senile or physically disabled. The task is complicated because the immaturity or state of mind of such individuals usually prevents them from participating in the decision. Absent appropriate facilities they must often be housed along with those charged with criminal offenses. As an alternative, police will commonly seek to arrange for housing with family or friends. But if an individual has family or friends he is less likely to be among those who come to police attention.

The decision to do nothing may seem obvious, but to the degree that it is a conscious choice it warrants close study. In analyzing police decision-making, it is important to look at the many cases in which the police record the fact that they chose to take no action in order to determine if some action should, in fact, have been taken. Likewise, in trying to develop a rational scheme for handling police business, the option of doing nothing should be recognized as an appropriate alternative in some situations.

Acknowledging the various dispositions used by the police in this manner achieves several desired objectives. It identifies the criminal justice system as but one of the several forms of disposition available to the police and, therefore, places the system in more appropriate perspective vis-à-vis the totality of police functioning. It reflects the abandonment of the concept that the system is the principal means by which the police operate. Identification of the alternative dispositions gives recognition and proper status to methods commonly and properly employed by the police which, in the past, have often been viewed as questionable or less satisfactory than the criminal justice system. And it makes more apparent the need to provide police with adequate forms of disposition for the matters they are called upon to handle.

While all of these actions are referred to as "dispositions" from the standpoint of the police, they do not, by any means, constitute *final dispositions* or *solutions* for the people involved. On the contrary, what the police conceive of as their final disposition may be viewed by the affected party as the first step in a more prolonged process. The police are in the business of administering "first aid"—of doing the best they can to prevent a bad situation from getting worse and then passing the case on to an individual or an agency better equipped to deal with the underlying problem in a more permanent manner.

Recognition of their broad role does not make social workers of the police. No one has seriously suggested that the police undertake to counsel individuals over a prolonged period of time, as a social worker does with his assigned case load. The police function, if viewed in its broadest context, consists of making a diagnostic decision of sorts as to which alternative might be most appropriate in a given case. In this respect the total role of the police differs little from their role in administering first aid to sick and injured persons. Medical first aid serves to prevent further deterioration until the patient can be turned over to more highly trained medical personnel. This function of the police is generally recognized as an extremely important one, and the need for appropriate training in order to perform it adequately has long been recognized.

Ramifications of Acknowledging the Multiple Functions of the Police

If separating out and acknowledging the various elements of the police function in this manner is accepted as a valid way of conceptualizing the police role, a number of related factors begin to fall into place.

The often-repeated contention that police functioning is an extremely complicated business—rather than a simplistic occupation—is indeed confirmed. The need to give high priority to developing alternatives to the criminal justice system in order to enable the police to achieve their objectives more effectively becomes even more evident. And the vast amount of discretion that must of necessity be exercised by the police—in choosing among objectives and methods for achieving these objectives—becomes strikingly obvious.

Beyond this, reflection on the impact that the multifaceted aspects of police functioning can have upon a community and upon the individual citizen underlines the need for more effective control over the behavior of individual police officers. It also points to the need for more effective avenues by which a community can issue directions to its police agency and hold it accountable for its actions.

This conceptualization holds many implications for the staffing, training, and organization of police agencies. It tells us, for example, that in recruiting personnel to be police officers we need individuals who will not only perform well in dealing with serious crime, but will also be capable in many other areas: resolving conflicts, protecting constitutional guarantees, and handling an incredibly wide range of social and personal problems; and, most important, who will have the ability to shift with ease from performing one of these functions to performing another. It tells us, too, that the training of such officers must equip them to make the difficult choices between alternative forms of action. And it raises serious questions as to the appropriateness of the military model by which police departments have traditionally been organized. Subsequent chapters will examine these and related implications in detail.

NOTES

1. See, for example, *Criminal Justice in Cleveland* (Cleveland: The Cleveland Foundation, 1922) and the various reports of the National Commission on Law Observance and Enforcement (Washington, D.C.: Government Printing Office, 1931; reprint ed., Montclair, N.J.: Patterson Smith, 1968).

2. It has since become available in published form: William A. Westley, *Violence and the Police* (Cambridge, Mass.: MIT Press, 1970).

3. The results of this study that pertain most directly to the police are reported in Wayne R. LaFave, *Arrest,* ed. Frank J. Remington (Boston: Little, Brown, 1965); Lawrence P. Tiffany, Donald M. McIntyre, Jr., and Daniel L. Rotenberg, *Detection of Crime,* ed. Frank J. Remington (Boston: Little, Brown, 1967); and Donald M. McIntyre, Jr., ed., *Law Enforcement in the Metropolis* (Chicago: American Bar Foundation, 1967). The last publication contains, in addition, a description of the project, including a list of other publications that, as of 1967, had emanated from it.

4. President's Commission on Law Enforcement and Administration of Justice, *The Challenge of Crime in a Free Society* (Washington, D.C.: Government Printing Office, 1967), pp. 7-12.

5. Elaine Cumming, Ian Cumming, and Laura Edell, "Policeman as Philosopher, Guide and Friend," *Social Problems* 12 (1965): 285.

6. James Q. Wilson, *Varieties of Police Behavior* (Cambridge, Mass.: Harvard University Press, 1968), p. 19.

7. Albert J. Reiss, Jr., *The Police and the Public* (New Haven: Yale University Press, 1971), p. 75.

8. Thomas Bercal, "Calls for Police Assistance," *American Behavioral Scientist* 13 (1970): 682.

9. An exception is the large-scale study of the police function, along with

other aspects of the criminal justice system, conducted in California. Project STAR (Systems and Training Analysis of Requirements for Criminal Justice Personnel), in which many police officials participated, was begun in May, 1971, and was expected to take 39 months. It was sponsored by the California Commission on Peace Officer Standards and Training (State Department of Justice, Sacramento, California) and conducted, under contract, by the American Justice Institute. One of the objectives of the study was to accurately define the police function so that training can be made more relevant. The results of the study are presently being disseminated. See, in particular, California Commission on Peace Officer Standards and Training, *Project Star: Police Officer Role Training Program* (Santa Cruz, Calif.: Davis Publishing Co., 1974). For an early description of the project, see "Report on Project STAR," by Sheriff Bernard J. Clark and Dr. Charles Smith in *The Police Yearbook: 1974* (Washington, D.C.: International Association of Chiefs of Police, 1974), pp. 99–116.

10. In addition to those previously cited, see Michael Banton, *The Policeman in the Community* (New York: Basic Books, 1964); Jerome H. Skolnick, *Justice Without Trial* (New York: John Wiley and Sons, 1966); Joseph M. Livermore, "Policing," *Minnesota Law Review* 55 (1971): 649–729; Jonathan Rubinstein, *City Police* (New York: Farrar, Straus and Giroux, 1973); John A. Webster, *The Realities of Police Work* (Dubuque, Ia.: Hunt Publishing Co., 1973).

11. This is the central point in Wilson's *Varieties of Police Behavior.*

12. The importance of this point, as it bears on contemporary policing, is discussed by James F. Richardson in his *Urban Police in the United States* (Port Washington, N.Y.: National University Publications, Kennikat Press, 1974). See especially p. x.

13. For a more detailed discussion of these points, see American Bar Association, *The Urban Police Function*, Approved Draft (Chicago: American Bar Association, 1973), pp. 47–53.

14. Egon Bittner, *The Functions of the Police in Modern Society* (Chevy Chase, Md.: National Institute of Mental Health, 1970), p. 40.

15. Ibid., pp. 52–62, 83–87. The entire monograph is highly recommended. It is a stimulating analysis of the use of force as the central element of policing.

16. Banton, *The Policeman in the Community*, p. 127.

17. Egon Bittner, "The Police on Skid-row," *American Sociological Review* 32 (1967): 701.

18. Wilson, *Varieties of Police Behavior*, pp. 4–5.

19. Ibid., pp. 17 and 21.

20. Crimes are categorized in various ways for administrative and statistical purposes (e.g., crimes against property as distinct from crimes against persons; or part I crimes as distinct from part II crimes under the Uniform Crime Reporting System), but these distinctions are extremely broad and even they are often lost in general discussions of the police role in relation to crime.

21. See, for example, *Papachristou* v. *Jacksonville*, 405 U.S. 156 (1972).

22. See, for example, Richard A. Myren, "The Role of the Police" (a paper submitted to the President's Commission on Law Enforcement and Administration of Justice, 1967). For an illustration of the position as commonly articulated

in the literature, see Rodney Stark, *Police Riots* (Belmont, Calif.: Wadsworth Publishing Co., Focus Books, 1972), pp. 231–234.

23. For a full discussion of these points, see American Bar Association, *The Urban Police Function*, pp. 39–42.

24. Ibid., pp. 53–71.

25. This list differs from that approved by the ABA committee in several respects. I have deleted the references to apprehending offenders, participating in court proceedings, and working to reduce crime through preventive patrol, on the assumption that these are more accurately characterized as methods employed by the police than ultimate objectives to which they are committed. I have dropped the objective of promoting and preserving civil order because this is covered adequately under resolving conflict. Some might want to add to this list the regulation and control of private morals, not because it should be a police responsibility but because the police are currently expected to devote substantial resources toward this end.

26. Reiss, *The Police and the Public*, p. 64. The distinction has become a part of police vernacular, primarily because of its use in the Kansas City patrol experiment (see chapter 3).

27. Wilson, *Varieties of Police Behavior*, pp. 16–17.

28. Egon Bittner, "Florence Nightingale in Pursuit of Willie Sutton," in *The Potential for Reform of Criminal Justice*, ed. Herbert Jacob (Beverly Hills, Calif.: Sage Publications, 1974), p. 30. This excerpt is reprinted by permission of the publisher.

29. See Kenneth Culp Davis, *Police Discretion* (St. Paul, Minn.: West Publishing Co., 1975), pp. 79–97. I examine selective enforcement, as one aspect of police discretion, in chapter 5 of this book.

30. Ronald S. Rock, Marcus A. Jacobson, and Richard M. Janopaul, *Hospitalization and Discharge of the Mentally Ill* (Chicago: University of Chicago Press, 1968), p. 87.

31. The police use of the criminal law and of the newly enacted statutes is described in Arthur R. Matthews, Jr., "Observations of Police Policy and Procedures for Emergency Detention of the Mentally Ill," *Journal of Criminal Law, Criminology and Police Science* 61 (1970): 284–287. For a critique of the operations under the new statute enacted in Michigan, see "Police Initiated Emergency Psychiatric Detention in Michigan," *Journal of Law Reform* 5 (1972): 581–598.

32. See, for example, Robert L. Derbyshire, "The Social Control Role of the Police in Changing Urban Communities," *Excerpta criminologica* 6 (1966): 315–321; and Cumming, Cumming, and Edell, "Policeman as Philosopher," p. 277.

Chapter 3

The Police and Serious Crime

Because the last chapter dwelled at some length on the problems that arise from the generic use of the term "crime," it must be emphasized that "crime" and "serious crime" are used in this chapter to describe those forms of serious misconduct—such as homicides, aggravated assaults, rapes, robberies, burglaries, and thefts—for which the police have traditionally been held responsible.

Because dealing with these offenses is the most widely recognized aspect of the total police function, one expects police operations in this area to be highly developed. And much in the daily operations of a police agency appears to confirm this expectation. Through a combination of skill, aggressiveness, determination, and the application of technology, many offenders are identified and apprehended. Victims are rescued from their attackers. And wanted persons are located. These successes reflect a vast accumulation of knowledge and expertise developed over the years. Some of this know-how is simply passed on informally through the police ranks; some of it, such as that relating to the scientific detection of crime, is recorded and transmitted through books, manuals, and established operating procedures.

Against this background it is somewhat paradoxical to observe that the police role in relation to serious crime is, in fact, not well developed. And yet this conclusion is forced on anyone who examines the bigger picture—the role of the police in relation to the totality of crime in the community. In this larger focus it is clear that the actual capacity of the police to prevent serious crime and to apprehend offenders is greatly exaggerated. Myths have prevailed over facts in dictating many aspects of current operations. Little has been done to take the problem of crime apart and to develop the police response to each aspect of it. Relatively few experiments have been conducted. And we have just begun to measure the effectiveness of practices in which fantastic amounts of economic and human resources have been invested—day after day, month after month, and year after year. The most troubling realization, given the current pressure to deal more effectively with crime, is that we simply do not know how to invest newly available police resources in ways that will produce predictably beneficial results.

In the pages that follow, a number of underlying problems that police face in dealing with serious crime are examined; attention is drawn to those assumptions and practices in police operations that are most in need of review; and suggestions are offered that might lead to more productive use of police resources.

UNDERLYING PROBLEMS

The Emotionalism Associated with Serious Crime

Violent crimes arouse intense emotions. A single well-publicized crime may result in indignation and outrage sweeping an entire community. Each crime affects a limited circle of people in the same manner, and hundreds of serious crimes are reported to the police every day in each large city in the country. So there is continuous reinforcement of the emotions caused by crime.

Because it is their business, the police must—and do—view crime in a more dispassionate manner, but their constant exposure to the suffering and loss experienced by victims of crime subjects them to some of the same emotional pressures generated in the community. The police administrator of a large city who, on a Monday morning, reviews the summaries of thousands of crimes reported over a weekend cannot help feeling a desperate sense of urgency that "something" be done. The suffering conveyed by these summaries of deprivations—of individuals preying upon one another—is often enough to make the administrator wonder if the police are justified in doing anything other than grappling in the most direct manner possible with the crimes that the statistics reflect.

As a result more and more police resources are poured into fighting crime— usually in the form of additional manpower—even though there is serious doubt about the actual value of what the police have traditionally done. And as the problem becomes more aggravated and pressures intensify, the community and the police are less willing to challenge the feasibility of what is being done, clinging tenaciously to the notion that a greater investment in familiar remedies will eventually produce desired results. Under these circumstances it is extremely difficult to discuss in rational terms, especially in the public forum, the police relationship to crime. Discussions of underlying problems are met with intolerance, and proposals for experimentation are impatiently rejected. So in an often-repeated cycle the myths are reinforced, operating problems are further compounded, more resources are wasted, and intelligent public discussion of the police relationship to crime becomes increasingly futile.

Actual Crime vs. Fear of Crime

Because violent crime generates community-wide concern and fear, the police are under constant pressure to provide protection of a kind that will relieve anxieties. But since general concern about the crime problem may differ from actual fear of being victimized, and both may be unrelated to the actual incidence of crime and the likelihood of criminal attack, it is extremely important for the police to know the specific nature of the problem with which they are dealing.

Some of the earliest studies of the fear of crime claimed that people least in danger were most afraid, suggesting that the problem of fear might be dealt with separately from the actual incidence of crime.[1] In a review of these early studies, however, Frank F. Furstenberg makes the point that those studies failed to distinguish between a broad general concern for crime and fear of actually being criminally attacked; that if these two factors are separated there is a much closer correlation between the actual incidence of crime and the fear of crime.[2]

In the long run it may be that the only effective way the police can deal with fear of crime is to reduce the actual incidence of crime. But in the day-to-day operations of a police agency it is frequently helpful to make the distinction.

If, for example, two women have been raped in the course of several days in a single city block, arrest of the rapist would, of course, put much of the fear to rest. But before the rapist is caught, the police have two quite different responsibilities: to identify and apprehend the rapist, and to meet the fears of residents. These responsibilities may conflict if efforts to provide security lessen the likelihood that the rapist will be caught.

When it is clear that there is little or no relationship between the actual incidence of crime and the fear of crime, the two problems are more easily separable. In some segments of the community, residents fear crimes that have rarely occurred. Here the police must deal with the fear, for they can do little to combat nonexistent crime.

Police agencies do not now consciously distinguish between the actual incidence of crime and the fear of crime in planning their services. Yet in a rational approach to policing, what the police would do to allay fears would probably differ significantly from what they might do to identify and apprehend offenders. Where the fears are indeed justified, based upon the crimes that take place, little that they do short of reducing the amount of crime is likely to have an impact. On the other hand, groundless fear can be allayed by accurate information regarding the actual incidence of crime. A police agency might put together an entirely different blend of services in dealing with fear, which would contain, in addition to a massive effort to educate the community, variations in the usual form of patrol, the increased use of technical surveillance equipment, and a campaign to acquaint citizens with methods for providing themselves with security at their own expense—all of which may be more efficient and more effective than the deployment of more police.

This distinction between the actual incidence of crime and the fear of crime must be recognized at the policy-making level in a police agency. Should a higher priority be given to programs aimed at dealing directly with crime, or those aimed at dealing with the fear of crime? How should a police agency respond to competing demands from different neighborhoods, one having a high incidence of crime and therefore good grounds for fear, and the other, while panicked, having no grounds for being as fearful as it is? Is a police agency justified in responding to the anxieties of citizens whose fears are groundless, if it means removing police from areas where crime is rampant? Many would argue that the local government is as obligated to deal with the fear of crime as it is to deal with the actual incidence; that it is important, whatever the basis for existing fears, that citizens feel secure in their homes and on their streets.

Real vs. Imaginary Capacity

Much of the police response to crime consists of building an exaggerated image of police capacities in an effort both to allay and to generate fear. While a good deal of policing is actually aimed at reducing the extent to which people fear criminal attack, police are, at the same time, striving to generate fear in the minds of those who contemplate committing a crime.

Dealing with fear—whether allaying it or generating it—is a delicate business. It forces police to be as concerned about their image as they are about their true capacity. It requires that they build illusions as a means of expanding their actual potential: that they construct ghosts with which to combat ghosts. I recall a sergeant in Chicago whose assignment required that he handle complaints from large numbers of persons who were, to the degree police can make such judgments, assumed to be mentally ill. He frequently met their concerns about imaginary forces that were threatening them by informing them he was assigning the invisible squad. His resources were unlimited and his callers were apparently very pleased, because they would often make repeated requests for the same kind of assistance. This sergeant may unwittingly have put his finger on what a good deal of policing is about.

Obviously the strength of an image is heavily dependent upon actual capacity. If police performance fits the image, it is reinforced. But if performance does not meet expectations, the image suffers. Thus, for example, a citizen who feels secure in his home because a police officer is present on the street, but who is robbed anyway, will—along with his neighbors and others who learn of the incident—feel less secure thereafter. Likewise, a first offender who gets away with a crime will be less fearful of detection in the future. While personal experience is important in determining a person's impression of police capability, prevailing knowledge in the community—gleaned from mass-media coverage of crime—is also important. Accounts of persons attacked and offenders who are not apprehended detract from whatever image the police may have constructed to reassure citizens and frighten prospective criminals. Public discussion of police operations and crime has the same effect. It is sobering for a citizen to learn, for example that in a city of approximately 200,000 there may be only twenty police officers on street duty during the early morning hours, making a ratio of one officer to every 10,000 people. And it must be gratifying for a person contemplating a crime to realize that the best available statistics indicate that the police succeed in clearing by arrest only 21 percent of all serious crimes reported to them.[3]

The plain fact is that the illusions of past years about the capacity of the police are rapidly being shattered. Improvements in education and communication have resulted in a better-informed public which questions much that previously was taken for granted. Police administrators may still be able to relieve public anxiety in some communities by traditional promises of "crackdowns" or by assigning more manpower, but the value of these responses is being challenged in many areas by operating police personnel as well as the public. The time is coming when there will be no point in refraining from open discussions lest the image of police capacity be damaged. Efforts to improve police functioning vis-à-vis crime must be designed to increase actual capabilities rather than to expand procedures that are of an illusory nature.

REALISTICALLY ASSESSING THE VALUE OF THE TRADITIONAL POLICE RESPONSE TO CRIME

The first step in developing a more rational police response to crime is to challenge the value of current police operations. Two major elements of such operations—common to most police departments, heavily influenced by tradition, and accounting for roughly 80 to 90 percent of the time and resources expended on crime—are examined here: patrol operations and follow-up investigations.

Patrol Operations

The vast majority of the police in a typical large city are deployed in patrol. The uniformed patrolling officer is the generalist in the police agency, having almost as many functions as the agency itself. While much of patrol is clearly unrelated to serious crime, it is nevertheless viewed primarily as a response to crime. A large part of the time devoted to patrol is consumed in responding to calls for police assistance. When a police officer is not answering calls, he has time for what is commonly referred to as preventive patrol. Preventive patrol, in some cities, is limited to making the presence of the police known, on the assumption that this in itself will deter crime. In other cities preventive patrol calls for the police to engage in an aggressive probing of suspicious circumstances. Thus, the most fully developed forms of patrol have three components: the answering of calls for assistance; the maintenance of a police presence; and the probing of suspicious circumstances. The last two constitute preventive patrol.

The use of patrol to respond to calls from citizens regarding crimes seems, on the surface, to raise the fewest questions, since it is rather obvious that the strategic deployment, throughout a city, of police officers in radio-equipped vehicles is the most efficient way in which to create the kind of police readiness that makes a quick response possible. Assuming that officers respond when summoned, this readiness increases the speed with which the police can come to the rescue of individuals subjected to criminal attack. And it increases the potential for apprehending individuals reported to be in the act of committing a crime.

Additional claims are made for the value of a quick response that are less obvious and therefore require careful study. It is, for example, claimed that getting to the scene of a crime within minutes after it occurs increases the likelihood that important information and evidence will be acquired and that witnesses will be located, thereby leading to the identification of the offender and to his quick apprehension—perhaps in the immediate vicinity. It is claimed, too, that widespread awareness that the police have the capacity to make a quick response deters people from committing crimes and that it contributes toward a greater sense of security in the community. A current project, conducted by the Kansas City, Missouri, Police Department, is designed to test some of these hypotheses.[4]

In major urban areas, especially when citizen requests for service are at their peak, patrolling police officers may spend most—if not all—of their time responding to calls. This results in little or no time being available for the other two components of patrol—police presence and probing suspicious circumstances —just when the greatest number of crimes are occurring. In the more efficiently operated departments, manpower is distributed to minimize this situation, assuring that some portion of the patrol officer's time remains uncommitted. And in smaller and less urban departments, large amounts of time typically are uncommitted.

The second component of patrol—making the presence of the police known— can be achieved with minimal effort. By merely sitting in his squad car in the area to which he is assigned, an officer demonstrates his presence, and he further demonstrates it in responding to calls for police assistance. But in order to maximize police presence officers have for years been taught to use their uncommitted time to repeatedly crisscross the area to which they are assigned, on the theory that a single, conspicuously marked squad car can thereby create an impression of police omnipresence and may come upon a crime in progress. More recently several people with backgrounds in operations research have sought to develop highly sophisticated mathematical models which they contend would maximize the value of such coverage.[5]

Within the closed circles of the police field, doubts have often been expressed as to the value of this form of preventive patrol. Obviously, not all criminal offenders seek to avoid detection of their act. Crimes committed in a moment of passion or in privacy are unaffected by cruising patrols. And even where a police presence may deter, patrol by its very nature cannot be comprehensive. It is, at best, spotty in coverage. Moreover, the whole concept is based on the rather naive assumption that criminals have no awareness of police strength and the probability of having their actions intercepted.

In the third component of patrol—the probing of suspicious circumstances—police are expected to check on the security of premises, be on the lookout for wanted persons and stolen property, watch over places where crimes have occurred with some frequency (such as taverns, bus terminals, unoccupied homes, and subway stations), and keep a special watch on individuals who have been subject to criminal attack or who are suspected of engaging in criminal activities. In its more aggressive form this aspect of patrol calls for an officer to stop and question people (commonly referred to as field interrogation), check on the ownership of vehicles, frisk to locate weapons, search vehicles, and in general to intensively investigate suspicious circumstances.

Police have long assumed that a probing form of patrol has value in detecting criminal activity and in identifying and locating offenders. It is assumed, too, that if the mere presence of police in an area has the potential for deterring crime, the presence of police who are known to be constantly checking, probing, and inquiring should have an even greater impact. Police officers will often cite personal experiences in support of these assumptions. They will describe incident after incident where inquiring into suspicious circumstances led them to discover criminal offenses: a strange truck parked at the rear of a warehouse in the early hours of the morning; a light on that is not normally left on; an individual carrying a number of appliances at night in a residential area where burglaries have occurred; a piece of tape holding a door open. But these are episodic incidents; their value must be related to the total cost of an operation in which the number of such incidents may be relatively small.

Just how much effort goes into preventive patrol and what form it takes depend upon the operating practices and policies of a given agency. In many police departments preventive patrol is viewed as busywork—what you do when there is nothing else to do. In others preventive patrol is characterized as the very core of the police job, the activity that holds the greatest promise for dealing directly with serious crime. Where this is the prevailing view, more and more resources are devoted to it and pressures are exerted on officers to dispose quickly of incidents to which they are summoned so that they can return to their preventive-patrol activities.

Despite the tremendous investment in preventive patrol, we have until recently known little about what it actually accomplishes. Prior to 1972 only a handful of studies attempted to measure the effectiveness of specific aspects of patrol.[6] These experimented with increases in police manpower, for it was generally assumed that it was not feasible to reduce the number of police on duty or remove them altogether. The value of these studies was seriously limited by the short duration of the experiments, the total dependence on reported crime as a measure of effectiveness, and the absence of an opportunity to compare an area in which patrol was intensified with an area in which it was eliminated or decreased under controlled conditions.

Against this background the year-long experiment undertaken by the Kansas City, Missouri, Police Department in 1972 with financial and staff support from the Police Foundation represented a major breakthrough. Under carefully controlled conditions, comparisons were made of the impact that different levels of patrol had on three areas of the city, utilizing a number of different measures including surveys to establish with accuracy how many people were victims of crime. Plans for the study called for one area to receive no preventive patrol; another to receive from two to three times the usual level of patrol; and the third to receive the same level of patrol as had been maintained in the past.[7] The study was significant not only because it corrected the deficiencies of previous studies, but because it demonstrated that police can undertake complex experiments that require altering routine operations, with results that are beneficial to the agency and, more broadly, to the entire police field.

The Kansas City project concluded that the variation in levels of patrol produced no significant differences in the amount of reported crime, the amount of crime as measured through community surveys, and the extent to which citizens feared criminal attack.[8] As has been pointed out repeatedly both by the authors of the study and more vehemently by its critics, great caution must be exercised in interpreting the results of the study and especially in applying its conclusions to the wide range of police practices that can be found in other communities.[9]

One of the most startling facts revealed by the Kansas City study is that, whereas 60 percent of the time of the police officers in the three areas studied was available for active patrol in that it wasn't spent in responding to citizen calls, only 14.2 percent of the officers' total time was devoted to activities that were labeled as "mobile police related"—the category that most closely approximates the description of a probing form of motorized patrol.[10] The balance of the time was spent in ways that may have made the presence of the officer apparent in the community, but that involved the officer in contacts with other officers, in administrative chores such as report writing, or in matters unrelated to police business. So in spite of the talk about preventive patrol in police agencies throughout the country, the actual time spent in a probing form of patrol may be much less than is commonly assumed.

On reflection it should not be surprising that police officers, like other occupational groups, will spend large amounts of time on administrative matters and in nonproductive ways. It borders on the inhuman to expect any individual to maintain for an eight-hour period the kind of drive, aggressiveness, and concentration that the police-manual definition of preventive patrol requires.

While there were no significant differences in the incidence of crime resulting from variations in the *level* of patrol as it is conducted in Kansas City, one wonders if the results would be the same if the *form* of patrol varied. Are there aspects of preventive patrol—some of which may not have been used in Kansas

City—that are more effective? Specifically, would officers produce any different results if the time they devote to patrol was spent in a more aggressive and intensive probing of individuals, places, and circumstances? Some police agencies have created special tactical units that do nothing else. What, if anything, can be said of their value? And what about the negative consequences of aggressive patrol? Does it alienate the community and thereby prevent the police from enlisting public support to prevent crime? Hopefully replications of the Kansas City study and other specially designed research efforts will produce answers to some of these questions.

Probing suspicious circumstances means recognizing departures from a norm. A police officer familiar with an area comes to know the activities and behavior patterns of its residents. In commercial areas, for example, he comes to know where people are working at night, how different facilities are secured, and how bank deposits are made. In residential areas he learns which people gather regularly on street corners or in parks, the hours and practices of small merchants, and the patterns with which people use and park their vehicles. Departures from these patterns alert police to the possibility that a criminal act has occurred.

Some circumstances are obviously suspicious and by their very nature demand investigation (two men exploring the entrances to a commercial establishment during the early hours of the morning, for instance). But difficulties arise when the situation is less clear. In a small suburb having a homogeneous population, the person walking the streets at three in the morning either is known to the patrolling officer or is suspect. In contrast the police officer in a large city witnesses a great deal of unusual and sometimes bizarre behavior that is in no way indicative of criminal activity. The mixture of cultures and life-styles makes it difficult to judge what is "normal."

It follows that the value of probing depends heavily upon the patrolling officer's familiarity with an area and the people residing and working in it. In a strange environment he may overlook situations that warrant probing. He may be extremely cautious and discreet in making his inquiries. There is a good chance, however, that he will err in the other direction and offend many citizens by investigating situations that are not suspicious by local standards. When first assigned to an area, patrolling officers drawn from the majority community tend to employ their own norms in deciding what is and is not suspicious in the course of their patrolling—failing to consider the cultures, life-styles, and living patterns of the residents. This accounts for much of the friction between police and minority groups.

The problem becomes especially acute when, under a program of "aggressive preventive patrol," police officers are pressured into aggressive probes. Experience has shown that more aggressiveness means greater numbers of citizens offended by police inquiries. The problem is even further compounded when special tactical units are assigned to aggressive patrol activities. Because tactical patrol officers are usually strangers to a neighborhood, they commonly misconstrue and investigate situations that are not suspicious to the regular patrol officers. And their desire to establish a reputation for being especially tough and effective often earns them a reputation for crude and brutish behavior. In its worst form, patrol by tactical officers consists of stopping and questioning numerous citizens just to get word out in the neighborhood that the tactical unit is around. The National Advisory Commission on Civil Disorders concluded that the assignment of task forces to aggressive preventive patrol was a major factor contributing to the hostility felt by black communities toward the police.[11] With criticism of this kind, the police have a heavy responsibility to assess the value of the various forms of probing patrols that have been in use.

In a commendable effort to do just this the San Diego Police Department undertook a nine-month experiment in 1973 to assess the value of their long-established program of field interrogation, which has been an integral part of their patrol operations and which has apparently been conducted in such a manner as to have been well accepted by the public.[12] The San Diego department defines a field interrogation as a contact initiated by an officer who stops, questions, and sometimes searches a citizen who he has reason to suspect may have committed, may be committing, or is about to commit a crime. For purposes of the experiment the prevailing practice was continued in one area of the city; in another area the practice was carried out by officers who had special training designed to minimize potential friction with the public; and field interrogations were suspended in the third area. It was found that "some level of field interrogation activity, as opposed to none, provides a deterrent effect on suppressible crimes in localized areas."[13] The suspension of field interrogations in the third area was associated in time with a significant increase in the frequency of suppressible crimes. It was also found that changes in the frequency and type of field interrogations during the experiment did not have a major effect on police-community relations. But the study concluded that there were some indications that negative public reactions might develop if the level of field interrogation activities was greatly increased.[14]

Like the Kansas City project, however, the results of the San Diego experiment are limited in their application to other cities. Field interrogation has been a traditional and well-accepted practice in San Diego for which police officers have received extensive training. The study has helped the San Diego department to gain insight into the effects of its policies. It has contributed significantly to other departments by demonstrating the desirability and feasibility of examining this aspect of police operations and by plowing new ground in developing the methodology by which such a study can be conducted.

Follow-up Investigations

In all large police departments, many police officers serve as detectives, conducting follow-up investigations on crimes reported to the police.* Although

---

*As this book goes to press, the results of a major study have become available that strongly support many of the points made in this section. In the study, conducted by the

there is great variation from one agency to another in the arrangements under which detectives operate, their major functions are essentially the same. When a serious crime occurs and the offender is immediately identified and apprehended, they prepare the case for prosecution by bringing all available evidence together for presentation in an organized fashion to the prosecuting attorney. When the offender is identified, but not apprehended, they try to locate him. When the offender is not identified, but there are several suspects, they conduct investigations aimed at either confirming or disproving their suspicions. And when there are no suspects, they start from scratch to determine who committed the crime.

The bizarre aspects of many crimes, the puzzle involved in discovering the perpetrator, the struggle between the forces of good and evil, and the ever-present possibility of danger—all of these elements together account for the public's fascination with detective operations. Few legends are as strong in this country as that of the clever heroic detective who, against great odds, gets his man.

The extent to which the police detective has been popularized—in fiction, in motion pictures, and on television—has had a profound effect upon the way police detectives actually operate. Many of the techniques employed by detectives today are more heavily influenced by a desire to imitate stereotypes than by a rational plan for solving crimes. The myths and fantasy that pervade detective operations deter the police and the public from examining the utility of what it is that detectives in fact do.

Part of the mystique of detective operations is the impression that a detective has difficult-to-come-by qualifications and skills; that investigating crime is a real science; that a detective does much more important work than other police officers; that all detective work is exciting; and that a good detective can solve any crime. It borders on heresy to point out that, in fact, much of what detectives do consists of very routine and rather elementary chores, including much paper processing; that a good deal of their work is not only not exciting, it is downright boring; that the situations they confront are often less challenging and less demanding than those handled by patrolling police officers; that it is arguable

Rand Corporation under a grant from LEAA's National Institute, detective operations were observed in 25 police agencies, and detective practices were surveyed in an additional 156 police departments. Among the major findings were these: most serious crimes are solved through information obtained from the victim or victims, rather than through leads developed by police investigators; in more than half the cases solved, the suspect's identity is known or easily determined at the time the crime is reported to police; an investigator's time is largely consumed reviewing reports, documenting files, and attempting to locate and interview victims on cases that experience has shown are unlikely to be solved; and many investigations are conducted without any hope of developing leads, but simply to satisfy victims' expectations. See Peter W. Greenwood et al., *The Criminal Investigation Process*, 3 vols. (Santa Monica, Calif.: Rand Corporation, 1976).

Also newly available as this book goes to press is an analysis by the Urban Institute of the manner in which detective operations are managed, including some recommendations for improving investigative effectiveness. See Peter B. Bloch and Donald R. Weidman, *Managing Criminal Investigations* (Washington, D.C.: Government Printing Office, 1975).

whether special skills and knowledge are required for detective work; that a considerable amount of detective work is actually undertaken on a hit-or-miss basis; and that the capacity of detectives to solve crimes is greatly exaggerated.

The last point is of special importance and requires elaboration. Practically all serious crimes are investigated by detectives. Yet with the exception of homicide, most serious crimes are never solved. In the compilation of uniform crime statistics for 1974, it was reported that nationwide only 51 percent of all forcible rapes, only 27 percent of all robberies, and only 18 percent of all burglaries reported to the police and recorded by them were cleared.[15] And of these, only a portion were solved by detectives. In many instances offenders remain at the scene of the crime or turn themselves in shortly thereafter; some offenders are apprehended by responding police officers; others are identified by the victim or by a witness. A study of robbery in Oakland concluded that "most robbery apprehensions are made as the result of immediate action by citizens and the police; between 60 and 90 percent in most cities. Detectives and follow-up investigations are rarely as central to the apprehension process as is commonly thought."[16] Many of the crimes reported as solved are multiple clear-ups, which may in part be attributable to detective work, but which are heavily dependent on the willingness of a person charged with one crime to confess others. Many were committed by juveniles or amateurs who presented no real challenge for the detectives. Obviously detectives are kept busy in processing such cases. They must invest long hours in court appearances and in assembling witnesses. Their role, however, in relation to these offenses does not approximate the Sherlock Holmes type role commonly attributed to them.

This is not meant to imply that what detectives do has no value. In a large number of cases good detective work identifies the perpetrator and results in an apprehension. The dogged determination and resourcefulness of some detectives in solving cases are extremely impressive. But in the context of the totality of police operations, the cases detectives solve account for a much smaller part of police business than is commonly realized. This is so because, in case after case, there is literally nothing to go on—no physical evidence, no description of the offender, no witness, and often no cooperation, even from the victim.

For many crimes, such as, for example, mugging, physical evidence subject to any kind of analysis is rarely found. And where it is found (e.g., blood or hair), its use is likely to be restricted to confirming the identity of an individual located through some other means. It is not, in other words, a way to directly identify the attacker as is, for example, a full set of fingerprints that match fingerprints already on file. If descriptions are furnished to the police, they are often so vague as to be applicable to thousands of people. And, given the tense conditions under which offenders are seen and the inexperience of victims and witnesses in describing strange persons, they are frequently inaccurate. If witnesses can be located, they are often unwilling to cooperate. The reluctance of citizens to become involved—in coming to the aid of victims, in providing information to the police, and in cooperating in a prosecution—has been the subject of a great deal of attention in recent years.[17] The absence of such cooperation, explainable on several grounds, is most apparent to the detective who must acquire information to solve a crime.

In police agencies that have a comprehensive record-keeping system, a detective completes a report that eventually takes its place in the files behind the initial report on the crime filed by the patrolling police officer who first responded to the call from the victim or complainant. There is perhaps no better indicator of the futility of much of a detective's work than a comparison of these reports. In a very high percentage of cases the report filed by the detective will simply restate the information acquired by the patrol officer, providing no new leads.

Why, then, do detectives routinely conduct follow-up investigations—even in cases in which past experience abundantly demonstrates that there is virtually no likelihood of a solution? They may hope that a double check will produce new information. But in most cases it appears that their primary motive is to maintain good public relations. Being burglarized or robbed is a traumatic experience. The victim expects the police to take an intense interest in the incident, to exhaust every lead, and to employ all the techniques that citizens have come to associate with detective work. Most police are of the view that it simply does not suffice, given such expectations, for them to inform the citizen that the circumstances in his case do not warrant the assignment of a detective.

One cannot dismiss lightly the public-relations value of detective work. It may fully justify the police resources that are invested. Persons treated sympathetically may offer greater assistance to the police in the future. The advice detectives provide victims (for example, suggesting that they get new locks) may effectively prevent a repetition of the crime. But we must see these objectives for what they are and not delude ourselves into believing that detectives spend all of their time solving crimes.

Refusing to face up to the realities of detective work is costly. The myth that detectives are the most important and highest-status members of a police agency has damaging repercussions. The job (and often the higher salary) attracts competent personnel away from much more important police tasks. The officer performing basic patrol work tends to get downgraded to the role of a "report-taker." The myth that detectives are capable of solving all crimes encourages them, on occasion, to engage in illegal and improper practices in order to satisfy public expectations (such as extorting information through physical force or the threat of arrest and prosecution). The myth also serves to lull the public into believing that nothing more need be done after a detective takes over. Were the public more conscious of the true capacity of the detective, there might be less abdication of responsibility and a greater investment of citizens' efforts in solving crime.

Recognition of the purposes detectives serve has many implications for the form that detective operations should take. Would it, for example, be desirable to concentrate detective personnel on crimes where the added investment of re-sources may lead to the identification of the perpetrator? Should follow-up in-vestigations intended primarily for public relations be conducted by persons—other than detectives—specially trained for this more limited task?

DEVELOPING NEW RESPONSES

It is relatively easy to raise broad questions about the value of traditional police responses to crime. It is more difficult, as evidenced by the magnitude and cost of the Kansas City Preventive Patrol Experiment, to conduct studies that will provide specific answers to the questions raised. And yet important as these ef-forts are, they are essentially negative enterprises, intended to expose myths and disprove assumptions without proposing viable alternatives. The most difficult task—and the ultimate challenge—is to devise programs for the police that can be substituted for existing programs with some assurance that they will be more ef-fective.

It is indicative of the state of affairs in the police field that no alternatives to past methods are readily available. Relatively few new approaches to the crime problem have been proposed, let alone tested.

One might be tempted to conclude that, if police responses to serious crime are of questionable value, the investment of public resources in the police should be reduced. But this is a terribly simplistic reaction to commendable efforts on the part of police to gain new insights into their operations and to share these in-sights—however embarrassing they may be—with the public. It ignores the fact that dealing with serious crime is but one of the responsibilities of the police. More important, it assumes that what the police have been doing is the most ef-fective program they are capable of mounting in dealing with crime. There are no grounds at the present time for such a conclusion.

In casting about for new methods by which the police might have an impact on serious crime, the most one can do is identify some directions that should be explored. First among them is to see all aspects of the job clearly. Not only must the police make meaningful distinctions between their real and illusory capacity; not only must they distinguish between crime and fear of crime; they must also take apart and analyze all the subcategories of serious criminal behavior and eval-uate the appropriateness of the various techniques they have been employing in dealing with them.

Distinguishing Between Different Forms of Criminal Conduct

Some of the problems that arise from our tendency to speak of crime as if all forms of crime had a homogeneous character were identified in the last chapter. But even if we take some elementary steps, as were suggested there, in removing some conduct from underneath the umbrella of crime (such as ordinance violations and those forms of conduct that appear to be labeled criminal primarily to convey authority to the police to do something when the public interest seems to warrant that something be done), what remains nevertheless constitutes a large assortment of quite different forms of prohibited conduct, carried out under widely varying circumstances. This is true even if one's concern is limited to the several categories of crime identified at the beginning of this chapter as being the most widely recognized aspects of the police function.

Unfortunately the public—and sometimes the police—tends to view this mass of criminal conduct in monolithic terms. This creates acute problems for the police. The public, for example, tends to hold them uniformly responsible for all criminal acts. All police officers are considered equally capable of dealing with all forms of crime. And the methods that have evolved over the years—intended to prevent and control crime, but rarely validated in their effectiveness—are commonly viewed as being equally applicable to all forms of criminal activity.

In actuality each form of criminal conduct occurs in a different setting, is likely to involve different types of individuals (both offenders and victims), and poses a challenge to the police that differs significantly from the problems presented by other forms of criminal conduct. The problems associated with rapes, for example, obviously differ from those associated with larcenies, and they call for radically different responses on the part of the police. But more important, within each of the traditional categories of crime (such as homicide, rape, robbery, burglary, and larceny) are equally significant subcategories. The homicide committed by unknown persons under mysterious circumstances presents entirely different problems from the so-called "smoking-gun" homicide committed by one member of a family upon another, where the offender often is the person summoning the police. Likewise, one cannot talk in the same breath about a syndicate that fills orders to steal cars and teen-agers who steal cars for joyriding. Robberies break down into numerous categories—from armed robbery of a bank to the forceful snatching of a purse by a juvenile—with each category calling for a different response. The subcategory of purse snatchings in which force is used may itself be broken down still further by way of identifying situations that differ significantly from one another.

An excellent example of the benefits to be derived from intensive examination of specific crime categories is *The Prevention and Control of Robbery,* a study conducted by the Center on Administration of Criminal Justice at the University of California at Davis.[18] The objective of the study was to describe the patterns of robbery in Oakland, California. The following two findings illustrate the study's value in planning a more rational police response to robbery:

   —First, the picture of robbery in fact is enormously different from that generally assumed. The variance within the city, for example, is particularly great. In a three-year period in which the robbery rate in Oakland was one of the highest in the country, two-thirds of the half-block sized areas in the city had no robberies or pursesnatches at all. Thus, for many parts of the city robbery was a rare event. On the other hand 25 percent of the robberies and pursesnatches occurred in four percent of the half-block sized areas in the city, and over 50 percent along 36 major streets. Even for these areas, however, only one half-block sized area averaged as many as one offense per month, and few were even close.

—Second, while some view robbers as bold and fearless, robbery attacks, in fact, prey heavily on the old and the weak. More than one-third of the noncommercial robberies and pursesnatches in Oakland involving females involved victims who were 65 or older and more than half involved victims who were over 55. Many occurred while the victims were shopping or doing other necessary chores.[19]

Utilizing the results of the Oakland study and other research that has focused on the problem of robbery, Richard H. Ward, Thomas J. Ward, and Jayne Feeley, with the support of LEAA, have recently produced a manual on robbery prevention and control that promotes the need for subdividing the robbery problem and developing a multifaceted response to it.[20] Likewise, Thomas Reppetto's study of residential burglaries and robberies directs attention to the need for distinguishing among the different types of offenses in fashioning an appropriate police response.[21] Harry A. Scarr does the same for just burglaries.[22] Together these studies represent the beginning of an important effort to take apart the traditional categories of crime. They provide a framework upon which individual police agencies can profitably build in analyzing their own crime problems and in developing more sophisticated methods for dealing with specific aspects of them.

The recent development of "crime-specific" projects should result in spreading the practice of subdividing the crime problem as a first step toward fashioning the police response to crime. Initiated in California in 1971, the crime-specific concept encourages agencies to apply their technical and financial resources to the reduction of specific crimes. The pioneering California project, which focused on burglary prevention and control, involved six of the major local law enforcement agencies in a coordinated analysis of the burglary problem, followed by the development and testing of strategies for dealing with it. The analysis itself was a very detailed one, separating the various forms of burglary and establishing the important characteristics of the offense as committed under different circumstances.[23]

Many agencies throughout the country have since adopted the crime-specific concept, stimulated by the support and encouragement of LEAA. It would seem essential for an agency that focuses on a specific crime category, such as robbery or auto theft, to take the problem apart prior to exploring new ways in which it can be attacked. Evaluations of the projects which are now under way will provide some indication of the degree to which this technique has been employed.

Subdividing Police Activity Relating to Crime

When crime was much less of a problem than it is today, the police function was simply defined as preventing crime and apprehending criminals—with enlightened folk placing emphasis upon the former. There never was any doubt over what was meant by apprehension, but what is meant by prevention? Does it mean dealing with the root causes of crime? Does it mean, less ambitiously, that the police should work to reduce the opportunities for people to commit crimes? Crime prevention, to which so much police effort is devoted, is in fact an ambiguous responsibility.

With the increase in crime and the growing complexity of the police role in relation to it, the dichotomy between prevention and apprehension has outworn its usefulness. It is no longer helpful to talk solely in these terms. Just as there is need to speak of specific types of offenses and subcategories of offenses, so there is need to break down and refine the various things police do in dealing with serious crime.

The police have at least ten different tasks or responsibilities in relation to crime: (1) reducing the opportunities of individuals to commit a crime (by giving protection to people and to property that may be the target of criminal attack); (2) interceding in situations which, if allowed to escalate, would most likely result in the commission of a serious offense; (3) creating an atmosphere that deters individuals from committing offenses (by developing an aura of police omnipresence); (4) detecting criminal activity before harm is done (uncovering plots to bomb a building, kidnap an individual, hold up a merchant, or steal a truckload of furs); (5) coming to the aid of persons when they are subjected to criminal attack (such as the victim of a rape or of a robbery being held at gunpoint) and aiding them afterwards in recovering from their experience; (6) apprehending criminals in the process of committing their crimes (such as house burglars, purse snatchers, street muggers); (7) investigating offenses reported to the police in an effort to solve them and to identify the responsible party; (8) locating and apprehending individuals identified as having committed an offense; (9) recovering property lost through criminal action; and (10) assisting in the prosecution of those against whom criminal charges are preferred.

If these ten tasks (and there may be more) are examined in relation to specific subcategories of criminal activity, it immediately becomes apparent that some police tasks apply to some forms of criminal activity, but not to others. And the potential for carrying out any of these tasks will vary a good deal from one subcategory of criminal activity to another. Moreover, the conflicts between different police tasks become clear, crystallizing the need to set priorities and to make policy judgments.

Thus, for example, police efforts to create a presence in a community aimed at deterring crime (#3) have little if any impact upon that category of homicides that involve persons known to each other and that are committed at a moment of great rage in the privacy of a home. On the other hand, police efforts to investigate such offenses (#7) are almost always successful in establishing the responsible party. Recent efforts to improve the police response to domestic disturbances suggest that the police may have much greater potential than previously recognized for preventing such offenses, by skillful intervention when conflict first comes to their attention (#2).

The vastly different characteristics that surround each of the subcategories of criminal conduct of concern to the police require that the police do much more than they have done in the past to tailor their response. If a particular form of police activity has little or no impact upon a specific form of criminal conduct it should not be used in that situation. It may be that the most effective thing police can do in some cases is simply to take a report of the incident. If, however, a specific form of activity appears to have an impact on the problem and could accomplish more if additional resources were available, an investment of additional resources would seem justified. Refining the police response in this manner would encourage police to take a greater interest in finding out what is known about different forms of criminal conduct. It would also provide a more rational basis for making the difficult policy decisions on how best to use available resources in dealing with crime.

Emphasizing Citizen Responsibility

Whatever the police do in attempting to control serious crime, they must recognize just how much their efforts depend upon citizen cooperation and participation. The presence of citizens, like the presence of the police, deters some crime. While the police discover some criminal activity on their own, they depend upon citizens for initially reporting most crimes. Citizens are often in a far better position than are the police to spot suspicious circumstances and make the inquiries that will lead to discovery of a crime. They often possess knowledge that is the clue to the identity of wrongdoers. And their testimony is essential in most cases in which alleged wrongdoers are prosecuted. The plain fact is that the police cannot possibly create a capacity that would approximate the collective capacity that the public has for deterring crime, for reporting offenses, for identifying offenders, and for assisting in their prosecution.

Police efforts to achieve a higher degree of citizen involvement may be the single most important means the police have available to them for coping with crime. A 5 or 10 percent increase in the involvement of all citizens in a community could possibly prove of much greater value in combating crime than a 50 or 60 percent increase in the number of police officers or an equally large investment in technical equipment.

Yet from the days when most laws were enforced by citizen action through the days when citizens took their turn policing, we have entered an era in which many citizens in large urban areas not only abdicate their responsibility for dealing with crime, in some instances they act to frustrate police functioning. The reasons for this alienation are as numerous as they are complex.[24]

Recent efforts to motivate citizens to cooperate with the police by reporting suspicious circumstances are not enough. They perpetuate the notion that it is the police who are primarily responsible for coping with crime and that the police can do the total job if only they have citizen cooperation. We must go further. We must restore a balance between citizen and police responsibilities that reflects a more accurate assessment of actual capacities and acknowledges that effective social control cannot possibly be achieved by hired hands alone.

In some cities community groups have begun to take a more active role in stressing the need for a sense of personal responsibility in combating crime.[25] The police can aid this movement in three ways. They can take the initiative, at every opportunity, to impress on a community the responsibility citizens have for dealing with crime and to inform them of the limited potential of the police. They can offer specific advice to citizens on how they can aid in protecting themselves and their property from criminal attack. And they can cultivate their relationship with the community so that the community will freely turn to the police for support in those situations in which the police are uniquely equipped to be of assistance.

To urge more citizen action in controlling crime is not to suggest that citizens undertake to apprehend criminals or that vigilante groups be created. It is difficult enough to exercise adequate control over the authority vested in the police. It would be a serious mistake to give police powers to self-appointed watchmen or to suggest that untrained citizens use force in attempting to overpower dangerous offenders. The role of the citizen in relation to crime can be greatly increased without altering the rather sound concept that a suitably trained police force is the appropriate repository for both the authority and the force to be used in carrying out police responsibilities in our society.

By-Products of a Quality Response to Other Than Serious Crime

The many contacts citizens have with the police on matters unrelated to serious crime—as complainants, as persons in need of help, as motorists, or even as demonstrators—give police the chance to develop positive relationships with citizens. If the police response to these highly individualized situations is polite, efficient, and, most important, effective, it is argued that this will engender trust and confidence and will result in the citizen being more inclined to work with the police in dealing with serious crime. This concept is reflected in recent experiments with community-based policing and team policing, whereby a group of officers is given permanent responsibility for all police services in an area.[26] It is, for example, a central component in Cincinnati's Community Sector Team Policing Program.[27]

If the apartment dweller who has a difficult problem with his landlord is given some helpful advice, he is less likely to slam the door in the face of the officer when the officer subsequently seeks knowledge that might lead to the identification of the person who burglarized a nearby apartment. Positive attitudes, it is assumed, will produce a greater willingness on the part of the citizen to report suspicious circumstances to the police, to provide information, and to cooperate as a witness in a criminal prosecution.

The police can, as well, learn a great deal from their contacts with citizens over matters unrelated to serious crime. They have the opportunity to observe their culture, their problems, and their interrelationships. A detailed understanding of the community and of its residents can be of tremendous value in making the judgments required to solve serious crimes and identify and locate perpetrators. An officer who has acquired extensive knowledge of an area, it is argued, will be in a position to make more discriminating distinctions in separating the suspicious from the nonsuspicious; the innocent from the potentially guilty.

And if progress is made in equipping the police to provide more effective solutions for the problems they handle daily that are unrelated to crime, they may be better able to prevent situations from escalating into serious criminal conduct, for many of the incidents police are called upon to handle contain the incipient elements of a serious crime. A minor conflict may hold the potential for a future stabbing or shooting. The deranged conduct of a mentally ill person may be symptomatic of a potential for dangerous behavior. And frequent complaints about a juvenile may be the clearest signal we have of the likelihood that the juvenile will commit a serious offense. How the police initially deal with such incidents may determine whether or not the situation grows worse. One of the major claims for recent efforts to improve police intervention in family quarrels, as discussed in chapter 4, is that skilled intervention and a referral to a social agency will prevent the situation from deteriorating into an assault or a homicide. So in a very real sense more adequate responses to the various tasks commonly defined as noncriminal may afford one of the best opportunities the police have for preventing serious crime in the community.

Public Education in Crime Prevention

For many years police agencies, as part of their responsibility for traffic control and safety, have instructed the public in how to prevent traffic accidents. Posters, brochures, and advertisements on mass media provide advice. Schools are organized for drivers and especially for traffic violators. Police officers teach traffic safety to youngsters at public schools.

The police have recently begun to apply these same techniques to crime. Presently in most large cities an organized effort is made to educate the public on how to prevent crime and, in particular, protect themselves from being victimized. Brochures—often in several languages—provide specific suggestions for preventing burglaries from private homes, for preventing cars from being stolen, and for minimizing the likelihood of being mugged. Police officers in many communities are assigned to meet with various community organizations to instruct citizens on elementary precautions they can take to protect themselves. Special instructional sessions are held for businessmen particularly vulnerable to certain crimes, such as jewelers, truckers, and warehouse operators. Several police departments maintain special squads that inspect business establishments and residences at an owner's request to evaluate security procedures and suggest improvements. Police agencies in some cities make a special effort when investigating crimes to suggest how similar incidents can be avoided in the future.

Educational programs of this type may not reduce the total amount of crime in the community. They may simply redistribute it. But it does appear that individuals who follow the advice will be less subject to criminal attack. This potential, by itself, would seem to warrant that the police, at least on experimental grounds, treat their public-education efforts as central to their function rather than peripheral.[28]

Police have available a mass of information reported to them by the victims of crime. With careful analysis (and allowing for the fact that certain forms of criminal conduct are consistently underreported), police should be able to tell a community in very precise terms the conditions that increase the likelihood of criminal attack. It is not enough to stage a broad advertising campaign to exhort citizens to lock their cars or to urge children to avoid strangers. Specific areas of a community in which certain subcategories of criminal activity are concentrated should be targeted for special attention. Those elements of the population (like the elderly) who are especially vulnerable to certain crimes should be alerted.

It is interesting that although the recent concern over rape initially took the form of criticism of the police, the prosecutor, and the courts for the manner in which they handled such cases, more intensive and balanced inquiry appears to have led to the distribution of information on how to avoid a rape attack, with police agencies providing the data upon which such advice is based. This affords a good example of the form that a highly developed crime-prevention effort can take.

Directed Patrol

If the results of the Kansas City study are widely accepted and confirmed in similar studies elsewhere, several major changes in the form of police patrol can be expected. It will of course still be necessary to disperse police officers about a city in order to make them readily available to respond to calls for assistance. But they may be required to spend more time on these calls in order to improve the quality of the response; and the time between calls may be spent in more fruitful ways.

What should patrolling officers do when not responding to calls for assistance? As an elementary step it may be profitable to allocate more time for officers to get to know their community and to educate the citizenry in the prevention of crime. These are important elements in the team-policing projects that have recently been launched. Beyond this it may be beneficial to structure a form of patrol that is highly specific and directed, for use in special missions based largely upon a continuing analysis of serious crime. These missions could be designed to identify and apprehend a particular offender, such as a car thief known to be operating within an area, based upon descriptions furnished by several victims. Or they could deal with a specific problem, such as the early-morning armed robbery of 24-hour gas stations. Clearly there are serious limitations on the use of patrolling officers in this manner, since they are plainly identifiable and must be prepared to interrupt their assigned activities in order to respond to the unpredictable demands for their assistance. But many missions would not require the continuity that would be necessary for surveillance, nor would the effectiveness of the officer be impaired by his being in uniform.

Special missions based upon up-to-the-minute analyses of crime patterns are a potentially effective use for police who are relieved of routine patrol responsibilities. Their full-time availability would make it possible to deploy them with maximum flexibility. Some police agencies have utilized tactical units in a manner that approximates what is suggested here. Officers are assigned to deal with specific crimes, with a decision made each day on the hours they will work and whether their dress will be uniform, plainclothes, or a disguise. One of the best examples of such an operation is that of the Street Crime Unit of the New York City Police Department created in 1971.[29]

The use of special missions in the past has not been as effective as it could have been because the missions were not sufficiently specific or adequately controlled. As the New York City project makes clear, effective use of a squad of police officers on a specific mission requires careful planning. It requires building on past experience. It requires disciplined officers who can work together as a group, curtailing the temptation to see their activities as a form of "hunt" in which individual officers compete against each other for the publicity and rewards that follow an arrest. And it requires sustaining these efforts against pressures to utilize the personnel to fill manpower shortages elsewhere in the agency. Because we know little about the value of such programs conducted over an extended period of time, this is an area that calls for much more in the way of experimentation and careful evaluation.

Investigative Effectiveness

The one area in which the uneven development of police agencies around the country is most apparent is in the effectiveness of their investigative procedures. Many agencies would benefit from adopting elementary procedures in use for years in the more progressive departments. Some agencies, for example, routinely make a thorough search of a crime scene for physical evidence. In contrast, other agencies conduct a search only in major cases. It is repeatedly pointed out that a greater number of cases could be solved if evidence were collected and analyzed more systematically.[30]

Crime analysis, by which reported crimes are systematically analyzed to determine common factors which link them to the same offender, is a basic and indispensable element in the operation of most police agencies and is crucial in a large agency where different units and personnel handle different segments of the total crime problem. Recommendations have been made for strengthening these operations, but at the present time the full potential of crime analysis has not been realized.[31] Some agencies have not taken the most basic steps to collate the data on related crimes. Illustrative of the apparent difficulty in designing an effective crime analysis system in a large jurisdiction where numerous units have investigative responsibilities was the recent acknowledgment of the New York City Police Department that it had failed to recognize the overall pattern in the murders of eight different women and the serious injury of two others that occurred in the same hotel over a period of only one and a half years. The pattern was discovered only when the offender confessed to the incidents upon being charged with still another murder that occurred two doors down the street.[32]

Considerable effort is now wasted because we commonly assume that investigative activity is of equal value with regard to all crimes reported to a police agency. In a current study of investigative effectiveness in the Rochester, New York, Police Department, an effort is being made to determine if there are identifiable factors that indicate whether a particular case can be solved and how much effort will be required to solve it. If solvability factors can be identified, limited resources can then be utilized more effectively. At the same time the Rochester department has conducted a project that has already demonstrated that police officers and detectives working in teams solved more crimes than did their counterparts who followed the traditional division of functions between officers and detectives.[33]

A number of police administrators have suggested that detectives follow the activities of known offenders rather than devote all of their resources to investigating reported crimes. They claim that it is far more logical and efficient to investigate the continuing activities of a professional burglar, for example, than it is to simply wait for him to commit his next crime and only then set out in search of evidence that will implicate him. The thesis has special merit in the case of the professional, given his capacity to operate without leaving clues.

Investigations that focus upon an individual before he commits a crime, although based on knowledge of previous criminal activity, raise extremely difficult legal issues if they interfere in any way with an individual's privacy. Understandably there is concern that such investigations will be made indiscriminately and, especially in the case of ex-convicts, that they will be used in ways that prevent them from establishing normal lives for themselves. Who is to be investigated in this manner? What grounds must the police have to justify their actions? And who in the police department makes the decision? This is a situation in which the potential for abuse is great, and yet a strong case can be made for some narrowly defined and reviewable authority to enable the police to take more initiative in meeting the audacity of the professional or hardened criminal whose past record of judicially proved criminal conduct is known and who, they have reason to believe, is continuing to prey on society in a predictable manner.

Willingness to Experiment

The great hope for the police in coping with serious crime is flexibility—a willingness to test new ideas. This will require that they assume some of the risks inherent in any experimentation; that they carefully evaluate their efforts; and that they willingly discard those ideas that prove to be ineffective.

A police administrator who introduces a new concept quite naturally becomes its advocate. Indeed, a new program is not likely to be put to a fair test unless it has strong support, not only from the administration, but from supervisory personnel as well. As a consequence, when, on the basis of an objective evaluation, a program fails, this often reflects negatively upon those who initiated and supported it.

It requires great maturity on the part of an administrative agency to engage in experimentation. As police agencies mature, their personnel will hopefully view experimentation in much more positive terms. The willingness to experiment is itself a characteristic of a healthy organization. Evaluation is an integral part of experimentation. And negative results are to be expected occasionally if experiments are conducted honestly and are evaluated objectively.

Few people are now equipped to evaluate police programs. This task requires research skills, an understanding of the complexities of police functioning, sensitivity to the peculiar problems in conducting research in a police agency, and the ability to interpret the results of studies in ways that are of practical value to the police administrator. More trained researchers, as well as more advanced methodology, are needed. There is need, too, for police personnel to acquire skills that will enable them to design and carry out evaluation projects on their own. As more effort and talent are devoted to evaluation, the procedures themselves will become more sophisticated and precise and, as a result, will have greater value in determining the most effective ways to invest police resources.

NOTES

1. See especially the results of a Louis Harris poll in 1969, as reported in Jack Rosenthal, "The Cage of Fear in Cities Beset by Crime," *Life Magazine*, 11 July 1969, pp. 16–23. See also Albert D. Biderman et al., *Report on a Pilot Study in the District of Columbia on Victimization and Attitudes Toward Law Enforcement* (Washington, D.C.: Government Printing Office, 1967); and Jennie McIntyre, "Public Attitudes Toward Crime and Law Enforcement," *The Annals* 374 (November 1967): 34–46.
2. Frank F. Furstenberg, Jr., "Public Reaction to Crime in the Streets," *The American Scholar* 40 (1971): 601–610.

3. Federal Bureau of Investigation, *Uniform Crime Reports for the United States, 1974* (Washington, D.C.: Government Printing Office, 1975), p. 42.

4. Sponsored by the National Institute of Law Enforcement and Criminal Justice (NILECJ), Kansas City's response-time analysis study was launched in the summer of 1975. A report on the study is not yet available.

5. The leading work is by Richard C. Larson, *Urban Police Patrol Analysis* (Cambridge, Mass.: MIT Press, 1972).

6. For a comprehensive summary and analysis of these studies, see James Q. Wilson, *Thinking About Crime* (New York: Basic Books, 1975), pp. 81–97. See also George L. Kelling et al., *The Kansas City Preventive Patrol Experiment: A Technical Report* (Washington, D.C.: Police Foundation, 1974), pp. 1–16.

7. George L. Kelling et al., *The Kansas City Preventive Patrol Experiment: A Summary Report* (Washington, D.C.: Police Foundation, 1974), pp. 6–10. For a more detailed description of the study and all of the supporting data, see Kelling et al., *The Kansas City Preventive Patrol Experiment: A Technical Report.*

8. Kelling et al., *The Kansas City Preventive Patrol Experiment: A Summary Report,* pp. 3–4.

9. Ibid., pp. 5, 48–49. For critiques of the study and responses to them, see the series of articles in *Police Chief*, June 1975, pp. 20–45; and the International Association of Chiefs of Police Position Paper on the experiment in *Police Chief*, September 1975, p. 16.

10. Kelling et al., *The Kansas City Preventive Patrol Experiment: A Technical Report,* pp. 498–510.

11. National Advisory Commission on Civil Disorders, *Report of the National Advisory Commission on Civil Disorders* (Washington, D.C.: Government Printing Office, 1968), pp. 159–160. See also President's Commission on Law Enforcement and Administration of Justice, *Task Force Report: The Police* (Washington, D.C.: Government Printing Office, 1967), pp. 183–186, 191.

12. John E. Boydstun et al., *San Diego Field Interrogation: Final Report* (Washington, D.C.: Police Foundation, 1975).

13. Ibid., p. 5.

14. Ibid., pp. 4–6.

15. FBI, *Uniform Crime Reports for the United States, 1974*, p. 42.

16. Floyd Feeney and Adrianne Weir, eds., *The Prevention and Control of Robbery*, 5 volumes and summary (Davis, Calif.: University of California Center on Administration of Criminal Justice, 1974), summary volume, p. 5.

17. The reluctance of citizens to "get involved" became the subject of national concern following the fatal stabbing of Catherine Genovese in New York before thirty-eight witnesses who did nothing to aid her. See A. M. Rosenthal, *Thirty-Eight Witnesses* (New York: McGraw-Hill Book Co., 1964). See also James M. Ratliffe, ed., *The Good Samaritan and the Law* (Garden City, N.Y.: Anchor Books, 1966).

18. Feeney and Weir, eds., *The Prevention and Control of Robbery.*

19. Ibid., summary volume, p. 4.

20. Richard H. Ward, Thomas J. Ward, and Jayne Feeley, *Police Robbery Control Manual* (Washington, D.C.: Government Printing Office, 1975).

21. Thomas A. Reppetto, *Residential Crime* (Cambridge, Mass.: Ballinger Publishing Co., 1974).

22. Harry A. Scarr, *Patterns of Burglary*, 2d ed. (Washington, D.C.: Government Printing Office, 1973).

23. For a summary of the results of the project, including a report on the evaluation of the different strategies, see System Development Corporation, *Crime-Specific Burglary Prevention Handbook* (Sacramento: State of California, Office of Criminal Justice Planning, 1974). The development of the project is described by Joanne W. Rockwell, "Crime Specific . . . An Answer?" *Police Chief,* September 1972, p. 38.

24. See, for example, *Report of the National Advisory Commission on Civil Disorders*, pp. 157–168.

25. For interesting reports of this trend, see "Blacks, in Shift, Organize to Combat Rise in Crime," *New York Times*, 13 November 1974; and "Blacks Are Developing Programs to Fight Crime in Communities," *New York Times*, 23 February 1976. See also National Advisory Commission on Criminal Justice Standards and Goals, *Community Crime Prevention* (Washington, D.C.: Government Printing Office, 1973).

26. Peter B. Bloch and David Specht, *Neighborhood Team Policing* (Washington, D.C.: Government Printing Office, 1973). See also Lawrence W. Sherman, Catherine H. Milton, and Thomas V. Kelly, *Team Policing* (Washington, D.C.: Police Foundation, 1973).

27. Alfred I. Schwartz and Sumner N. Clarren, "Evaluation of Cincinnati's Community Sector Team Policing Program: A Progress Report—After One Year," mimeographed (Washington, D.C.: The Urban Institute, 1975).

28. In an interesting experiment, the FBI, the Police Foundation, and the chiefs of four local police departments announced on July 22, 1975, that they were jointly planning programs to encourage citizens to deter crime through their own low-cost efforts.

29. Andrew Halper and Richard Ku, *New York City Police Department: Street Crime Unit* (Washington, D.C.: Government Printing Office, 1975).

30. See, for example, Joseph L. Peterson, *The Utilization of Criminalistics Services by the Police: An Analysis of the Physical Evidence Recovery Process* (Washington, D.C.: Government Printing Office, 1974), pp. 7–10.

31. Law Enforcement Assistance Administration, *Police Crime Analysis Unit Handbook* (Washington, D.C.: Government Printing Office, 1973).

32. "Case of the 8 Dead Women: Detective Is Transferred," *New York Times*, 24 September 1974.

33. Peter B. Bloch and Cyrus Ulberg, *Auditing Clearance Rates* (Washington, D.C.: Police Foundation, 1974).

Chapter 4

Developing Alternatives to the Criminal Justice System

It is ironic that there is so inverse a relationship between the diverse array of tasks the police are expected to perform and the extremely limited methods formally available to them for getting the job done. If the police are to fulfill their responsibilities in a fair and effective manner, they must be provided with a set of alternatives, in the form of authority and resources, sufficient in number and variety to enable them to deal appropriately with the situations they commonly confront. This means that informal alternatives now in use must be evaluated—legitimated and refined when necessary, or discarded. And it means that new alternatives must be designed. It should not be necessary to label conduct criminal in order to authorize the police to deal with it. Nor should it be necessary for the police to make informal use of other systems, or improvise, or function in a sub-rosa or illegal manner.

If the focus in improving police operations is on the quality of the services delivered to the citizenry, as it should be, the design of new responses to commonly recurring situations holds tremendous promise. It is possible to visualize the day when a police officer will be provided with a wide range of alternatives for both immediate intervention and the disposition of cases, and when he will be highly trained in their use. Some of these alternatives may simply consist of new techniques and procedures; others may call for invoking some carefully limited forms of police authority; still others might consist of new community services with which the police can integrate their efforts. Whatever their form the alternatives would result from careful study and imaginative planning; and they would be molded to fit the situations to which they were intended to apply, have proper legal underpinnings, be accompanied by adequate procedural safeguards, and be fully recognized as appropriate methods for handling police business.

IMPEDIMENTS TO DEVELOPING ALTERNATIVES

Reluctance to Give Police Additional Authority

How can one responsibly propose that the police be granted any additional powers, given the extent to which police authority has been abused in the past? Police administrators striving to improve police functioning are constantly faced with this query, burdened by the record of past abuse and continually blamed for the wrongs committed in other police agencies. Sadly, ample justification exists for distrusting the police, and proposals for giving the police additional authority are therefore understandably greeted in many quarters with skepticism and even alarm.

Combating this distrust requires getting across the rather complicated message that granting the police specific forms of new authority may be the most effective means for reducing abuse of the authority which is now theirs; that it is the absence of properly proscribed forms of authority that often impels the police to engage in questionable or outright illegal conduct. Before state legislatures enacted statutes giving limited authority to the police to stop and question persons suspected of criminal involvement, police nevertheless stopped and questioned people. It is inconceivable how any police agency could be expected to operate without doing so. But since the basis for their actions was unclear, the police—if they thought a challenge likely—would use the guise of arresting the individual on a minor charge (often without clear evidence) to provide a semblance of legality. Enactment of stopping-and-questioning statutes eliminated the need for this sham. In some jurisdictions, moreover, police administrators acquainted officers with their new authority to stop and question by providing specific guidelines for making use of an investigative process which—up to that time—was employed without any guidance whatsoever.

Many other areas of police functioning would be similarly improved if specific forms of carefully defined authority were granted. Why should a police officer arrest and charge a disorderly tavern patron if ordering him to leave the tavern will suffice? Must he arrest and charge one of the parties in a lovers' quarrel if assistance in forcing a separation is all that is desired? It is of course arguable that specific authority to require a person to leave in these situations might be abused. But the abuse could hardly be greater than that which results from applying the criminal justice system to such incidents. From the administrative standpoint it is much easier for a police chief to gain meaningful compliance with an explicit grant of authority than for him to seek to improve police functioning by an awkward adaptation of the criminal justice system.

Another objection to authorizing police to do things outside of the criminal justice system is that it exempts their actions from the reviews and controls inherent in the system. But this view fails to recognize how ineffective these controls have been in many jurisdictions, especially when an officer's intent is to achieve some objective other than prosecution. The street prostitute who is illegally arrested for purposes of harassment may eventually be acquitted or have her case dismissed, but she receives no redress for having been unjustly processed through the system. Indeed, programs such as the wholesale harassment of street prostitutes and other petty offenders through illegal arrest and the confiscation of weapons through illegal search have often taken place with the full knowledge of the prosecutor and judges who review such cases. None of the checks built into the criminal justice system seems to curtail these illegal practices where they have been known to exist. We must ask if the review provided by the criminal justice system—with all its apparent inadequacies—is so superior to one which might be provided by an alternative system that it justifies continued use of the criminal justice system, even when its use seems inappropriate and excessive.

Growing Disenchantment with Social Service Programs

Developing new and more helpful responses to the massive volume of police business is generally recognized as an enlightened approach to policing. This comes at a time, however, when there is increasing questioning of the use being made of both the criminal justice system and related systems to provide social services.[1] Most familiar, perhaps, are the recent challenges to the operation of the juvenile justice system. Launched as a novel effort to act in the interest of the child, the system has been under increasingly severe attack for its failure to afford adequate protection for the rights of the child, for the absence of adequate treatment, and for using a form of custody that, in many situations, amounts to penal incarceration. Thus, in the name of helping children, the juvenile justice system has, in some jurisdictions, fostered undesirable practices that are alien even to the system it was designed to supplant.

The civil commitment for "treatment" of mentally ill offenders who are adjudged unfit to stand trial is another example of a program designed to be more humanitarian that has backfired in many instances. Offenders detained as patients in mental institutions have received no more help than they would have received had they been imprisoned.[2] At the same time they have often been denied recourse routinely afforded prison inmates.

In the light of these experiences, proposals to establish programs to help chronic alcoholics, drug addicts, and other troubled people with whom the police come in contact are often viewed with deep suspicion—with fear that the needed assistance may not be delivered and, worse, that government power will be used in ways that may adversely affect the person being "helped." Moreover, if professionals such as judges, social workers, psychiatrists, and correctional officials misuse power in administering programs, what will happen if the police, who are viewed as much more punitive and coercive, are entrusted with more authority to help people than they now have?

Yet it is unacceptable to conclude that because social services run into difficulties, the police should, for example, have no alternative but to transport the down-and-out drunk to a jail in which he is housed with large numbers of other inebriates, often in such crowded, smelly, and unsanitary conditions that the whole process seems subhuman. It is equally unacceptable to conclude that a police officer who, through no choice of his own, is forced to intervene in a domestic quarrel should have no alternative but to charge one of the participants with a criminal offense—an act that can only exascerbate an already aggravated situation.

But in fashioning more humanitarian responses to old problems, the police and others working to improve police functioning must move gingerly, with an awareness of the many pitfalls to be avoided. The initial criteria for police use of any new alternative must be carefully worked through; the degree of coercion in the application of new alternatives must be carefully weighed; the police judgment must be subject to review; and the police must have some assurance of the adequacy of the resources or systems to which referral is made, lest they be placed in the position of offering a helping service that does not help and that may unwittingly cause harm.

Resistance of Operating Personnel

The initial reaction of the police to proposals that they be equipped with various alternatives for handling their work load is often hostile. The process of admitting an intoxicated person to a detoxification center, for example, may appear to be more bother than it is worth; personnel understandably cling to the familiar and uncomplicated procedure of locking up drunks. Moreover, many police consider it demeaning to admit that some aspects of the police task require "softer" approaches than those associated with serious crimes.

Some of this initial resistance can be overcome by an appeal to an officer's pride in the importance and complexity of his work. Little skill and talent are required to crudely apply a uniform solution (the criminal justice system) to an array of different problems. Diagnosing a situation and selecting an appropriate method for dealing with it are much more challenging tasks. Additionally, it can be argued that it is an affront to the self-respect of a police officer to be held responsible for problems that society not only has not solved, but to which it has blinded itself, and to be required to deal with these problems, many of them unpleasant, day in and day out, in a useless and ineffectual manner. It is especially offensive to be forced to use procedures that literally subject the officer to being sued, prosecuted, and dismissed from his job in order to do what is expected of him. It is difficult to think of another profession or occupation that tolerates such a situation.

But rank-and-file objection to new alternatives is not simply objection to the alternatives themselves, but to accepting responsibilities from which many police would prefer to be relieved. The police must be persuaded of the desirability—and perhaps the inevitability—that they continue to handle most of the problems for which they are now responsible. It is encouraging that police administrators are increasingly indicating a willingness to accept this position and that rank-and-file officers, in the context of some of the new projects, also have demonstrated their support for the concept.[3]

The initial resistance to introducing alternatives to the criminal justice system makes it doubly important that the alternatives work. There are great dangers in overselling a new form of response lest it not meet the hard tests to which police will put it. This problem will be discussed in detail later.

RECENTLY LAUNCHED PROGRAMS

Much progress in developing new alternatives to the criminal justice system has been made in recent years. This progress is particularly encouraging because it reflects a willingness of some police agencies to engage in limited experiments and a willingness of local governments, state legislatures, private organizations, and federal and state funding agencies to provide the authority, the money, and often the guidance that have made the projects possible.

In discussing such experiments, distinctions must be made between efforts to decriminalize certain forms of behavior, efforts to divert the handling of some forms of conduct from the criminal justice system after initial processing, and efforts to supply alternatives that bypass the system altogether.

Decriminalization may or may not involve creating new police responses. Obviously if a legislature decides to decriminalize adultery it will not be necessary to create any alternatives for the police, since police are under no pressure to deal with adultery. But if a legislature decriminalizes drunk and disorderly conduct, the police will, as a minimum, need some alternative for dealing with the "down-and-out" who requires care. The legislature may or may not provide it.

Most diversion projects are designed to take cases out of the crowded and overworked criminal justice system after they have entered the system and usually after a prosecutor has concluded that probable cause existed for the arrest.[4] In these projects the police practices in bringing cases into the system do not necessarily change. The police are, however, generally assigned some role in selecting the cases that are to be dropped out of the system, once admitted. A diversionary project of this kind tends to perpetuate police use of the criminal justice system, at least in its initial stages, whereas legislation that gives police specific new authority, such as empowering them to take intoxicated persons to a medically operated facility, is a much more clear-cut alternative to prevailing practice. When police are authorized or expected to act in some manner other than by an arrest, the process is sometimes labeled prearrest diversion—a form of diversion that does constitute a clear alternative to the use of the criminal justice system.

The new alternatives are quite varied. They include such dissimilar developments as the explicit authority many legislatures have given the police to stop and question persons suspected of a crime, the new conflict-management techniques police have employed in handling interpersonal disputes and confrontations between opposing groups in the community, and the programs to respond more suitably to the public inebriate, the mentally ill, the drug addict, and the juvenile delinquent. Such programs may have been launched for some other purpose and thus have not always been characterized as alternatives to the criminal justice system, but their availability nevertheless affords police new options for handling commonly recurring situations.

Progress in the development and use of these alternatives has been uneven, reflecting varying degrees of commitment in the first instance and radical changes in commitment as specific projects have been pursued. A number of projects have been abandoned or substantially redirected, as when, for example, a new chief or commissioner is appointed. And, as one could anticipate, even those projects having the benefit of continuous administrative support have suffered serious setbacks because of errors and omissions that quite naturally occur in exploratory efforts of this kind. But the results of experimentation in one jurisdiction have stimulated other agencies to pick up an idea and develop it, so proliferation and additional development have taken place even though the original project may have been abandoned. Our tendency to view police in a parochial manner and to be disappointed by setbacks in specific agencies blinds us to the fact that the overall picture is often much more encouraging.

In view of their variety, no attempt will be made here to describe and analyze these projects in detail. Their diversity makes generalizations impossible, and their complexity makes brief analysis impractical. Many of the projects have been described and evaluated in readily available publications.[5] From among the various alternatives that have been tried, those aimed at improving the police response to conflict (particularly the domestic disturbance) and to the public inebriate currently appear to be receiving the greatest amount of attention. They are discussed here because the experience in implementing them affords an illustration of the issues likely to arise when alternatives are developed. The popularity of projects in these two areas is quite natural, since the domestic disturbance ranks among the most common incidents the police are called upon to handle; and approximately 15 percent of all arrests made for other than traffic offenses in 1974 in the United States were for public drunkenness.[6] So while the attention recently concentrated on the domestic disturbance and the public inebriate sometimes wears on the patience of traditional police officers, who see these problems as relatively unimportant, the volume of such cases and the sense of frustration commonly experienced in coping with them have apparently contributed to a readiness on the part of many police agencies to experiment with alternative approaches. A cluster of other alternatives has developed around these two major efforts—some are an outgrowth of family-crisis and detoxification projects and others have evolved independently.

The Conflict-Management Programs

The typical family-crisis intervention project is designed to augment an officer's options by providing him with training in skillful mediation as a form of immediate intervention, and by enabling him to make selective referrals to social agencies. The pioneering effort in family-crisis intervention was conducted by Professor Morton Bard in collaboration with the New York City Police Department.[7] The much-cited project involved the intensive training of eighteen officers who were then assigned to a precinct where they handled all complaints which could be predetermined to involve a family disturbance. An important element in the program was constant development of the officers' skills through frequent consultation and additional training while in the field. The project cautiously concluded that, among other things, sensitive and skillful police intervention in family quarrels may reduce the number of family assaults and family homicides, may have a positive effect upon police-community relations, and may greatly increase the safety of police officers in handling these highly charged situations.[8]

Since 1970, family-crisis intervention projects have been initiated in many police agencies throughout the country. Many have been federally funded. The Law Enforcement Assistance Administration's research arm, the National Institute of Law Enforcement and Criminal Justice, has been attempting to systematically evalute their success and to provide more refined guidance for their implementation.[9] As one would expect, the projects vary greatly—especially in the kind of training provided and in the use made of social agencies for referral. Unfortunately, like all new efforts of this kind, many of the projects are primarily public-relations efforts and do not significantly change the way police respond to domestic disturbances.

Some of the basic concepts initially set forth in the family-crisis projects have been adapted to other areas of police operations. Bard himself experimented with the application of family-crisis intervention techniques to a broader range of conflicts that came to the attention of special housing police in a public-housing project in New York City.[10] The Oakland, California, Police Department, in addition to developing a new response to family crises, initiated a project in 1969 to furnish a more effective response to conflicts between landlords and tenants.[11] In this project emphasis was placed on providing the officer with the legal knowledge to understand and settle disputes. When he was unable to solve their problems the officer referred landlords and tenants to appropriate agencies. A number of other police departments have since taken similar steps to improve their response to landlord-tenant conflict.

Illustrative of an interesting variation on these conflict-management programs is the citizen-dispute settlement program in Columbus, Ohio, which was cited by the National Institute of Law Enforcement and Criminal Justice as an exemplary project.[12] Under this program the disputing parties in family and neighborhood conflicts are scheduled for an administrative hearing before a hearing officer, who is a law school student working under the supervision of a member of the prosecutor's staff. No arrests are made. The formal objectives of the program are to reduce the work load of police and judicial officers, to ease interpersonal tensions by finding equitable solutions to problems without resort to a formal judicial remedy, and to avoid giving minor offenders an arrest record. The program apparently does not attempt to alter the initial on-site contact of the police with the disputing parties, but it does afford the responding officer the choice of an alternative disposition that seems ideally suited for many minor disputes.

All of the preceding are responses to conflicts of an interpersonal nature. Of equal significance are the efforts to develop more effective responses to large-scale conflicts between groups of people—disputes, for example, between political dissenters and government authorities, between students and university administrations, between striking employees and management, and between black and white students attending the same high school. As the large-city police agencies were drawn into the increased racial conflict of the 1960s, some of them established special police-community relations units which initially were limited in their objectives to keeping better informed on the troubles brewing in their communities. They attempted to maintain positive open communication with groups often considered hostile toward the police. On many occasions in the 1960s, the informal mediating efforts of these units prevented violent conflict.

But as civil-rights groups became more militant and as anti-war groups began to demonstrate in the streets, the special units lost their effectiveness. It became evident that, when public pressures demanded traditional responses, these units did not have sufficient influence over police operations—either in the provision of routine services or in a riot or demonstration situation. Subsequently, however, as police administrators found they could not cope with large-scale conflicts, a search began for alternatives, and some of the previous efforts to communicate with conflicting groups were reinstituted. In addition some police administrators experimented with "softer" responses to disturbances and demonstrations—responses that required extensive planning and usually called for getting officers to the scene before tensions developed, using fewer uniformed officers, and instructing them to act in a more casual, less threatening manner. Officers who facilitated peaceful demonstrations thereby lessened the likelihood that the police would become the target of attack. So what previously was only a staff concept gradually became an operational concept that constituted an alternative way to handle major confrontations.

In Dayton, Ohio, the conflict-management concept, under the administration of Robert Igleburger, was made a standard response to group conflicts, and officers were urged to employ the technique in handling individual cases as well.[13] Dayton police used the approach in responding to a variety of potentially explosive situations, such as the announced intention on the part of black organizations to shut down a construction site in protest over the failure of building-trades unions to hire more members of minority groups; the conflicting demands and outbreak of physical attacks in a newly integrated high school; the traditional conflicts between labor and management at the site of a strike; and the annually recurring tensions, mostly of a racial nature, between youths and itinerant operators of a heavily attended county fair. Community reaction to the police response in these situations was overwhelmingly positive. Even those groups involved in the conflicts appeared to be satisfied.

While many departments have employed the same techniques used as part of the Dayton program in handling specific incidents, few have done so consistently, and not even Dayton has succeeded in institutionalizing the response. In some cities this is because major conflicts do not arise with sufficient frequency to warrant standardizing department methods for dealing with them. In other cities a change in administration results in a change in approach. And in still others the political climate or the magnitude of a given conflict results in abandonment of the concept even though it has previously been used with success. Thus, for example, the Metropolitan Police Department of Washington, D.C., utilizing conflict-management techniques, was widely acclaimed for its handling of the march by anti-war groups on the Pentagon in October of 1967 and for its handling of the counter-inauguration activities staged by similar groups in January of 1969.[14] But the department adopted a traditional response to the anti-war demonstration staged in May, 1971, which resulted in the arrest of approximately 13,500 persons and considerable on-the-street violence.[15]

Detoxification Programs

After many years of disregarding the problem of the public inebriate—especially the skid-row resident—there is now a flurry of activity to develop more satisfactory responses. Some of the programs that have emerged afford the police a clear alternative to arrest and jailing of the homeless alcoholic. Others are responsive to some aspects of the skid-row problem, but are so limited in their objectives and resources that they cannot be accurately characterized as a viable alternative for the police. Whatever their limitations, these programs are a most welcome development, for they reflect a concern with the extraordinarily frustrating skid-row problem which has been left, in the past, almost exclusively to the police and missionary groups.

The new projects have much in common. They are all based on the premise that the criminal justice system is not an appropriate vehicle for dealing with the alcoholic who violates no other laws; that it should not be necessary to label the alcoholic a criminal in order to help him. All of the projects maintain some kind of facility to which alcoholics are taken. But beyond these basic similarities the projects take many different forms. Each project reflects a different degree of commitment to the various elements that together might constitute a comprehensive approach toward dealing with the public inebriate. Some place heavy emphasis upon providing an improved form of initial on-the-street contact with the alcoholic; others stress the provision of critically needed medical care and temporary shelter; some emphasize the detoxification process and the provision of care for from seven to ten days; and others place primary emphasis upon efforts to enroll detoxified alcoholics in an extended program designed to assist them in controlling their drinking habits.[16]

Of special interest to the police are the provisions of the programs that relate to the initial contact with the inebriate. A number of them require that all admissions to a detoxification center be voluntary. Voluntariness appears to be an essential requirement if a program is to succeed, although there is serious question as to how much importance can be attached to the "voluntary" decision of one who is incapacitated or in a state of physical distress.[17] In the often-cited St. Louis project, the intake procedure was described as "voluntary or else," it having been made clear to the alcoholic that if he failed to volunteer, he would be arrested and prosecuted.[18] In some jurisdictions the alcoholic is arrested in the traditional manner, but transported to a detoxification facility rather than a jail. If the duration of the alcoholic's stay in a detoxification facility is no longer than it would have been in a jail, some progress may have been realized by this method, even though procedural safeguards are lacking and the inebriate still gets an arrest record. But if an arrest results in prolonged custody and treatment, it may be that one crude use of government authority is being replaced by an even more questionable one.

An increasing number of states have attempted to solve this problem by enacting legislation that decriminalizes public intoxication, gives police explicit authority to take incapacitated alcoholics into protective custody for transportation to a treatment center, and authorizes detention for a limited period of time. The programs provide an opportunity for initiating a continuum of treatment on a voluntary basis or by a commitment proceeding that incorporates all due process requirements.[19]

Some of the problems raised here are avoided or at least reduced if all pickups for detoxification programs are, in fact, voluntary, and if, in addition, civilian rescue teams are used in lieu of the police—thereby divorcing the program from the coercive element implied by police involvement. Raymond T. Nimmer strongly recommends this method.[20] Charles W. Weis goes further, arguing that "citizens suffering from drinking problems and from homelessness are not the proper concern of the police, no matter how humanitarian the latter's efforts may be."[21] Given the inherently concentrated nature of the skid-row problem, it may well be both more efficient and more effective to utilize civilian rescue teams in some cities. It is misleading, however, to suggest that a detoxification program or a civilian rescue team will eliminate the need for police involvement. Police must continue to deal with the often related and sometimes independent problems stemming from a high incidence of violence; from lack of food and shelter; from injuries and illness in need of medical attention; and from the nuisance created for permanent residents, business establishments, and passers-by. They must continue to be involved in various ways with inebriates who refuse help or who, for some reason, cannot be helped by established detoxification programs.

ISSUES RAISED BY RECENT PROGRAMS

When related to the total need, the new alternatives for dealing with problems the police routinely confront—even if one includes those not described here—seem pitifully few. And only a scattering of police agencies have experimented with them. But much has been learned that will be of value in improving upon these relatively modest efforts and in designing additional alternatives. Particularly helpful at this stage are the identification of pitfalls to be avoided and the crystallization of some basic issues that had not previously surfaced.

Tailoring Alternatives to the Needs

The need to develop new alternatives calls attention, once again, to the importance in policing of taking large problems apart in order to deal more effectively with them. Bard's family-crisis experimentation is a good example of such an approach. It not only focused, at the outset, on but one form of conflict; some effort was made, within the project, to develop different responses to different forms of family disputes.[22]

The detoxification projects have suffered because they have often been presented as a total response to the problems of the public inebriate, when in fact they are extremely limited or have been designed to achieve a number of different objectives—among which the improvement of the police response is but one. The situation has been aggravated because some treatment centers make it clear that they want only those alcoholics who have the greatest potential for rehabilitation. The police often complain that such programs cater to the least troublesome part of the total problem. They see themselves as being left to struggle with the large volume of public inebriates in whom the centers are not interested.

If one were to start fresh to fashion a more effective response to the problem of the public inebriate as it is confronted by police agencies, the response would, of necessity, consist of several elements.

A detoxification program is important for some inebriates, affording them the opportunity to sober up under medical supervision and the opportunity, while in a sober state, to consider entering a treatment program. For others, suffering from injuries or disease, the most critical need is for immediate medical assistance. For those inebriates who have a home, the police need both the authority and the means to transport them there. Many of the homeless simply need a more decent form of shelter than is provided by a jail, but less elaborate and less costly than a hospital, with the offer of assistance in gradual withdrawal if the alcoholic desires it. For those who commit crimes or who routinely prey upon other alcoholics, prosecution may be in order. And some form of institutionalizing is required for those whose physical condition deteriorates to the point where they can no longer function at the minimal level required on skid row.

In his analysis of the various detoxification programs, Nimmer concludes that it is a mistake to assume that arrests cannot be terminated unless new systems are developed to provide care for the public inebriate.[23] The arrest process has often been viewed as affording shelter and thus, in a minimum way, providing care for the unconscious inebriate who might otherwise die (as, for example, from exposure). But Nimmer argues that the number of inebriates on the streets in this condition is but a small fraction of the total skid-row population.[24] Thus, as to some inebriates under some conditions, Nimmer contends that the police should simply let them be. While this is an alternative the police should have, police experience suggests that it is an unsatisfactory alternative where the presence of inebriates is in conflict with other uses made of the public areas they frequent.

In measuring the value of new alternatives used by the police, expectations must be defined realistically. If the public inebriate who desires shelter is provided with an opportunity for a decent, sanitary overnight acccommodation rather than space on the floor of a crowded and stench-ridden jail, the police function in relation to the alcoholic in need of shelter will have been improved, though little if anything is done toward rehabilitation. Likewise, if an improved police response to the domestic disturbance reduces the number of deaths and serious injuries resulting from such quarrels, the program will have been a success even though the marriages may subsequently be dissolved. Because the problems that police confront are among the most exacerbated to be found in society, one must often be content with the minimal goal of preventing a bad situation from getting worse.

Formalizing the Informal

In searching for new alternatives, police would be well advised to look carefully at the informal techniques some of them now employ. With imagination and resourcefulness, officers often work out ingenious solutions to frequently recurring problems. The quality of police services would be greatly improved if some of these responses were more widely employed.

An officer in Detroit, for example, concluded that a major factor in domestic disputes was the presence of a gun in the home. In his view it added to the fear, to the tensions, and to the possibility of injury or death if the conflict escalated. So when called to a serious domestic dispute, he discreetly offered to remove any weapons, to hold them in his personal custody, and to return them in two or three days. Even though the officer's thesis cannot easily be proved, it seems likely that a distraught spouse would be relieved to know that a gun was not readily available. Obviously removal of a weapon is not a solution to domestic quarrels, but it might be among the techniques used in dealing with them when they escalate to a point requiring police attention. Interestingly, in developing a departmental policy on domestic quarrels a citizen member of a task force in the Dayton, Ohio, Police Department made just such a suggestion, and the procedure was incorporated in department policy.[25] The legal implications of the action were studied, and a form was drawn up which the citizen signs authorizing removal and which serves as a receipt. The weapons are then stored by the department.

The value of examining what police currently do is reflected in other recently implemented programs. The improvised practices of experienced officers in mediating conflicts contained some of the basic elements of the conflict-management programs now popular in police departments. And the practice of referring troubled people to various agencies in the community was employed informally by many officers long before they were urged to use manuals containing lists of available services. Not only were these improvised practices not recognized, they were, to some degree, secret, because they were not considered proper procedures since they lacked formal departmental sanction.

Among existing alternatives that should be carefully reviewed to determine if they are being utilized to the fullest extent is the practice of charging an individual with violation of a city ordinance rather than a state statute, where the option exists. The criteria currently used in making this choice are often questionable, but the consequences may be more beneficial than has been assumed. This is especially so in small communities and in suburban areas where charging a city-ordinance violation results in an adjudication that is much more informal and thus allows for greater flexibility in working out dispositions. The proceeding usually takes place before a local judge (rather than a judge at the county seat or in the centralized courts of a large city). The offender does not always receive an arrest record. The stigma of a criminal prosecution is usually avoided. And yet the individual's behavior is subject to judicial review and, where there is a finding of guilt, to the imposition of some punishment. Should greater use be made of city ordinances to deal with forms of behavior that are not sufficiently serious to warrant criminal prosecution?[26]

Absence of Adequate Community Resources

Efforts to improve police functioning inevitably lead to the identification of larger unmet community needs. Police programs to provide direct assistance to juvenile offenders, in lieu of juvenile court, long ago pointed up the critical need for counselors, psychiatrists, and various other specialists to whom juveniles could be referred—not that all juvenile offenders require such services. The continued absence of such resources when they are needed, however, is among the factors accounting for the difficulty police experience in arranging satisfactory dispositions for juveniles.

As new alternatives have been developed, additional needs have been exposed. Police efforts to handle tenant complaints draw attention to the need for more vigorous enforcement of building codes; efforts to cope with vagrants expose the need for shelter and medical facilities; and the programs aimed at resolving disputes disclose the critical need that indigents, in particular, have for marriage counselors and routine legal services. Police often find, for example, that misunderstandings over purchase agreements, credit arrangements, and leases are at the heart of the disputes they are called upon to handle.

Although the need for agencies to which individuals requiring help can be referred is obvious, the amount of help these agencies can supply tends to be over-estimated. A police officer may be as effective as—if not more effective than—an independent agency. The officers engaged in the New York Family Crisis Intervention Project got the impression that the agencies to which cases were referred were not only overburdened, but were unable or unwilling to provide the kind of flexible crisis services the frontline operational group needed.[27] This is not surprising, for the agencies to which referrals were made had probably not previously handled the end-of-the-road cases police commonly see. So even though the agencies were formally available as a resource in the project, police tended over a period of time to make less use of them and to depend more heavily upon their own mediation skills.

Somewhat the same problem has arisen with regard to the public inebriate where states have substituted the health care system for the criminal justice system. In Wisconsin, for example, legislation enacted in 1974 provided that, as an alternative to arrest, all persons incapacitated by alcohol be taken into protective custody and be transported to a treatment facility at which they were to be initially examined by a physician and then provided with optional forms of treatment.[28] After the law went into effect, it quickly became apparent that many inebriates did not need medical care; and as for others, the medical or mental health system had little to offer. The ability of physicians, psychiatrists, and other mental health workers to effectively treat chronic alcoholics who are repeatedly picked up by the police is extremely limited. The net effect of the new program may simply be to process chronic alcoholics through a different and more costly revolving door, returning them to the street where they again become the concern of the police.[29]

These experiences call attention to the peculiar nature of police work. Many of the problems the police confront—in dealing, for example, with the alcoholic, the mentally ill, and the parties in a dispute—are the residual problems for which no solution has been found. Indeed, this is precisely why they become police business. It follows that any improvement in dealing with them, to the extent that improvement is possible at all, requires innovative techniques. Little will be gained by merely substituting another process for the criminal justice system if the new process is no more effective in solving the problem. The inability of various service agencies to carry out the tasks that the police are led to expect from them can be fatal to a program in which referral is the major element. Police stop using alternatives that appear to them not to accomplish anything, and they revert to improvising responses as they have done in the past.

The need for tying police operations into other social services and—more especially—the need to establish new services and to improve existing ones so that they can respond adequately to the kind of cases surfaced by the police require that police administrators articulate their needs more aggressively. As long as the police are willing to cope with their common problems as they have in the past, it is unlikely that there will be any public clamor to provide more suitable and costly alternatives. The most annoying aspects of the problems are taken care of, as, for example, by arresting the unsightly derelict; and the negative effects of the programs, such as harm caused by a long record of arrests for minor offenses, are not plainly visible. Police administrators should not be expected to help bury recurring problems but should instead assume a positive role in calling them to the public's attention.

Equipping Police to Use Alternatives

If new alternatives are to have any chance of succeeding, police officers must be trained in their use. It is not surprising that some carefully devised programs for using alternative responses to commonly recurring incidents have failed, when one considers that all that was done, on implementation, was to announce the availability of the new alternative to officers through formal channels of communication. Many officers, conditioned to operating in one manner for years, will ignore communications that inform them that they now have the opportunity, for example, in lieu of making a physical arrest, to request an offender accused of a petty crime to appear in court; or that they may now deliver intoxicated persons to a special shelter or medical facility; or that tenants having disputes with their landlords may be referred to a number of agencies. This is especially so since the whole concept of employing alternatives to the criminal justice system is relatively novel and is perceived by some officers as being in conflict with their own idea of the police function.

Training is required that not only will acquaint an officer with the specific provisions of a given alternative, but also will tell him the rationale that resulted in its being made available, in the hope that increased understanding will lead to intelligent full use. Officers must be equipped with criteria to help them decide when to make use of the alternative. Some new alternatives, such as family-crisis intervention, may require prolonged and intensive training. Many agencies have erred in attempting to implement family-crisis programs without providing anything approaching the kind of intensive training given to the officers who participated in the pilot program.

Motivating police officers to make wise use of alternatives—especially in light of the antagonism some alternatives will engender—requires strong signals from top administrators that such use is indeed desired. Rank-and-file officers will ig-

nore newly established procedures that they sense were reluctantly implemented
by top administrators on the insistence of outside interests, such as the courts,
neighborhood groups, or academicians. But support will be forthcoming if administrative and supervisory personnel demonstrate their own desire to make the
alternatives work.

It follows, very directly, that formal systems for measuring an officer's performance must be changed so that the officer who strives to use available alternatives is rewarded with advancement and status in the organization. It makes no
sense to perpetuate a system in which an officer is urged to deal with a situation
by avoiding an arrest, but whose performance is then judged by the number of
arrests he makes; nor does it make sense to urge an officer to develop a special
skill and take on a special assignment which may then preclude promotion and
raises.

The Need for Specific Grants of Limited Police Authority

Since police so often employ the criminal justice system solely for the authority it gives the officer to make an arrest, one would expect that any alternatives
to the criminal justice system must, of necessity, include some substitute form
of authority. But proposals for new forms of police authority have been slow to
emerge.

In the conflict-management programs one gets the impression that the emphasis upon using persuasion and mediation is so great that any talk of authority
seems, at this point, antithetical. And yet if conflict-management techniques are
to be routinely utilized in handling domestic quarrels, for example, some difficult questions of authority must inevitably be faced. What happens if the police
are refused entry? What happens if the parties fail to separate or refuse to obey
the order of a police officer to leave a room or an apartment? Should a police officer, in such situations, simply revert to the criminal process and his aura of
omnipotence? Would it be consistent for police officers who are committed to a
more sophisticated form of intervention to resort to using their arrest powers
when challenged? Whether specific forms of limited police authority will be
needed will probably not be known until we have had much more widespread
and continuous experience with family-crisis projects.

As previously noted the legal basis for delivering an inebriate to an established
detoxification facility is fuzzy in many jurisdictions, but nineteen states and the
District of Columbia have given specific authority to the police to take persons
incapacitated by alcohol into custody without arresting them.[30] The Wisconsin
statute, which is adapted from the Uniform Alcoholism and Intoxication Treatment Act, reads:

> A person who appears to be incapacitated by alcohol shall be taken into
> protective custody by a law enforcement officer and forthwith brought to

an approved public treatment facility for emergency treatment. If no approved public treatment facility is readily available he shall be taken to an emergency medical service customarily used for incapacitated persons. The law enforcement officer, in detaining the person and in taking him to an approved public treatment facility, is taking him into protective custody and shall make every reasonable effort to protect his health and safety. In taking the person into protective custody, the detaining officer may take reasonable steps to protect himself. A taking into protective custody under this subsection is not an arrest. No entry or other record shall be made to indicate that the person has been arrested or charged with a crime.[31]

New forms of authority are bound to be slow in developing. It is an extremely difficult undertaking to draft a specific form of authority that will withstand legal attack and to devise a system to assure ample opportunity for review of its use. Given the complexity of the task, further refinements seem a long way off. One development that may provide a catalyst for more rapid progress, however, is the increased challenge by appellate courts of the broad uses made of the criminal law. As statutes and ordinances defining disorderly conduct or vagrancy, for example, are increasingly declared void for vagueness, and as such statutes and ordinances are redrafted in more exact terms, police will no longer be able to fall back upon them as a basis for their actions when more specific authority is lacking.[32]

Some Underlying Legal Problems

A number of recent efforts to furnish additional alternatives for handling police business have collided with the common assumption that the police are required to enforce all laws.

This was illustrated in the various proposals to structure a more rational police response to drugs. In handling the drug problem, police must deal with extremely varied situations: with both the pernicious peddler and the innocent experimenter; with the extremely dangerous drugs and the relatively harmless ones; with large international shipments and with infinitesimal quantities incidentally found on persons coming into police custody. The most highly developed legislative provisions did not give the police sufficient specific guidance on how to tackle so large and varied a problem, and as a result informal policies emerged. To improve on these informal policies, some police agencies, in collaboration with other community service agencies, sought to provide a more suitable disposition for those accused of petty offenses by offering to refer them to a drug clinic as an alternative to criminal prosecution. Although referral was hailed initially as an enlightened approach to a complicated problem, these efforts raised difficult questions.

If the referral was made by the prosecutor, it was assumed the legal basis for the arrest would be reviewed; and the prosecutor's discretion to decide not to prosecute is firmly established. But some of the programs called for referral prior to involvement by the prosecutor. The question then is whether a police officer has the authority to release a person who has been arrested. Would failure to prosecute subject the officer to any liability? Specifically, would the officer's action in searching the individual—a search that probably produced the narcotics—subject him to any liability if the officer chose not to pursue the arrest, which provided the legal basis for the search? In addition, the arrangements raised other questions about the status and civil rights of the alleged offender. Under what control or obligation, if any, is the person who accepts referral in lieu of prosecution? What happens, for instance, if the arrestee fails to appear for referral? Is he or she then subject to prosecution? The questions related to the status of the alleged offender are receiving attention now as part of the rapidly expanding movement to implement diversion projects, although the answers to them are not clear by any means.[33]

Questions about the meaning of arrest and the consequences of arrest, as they bear on police operations, are also raised by the move to encourage the police to allow alleged offenders their freedom at the scene of an offense, with the understanding they will appear in court, rather than take them into custody pending release on bail or personal recognizance. The intent in advocating this procedure is not only to reduce the harsh effect of the criminal process when it seems appropriate to do so (for example, in minor cases such as shoplifting), but to eliminate the need for police officers to transport a person to a booking facility. The option is provided for by statute in some jurisdictions.[34]

But even where authorized, the procedure is not used as much as it could be.[35] One reason for this is the tendency to label contact with an offender an arrest if the person is under some legal obligation to appear subsequently either at a police facility or in court. But some argue that no arrest has in fact been made if the officer does not intend to take the person into immediate custody. If the contact is viewed as an arrest, the officer is often reluctant to release the offender, since the statutes generally provide no basis for release of an arrested person except when the grounds for the arrest are found to no longer exist or when the release is authorized by a court. On the other hand, if subsequent appearance is not required and not enforceable, the use of the notice to appear is seen as being in conflict with the statutes that mandate arrest whenever an offense has occurred.

So full-enforcement statutes continue to impede the development of new clear alternatives, even though the statutes are widely ignored in the daily operations of police agencies. The problems to which they give rise lend support to the arguments for a more forthright legislative recognition that it is neither feasible nor desirable for the police to be required to enforce all laws. Indeed, the very concept of alternatives to the criminal justice system requires formal recognition of the discretionary nature of the police function—the subject matter of the next chapter.

NOTES

1. The issues of concern today are essentially the same as those raised by Francis A. Allen in his provocative work, *The Borderland of Criminal Justice: Essays in Law and Criminology* (Chicago: University of Chicago Press, 1964).

2. See, e.g., most recently, *O'Connor* v. *Donaldson*, 95 S. Ct. 2486 (1975).

3. It is significant, for example, that the Board of Officers of the IACP joined with the House of Delegates of the American Bar Association in endorsing a set of standards relating to the urban police function that urged recognition of the wide range of police responsibilities and advocated that the police be given the means to carry out their responsibilities effectively. American Bar Association, *The Urban Police Function*, Approved Draft (Chicago: American Bar Association, 1973), pp. 1–4, 22.

4. For the most current summary of such projects, reflecting their diversity and some of the problems they raise, see Raymond T. Nimmer, *Diversion: The Search for Alternative Forms of Prosecution* (Chicago: American Bar Foundation, 1974).

5. Some of these projects are cited in the bibliography of this chapter. For an interesting analysis of the problems that surfaced when such projects were used as demonstration projects designed to effect change in police operations, see Catherine H. Milton, "Demonstration Projects as a Strategy for Change," in *Innovation in Law Enforcement* (Washington, D.C.: Government Printing Office, 1973), pp. 115–133.

6. The percentage was computed from statistics compiled by the FBI. See FBI, *Uniform Crime Reports for the United States, 1974* (Washington, D.C.: Government Printing Office, 1975), p. 179.

7. For a detailed description of the project and its evaluation, see Morton Bard, *Training Police as Specialists in Family Crisis Intervention* (Washington, D.C.: Government Printing Office, 1970).

8. Ibid., p. 35.

9. LEAA has published a helpful summary of the concept and the pitfalls to be avoided for the benefit of police agencies contemplating such a project. See Morton Bard, *Family Crisis Intervention: From Concept to Implementation* (Washington, D.C.: Government Printing Office, 1974). For an interesting account of the continuing effort to evaluate the projects, see Gerald M. Caplan, "Evaluation: A Vital Step in Criminal Justice Programs," *LEAA Newsletter*, March 1975, pp.8–11. Some of the programs that have been established in recent years are summarized and critiqued in Donald A. Leibman and Jeffrey A. Schwartz, "Police Programs in Domestic Crisis Intervention: A Review," in *The Urban Policeman in Transition: A Psychological and Sociological Review*, ed. John R. Snibbe and Homa M. Snibbe (Springfield, Ill.: Charles C. Thomas, 1973), pp. 430–436.

10. See Morton Bard, Joseph Zacker, and Elliot Rutter, "Police Family Crisis Intervention and Conflict Management: An Action Research Analysis," mimeographed (prepared for the Department of Justice, LEAA, 1972).

11. For a description of this project, see Linda A. Moody, "Landlords and

Tenants: Oakland's Landlord/Tenant Intervention Unit," *Police Chief*, March 1972, pp. 32–34.

12. See John W. Palmer, "Pre-Arrest Diversion: Victim Confrontation," *Federal Probation*, September 1974, pp. 12–17. For those who wish to replicate the project, the National Institute of Law Enforcement and Criminal Justice has published a manual: *Citizen Dispute Settlement: The Night Prosecutor Program of Columbus, Ohio* (Washington, D.C.: Government Printing Office, 1974).

13. The Dayton experience is described by the head of the conflict-management unit, Tyree S. Broomfield, in "Conflict Management," in *The Police and the Behavioral Sciences*, ed. J. Leonard Steinberg and Donald W. McEvoy (Springfield, Ill.: Charles C. Thomas, 1974), pp. 85–95. For an evaluation of the program, see Community Research, Inc., "Evaluation of the [Dayton, Ohio] Conflict Management Program, 1971, " mimeographed, n.d.

14. See National Commission on the Causes and Prevention of Violence, Task Force on Law and Law Enforcement, *Law and Order Reconsidered* (Washington, D.C.: Government Printing Office, 1969), pp. 343–351.

15. See Michael S. Wald, "Mayday Revisited: Parts I and II," *Criminal Law Bulletin* 10 (1974): 377–435, 516–643.

16. For an excellent description and analysis of the earliest projects, including those conducted in St. Louis, in Washington, D.C., and on the Bowery in New York City, see Raymond T. Nimmer, *Two Million Unnecessary Arrests* (Chicago: American Bar Foundation, 1971). A series of recommendations for implementing new projects, based upon a more recent review of the various efforts that have been launched across the country, is presented in Charles W. Weis, *Diversion of the Public Inebriate from the Criminal Justice System* (Washington, D.C.: National Institute of Law Enforcement and Criminal Justice, 1973).

17. Weis, *Diversion of the Public Inebriate from the Criminal Justice System*, p. 11; Nimmer, *Two Million Unnecessary Arrests*, pp. 135–137.

18. Raymond T. Nimmer, "St. Louis Diagnostic and Detoxification Center: An Experiment in Non-Criminal Processing of Public Intoxicants," *Washington University Law Quarterly* 1970: 1, 8. See also Nimmer, *Two Million Unnecessary Arrests*, p. 85.

19. Most of these states have adopted, with some modifications, the provisions of the *Uniform Alcoholism and Intoxication Treatment Act* drafted by the National Conference of Commissioners on Uniform State Laws, Committee Print prepared for the Subcommittee on Alcoholism and Narcotics of the Committee on Labor and Public Welfare, U.S. Senate (Washington, D.C.: Government Printing Office, 1971).

20. Nimmer, *Two Million Unnecessary Arrests*, pp. 150–152.

21. Weis, *Diversion of the Public Inebriate from the Criminal Justice System*, p.11.

22. Bard, *Training Police as Specialists in Family Crisis Intervention*, p. 30.

23. Nimmer, *Two Million Unnecessary Arrests*, p. 151.

24. Ibid., p. 142.

25. Dayton, Ohio, Police Department Manual, General Order 2.01-2 "Domestic Disputes," section V C 1 (revised 6/74).

26. In a variation of this alternative, Oregon enacted legislation in 1973 that made possession of less than one ounce of marijuana a civil rather than a criminal offense, with a maximum penalty of $100. At the local level, Ann Arbor, Michigan, and Austin, Texas, are among the cities that have sought to deal with possession of small amounts of marijuana as an ordinance violation.

27. Bard, *Training Police as Specialists in Family Crisis Intervention*, p. 30.

28. *Wisconsin Statutes* §51.45 (11) (1973).

29. Memorandum from Chris Moraski and Jim Klein, Committee Staff for Alcohol and Drug Abuse, Senate Committee on Agriculture, Human Services, Labor & Taxation and Assembly Committee on Health & Social Services, Wisconsin Legislature, to Committee Members re Implementation of Chapter 198, 1973 (29 September 1975).

30. The states that have adopted the Uniform Alcoholism and Intoxication Treatment Act with but minor modifications are: Alaska, Colorado, Georgia, Idaho, Illinois, Kansas, Maine, Montana, South Dakota, Washington, and Wisconsin. Those that have adopted an act very similar to the uniform act are: Connecticut, Florida, Iowa, Maryland, Massachusetts, Michigan, Minnesota, and New Jersey. Also in the second category is the District of Columbia.

31. *Wisconsin Statutes* §51.45 (11)(b) (1973).

32. For an analysis of the need for new forms of limited authority and for an overall review of recent efforts along these lines, see ABA, *The Urban Police Function*, pp. 87–114.

33. See, e.g., Daniel L. Skoler, "Protecting the Rights of Defendants in Pretrial Intervention Programs, " *Criminal Law Bulletin* 10 (1974): 473.

34. See, e.g., *Illinois Revised Statutes* ch. 38, §107.12 providing for issuance of a notice to appear. See also the model provision recommended in the American Law Institute, *A Model Code of Pre-Arraignment Procedure*, Proposed Official Draft (Philadelphia: The American Law Institute, 1975), §120.2, pp. 15–17. For interesting analyses of the police citation procedure in several jurisdictions, see Mark Berger, "Police Field Citations in New Haven," *Wisconsin Law Review* 1972: 382–417; Floyd F. Feeney, "Citation in Lieu of Arrest: The New California Law," *Vanderbilt Law Review* 25 (1972): 367–394; Jeffrey M. Allen, "Pretrial Release under California Penal Code Section 853.6: An Examination of Citation Release," *California Law Review* 60 (1972): 1339–1370.

35. See, e.g., Marvin E. Aspen, "Arrest and Arrest Alternatives: Recent Trends," *University of Illinois Law Forum* 1966: 241, 249–250.

Chapter 5

Categorizing and Structuring Discretion

That the police exercise broad discretion in carrying out their multiple functions should, by now, be patently clear. That the quality of police service depends on the manner in which this discretion is exercised should be equally obvious. Yet it was only approximately fifteen years ago that the existence of discretion in police work was first openly recognized. We are, therefore, still in the earliest stages of working through the many problems that arise from viewing the police as an agency of municipal government having major policy-making responsibilities and as an agency whose employees themselves are required to make many important discretionary judgments in the course of their daily work.

In the past the prevalent assumption of both the police and the public was that the police had no discretion—that their job was to function in strict accordance with the law. In fostering this image of themselves as ministerial officers, doing precisely what they were mandated by law to do, the police were responding to their understanding of what was expected of them by legislatures, by the courts, and by a substantial segment of the general public. But behind this facade, in sub-rosa fashion and with an air of illegitimacy and impropriety, the police have, of necessity, functioned in a much looser and more informal manner —making frequent choices and exercising broad discretion in order to carry out their multiple responsibilities.

This business of formally subscribing to one concept while operating on the basis of a conflicting one has had a profoundly negative effect upon police services. It has, as one commentator put it, stunted the healthy growth of police organizations.[1] It has placed a curb on forthrightness in dealing with the public and has forced the police to violate the law in order to do their jobs. And it has put a premium on duplicity in the relationship of police officers with each other and with the community.

We are not completely out from underneath this yoke by any means. Many people—including some police leaders—tenaciously adhere to the notion that the police do not exercise discretion. And others, while they recognize the discretion currently being exercised, nevertheless conclude that it should be eliminated. This presents a major problem that will be examined later in this chapter.

On the more positive side there is today a steadily growing recognition of police discretion and increasing support for the contention that it is not only necessary and desirable, but should be openly acknowledged, structured, and controlled. This chapter looks at the issues raised by this more forthright approach to police functioning.

THE DIFFERENT FORMS OF DISCRETION

Like all new concepts that carry a one-word label, "discretion" has come to mean different things to different people. As a result it is not unusual to find a police agency that claims to support the general thesis that police exercise discretion, but manifests little evidence that this concept has been incorporated in operating policies. In some departments discretion means merely using good common sense in exceptional circumstances. It connotes a degree of flexibility in an unusual situation when more formal treatment would bring embarrassment to the police officer and the agency. In other departments discretion is thought to apply solely to the judgments police must make in using the criminal process —in searching suspects and vehicles, in obtaining search warrants, in conducting lineups, and in seizing property. And in still others discretion refers primarily to selective enforcement—when to take action against conduct defined as criminal.[2]

Selective enforcement does pose, in clear form, a wide range of the problems that must be confronted in coming to grips with police discretion. Police are usually mandated to enforce all laws. They generally claim that this is what they do. But in reality they systematically ignore many violations, and they enforce other laws only under certain conditions. By examining selective enforcement one can explore both the feasibility and the legality of police discretion and can formulate specific methods for better structuring the discretion that is exercised.[3] But concentrating on selective enforcement, by itself, as a way to examine discretion in police agencies, has serious drawbacks.

First it tends to result in viewing police functioning with regard to all criminal violations—from the most petty to the most serious—in uniform terms. Police discretion in enforcing a city ordinance prohibiting the consumption of beer in a public park is looked at in the same light as the discretion involved in not arresting an assailant, absent the cooperation of the victim. This puts in one basket the various uses of the criminal law that, as argued in chapter 2, should be distinguished, and it tends to reinforce the simplistic notion that the job of the police is to enforce the law. The issues that arise from the discretion exercised in enforcing the disorderly conduct statutes are significantly different from those connected with enforcing a city ordinance prohibiting smoking on mass transit, and both differ significantly from the issues that arise in enforcing the statutes prohibiting assault or burglary. Because the law, in reality, is a means to an end, selective enforcement must be examined in the context of the various objectives of the police. Whatever guidance a police administrator provides his officers in deciding whether to arrest for disorderly conduct, for example, should be contained in broader policies on such problems as street gatherings, domestic disputes, and public inebriates, rather than in a specific policy or rule on the enforcement of the disorderly conduct statute.

The second serious drawback in focusing exclusively on selective enforcement is that it ignores the vast areas of discretion that do not directly involve a decision whether or not to enforce a law. An examination of selective enforcement does not, for example, include discretionary decisions on when to use force, on appropriate uses for surveillance and undercover techniques, or on stopping-and-questioning practices. Nor does it cover the decision to dispose of police business by some means other than prosecution. Kenneth Davis, though he has concentrated on selective enforcement, nevertheless acknowledges the importance of these other decisions as part of the total picture of police discretion:

> A public officer has discretion whenever the effective limits on his power leave him free to make a choice among possible courses of action or inaction.
> Some elements of this definition need special emphasis. Especially important is the proposition that discretion is not limited to what is authorized or what is legal but includes all that is within "the *effective* limits" on the officer's power. This phraseology is necessary because a good deal of discretion is illegal or of questionable legality. Another facet of the definition is that a choice to do nothing—or to do nothing now—is definitely included; perhaps inaction decisions are ten or twenty times as frequent as action decisions. Discretion is exercised not merely in final dispositions of cases or problems but in each interim step; and interim choices are far more numerous than the final ones. Discretion is not limited to substantive choices but extends to procedures, methods, forms, timing, degrees of emphasis, and many other subsidiary factors.[4]

To appreciate the extent to which police exercise discretion it is necessary to identify the full range of discretionary decisions and to begin to distinguish the different categories of such decisions. Six such categories will be examined here, the first three of which relate to the conceptual framework of the police function developed in chapter 2.

Choosing Objectives

Because the police have a number of different objectives (such as preventing and controlling serious crime, aiding individuals in danger, facilitating the movement of people and vehicles, and assisting those who cannot care for themselves), both administrators and officers at the operating level must continually make judgments as to what they are seeking to achieve in a given case or category of cases. The administrator, for example, must decide how much of the agency's resources should go into dealing with serious crime as compared with such other objectives as investigating traffic accidents, providing protection to persons who feel threatened, and coping with public inebriates. A decision must be made, too, about how intensively the police should apply themselves to their objectives and what happens if two objectives conflict. The officer at the operating level also must often decide what he or she should attempt to achieve. Given the nature of police operations, administrators and officers may not realize that they are making important decisions. And even if they do, the judgments that go into them are rarely articulated. One can, however, identify some of these decisions and gain some understanding of how they are made by looking at different aspects of the routine operations of a police agency.

The organization of the agency, which usually includes specialized units of differing size to deal with traffic, youth, and organized crime, for example, provides a good indication of the relative importance attached to different functions. The factors weighed in distributing the patrol force—such as the number of arrests, reported crimes, or service-oriented calls—are significant. When the police wait for a complaint to be filed or a violation to occur before taking action, they obviously do not think the matter is as important as when they aggressively seek out complaints and identify violations. Important discretionary judgments are reflected in the measures used to evaluate the operating efficiency of police officers, such as traffic-ticket quotas, arrests, or the amount of time taken to handle specific kinds of calls. One can learn a great deal by observing the responses of personnel to telephone requests for police assistance. Are there calls to which police refuse to dispatch officers? Are there others to which they consistently respond by making referrals to other agencies? What are the priorities when more calls are received than can be handled immediately? And, finally, much can be learned from an examination of training programs. For example, in the training of recruits, how much time is devoted to criminal investigation, to dealing with social problems, and to the protection of constitutional rights?

Observation of police handling of incidents on the street often provides the most accurate indication of the choices made from among competing objectives. In the massive demonstrations in recent years, the tactics of the police clearly indicated whether their primary goal was to deal with wrongdoing, to protect constitutional rights, or to resolve conflict and maintain the tranquility of the larger community. Their choices, however, are not as obvious in routine day-to-day operations. In daily patrol activities, for example, does a police officer attach more importance to ferreting out criminal activity or to providing a sense of security to those in the area he patrols? In responding to an armed robbery, is the primary objective of the officer to aid the victim or to apprehend the robber? And in responding to a domestic argument, does the police officer see his primary goal as determining whether a crime has been committed, as restoring peace, or as working to improve a strained relationship? Police administrators make some of these decisions and provide varying degrees of guidance to their personnel on questions of this type. But in most instances the operating personnel are left to make such decisions for themselves, and the action they take is based on their personal concept of what policing is all about.

Choosing from Among Methods for Intervening

A second major category of discretion is reflected in an officer's choice of action upon initially responding to an incident. As was pointed out in chapter 2, the officer must often decide, under great time pressure, whether to conduct an investigation, whether to freeze a situation, whether to stop and question, whether to frisk, whether to make an immediate apprehension, or whether to use force. And once the initial determination is made, several of these alternatives require additional discretion. Thus, if the officer decides to investigate, determination must then be made about the scope and intensity of the investigation to be undertaken.

Some forms of immediate intervention, such as the use of force, are authorized by statute. But the language is quite general, leaving much room for the police officer to exercise discretion. This is highly significant, given that force—especially deadly force—constitutes the ultimate form of police authority. Its use under questionable circumstances often leads to vigorous public debates; many communities have held special inquiries into deaths caused by police gunfire where the circumstances leading up to the use of force were not clear. (See, for example, the Evanston, Illinois, case described in chapter 6.) Despite the importance of this decision, however, police officers, until recently, were rarely given any more specific guidance than the literal statutory provisions. Policies on the use of deadly force that provide more specific guidance than the statutes are now being promulgated by many of the larger departments.

As for most of the other forms of immediate intervention, little if any guidance is provided either by statute or by police department policy. An officer is left largely on his own to improvise in gaining control of a situation, leaning heavily upon the image of authority his uniform conveys. Thus, for example, there is little if any legal basis for an officer's action in ordering street loiterers to disperse, instructing a man to stay away from his wife for a night, or, absent an arrest, seizing the small knives found on a group of teen-agers or confiscating the beer being drunk by juveniles. But police are making these decisions all the time.

Choosing from Among Alternative Forms of Disposition

As was noted in chapter 2, police must, after their initial involvement in a case, decide how to dispose of it. They may decide to arrest and prosecute, or to use some alternative to the criminal justice system—to warn, mediate, or make a referral; to use the juvenile justice system or the mental health system. They may decide to charge a person with violating a city ordinance rather than a state statute, or they may decide to do nothing.

Where evidence exists to support a charge of violating a statute or ordinance, the decision whether or not to prosecute is a selective enforcement decision. Such is the case, for example, when a police officer warns rather than arrests a driver who has exceeded the speed limit. But in many incidents in which the police become involved, there is no basis for a prosecution. As for these, police may choose from among the nonprosecution alternatives or—as was discussed in earlier chapters—they may nevertheless use the criminal justice system for a purpose for which it was not intended, cognizant of the fact that whatever charge is brought will be dismissed.

Little can be observed at the administrative level of a police agency to provide insight into the way this form of discretion is exercised. This is understandable, for if the discretion is a matter of selective enforcement, it is difficult to acknowledge it because it conflicts with the pretense that police enforce all of the laws all the time. And if the discretion involves using the criminal justice system without adequate basis or without intent of prosecution, acknowledgment would be tantamount to pleading guilty to misuse of authority.

Yet the activities of police officers at the operating level provide example after example of the discretion exercised in disposing of matters coming to their attention. Having intervened in a fight, an officer may arrest one or both of the parties, or may suggest one of them take legal action against the other in the form of a private prosecution, or may admonish the combatants to refrain from fighting in the future, or may do nothing. The choice is largely a matter of individual style and varies greatly from one officer to another. This results not only in unequal treatment of individuals in similar situations, which is itself a serious consequence, but also in the creation and fostering of an atmosphere in which a decision of vital importance to a citizen may be based on irrelevant considerations, such as which alternative is most convenient to the officer.

Choosing Investigative Methods

An important segment of police activity, requiring many discretionary decisions, involves efforts to acquire evidence of certain kinds of criminal behavior while it is going on and, in some cases, before a victim recognizes that he or she has been victimized. The police in most large cities follow the activities of known professional burglars; lie in wait for street robbers and muggers; trace the sale and distribution of narcotics; check out individuals encountered under suspicious circumstances; keep tabs on suspected subversives; and acquire information on the activities of persons thought to be involved in organized crime.

Most of the methods commonly employed in these self-generated activities involve some degree of intrusion—albeit legal—into the affairs of private individuals. The decisions to utilize these methods, therefore, constitute one of the most important forms of police discretion. Officers conducting such investigations are constantly making important choices. They can decide to frisk; stop and question; search persons and property; use informants; conduct surveillances; eavesdrop or wiretap; take photographs and motion pictures; go undercover; infiltrate an organization; employ decoys; or in other ways place themselves in a situation that invites a person intent on committing a crime to attempt it.[5]

The actual amount of discretion a police agency and police officers have in choosing from among these methods varies a great deal. Statutes and case law are very specific in setting forth the criteria for conducting searches, but, short of prohibiting entrapment, say nothing, for example, on the use that can be made of decoys. Administrators have not filled the policy vacuum, with the result that the decision to employ these techniques is left to supervisors or, most commonly, to personnel at the operating level.

Many of the most publicized controversies over police functioning in recent years have centered on the use made of these investigative methods: the photographing of political demonstrators; the assigning of decoys to apprehend street robbers (the practice has resulted in a number of the robbers being killed in the scuffle following an attack); the hiring of informants, especially to acquire evidence of narcotics sale and use; the planting of police officers and informants in militant groups and in university programs and classrooms; the extensive use of wiretapping without court authorization; and wholesale frisking to confiscate weapons and narcotics.

Determining Field Procedures and Matters of Internal Administration

A quite different category of discretion involves the decisions of an administrative nature relating to the internal management of a police agency. Police exercise the least discretion in this area—a situation that has wrongly led some to conclude that theirs is a highly structured job. For example, police officers have always been told exactly where they must wear their weapons, though only recently have they been told with any preciseness when to use them. They are told exactly how to stop a traffic violator, but have wide discretion in determining what to do with that violator. And they are given very specific instructions on the forms to be completed upon making an arrest, though whether the arrest itself is made is often up to them. The fact that police officers are usually provided with huge volumes containing detailed operating procedures is often cited as belying the contention that the police function without adequate guidance most of the time. It is ironic that an agency which, by tradition, spells out its operating procedures in infinite detail, leaves vast areas of its most important functioning to the discretion of individual officers.

Limited as this form of discretion is, it is mentioned here for two reasons. First, some police officials have interpreted recent prodding to structure discretion as meaning that they should provide still more comprehensive and more detailed administrative procedures. In response to the urging that they articulate their policies, therefore, a number of police agencies have recently produced "policy manuals" that consist of little more than a recodification and modernization of rules governing police conduct (such as drinking on duty, absence from post, acceptance of gifts, care of equipment) and standard operating procedures (such as forms to be completed, uniform to be worn, procedures to be followed in booking a prisoner). Regulation of police functioning is obviously needed in these areas, but meeting this need should be distinguished from efforts to structure the other categories of discretion that have been identified. Second, whereas some future developments in the police field may bring about an increased structuring of existing discretion, there is good reason to believe that other changes will produce a loosening-up of police organizations, resulting in an increase in freedom in areas now tightly controlled by administrative regulations. Thus police officers may soon exercise more discretion than is currently allowed by regulations covering the wearing of their uniforms, the completion of certain forms, and the conditions under which they can leave their beat or go to lunch.

Issuing Licenses and Permits

Police agencies are often charged with the responsibility of approving the issuance of certain licenses, such as for selling intoxicating beverages, operating a taxicab, or running a private detective agency. They are also commonly charged with the responsibility for issuing permits, such as for carrying concealed weapons, for parades, or to give members of the press access to restricted areas. Less formally, police act on numerous requests from citizens for "certificates of good behavior," often required, for example, by some foreign countries prior to their issuing of a visa.

The discretion exercised in acting upon these requests differs significantly from all other forms of police discretion in that it is highly centralized. A single individual or a single unit of the police department may be responsible for all the decisions relating to a given type of license, permit, or record clearance. Nevertheless the criteria for making the decisions may be no more rationally developed than are the criteria in other areas. Problems most commonly arise when the action taken on a given application for a license or permit is based not simply on the factors considered relevant by the legislature in establishing the licensing process, but on unrelated factors of broader concern to the police agency in which the issuing function is housed. Thus, for example, protesting groups have been denied permits to parade or to block a street for a demonstration, not because of the effect this would have upon the flow of traffic, but because the police agency or the local government wanted to prevent the protest from taking place.

This aspect of police discretion is more widely recognized than other forms by people outside police agencies, for it has its parallel in many other administrative agencies that issue licenses and permits. Because comparable situations exist, and because police judgments relating to permits and licenses can affect large numbers of individuals in a given occupation or profession, police actions in this area have been especially vulnerable to challenge in recent years.[6]

PRESENT PRACTICE

The Concentration of Discretion at the Operating Level

The pattern of decision-making that evolves in a police agency tends to reflect the size of the agency, the nature of its leadership, and the frequency with which personnel are called upon to handle similar incidents. In almost all police agencies, as was pointed out, administrators have assumed responsibility for establishing administrative procedures. They also have a major influence on an agency's objectives through their allocation of resources and through their control of the system of rewards. The administrator or specific officers may exercise all the discretion involved in the issuance of licenses and permits. But in the other discretionary areas much discretion is delegated—largely by default—to the police officer. Unlike the military, on which they claim to model themselves, police agencies allow their lowest-ranking officers to make some of their most important decisions.

What typically happens is that officers discover, upon graduating from their recruit training and taking their first assignments, that they are constantly being called upon to make decisions; that relatively little of what they were taught seems to apply to the situations they confront; and that they are often without guidance in deciding what to do in a given situation. They gradually learn, from their association with more experienced personnel and from their supervisors, that there is a mass of "know-how" upon which they must draw. Practices, they find, vary a great deal. Some seem so well established that they take on the quality of a standard departmental operating procedure utilized uniformly by all personnel. Though these may not have any legal basis (some may, in fact, be clearly illegal) and are not formally recognized, they are employed so routinely that reference to them commonly creeps into departmental reports and forms, into exchanges between supervisors and subordinates, and occasionally even into court testimony. In contrast officers find that other informal practices are common only to the personnel working within a single area or under a particular supervisor.

Whatever guidance may be provided by their supervisors and by their peers, officers assigned to routine patrol activities—especially if they work alone—usually develop distinctive styles that reflect a blend of practices learned from their associates and supervisors that are modified by their own values, the kinds of incidents they handle, and the individuals to whom they must relate. Thus, although the socializing process that goes on within a police agency accounts for some forms of discretion being uniformly exercised, officers nevertheless tend to make the bulk of their decisions on their own. Persons who have accompanied several different police officers on routine assignments in the same area are often startled by the different ways in which similar incidents are handled. One officer may leave the scene of a quarrel among neighbors almost immediately upon establishing that an offense has not been committed, whereas another officer, in the same situation, may spend some time trying to solve their problem.

Even when an officer's style is firmly established, the manner in which he or she handles similar situations may not always be consistent. Under the pressures of time and volume of work, officers in many areas—especially in the congested sections of large cities—end up improvising responses to calls and taking short-cuts as they are forced to move rapidly from one incident to the next. So under the most intense pressures decisions are made on an ad hoc basis.

The Potential for Abuse

It should come as no surprise that discretion exercised in this manner lends it-self to abuse. When administrators and supervisors make the necessary decisions, they may do so in ways that improve the overall quality of police service by, for instance, providing for a rational and fair distribution of police manpower, con-trolling the use of force, and increasing the effectiveness of the police officer's response to a call for assistance. Many discretionary judgments made at this level, however, are influenced primarily by a desire to placate special-interest groups, to bend to highly partisan political pressures, and to become aligned with the most powerful segments of the community, with the result that minority inter-ests tend to be ignored. Without strong leadership dedicated to a form of policing that is both fair and effective, a police agency is likely to have its discre-tionary decisions made for it by pressure groups.

The decisions of individual police officers often reflect a desire to make the best of a troublesome situation. Through the exercise of discretion, police offi-cers—against great odds—often demonstrate a remarkable ability to arrive at effective and fair solutions to the problems they must handle. But it is perfect-ly clear that, while the welfare of the individual and the achieving of some social good may be dominant considerations, individual officers are often influenced by the degree of cooperation they receive and by such irrelevant factors as the desire to get by with a minimum amount of work, to please superiors, to avoid filing forms, or to be paid overtime for appearing in court. The worst abuses of discretion occur when decisions are based primarily upon personal prejudices, upon partisan political considerations, upon a desire for personal power, or, in a corrupt setting, to realize monetary gain.

CONTROVERSIAL POLICE PRACTICES AND THE DISCRETIONARY ISSUES BEHIND THEM

If present practices have prevailed for so long, why be concerned with the whole discretion issue? Why not let sleeping dogs lie? The answer, very simply, is that the public is demanding a higher quality of service from the police. And most of the criticism directed against the police within the past decade has related to the manner in which they have used their discretion, though this may not always have been apparent to those who have complained. An examination of some of the practices that have caused the greatest amount of controversy in recent years illustrates these discretionary issues.

Intelligence Gathering

Local police have been severely chastised in the past several years for the methods some agencies apparently used in collecting intelligence on political activists. Investigations and court cases have exposed to public view police practices in conducting surveillances, in infiltrating organizations, and in compiling extensive records on individuals—many of whom, while politically active, had no ties to criminal activity.

Police have great latitude in gathering intelligence, but the line between legal and illegal conduct is clearly drawn. The inquiries, therefore, have tended to focus most directly upon gross illegalities—upon the commission of burglaries, the use of eavesdropping, and the actions of undercover police officers in inciting violence or in planning and financing specific crimes.

As these inquiries have grown in number, however, it has become clear that public concern with police functioning in this area is not limited to the legality of individual acts, but extends to the propriety of the overall programs in which police have become involved. It is generally recognized that police need to gather certain types of intelligence. They are expected to seek information regarding criminal activity to prevent crimes from occurring and to solve those that occur. But what types of activities are likely to lead to commission of a criminal act? What organizations and individuals are to be kept under surveillance? And what criteria are to be employed in decided on the methods to be used in gathering intelligence data? The police exercise a tremendous amount of discretion in making these judgments.

The shift in public attention from acts of individual wrongdoing to the broad discretion exercised in fashioning an intelligence-gathering program is illustrated in the report filed in 1975 by a grand jury that spent seven and one-half months investigating the intelligence-gathering activities of the Chicago Police Department.[7] The jury concluded that thirteen police officers had acted far beyond their authority. But it did not indict them, claiming among other reasons that their trial would obscure the culpability of officers of much higher rank whom the jury accused of either condoning the actions of their subordinates or grossly neglecting their supervisory duties. The grand jury asserted, as another reason for its decision not to indict operating personnel, its belief that doing so would shift public attention away from the grave threat to individual rights and freedoms posed by the activities of the intelligence unit. The jury apparently concluded that its main function was to call public attention to the manner in which the police department exercised its discretion in carrying out its intelligence-gathering function.

Handling of Riots and Mass Demonstrations

Although the inquiries that almost routinely followed each major disturbance in the late 1960s and early 1970s usually became preoccupied with establishing who did what to whom once a confrontation had taken place, the real issue—commonly overlooked—was the propriety of the tactics employed as the police prepared to handle the disturbance and as they brought it under control. Assigning blame for specific acts was a rather futile exercise since, once a decision had been made to adopt a form of action which the police could not possibly carry out in a discriminate manner, there was bound to be trouble, resulting in charges and countercharges. Focusing upon the hard choices that were made prior to an actual confrontation would have been a more profitable exercise. The choice of tactics in handling mass conflict is a highly discretionary decision, and it is usually based on a more fundamental judgment by the police as to what they conceive to be their function in relation to the incident.

Unequal Enforcement

Some of the hostility that minorities have expressed toward the police reflects their belief that the police, in their enforcement of the law, discriminate against them. It is no response to such complaints for the police to argue that they enforce the law in an objective manner, based upon evidence of violations that come to their attention, when they are in fact constantly engaged in selective enforcement. The complaints raise questions about the choices the police have made in deciding which laws are to be enforced, to what extent they are enforced, and under what conditions they are enforced. Do the police aggressively investigate and prosecute all forms of gambling in the minority community while ignoring gambling elsewhere in the city? Do they respond differently to reports of robberies, shoplifting, larceny, petty thievery, or delinquent youth depending on where they occur? There is abundant evidence that the police response does differ in some cities; that behavior tolerated in some areas—social gambling, for example—is dealt with more severely in the inner core of the cities and, at the same time, that behavior tolerated in these areas, such as aggravated assaults, is dealt with more severely elsewhere.

Are these distinctions justified? The informal practices that commonly prevail and that dictate the manner and extent to which existing laws are enforced have evolved over the years and, therefore, do not appear to be an exercise of discretion—appropriately subject to challenge and change—and yet, of course, they are.

Arrests on Petty Charges

The police occasionally use laws that lie dormant through nonenforcement in order to deal with specific situations they feel compelled to handle, but for which they have no legal authority. In recent years, for example, persons engaged in various forms of militant demonstrations were prosecuted for posting notices, for littering, for violation of the pedestrian ordinance, and for disposing of lighted cigarettes in the public way. And, as previously noted, extensive use has been made of vagrancy and disorderly conduct statutes for the same purpose. The petty nature of the charge understandably leads to an allegation of harassment. In their defense the police will often cite their responsibility for enforcing all laws. Behind this superficial exchange the real issue is the discretion being exercised. Did the situation call for any form of police action? And if it did, was the choice from among available alternatives the proper one?

Programs of Wholesale Harassment

When police officers become frustrated in accomplishing what they conceive to be their objectives, they tend to develop new and more direct responses to immediate pressures. This is especially true when they are called upon to deal with incidents that involve many people and recur frequently. Some police agencies have engaged in wholesale programs in which they have chased prostitutes off the streets or locked them up overnight without prosecution; disrupted and dispersed groups of gamblers; disrupted persons engaged in the illegal manufacture and sale of liquor, destroying their equipment and supply; and stopped and searched large numbers of individuals on the street, confiscating any weapons, narcotics, or other contraband found in their possession. Police often justify such programs on the grounds that the criminal justice system does not work effectively and that the most pressing needs of the community are temporarily met: guns are removed from the street, the nuisance created by prostitutes is ended, and gambling is disrupted.

Many such programs are illegal. Others, while perhaps legal, are nevertheless offensive to large segments of the community. By their very nature they tend to become indiscriminate. Many individuals are stopped, questioned, searched, and occasionally taken into custody who are in no way involved in the activity against which the programs are directed. That the police are engaged in such programs is obvious to individuals residing in the area in which they are carried out. With increasing frequency, persons subjected to the police practices as well as those who observe them are asking why they are allowed to go on and who is responsible for them. There is good reason to believe that the chiefs of some of the larger police agencies are in fact ignorant of the practices of their personnel on the street. As a result they commonly deny that such practices exist when confronted with citizen complaints. This kind of a reaction only serves to intensify the frustrations of the aggrieved communities; it is among the factors that contributed to the demands for neighborhood control of the police. The central message of these demands was that many residents were angered by the continuation of practices which, legal or illegal, were ways in which the police were exercising discretion that were considered objectionable by the community.

SHOULD POLICE DISCRETION BE RECOGNIZED AND STRUCTURED?

Objections to the Concept of Police Discretion

Given the massive amount of discretion that the police exercise and the extent to which it pervades all aspects of the police function, it seems incredible that there are those who cling to the notion that the police do not have discretion—or, if they do, should not. Almost invariably, however, when the subject is initially explored with people who have not previously reflected upon the discretionary nature of the police job, they express great alarm. The tradition for viewing the police as a ministerial agency is deeply embedded, long standing, and widely accepted. Suggestions that so basic a concept be modified or cast aside are often rejected out of hand. It follows that serious consideration of the problems raised by the discretionary powers of the police requires, as a first step, acceptance of the fact that discretion exists.

Unfortunately, some of the individuals who reject the concept that the police do and must exercise discretion are in positions directly influencing police service:

A local chapter of the American Civil Liberties Union challenges the policy of a police administrator intended to regulate the use made of street interrogations, arguing that police have no basis for questioning citizens unless there are grounds for making an arrest.

A state supreme court finds a law enforcement officer guilty of nonfeasance for his failure to initiate a criminal prosecution where evidence of the violation came to his attention.

A state attorney general holds that a police chief cannot limit the authority of his personnel to use deadly force within the bounds of existing statutes.

A newspaper editorial condemns the local police chief for rising above the law in setting down guidelines that would result in his officers arresting curfew violators only under certain conditions.

Another newspaper editorial condemns a chief for pointing out that the enforcement of a newly enacted ordinance regulating massage parlors will have to compete with other demands for police manpower.

In November, 1974, the United States Attorney for the District of Columbia announced that his office would no longer prosecute persons arrested with less than one gram or five cigarettes of marijuana. The authority of a prosecutor to make such policy decisions is much more firmly established than is that of the police, and yet it was reported that the policy was apparently overridden by the attorney general, who is quoted as having said that the prosecutor was not going to change the law by administrative fiat; that he felt the United States Attorney had to enforce the law.[8]

In another interesting case a group of citizens in Berkeley, California, in 1973, obtained enough signatures to have an ordinance placed on the ballot that in effect instructed the Berkeley Police Department to give a low priority to the enforcement of marijuana laws. After its adoption, however, the attorney general of California filed suit to invalidate the ordinance on the grounds that the California Penal Code preempted the field with respect to the enforcement of criminal laws. A permanent injunction, which kept the ordinance from going into effect, was issued against the city, and the city appealed the decision. The matter is still pending.[9]

Many police chiefs themselves object strongly to the notion that the police be recognized as having broad discretion, arguing that this would detract from their image of objectivity and would open them up to charges of partiality, that it would increase the potential for corrupt practices, and that it would subject to public debate aspects of the police function that might better be left in their current state. As one chief put it recently, "A police officer does not have the discretion to arrest or not to arrest any more than a judge has the discretion to judge or not to judge. . . . When some people advocate the philosophy that a police officer has discretion in the field to arrest an individual or to take him home, they are talking about *discriminatory law enforcement* which is *police corruption*."[10]

By far the most common objection to police discretion is the contention that ours is a government of laws and not of men; that the police, as an agency in the executive branch of government, must be restricted to doing those things that are assigned by legislative bodies—and to doing them in a manner prescribed by these same bodies. Any exercise of discretion by the police, it is argued, opens the door for the arbitrary wielding of government power. Yet all around us are administrative agencies that exercise broad discretion. Legislatures have told them in general terms what to do and have left it to them to work out ways in which to get the job done. If administrative agencies were stripped of their discretion, government operations would come to a standstill.[11]

Those who recognize the need for discretion in other administrative agencies of government, but do not want to grant discretion to the police, base their reluctance on these factors: (1) the awesome power of the police, as exemplified by their authority to deprive an individual of his freedom and to use deadly force; (2) the reputation the police have established in many areas for exceeding their legal authority; and (3) the extent to which existing discretion—reluctantly acknowledged—has been abused. The first factor is a distinctive characteristic of the police and thus a very valid concern. As for the other two, the failures of the police to use their authority properly in the past should not be taken as an indication that they will not be able to handle legislatively delegated discretion in a responsible manner in the future. On the contrary it can be convincingly argued that failure to acknowledge the discretionary nature of police functioning accounts, at least in part, for some of the most common abuses and shortcomings in police operations.

Discretion is normally viewed in government agencies as that area of decision-making that falls within the bounds of legislative determinations. Under normal circumstances no one would seriously defend a decision on the part of an administrative agency that violated either the language or the intent of legislative enactments. But it is difficult to apply this rather neat definition of the limits of administrative discretion to the police field, primarily because of the crude state of current legislation pertaining to the police and the police function. Statutes and ordinances—if interpreted literally—impose unrealistic, and often conflicting, responsibilities on police agencies and upon individual police officers. Their language frequently leaves no room for discretion. Two consequences of this situation are particularly troubling. First, many of the actions that the police are forced to take are not, in fact, merely an exercise of discretion in the usual sense of this term, but are in open defiance of legislative mandates. Second, since all legislation relating to the police has come to be viewed as not intended to be applied literally, legislatures find themselves without an effective vehicle for mandating police action and narrowing discretion when they desire to do so.

The situation is most acute and best illustrated with regard to the responsibility of the police to enforce the law—the selective enforcement problem. Most states continue to mandate that the police will enforce all laws. Congress has even gone so far in the District of Columbia as to subject a police officer to criminal prosecution and to imprisonment up to two years for failure to make an arrest for an offense committed in his presence.[12] With such laws on the books, is it defensible for police agencies to announce that they will not, for example, proceed against social gamblers, or that they will not proceed against curfew violators, pedestrian violators, homosexuals, fornicators, or narcotics addicts except under certain conditions? Are the police usurping legislative authority in deciding not to take action in such cases, especially when a violation occurs in their presence?

The answer is likely to depend upon the language of a particular statute and upon the legislative history of the specific prohibitions. In the case of gambling, for example, it could be argued in many states that the legislature did not intend for its prohibition to apply to petty social gambling. But it is unlikely that one could find any support for an argument that a legislature intended that the police exercise discretion in deciding whether or not to proceed against a known rapist.

Ideally the whole problem could be resolved by requiring legislative bodies to clarify their definitions of criminal conduct; to consider enforceability, to be more precise in their language, and to recognize the propriety of police discretion when they desire that it be used. It is realistic to expect legislators to do some of these things, but they are likely to avoid the thorniest problems that the police confront—primarily because, as elected officials, they are reluctant to endorse legislation that puts them on record as tolerating forms of conduct widely condemned.[13] Thus, although unenforceable laws could be changed by legislative action, they are bound to remain a police problem for some time. Recognizing this situation, Kenneth Davis makes this observation:

> If a choice can be freely made between full fidelity to enacted law and police illegality through a rule specifying what will and will not be enforced, the enacted law clearly should prevail. But realistically, that choice is not open to the police if the community refuses to tolerate full enforcement, as many communities do, and if the legislative body refuses to amend the statute, as many do. If the only realistic choice for the police is between (1) secret policies through ad hoc decisions of individual officers often resulting in flagrant denials of equal justice and (2) open policies adopted through rule-making proceedings with something approaching even application in all like cases, then the second choice is clearly better than the first.[14]

In his most recent writings on the subject, Davis goes further in supporting the legality of a rule or formal policy that spells out a practice that appears to be in conflict with a statute:

> The legislative body speaks with three voices. The first is the statute. The second is long-term knowledge of and acquiescence in nonenforcement in absence of a commercial element. The third is appropriation of funds insufficient for complete enforcement, compelling the police to create a system of enforcement priorities. The argument that the second and third voices speak louder than the statute and express the true legislative intent is based on realism and cannot be brushed aside. Furthermore, if the rule accurately states the longstanding practice, it can be no more illegal than the practice. . . .[15]

While the questionable legality of selective enforcement is often held out as the major obstacle blocking fuller recognition of police discretion, difficult legal issues of a different kind arise in coming to grips with other forms of discretion. For example, can a police department, by adopting a written policy, narrow an officer's statutory authority to use deadly force or to operate an emergency vehicle? It would seem that it can, for otherwise one would have to conclude that an officer was under some mandate to use all of his authority to the fullest. Nevertheless, there have been some holdings that police administrators erred in narrowing police authority through administrative regulation.[16] That attorneys general, city attorneys, or arbitrators should rule in this manner is not so much an indication of the state of the law as it is an indication of their lack of awareness of the complexity and dynamics of police operations. It falls to the police administrator to provide such officials with the background that will enable them to see in a more realistic context the issues on which they are asked to rule.

Benefits to Be Gained from Structuring Discretion

Because police discretion has been covert and disavowed, no system exists for structuring and controlling it. So the police really suffer the worst of all worlds: they must exercise broad discretion behind a facade of performing in a ministerial fashion; and they are expected to realize a high level of equality and justice in their discretionary determinations though they have not been provided with the means most commonly relied upon in government to achieve these ends.

If discretion is to be exercised in an equitable manner, it must be structured; discretionary areas must be defined; policies must be developed and articulated; the official responsible for setting policies must be designated; opportunities must be afforded for citizens to react to policies before they are promulgated; systems of accountability must be established; forms of control must be instituted; and ample provisions must be made to enable persons affected by discretionary decisions to review the basis on which they were made.

Structuring police decision-making has other value beyond assuring fairness in the use of government authority. A police administrator's capacity to administer his agency effectively and to improve the quality of policing depends heavily upon his being able to exercise effective control over the infinite number of decisions that are constantly being made by his personnel at the operating level. If discretion were structured, many of the decisions now being made at the lowest levels in the organization would be made at higher levels and would therefore hopefully be based upon a more careful and more defensible weighing of competing considerations. Operating personnel would be provided with guidance in areas in which they now have none. Supervision would be made easier. Solutions would be worked out to problems that are now not even identified. Corruption would be curtailed if police officers were not in a position to threaten maximum and unpredictable use of their statutory authority (see chapter 8). Training could be more realistic, with police officers receiving guidance in the making of important decisions rather than being provided with an unreal concept of the police function that is of no help on the job (see chapter 10). Operating personnel could be held to preannounced standards. This is of special importance since, in the absence of policies in many areas today, a police chief is simply not in a position to proceed against a police officer who, in the judgment of the chief, acted improperly, but whose action did not constitute a violation of the law or of department regulations (see chapter 7).[17]

Additional benefits of a general nature are bound to accrue from the open discussion of issues and the resolving of ambiguities and conflicts as discretion is structured. Levels of service and enforcement could be related much more directly to legislative appropriations. City councils could be given the choice of different enforcement policies relating, for example, to narcotics, based upon the amount of funds they are prepared to budget. The complex and important nature of the police officer's job in choosing from among available alternatives would be brought into focus. And the expertise that the police have developed could be more systematically utilized in deciding upon operating policies.

Perhaps most important, the police would be provided with a more realistic and healthier atmosphere in which to function. It would no longer be necessary for a police administrator to dodge issues, to maintain an image that is unsupported by practice, or to be less than forthright in his dealings with the public. Openly structuring discretion should encourage greater integrity on the part of the administrator and make it possible for police agencies to realize a much higher level of credibility in the community. Both the community and the police should recognize that the police must make difficult choices, that the police must take risks, and that the police will occasionally make mistakes.

PROBLEMS IN STRUCTURING DISCRETION

Structuring discretion will be no easy task. Most agencies will have to start almost from scratch. It will require time, perseverance, and experimentation to develop the needed guidelines and to provide adequate mechanisms for their implementation. A number of proposals have been made for approaching the task, but the problems involved in applying them have not been fully worked out.

How Much Structuring

The implication in most of the discussions of the need for structuring discretion is that ideally police officers would be provided with the greatest possible amount of guidance in all areas in which they operate. This has led to the impression, especially among police personnel, that extensive structuring of discretion would reduce a police officer to an automaton of sorts, weighted down by volumes of standard operating policies, who would then more accurately fit the ministerial image now incorrectly ascribed to him. Is it desirable to provide detailed direction for all frequently recurring incidents? Is it feasible to do so?

Structuring discretion does not mean eliminating discretion. It would be impossible to carry out the varied and often unpredictable tasks of the police without affording substantial discretion to officers at the operating level. Moreover, anyone who has tried to develop a detailed policy covering a common aspect of police functioning—such as, for example, the manner in which police are to handle street gatherings or domestic disputes—quickly discovers that it is impossible to prescribe with any precision what should be done, since an infinite number of possible circumstances could occur. At best, preformulated guidance can alert officers to the alternatives available for dealing with a given situation, to the factors that should be considered in choosing from among available alternatives, and to the relative weight that should attach to each factor. It is possible to be much more specific in setting forth what should not be done in some situations—in establishing factors that should not be considered, such as racial distinctions, and in prohibiting some courses of action as, for example, shooting at a suspect in a crowded area.[18] There is plenty of room for narrowing discretion without eliminating it. The major challenge, in each area of police operations, is in deciding on the appropriate level of specificity for a given set of guidelines.

As a minimum it would seem desirable that discretion be narrowed to the point that all officers in the same agency are operating on the same wavelength. The limits on discretion should embody and convey the objectives, priorities, and operating philosophy of the agency. They should be sufficiently specific to enable an officer to make judgments in a wide variety of unpredictable circumstances in a manner that will win the approval of top administrators, that will be free of personal prejudices and biases, and that will achieve a reasonable degree of uniformity in handling similar incidents in the community. As Davis has pointed out:

> The sensible goal . . . is not to try to replace discretion with rules but to locate the proper balance between rule and discretion. I think that in many areas our existing practice misses that proper balance by a wide margin; the usual need is for reduced discretion and more elaborate rules. But on many subjects we cannot eliminate all discretion, and on other subjects we should not even when we can.[19]

As an example it would certainly be a major advance if a police administrator clarified his agency's objectives in handling minor disputes. If the prime objective is to resolve the dispute, as it should be, the efforts of the officer who attempts to do this through the use of a variety of different techniques will be legitimated and supported, and the officer who seeks only to make an arrest or who limits his concern to deciding whether an offense occurred will be expected to alter his behavior in order to conform. Here a policy could be more specific without becoming unduly restrictive.

Who Should Decide What?

The implication in most of the discussions of police discretion is that it is the police administrator who should undertake to spell out policies and rules. For many discretionary decisions he may be the most logical official to do the job. But it could be argued that a city council or a municipal chief executive should have final say on the objectives of the police—in determining, for example, the proportion of available resources that should be devoted to handling traffic, as compared with dealing with serious crime. And it could be argued that the trial judiciary should have the final say in deciding on the detailed guidelines covering those matters on which higher courts have not yet ruled, such as on fine points that arise in making arrests and conducting searches.

A complete listing of bodies and officials who might logically be given the ultimate responsibility for different discretionary decisions in any more formal structuring of police discretion would include: state legislatures, state attorneys general, governors, city councils, mayors, city managers, specially designated neighborhood representatives or councils, prosecutors, city attorneys, judges, police boards and commissions, police chiefs, supervisory personnel, and operating police officers and their associations. From among these bodies and individuals, who should decide such varied questions as, for example, the following:

Whether police officers should seek to make mass arrests of illegally assembled demonstrators.

Whether patrolling police officers should be routinely armed with shotguns.

Whether police officers should shoot at individuals looting stores in a riotous situation.

What the response of the police should be to social gambling.

The kinds of requests for assistance to which the police will not respond.

The extent to which arrest records maintained by the police should be made available to others.

The amount of police resources to be devoted to investigating organized crime.

Whether police officers should be required to wear nameplates.

The manner in which parking regulations are to be enforced.

Whether police officers should seek to prosecute a known assailant when the victim refuses to cooperate in the prosecution.

The extent to which police pay informants for information.

The content of police training curricula.

The procedures for investigating complaints against police officers.

Whether an intoxicated person should be taken home, to jail, or to a detoxification facility.

Whether a speeding motorist should be warned, issued a summons, or taken into physical custody.

Although most of these questions have traditionally been viewed as clearly within the province of the police, detailed exploration of each question is likely to lead to the conclusion that the officials mentioned above have a direct legitimate interest in the issues that are raised. How can these interests be accommodated at the same time that the decision-making responsibility is concentrated in a way that provides the necessary degree of accountability? One of the interested parties must obviously assume primary responsibility—a matter explored in detail in chapter 6. The choice of who this should be, however, is heavily influenced by the specific method by which such decisions are to be made.

Alternative Methods for Structuring Discretion

The most common proposal for structuring police discretion calls for policy development or rule-making by the police agency. This process may turn out to be the most satisfactory. But a number of other methods could, with some adaptations, be utilized to introduce some order into what is currently an almost totally uncharted area.

If, for example, it is appropriate that city councils make broad policy decisions, the existing processes by which municipal legislative policy is enacted may be employed. Most police chiefs would welcome an ordinance to clarify the function of a police agency and provide priorities between different tasks. In an interesting venture into police policy-making, the city council of Evanston, Illinois, prompted by alleged mistreatment of one of its own members, recently used a resolution to give its approval to a set of detailed guidelines covering police conduct in stopping and questioning.[20]

Increased use can also be made of a city council's budget-making process, especially in the light of recent efforts in the municipal finance field to relate appropriations directly to actual programs. The amount of money a city council appropriates determines, to a great extent, the services the police will provide. Obviously the effectiveness of this process as a means for deciding upon and articulating policies is heavily dependent upon the capacity of police administrators, mayors, city managers, and budget officials to translate dollar expenditures into specific programs and goals.

If trial judges were to assume a greater responsibility for clarifying uncharted areas in criminal procedure, they could make use of judicial rule-making as, for example, was done in England through promulgation of the "Judges' Rules."[21] Certainly rules made by trial courts—especially in the larger cities—or even by state supreme courts are preferable to a system whereby legislatures or the appellate courts refine criminal procedure on a sporadic basis in response to problems that come before them.[22]

But there are many questions on how a system of judicial rule-making might fit into a rational scheme for systematizing police decision-making. How detailed can court-enacted rules be without unduly restricting the flexibility required at the operating level? Would judicial rule-making apply only to those aspects of police functioning that are subsequently subject to judicial review, or could judicially made rules apply as well to decisions whether to make use of the criminal justice system? Would a formal system by which rules are promulgated by a supreme court and approved by the legislature be appropriate, or would it be preferable for local trial courts—especially the multiple trial courts in the larger cities—to devise a system for promulgating rules directly applicable to local problems?

If it is determined that a mayor or a police administrator should be the official to make policies and rules, the most logical process for doing so would be through administrative rule-making procedures paralleling those used by federal and state administrative agencies.[23] Kenneth Davis, who is a strong advocate of administrative rule-making, argues that the process is particularly applicable to the discretion exercised by the police and that the police should make extensive use of it.

> In our entire system of law and government, the greatest concentrations of unnecessary discretionary power over individual parties are not in the regulatory agencies but are in police and prosecutors. Unfortunately, our traditional legal classifications—"administrative law," "the administrative process," and "administrative agencies"—have customarily excluded police and prosecutors. The terminology as such is unimportant, but it has carried with it a failure to transfer know-how from advanced agencies, such as the federal regulatory agencies, to such backward agencies as the police departments of our cities. I think that both police and prosecutors, federal as well as state and local, should be governed by many principles that have been created by and for our best administrative agencies.
>
> The police are among the most important policy-makers of our entire society. And they make far more discretionary determinations in individual cases than any other class of administrators; I know of no close second. Comparing police decisions with regulatory agencies' decisions is as baffling as comparing murder with a million dollars, but the amount of governmental activity through the police, measured by man-hours, is more than forty times as much as the amount of governmental activity through all seven of the independent federal regulatory agencies; those agencies in the aggregate have about 10,000 employees but the nation has about 420,000 policemen, exclusive of supporting personnel in the departments.[24]

Specifically, administrative rule-making is a procedure by which an administrative agency undertakes to confine and structure its discretion by articulating its operating policies in the form of rules. The first step usually consists of an extensive study in order to produce a proposal for consideration. The study is made in consultation with various interested parties which, in the case of the police, might be the prosecutor, the judges, city agencies, local community groups, and the special interests that may be involved. The proposed rules are then published, and reactions to them are solicited. The agency then revises its proposal in the light of the criticism received. Implicit in the procedure is a process of drafting, redrafting, and redrafting again in an effort to best meet the situation to which the rules are intended to apply. Once a start is made on the process, it calls for building upon precedent.

The major control on the procedure is its open quality—openness commonly being viewed as the natural enemy of arbitrariness. Policies and rules are published. Findings and reasons are made known. A system of checks is provided to assure that the administrative agency is making proper use of its power and that once rules are adopted they are followed.

Not all policies need take on the specificity implied by "rule-making." As Davis indicates, the movement from vague standards to definite standards to broad principles to rules may be accomplished by policy statements in any form. "When rule-making procedure is used, even a statement which changes a vague statutory standard into an administrative standard which is as vague or only slightly less vague is called, in our somewhat confusing language, a 'rule.' "[25] As previously noted it will be difficult in the police field to do more in many areas than develop very general guidelines which, in their language, will necessarily be broad and ambiguous. These, nevertheless, would narrow discretion and make it possible to improve—however slightly—accountability and control.

In the next several years all of the policy-making processes identified here— legislation, budgeting, judicial rule-making, and administrative rule-making— will probably be used more frequently. What use is made of what process will depend in large measure on who takes the initiative and on the results of these first efforts.

THE MOVEMENT TOWARD USE OF ADMINISTRATIVE RULE-MAKING

From among the several methods by which discretion can be structured, the strongest support, so far, has been for making use of administrative rule-making or a less formal adaptation of the rule-making process. The support has come from many quarters. The President's Commission on Law Enforcement and Administration of Justice urged that police departments enunciate policies to give police personnel specific guidance for the common situations requiring the exercise of discretion.[26] A series of specific proposals was presented in the report of the commission's task force on the police.[27] The general concept of developing and articulating policies in discretionary areas was also endorsed by the National Advisory Commission on Criminal Justice Standards and Goals.[28] And the American Bar Association, with the endorsement of the Board of Officers of the International Association of Chiefs of Police (IACP), not only advocated that discretion be structured and controlled, but specifically recommended that it be done through the process of administrative rule-making.[29]

In addition to these national groups it is significant that so many individuals who have immersed themselves thoroughly in the problems of policing have, despite their varied backgrounds and sharply differing perspectives, joined in support of applying administrative rule-making to police operations: Judge Carl McGowan of the District of Columbia Court of Appeals;[30] Gerald M. Caplan, formerly general counsel for the District of Columbia Metropolitan Police and now director of the National Institute of Law Enforcement and Criminal Justice.[31]

Wayne W. Schmidt, formerly director of the Legal Center of the IACP and now supervising attorney of the Legal Defense Center of the Americans for More Effective Law Enforcement;[32] Professor Anthony G. Amsterdam, an authority on constitutional law, who has worked and written extensively on defending the rights of suspects;[33] and, of course, Professor Kenneth Culp Davis, widely recognized for his expertise in the field of administrative law.[34]

In response to these urgings, and sometimes on their own initiative, a number of police agencies—most notably those in Washington, D.C., Dayton, Ohio, Madison, Wisconsin, and Boston, Massachusetts—have embarked upon ambitious efforts to develop guidelines for their personnel.[35] In addition the Arizona State University Project on Law Enforcement Policy and Rulemaking has produced a set of model guidelines to be adapted by local departments.[36] And the Texas Criminal Justice Council, with staff assistance from the IACP, has published a set of model rules for law enforcement officers.[37]

Much of the emphasis in these efforts has been upon structuring police discretion in conducting searches, holding lineups, and stopping and questioning suspects—areas of police functioning to which the courts have spoken in great detail and in which the policy choices, as a result, are extremely limited. But outside these rather traditional concerns, interesting efforts have been made to develop policies for handling domestic conflicts, labor-management strife, the public inebriate, the mentally ill, and the juvenile offender. In some of these projects an attempt has been made to face up to the most difficult aspects of articulating policy by actually asserting a policy of nonenforcement, or by involving citizens in the formulation of policy, or by submitting drafts for public comment. Although none of the efforts to date contains all the elements of administrative rule-making, the experiments have been valuable in surfacing some of the problems that must be addressed if the administrative rule-making model is to be utilized more fully.

Developing and Documenting Police Expertise

In turning to an administrative agency to formulate detailed operating policies, one assumes that the agency is best equipped to undertake this task because its personnel have developed expertise in handling the problems they confront. Specifically this means that employees at the operating level possess special knowledge and skill to which one is prepared to defer and that the agency itself has the capacity to undertake studies and make recommendations.

Those who are familiar with police operations tend to conclude that police officers do, indeed, have a tremendous body of expertise that they routinely tap in making their daily decisions. It is a kind of know-how that results in a police officer reacting to situations differently from the way a layman would. This expertise, however, is rarely shared with others in a systematic way or reflected in formally adopted operating policies. It is, rather, informally communicated from one officer to another.

Since police expertise has not been documented, it follows that it has not been subjected to careful analysis. In part this is because the police have not had to justify many of their decisions. In those instances in which police practices have been subject to review by the appellate courts, police expertise has seldom been cited to support the questioned practice. And when it has, the evidence offered to document it has tended to be extremely thin.

How much expertise exists and how much of it can be communicated will not be determined until current police practices are increasingly questioned. But this challenge need not come from the outside—from courts, legislatures, or citizen groups. Police agencies themselves can take the initiative in examining existing practices and policies and in determining the basis for them. The process should reveal to what extent police decisions are based upon actual knowledge, skills, and experience peculiar to those in the field.

By way of illustration it is frequently pointed out that a police officer, under certain conditions, always frisks an individual. The implication is that past experience indicates to the police that persons encountered under these conditions are likely to be armed. Any reasonable person is prepared to defend the right of a police officer to protect himself by searching for weapons. But frisking—especially in the presence of others—is offensive, degrading, and certainly an invasion of privacy. If the action is challenged, what can the police agency say is the basis for instructing police officers to frisk in a given set of circumstances? How often have persons encountered under similar conditions been found to be armed? Data indicating that such encounters in the past have produced weapons would probably support the current practice. But if no weapon has ever been found on persons encountered under these conditions, perhaps the practice should be discontinued or modified. Establishing these facts need not await the filing of a complaint or a court challenge.

In addition to supporting the expertise of individual officers through detailed studies, police agencies will increasingly find it necessary to undertake in-depth inquiries in support of policies and rules they decide to promulgate. It will not suffice, in establishing a policy, simply to assert an often-repeated but untested claim as to its value. It is often said, for example, that selective arrest of street prostitutes reduces the amount of prostitution, the incidence of venereal disease, and the number of related robberies; that removing guns from the streets reduces the number of assaults and robberies; and that partial enforcement of the gambling laws combats organized gambling. No doubt many of the assumptions on which police operate are correct. Having to articulate policies based on them, however, will require that the police go through the healthy exercise of validating their theories.

In designing studies to support policies of selective enforcement, police might profit from an examination of some of the practices that they themselves have already developed in the traffic area. Many departments, for example, base the decision on when and where to use radar units on an analysis of reported accidents attributed to speeding. Assuming it is possible to validate the premise that speeding, under some conditions, causes accidents, policy of this type goes along way toward eliminating arbitrary use of this detection device.

Openness

Although police chiefs are not at all averse to providing their personnel with more formal guidance, they balk at the suggestion that policy-making be done openly and that operating policies be published. Yet without the element of openness, according to those who support administrative rule-making, its value and effectiveness cannot be fully realized. The proponents of administrative rule-making see it as a process for both improving the quality of administration and providing a system of accountability for the exercise of governmental authority, whereas police administrators view the process primarily as a vehicle for achieving the first of these two goals.

It is difficult to establish how much of the police objection to openness is justifiable and how much is a habitual response to any outside inquiry into how the police conduct their business. Secrecy pervades police functioning and is often applied to areas where there is no need for it. One of the reasons the police have become so secretive is that they have been forced over the years to maintain a false facade in their relations with the community. If a police administrator did formulate a policy in the past and if the policy was leaked, let alone published, the administrator ran the risk of being attacked for usurping legislative authority and for acting illegally. Against this background a proposal for the systematic publication of operating policies represents a radical change. It is understandable, therefore, why—at least initially—it is so strongly opposed.

If one overcomes the blanket objections to openness, problems arise in a number of specific areas. One such area is illustrated by the so-called tolerance manuals some police agencies have adopted to guide their personnel in the enforcement of traffic laws. Almost without exception the police have gone to extremes to keep these manuals confidential. They fear that widespread knowledge that an officer, for example, will not take action unless a motorist is exceeding the speed limit by five miles an hour will result in raising the average speed by five miles an hour. They also fear that officers who, for some reason, take action against violators who are within the tolerance limit will be subject to challenge in the course of their prosecution. Thus the police see publicly announced policies as reducing the likelihood that citizens will obey the law as written, and they see publicized policies as providing a violator with additional grounds for contesting a prosecution.

The articulation of police policies, however, is a way of bringing police practice into line with public expectations, and vice versa. Police concerns stem from their traditional obligation to achieve full enforcement. If it is generally accepted that full enforcement is not achievable, compliance with established policies— rather than the terms of a statute or ordinance—would become the measure of police success.

A more difficult problem is presented by those policies relating to the use of investigative techniques designed to ferret out evidence of wrongdoing. Obviously the objectives of the police would be thwarted if they publicized the detailed criteria by which they decided to conduct such investigations and if they were held to strict compliance with these criteria. Police effectiveness often depends on the uncertainty and unpredictability of their actions, just as the effectiveness of the Internal Revenue Service depends to a large degree upon the inability of the taxpayer to predict whether his return will be audited. One could make a case for confidentiality when it is essential, perhaps substituting review by the judiciary or by a specially constituted body. In any event the burden for proving the need for confidentiality should rest with the police.

Community Involvement

The police are deeply concerned that greater openness in the formulation of police operating policies will inevitably lead to increased pressures upon them. As they see the situation, they are already subject to too many conflicting pressures. They have been struggling over the years to shelter their operations from external influences, especially those of a partisan political nature, so that they might be free to do a more "objective" job of policing. Although they agree that the public should be consulted, most police feel strongly that the public should not be directly involved in making decisions that determine the manner in which police discretion is to be exercised.

Anthony Amsterdam, writing on the use of rule-making as a way of better protecting suspects' rights, contends that there is value in the process even without community involvement:

> Even if there were no citizen participation in the formulation of these regulations, their enunciation would mark a significant advance in suspects' rights. They would bring the major issues up to visibility, and would subject police resolution of those issues to correction by political and (to a lesser extent) by judicial process. Also, it is likely that police administrators themselves would resolve the issues in a fashion more considerate of individual rights, when designing rules of general application posted for public scrutiny, than do individual policemen in their unguided, invisible and adrenalin-stimulated treatment of particular suspects.[38]

One of the major goals of those pressing for more openness on the part of the police, however, is greater citizen involvement in decisions affecting police operations. Indeed, a key objective of any system for structuring discretion is to afford opportunities for citizens to challenge discretionary decisions and influence the manner in which they are made.

It would appear, at first, that the two viewpoints are irreconcilably opposed, but this may not actually be the case. In the minds of police personnel, citizen involvement conjures up an image of endless ad hoc citizen groups telling the police how to carry out their job—including its most mechanical aspects. A great deal of time is already devoted to achieving some kind of consensus among such groups on an informal basis. The task of administering a police agency, especially in a large city, would become all but impossible if detailed operating policies on all aspects of police functioning were subject to approval by numerous citizen groups at the neighborhood level.

The police idea of what greater citizen involvement is likely to mean stems in large measure from proposals that were made in the 1960s for so-called community or neighborhood control over the police. Several of these proposals, in particular, called for an unusually high degree of citizen involvement in the detailed decisions that must be made in the day-to-day running of a police agency.[39] The authors of these proposals may well have been serious in seeking to place such decisions in the hands of elected citizens. There is, however, some reason to believe that they overstated their desires for rhetorical purposes; that the rather crudely worded proposals were intended primarily to dramatize the more basic contention that the citizenry should have a greater voice in determining police policies.

No one—including the police—can seriously question the propriety of having some means by which the discretionary actions of government employees are subject to influence, control, and review by the citizenry. But such methods must themselves be structured. The police cannot simply be buffeted about by the many interests and pressures in the community. Indeed, in many instances it would be appropriate for the police to be much more responsive than they are to the diverse interests of different neighborhoods, groups, and even individual citizens; but in other instances the police should be sheltered from citizen influence, even if the majority of the community opposes their action.

Crudely drawn arrangements do not make these important distinctions. An elaborate and carefully developed governmental process for considering citizen interests should accommodate appropriate influences while insulating the police from those which are inappropriate. This complex problem is examined in detail in chapter 6.

If proposals for structuring discretion are also viewed as means for structuring community involvement in police decision-making, it could be persuasively argued that they would, in the long run, actually relieve rather than increase the pressures upon the police. Today a police chief must deal with various influences without any formal process by which conflicting pressures can be resolved. The structuring of discretion would provide such a process. Additionally, more direct involvement of citizens may contribute to better policies, to better day-to-day relations with the community, and to increased public understanding of police functioning. The Dayton, Ohio, police experimented with the use of task forces consisting of police officers and citizens to study various aspects of police operations and to propose improved operating policies. Initially opposed by the Fraternal Order of Police, the project won the enthusiastic support of the community and eventually won the support of the majority of police officers, including the FOP. Citizen members of the task forces contributed many helpful suggestions, developed a deep respect for the complexity of police operations, and, as a result, helped build bridges between the police and the community. The police became more relaxed about citizen involvement, seemed to appreciate the constructive criticism that was offered, and most particularly liked having an operating policy that had the prior approval of the citizens.[40]

In summary, the real question of citizen involvement is not whether the citizenry have a legitimate role in contributing to and influencing the rules and policies of the police. They obviously do. The real question is how this influence should be expressed and channeled—an issue that is explored in detail in the next chapter.

Status and Force of Rules, Policies, or Guidelines Aimed at Structuring Discretion

If discretion is structured, one must assume that operating personnel will be held to the guidelines that are promulgated. But with what degree of force? Is a police officer to be disciplined, for example, if it is established that he took an intoxicated person into physical custody when strict application of administratively adopted rules would have resulted in his having taken the individual home? Will police administrators and officers be more vulnerable to civil suit if a police officer violates the agency's own rules than they would be if no such rules or guidelines existed? Is evidence obtained within the bounds of statutory and case law, but in violation of a department's self-proclaimed guidelines, to be excluded as having been obtained illegally?

Police officers should be required to conform with the guidelines that are established. Certainly this is the expectation where an agency has formally adopted its rules through the administrative rule-making process. Even in those situations in which the process is less formal, courts have insisted, in the case of federal agencies, that an agency cannot then ignore the regulations and procedures that it, itself, lays down.[41]

The IACP, in furnishing police administrators with a model set of guidelines governing the use of firearms, includes this provision:

> If an officer disobeys a written, internal directive prohibiting the use of firearms in any of the above cases, he will be subject to disciplinary action and possible civil liability. This will be true even if the use of deadly force under these circumstances is lawful under the state penal code.[42]

Faced with this same issue in a recent case before it, the Florida District Court of Appeals for the Fourth District concluded that a local police department regulation limiting the use of deadly force would be an applicable standard for use in a disciplinary proceeding, but not in a criminal or civil action stemming from an incident involving the use of such force.[43]

Attractive as it is to conclude that an agency that adopts rules should be held to those rules, it can be argued that application of the full range of available sanctions is neither appropriate nor desirable, given the peculiar nature of police discretion and especially the primitive state of its development. At least initially police guidance in some areas must be very general and, as a result, vague. Furthermore, police administrators view some written guidelines as administrative devices for "pulling" the agency to function in a given manner; to change police conduct over a period of time. This is a commendable use of the process, and they would obviously not want to commit themselves to punishing officers nor would they want to make the agency vulnerable to suit if the behavior of an officer did not immediately conform to their standards. Likewise, police are fearful that one of the consequences of articulating policies will be that evidence obtained legally, but in violation of an administrative policy, would be declared inadmissible in a criminal proceeding. Clearly a blanket application of all existing sanctions would, in the current situation, discourage the police from articulating policies.

In the several cities in which police have begun to spell out their policies, the procedure has been a matter of concern to city attorneys, whose job it is to defend the city in lawsuits. If a police agency makes itself increasingly subject to suit whenever it specifies its operating policies, city attorneys are likely to instruct the police to refrain from further policy-making. Tort liability is not, however, automatic. Kenneth Davis observes:

> One factor to take into account is that such rules may be interpretative and may lack the force of law that legislative rules would have. Even if the rules were legislative, violation of police rules governing or guiding selective enforcement could not automatically constitute a tort; for instance, in a suit for malicious prosecution, the court should determine whether or not the officer abused his discretion and in making that determination the violation of a rule should usually be only one vital factor for the court to consider.[44]

In its study of the urban police function, the American Bar Association, anticipating the problems likely to arise by application of both the exclusionary rule and tort liability to violations of administrative rules, recommended:

> To stimulate timely and adequate administrative policy-making, a determination by a court of a violation of an administrative policy should not be a basis for excluding evidence in a criminal case unless the violation of administrative policy is of constitutional dimensions or is otherwise so serious as to call for the exercise of the superintending authority of the court. A violation per se should not result in civil liability. . . . [45]

The concerns of both city attorneys and police chiefs may be overstated. One of the most outspoken police administrators, Chief Edward Davis of Los Angeles, strongly supports an aggressive posture by police in spelling out their policies. He responds to the concerns of city attorneys by contending that, while the existence of policies may cause some additional problems for them in the immediate future, the better guidance that policies convey to operating personnel will, in the long run, reduce the kind of behavior that gives rise to citizen complaints and subsequent legal actions.[46]

The great need in dealing with this issue, as with so many other issues in the police field, is to refine our thinking; to determine, specifically, when sanctions are appropriate. In all probability there are some rules and policies which all parties might agree should be enforced by full application of available sanctions. In many instances, however, it may be desirable for a police administrator to employ internal discipline to assure conformity with his policies without, at the same time, increasing the vulnerability of his agency to civil action. And there are probably other areas where—because of the need for maximum flexibility or because of the difficulty in attempting to provide anything more than the most general guidance—no sanctions should be applied.

PROMOTING THE STRUCTURING OF DISCRETION

After these many years in which next to nothing has been done to structure police discretion, it seems appropriate to inquire about the future. If there is to be greater movement along the lines suggested here, who will provide the necessary impetus? To the extent that it is agreed that certain discretionary decisions are properly the province of police administrators, these administrators themselves should increasingly recognize the value of clearly formulated policies. But it must be acknowledged that a police chief takes on many problems when he moves in this direction—resistance from operating personnel, opposition from community groups, and opposition from city attorneys. So whether a chief undertakes to address policy issues, is dissuaded from doing so because of the opposition he is likely to encounter, or simply procrastinates, outside pressures and support are needed.

In his enthusiasm for the application of rule-making procedures to the police, Kenneth Davis argues:

> All concerned should push administrators toward earlier and more diligent use of the rule-making power: Affected parties should push, legislators and legislative committees should push, appropriations committees should push, bar groups should push, and reviewing courts should push.[47]

Several courts, in recent years, have urged that the police adopt regulations governing their conduct.[48] Some have complimented the police for having adopted administrative regulations.[49] And in a few cases the courts have gone so far as to require the police to develop rules or procedures.[50] It is worth noting that these cases do not relate to discretion in selective enforcement, but rather to several of the other forms of discretion exercised by the police. In a few isolated instances, local groups have initiated court actions in an effort to press police agencies into articulating their operating policies. These efforts, which were usually begun in an effort to control police conduct, but which if successful would have the effect of forcing a structuring of discretion, are discussed in chapter 7.

Legislatures have been urged to recognize the discretionary nature of the police job. With increasing frequency they are being pressured to go beyond recognition and specifically authorize the police to establish policies and to adopt rules as a way of structuring their discretion.[51] Davis argues that this is unnecessary; that police now have whatever authority is required.[52]

The need for legislative action, however, is not simply to provide sound legal underpinnings for police rule-making. Equally important is the need to clear the air by acknowledging as a matter of public policy that police departments are administrative agencies having important policy-making responsibilities. This would answer, most directly, those who so strongly resist the application of rule-making to the police.

Some have argued that legislatures should go further by requiring the police to spell out their policies in areas in which the legislature has spoken in broad terms. This general concept is incorporated in the American Law Institute's *Model Code of Pre-Arraignment Procedure*, though it is the chief law enforcement officer of the state rather than the police on whom the primary responsibility is placed.[53] The choice of a state official is intended to deal with the problem created by the multiplicity of police agencies, many of which may be too small to engage in rule-making on their own. Anticipating the same problem, Wayne Schmidt, arguing that rule-making should be mandatory, proposes to create a statewide law enforcement administrative law council "to promulgate rules governing the conduct and behavior of the police, to guide their activities, and to delineate their discretionary practices."[54]

Inevitably the question is raised whether structuring police discretion will be to any avail when it is often difficult to keep police operations within the broad bounds of the Constitution and the limitations established by legislation, case law, and existing department regulations. Would not the intentions of new guidelines be subverted in many communities in the same manner as other instructions and changes are subverted by the existing police subculture? Is policy-making a naive and overly mechanistic approach to a problem that cannot be solved by further enactments, directions, and exhortations? In isolation the mere development of more specific standards where general ones are now ignored would obviously be futile. But the structuring of discretion discussed in this chapter is but one element in a much broader program that involves clarification of the police function, creation of new alternatives and resources, development of new systems of accountability and control, and changes in the leadership, staffing, and training of police personnel. Its potential depends on simultaneous progress in these other areas—on progress in effecting changes that will enable the police to function in a legitimate and straightforward fashion.

NOTES

1. See Kenneth Culp Davis, *Police Discretion* (St. Paul, Minn.: West Publishing Co., 1975), pp. 96–97. This volume by Davis is a major contribution to the literature on police discretion, pursuing a line of inquiry initiated in his earlier work, *Discretionary Justice* (Baton Rouge, La.: Louisiana State University Press, 1969). Frequent reference will be made in this chapter to both volumes.

2. The term "selective enforcement" is used here broadly to apply to all offenses against which the police commonly take action. It is recognized that in police agencies the term has so often been used to describe the practice of enforcing traffic laws where accidents most frequently occur that it has come to be viewed in some quarters as limited to this one aspect of police activity.

3. This is the approach taken by Davis in *Police Discretion*.

4. Davis, *Discretionary Justice*, p. 4.

5. Two recent articles that explore the use made of these investigative techniques are of special interest: Gary T. Marx, "Thoughts on a Neglected Category of Social Movement Participant: The Agent Provocateur and the Informant," *American Journal of Sociology* 80 (1974): 402-442; and George E. Dix, "Undercover Investigations and Police Rulemaking," *Texas Law Review* 53 (1975): 203-294. Also see the materials on encouragement and entrapment in Lawrence P. Tiffany, Donald M. McIntyre, Jr., and Daniel L. Rotenberg, *Detection of Crime*, ed. Frank J. Remington (Boston: Little, Brown, 1967), 208-282.

6. See, e.g., *Quad-City Community News Service, Inc.* v. *Jebens*, 334 F. Supp. 8 (S.D. Iowa 1971), in which police standards providing for issuance of press passes to "established" media only were declared too vague to meet due process requirements.

7. Cook County Grand Jury, "Improper Police Intelligence Activities," mimeographed (A Report by the Extended March 1975 Cook County Grand Jury, Chicago, 10 November 1975).

8. This interesting chain of events is traced in *Narcotics Control Digest*, 20 November 1974, pp. 1-3; and *Narcotics Control Digest*, 4 December 1974, pp. 1-4. The attorney general's views were presented by a Justice Department spokesman. See *Washington Post*, 30 November 1974, p. 1.

9. The injunction preventing the Berkeley ordinance from going into effect was issued by the Superior Court of Alameda County, Judge Lionel Wilson, on August 1, 1973 (case no. 435827). The status of the appeal is uncertain at the present time.

10. A. O. Archuleta, "Police Discretion v. Plea Bargaining," *Police Chief,* April 1974, p. 78.

11. For a persuasive response to the argument that administrative discretion violates the rule of law and, more generally, for a detailed examination of the need for administrative discretion, see Davis, *Discretionary Justice*, pp. 27–51.

12. *D.C. Code Ann.* §4–143 (Supp. III 1970). New life was given to this provision in 1968 when Congress amended it to allow the police to transport intoxicated persons to an alcoholic treatment center rather than to jail under the provisions of the newly enacted Alcoholic Rehabilitation Act.

13. Other reasons for legislative failure to make criminal statutes less ambiguous include the legislative intention to provide administrative flexibility, the increased likelihood of loopholes as statutes are made more specific, and the limitations inherent in the effectiveness of language. See Frank J. Remington and Victor G. Rosenblum, "The Criminal Law and the Legislative Process," *University of Illinois Law Forum* 1960: 481–499.

14. Davis, *Discretionary Justice*, pp. 93–94.

15. Kenneth Culp Davis, "An Approach to Legal Control of the Police," *Texas Law Review* 52 (1974): 715. For further elaboration of Davis's argument for the legality of rules that are in conflict with statutes, see Davis, *Police Discretion*, pp. 79–97.

16. See, e.g., Florida Attorney General Robert L. Shevin's opinion in response to Miami Police Chief Bernard L. Garmire's effort to develop policy regarding use of deadly force, *Annual Reports of the Attorney General of Florida* 1971: 68–75 (#071–41).

17. For elaboration on all of these points, see Herman Goldstein, "Police Policy Formulation: A Proposal for Improving Police Performance," *Michigan Law Review* 65 (1967): 1130–1135; Davis, *Police Discretion*, pp. 143–148; Davis, *Discretionary Justice*, pp. 90–91; President's Commission on Law Enforcement and Administration of Justice, *Task Force Report: The Police* (Washington, D.C.: Government Printing Office, 1967), pp. 18–21.

18. For an example of the kind of guidance that can be given to a police officer for the handling of domestic disturbances, see Frank J. Vandall, "Training to Meet the Police Function," *Wisconsin Law Review* 1971: 562–575. Among the police agencies that now have manuals containing a good sampling of the kind of guidance that can be formulated relative to various aspects of police business are Madison, Wisconsin, and Dayton, Ohio. See also Texas Criminal Justice Council, *Model Rules for Law Enforcement Officers: A Manual on Police Discretion* (Gaithersburg, Md.: International Association of Chiefs of Police, 1974). For an interesting exploration of the complexities in attempting to formulate policies governing such matters as the use of undercover investigations, see Dix, "Undercover Investigations and Police Rulemaking."

19. Davis, *Discretionary Justice*, p. 44.

20. See "Evanston Council Votes 'Stop and Frisk' Guidelines," *Chicago Sun-Times*, 28 November 1973.

21. Examples of what can be achieved through use of the judicial rule-making power can be found in J. Edward Lumbard, "Criminal Justice and the Rule-Making Power," *West Virginia Law Review* 70 (1968): 151; and Council of Judges, *Model Rules of Court on Police Action from Arrest to Arraignment* (New York: National Council on Crime and Delinquency, 1969). For an interesting discussion of the "Judges' Rules," see Ben Whitaker, *The Police* (London:

Eyre and Spottiswoode, 1964), pp. 67–86. Whitaker reprints the rules themselves, along with administrative directions on interrogation and the taking of statements, on pp. 217–224 of his book.

22. The particular problem of appellate courts ruling on police policy without really being informed on current needs of law enforcement is discussed in Frank J. Remington, "The Role of the Police in a Democratic Society," *Journal of Criminal Law, Criminology and Police Science* 56 (1965): 363–364.

23. For the procedures at the federal level, see Administrative Procedure Act, 5 *U.S.C.* §553.

24. Davis, *Discretionary Justice*, pp. 222–223.

25. Ibid., p. 56.

26. See President's Commission on Law Enforcement and Administration of Justice, *The Challenge of Crime in a Free Society* (Washington, D.C.: Government Printing Office, 1967), p. 104.

27. President's Commission on Law Enforcement and Administration of Justice, *Task Force Report: The Police*, pp. 25–35.

28. See National Advisory Commission on Criminal Justice Standards and Goals, *Police* (Washington, D.C.: Government Printing Office, 1973), pp. 53–55.

29. See American Bar Association, *The Urban Police Function*, Approved Draft (Chicago: American Bar Association, 1973), pp. 121–133.

30. See Carl McGowan, "Rule-Making and the Police," *Michigan Law Review* 70 (1972): 656–694.

31. See Gerald M. Caplan, "The Case for Rulemaking by Law Enforcement Agencies," *Law and Contemporary Problems* 36 (1971): 500–514.

32. See Wayne W. Schmidt, "A Proposal for a Statewide Law Enforcement Administrative Law Council," *Journal of Police Science and Administration* 2 (1974): 330–338.

33. See Anthony G. Amsterdam, "The Supreme Court and the Rights of Suspects in Criminal Cases," *New York University Law Review* 45 (1970): 785–815; and Anthony G. Amsterdam, "Perspectives on the Fourth Amendment," *Minnesota Law Review* 58 (1973–74): 349, 417–428.

34. See Davis, *Discretionary Justice*, and Davis, *Police Discretion*.

35. See Caplan, "The Case for Rulemaking by Law Enforcement Agencies," and Robert M. Igleburger and Frank A. Schubert, "Policy Making for the Police," *American Bar Association Journal* 58 (1972): 307–310.

36. Arizona State University Project on Law Enforcement Policy and Rule-Making, *Eyewitness Identification*; *Search Warrant Execution*; *Stop and Frisk*; *Searches, Seizures and Inventories of Motor Vehicles; Release of Arrest and Conviction Records*; *Warrantless Searches of Persons and Places*, Model Rules for Law Enforcement Series (Washington, D.C.: Police Foundation, 1974).

37. Texas Criminal Justice Council, *Model Rules for Law Enforcement Officers*. See also Saadi Ferris, "Administrative Rulemaking—Police Discretion," *Police Chief*, June 1974, pp. 70–71.

38. Amsterdam, "The Supreme Court and the Rights of Suspects in Criminal Cases," p. 812.

39. See, e.g., Berkeley, California, Charter Amendment No. 1, defeated 22,712 to 16,142 at the general municipal election held April 6, 1971.

40. More information on the use of police-public task forces is available in Igleburger and Schubert, "Policy Making for the Police"; Dayton Police Department, *Dayton Police Policy-Making Proposal* (Washington, D.C.: Police Foundation, 1972); and Dayton Police Department, *Citizen-Officer Policy-Making System: The Dayton Program* (Dayton, Ohio: 1974).

41. See, e.g., *Smith* v. *Resor*, 406 F.2d 141, 145 (2d Cir. 1969); *United States* v. *Heffner*, 420 F.2d 809, 811 (4th Cir. 1970). The *Accardi* doctrine states that an agency of the government must scrupulously observe rules, regulations, or procedures which it has established. *United States ex rel. Accardi* v. *Shaughnessy*, 347 U.S. 260 (1954). However, the issue of applicability of the *Accardi* doctrine to police agencies has not yet been decided by the courts. See Caplan, "The Case for Rulemaking by Law Enforcement Agencies," p. 511.

42. International Association of Chiefs of Police, "Use of Deadly Force—III," *Legal Points* #37 (Gaithersburg, Md.: IACP, n.d.), p. 3.

43. *Chastain* v. *Civil Service Board of Orlando*,—So.2d—(1976). See also *City of St. Petersburg* v. *Reed*, 19 CrL 2113-2114 (1976).

44. Davis, "An Approach to Legal Control of the Police," p. 723.

45. See American Bar Association, *The Urban Police Function*, standard 4.4 (b)(ii) on p. 8 of the Supplement. For a discussion of this recommendation, see pp. 137–138 of the text and p. 31 of the Supplement.

46. *Report of Proceedings of the Federal Bureau of Investigation, American Bar Association, and International Association of Chiefs of Police Symposium on the ABA Standards Relating to the Urban Police Function*, October 28–30, 1973 (Quantico, Va.: FBI, 1973), p. 106.

47. Davis, *Discretionary Justice*, p. 57.

48. See, e.g., *United States* v. *Wade*, 388 U.S. 218, 239 (1967); *Clemons* v. *United States*, 408 F.2d 1230, 1237-1238 (D.C. Cir. 1968); *Dancy* v. *United States*, 395 F.2d 636, 638 (D.C. Cir. 1968); *Hughes* v. *Rizzo*, 282 F. Supp. 881, 883-884 (E.D. Pa. 1968); *United States ex rel. Guy* v. *McCauley*, 385 F. Supp. 193, 200-201 (E.D.Wis. 1974); and *United States* v. *Barbera*, 514 F.2d 294, 302-304 (2d Cir. 1975).

49. See, e.g. *United States* v. *Perry*, 449 F.2d 1026, 1037 (D.C. Cir. 1971).

50. See, e.g., *United States* v. *Bryant*, 439 F.2d 642, 652 (D.C. Cir. 1971), where the court requires investigative agencies to control the discretionary authority of investigative agents by establishing regular procedures for preserving evidence. The court noted the trend toward requirement of rule promulgation (n. 22). See also *Washington Mobilization Committee* v. *Cullinane*, 400 F. Supp. 186, 217 (D.C.D.C. 1975), where the court ordered the Metropolitan Police Department of the District of Columbia to formulate a comprehensive written plan of policies and procedures to be followed in mass demonstrations. In *Cullinane* the court cited the precedent established in *Council of Organizations on Philadelphia Police Accountability and Responsibility* v. *Rizzo*, 357 F. Supp. 1289, 1321 (E.D. Pa. 1973), where the federal court ordered the police agency to submit a plan for handling citizen complaints. The court's decree was affirmed by the Third Circuit Court of Appeals. *Rizzo*, aff'd 506 F.2d 542 (1974). The case was reversed, however, on appeal to the Supreme Court on several grounds, including the belief that the order to revise the internal disciplinary procedure

was an unwarranted intrusion into the operation of a local government agency, given the facts in this case. *Rizzo* v. *Goode*, 18 CrL 3041 (1976). See the detailed discussion of this case in chapter 7.

51. American Bar Association, *The Urban Police Function*, pp. 133–134.

52. Davis, *Police Discretion*, pp. 107–112.

53. American Law Institute, *A Model Code of Pre-Arraignment Procedure*, Proposed Official Draft (Philadelphia: The American Law Institute, 1975), pp. 1–2.

54. Schmidt, "A Proposal for a Statewide Law Enforcement Administrative Law Council," p. 332.

Chapter 6

Directing Police Agencies Through the Political Process

To whom are the police accountable? How do we give meaning to the widespread assumptions that the police are subject to control by the citizenry and that they are fully answerable for the manner in which they use their authority?

Establishing new mechanisms for the review and control of police discretion, as examined in the preceding chapter, contributes toward achieving greater accountability. But it cannot, by itself, provide the total government apparatus that is required to assure accountability with regard to all aspects of an agency's operations. Accountability, in its broadest sense, includes much more than responsibility for determining policies in discretionary areas. It covers every aspect of administration of an agency, including, for example, its operating efficiency, its hiring and promotion practices, and its financial management. Accountability encompasses as well responsibility for the conduct of individual employees—for the use which they make of their authority and for their integrity. These two concerns are so important and raise such complicated issues that they are dealt with separately in chapters 7 and 8. This chapter examines the processes by which citizens can, in a positive way, influence and sometimes alter the policies and administration of a police agency.

THE BASIC SYSTEM AND THE PROBLEMS IT PRESENTS

Compared to other nations the most distinctive characteristic of policing in the United States is the extent to which the police function is decentralized. The President's Crime Commission estimated that there are approximately 40,000 police departments in the country and that all but 250 of these are local agencies.[1] This organizational arrangement reflects the widely held belief that maintaining local control over police operations is the most effective means for avoiding abuse and assuring a popular voice in directing the police. Almost invariably, proposals for the consolidation of small agencies and for the creation or expansion of agencies at the federal, state, and regional levels have been strongly opposed. Even when the trend has been to consolidate units of government, such as school districts, to increase efficiency and reduce costs, the public has clung tenaciously to the practice of organizing police services at the lowest level of government.[2]

The traditional means by which citizens are assumed to exert positive influence on the police is through their elected officials. The influence is most direct in the case of sheriffs, who continue to be selected by popular election in most jurisdictions. At the municipal level a police chief who is by legislation required to function under the direction of an elected mayor and who is appointed by the mayor, is obviously considered responsible to the mayor for all aspects of police operations. The mayor, in turn, is considered by the electorate to have the ultimate responsibility for the police. Theoretically, then, citizens who want to influence police operations should be able to do so, in a general way, through their vote for mayor and subsequently by directing their complaints and suggestions about the police to the mayor.

But the lines of accountability to the citizenry and the formal channels for influencing police operations are rarely so open or so clearly defined. And herein lies one of the major paradoxes in policing in this country. We have insisted on maintaining the police as a responsibility of local government in order to assure accountability and an opportunity for local influence over so potentially powerful a government activity. Yet at the same time we have constructed various devices which, in attempting to protect the police from pernicious influences at the local level, effectively shield the police from the communities they serve. The net result of these conflicting aims is that considerable ambiguity exists as to who in fact is responsible for the many decisions that are made in the running of a police agency, and there is a great deal of uncertainty over how the public is supposed to control police operations.

Various Administrative Arrangements for Achieving Accountability

Much of the current ambiguity regarding the arrangements for supervising police operations is traceable to the pervasive influence that partisan politics had on police agencies in this country from the early years of their development and lasting well into this century. Not only were jobs filled by patronage. The police—and police authority—were used in various ways to enforce party loyalty and even to deliver elections. Friends were rewarded by lax law enforcement. Enemies were harassed. And honest efforts to provide equitable police service were constantly undermined. The fact that the police were beholden to a political party rather than the electorate often made a shambles out of their operations.[3]

In attempts to gain more effective control over the police so they would better serve the needs of the total community, various organizational arrangements were tried. Experiments were carried out in the second half of the nineteenth century with independent administrative boards, with elected boards, with bipartisan boards, and with state control over municipal police. By 1900 most municipalities whose police had been placed under state government won back control. But experimentation with the various forms of administrative boards continued into the first several decades of this century. These schemes not only failed to achieve the desired objectives, they were actually used to gain political control as often as they were used to insulate the police from partisan considerations.[4]

Starting early in the 1900s, as part of a general trend in city government, gradual support developed for the appointment of a single executive to head a police agency who would be protected from political influence through tenure. But this movement drew opposition because of the immunity that such an individual would have from appropriate citizen influence. Noting this resistance, the Wickersham Commission, which published the results of its investigation of police operations in 1931 and which reflected the viewpoint of the new breed of professional police administrators who were emerging at the time, observed:

> Seeking to avoid repression and to preserve democratic ideals, the people have virtually turned over their police departments to the most notorious and frequently the most dangerous persons in their communities, who do not hesitate to use them for every type of oppression and intimidation. Therefore, their attempt to protect themselves from a powerful autocratic chief of police has served to place them and the government in the hands of unscrupulous cut-throats, murderers, and bootleggers.[5]

When the commission was conducting its investigations, a strong movement was already under way to reform city government. Primarily in order to increase operating effeciency, independent administrative boards were gradually being eliminated as three forms of city government became popular—the commission, the strong-mayor, and the city-manager plans. All three called for the police chief to be more directly accountable to an elected official. Under the commission form of government the police were directed by one of the elected commissioners. Under the strong-mayor form the chief was under the direct supervision of the mayor. And under the city-manager plan the chief was accountable to the city manager who, in turn, was accountable to the city council. Interestingly, the Wickersham Commission saw these changes as steps backward unless special measures were taken to guarantee the chief's independence.

Limiting the powers of the police executive by placing absolute control of police under the mayor, commissioners, or city manager has opened wide the door for every conceivable type of incompetency, political corruption, and organization demoralization. The theory that the mayor, representing the people, will exercise wisdom in conducting the business of the city and, being directly responsible to the electors, will do his utmost to protect the lives and property of inhabitants and preserve the peace, has been badly shattered, judging by the caliber of the police service which is to be found in the majority of the communities in this country. . . .

The chief must be surrounded with every protective civil service device imaginable. When that is done the citizens may take more interest in the appointment of their chief police executive. With security of tenure, with intelligence, with training, with honesty, and with sincerity of purpose, the criminal element can be controlled. Without these virtues and with political control as it now exists, police departments must go on unorganized, inefficient, and corrupt.[6]

Today most police agencies are headed by a single administrator. In a survey of 1,774 cities having a population in excess of 5,000, the International City Management Association reported in 1972 that the chiefs in 1,018 were appointed by the mayor, city manager, or other chief administrative officer; 252 were appointed by the mayor and city council; 195 were appointed by the council; 199 were appointed by a civil service commission; 80 by independent boards; and 30 were elected.[7]

Included among these are some vestiges of the older arrangements where the channel of accountability is unclear. Boards with varying degrees of authority can be found, for example, in Chicago, Los Angeles, San Francisco, and Milwaukee. And the police departments of such large cities as Kansas City (Missouri) and St. Louis not only have boards but, along with Baltimore, continue to operate under state control.

Even where they are directly appointed, however, most chiefs enjoy some form of protection from political influence through civil service. So, although the vast majority of chiefs are, in a formal sense, directly responsible to the municipal chief executive and, through him, to the citizenry, accountability is in fact limited in a variety of ways.

Emergence of Police Autonomy as a Virtue

The effect that partisan political pressures had on the police through much of their history was apparently so catastrophic that fear of a recurrence has given rise to a fetish of sorts that equates any form of citizen involvement in directing police agencies with the most nefarious form of political corruption. As a result, even though most police chiefs are now directly responsible to the chief executive officer of a municipality, the chief executive tends to refrain from exercising the authority granted to him. In contrast with their relationship with other departments of city government, mayors and city managers have sought to avoid involvement in police business—especially as it relates to the way in which the law is to be enforced—deferring to the autonomy of the department or to the prosecutors, judges, and legislatures from whom the police are commonly assumed to receive their instructions.

Those running for the office of mayor for the first time often promise to grant autonomy to the police. And it is not uncommon for mayors running for reelection to brag about the degree of independence they allowed their police departments. Mayors often take pains to disassociate themselves from decisions upon which controversial police actions are based.

The startling result of this aversion to putting any political pressure on the police is that the police now actually have greater autonomy than other agencies of government that exercise much less authority. Yet most people seem unconcerned over this rather curious state of affairs. Apparently holding the traditional view that police are merely automatons and that the law defines their authority and function in precise terms, citizens are likely to support the mayor who, in disclaiming responsibility for police actions, is abdicating a responsibility which is clearly his. And they are likely to join in allegations that a mayor who questions police policies or attempts to influence the manner in which the police function is guilty of "political interference."

Negative By-Products of Autonomy

The intense concern over improper pressures has affected more than the system of accountability; it has had a major influence on all efforts to improve the police and has profoundly affected the internal arrangements for running a police agency. Indeed, freedom from partisan political influence has come to be synonymous with the professional movement among police personnel. Some of the consequences of this pervasive concern with neutrality and objectivity have only recently become obvious.

Because the professional movement evolved as a reaction to politically dominated policing, it naturally followed that little heed was paid to facilitating communication between the citizenry and the police. On the contrary, every effort was made to destroy existing relationships and to frustrate continuing contacts through rules or other administrative devices. Thus, for example, police officers were prohibited in some jurisdictions from talking to citizens except "in the line of duty." In the larger departments they were prohibited from working in the neighborhoods in which they resided, lest they be improperly influenced by those with whom they were most familiar. State police agencies were held up as models because of the extent to which they achieved objectivity through their policies of assigning personnel to areas away from their homes. Personnel in all agencies were transferred frequently in order to minimize the likelihood that familiarity with the citizens in an area would give rise to corrupt relationships. As police operations were centralized in order to achieve greater efficiency, the breaking of a network of relationships between locally organized police and the community they served was seen as having positive value. Subsequent events have made it clear that the highly impersonal form of policing that these changes produced has been among the major factors contributing to the hostility demonstrated toward police in recent years.

The priority placed on autonomy has also had a negative impact, in many situations, upon the capacity of police leaders to lead. In their study of the problems in governing New York City, Wallace Sayre and Herbert Kaufman observed that police commissioners in that city have long sought freedom from supervision by the mayor, from interventions by party leaders, and from jurisdictional invasions by other government agencies. But they point out that autonomy for the department has also meant isolation for the commissioner from sources which might help him in his difficult task of securing internal control.[8] Writing fifteen years ago, Sayre and Kaufman concluded that the overall effect of isolation, in the case of New York City, was to limit seriously a commissioner's potential for achieving change. The commissioner, they claim, must "yield to the necessity of being more the spokesman and the advocate than the leader and the innovator."[9] Although the experiences of New York City police commissioners may be assumed to be unique because of the size of their operations, the description of the commissioners' position, with some modifications, aptly fits many other police administrators in the country.

RECENT DEVELOPMENTS POINTING TO INADEQUACIES IN THE PRESENT SYSTEM

Until the 1960s the ambiguity of the procedures by which police agencies were subject to influence and control went largely unnoticed by the public. But the social turbulence of the sixties gave rise to numerous controversies regarding police functioning, and these in turn stirred citizen interest in the police. In their attempts to establish responsibility for past actions and to influence future police functioning, aroused citizens found, often to their surprise, that the channels for influencing police operations were poorly defined and, in some cases, totally blocked. Interest in the accountability of the police peaked in the late 1960s, but it has remained high as controversial issues involving the police continue to arise in cities across the country.[10] What, specifically, are some of the developments that have brought the problem to the surface?

Frustration of Minorities

Blacks and other minority groups became increasingly frustrated at having failed to bring about changes in police practices. For years the police in many jurisdictions had provided inadequate services to minority communities; beyond this, they had engaged in indiscriminate and often illegal actions in the policing of such areas. In the period from the 1950s to about 1965, criticism of police practices tended to take the form of a specific allegation of brutality or illegality. To eliminate such incidents, campaigns were mounted to improve police functioning by conducting a more thorough screening of police personnel and by providing human-relations training to police officers. There was, as well, a major effort to establish civilian boards to review allegations of police misconduct (see chapter 7). But these projects did not solve the problems. The quality of police service remained inferior in many jurisdictions, and indiscriminate street searches, harassment of persons committing petty offenses, and other police practices that offended minority communities went on unabated. From 1965 on, it became increasingly apparent to the most militant groups that the basic policies and overall attitude of some police administrators would have to be changed in order to affect the actions of the police at the operating level. But attempts to bring about such changes were frequently thwarted. Meetings with the police (often in the form of community-relations programs) were commonly used by the police to convince complainants that the prevailing police practices were in fact beneficial to the community. Police officials would deny categorically that illegal or improper practices were condoned. Mayors and city council members, when appealed to, claimed either that they were without authority to influence the police or that they thought it improper to interfere with police operations. The frustration such experiences produced contributed in no small measure to the violence that erupted in the late 1960s. It found expression, too, in the demands for neighborhood and community control of the police—a development that is discussed in more detail later.

But not all reactions were so volatile or so radical. In Evanston, Illinois, in 1969, the shooting of a black teen-ager by a police officer resulted in a lengthy investigation that produced a report in which questions were asked that, in a calm and thoughtful manner, reflect the same frustrations and illustrate the quest for clearer lines of accountability:

Who is Responsible for the Shooting?

The Police Officer? Ultimately, of course, it was his decision. But it is too simple to blame only him. He made his decision within a framework of "duty" supplied by the Evanston Police Department. He acted as he was trained to act, and the officer that takes his place will be trained in the same way.

The Chief of Police? According to his testimony, the Chief of Police makes the policy decisions for the Evanston Police Department. This includes the policy governing the use of firearms. Although he referred to no higher authority involved in shaping police policy, the Department is not entirely autonomous. If his policies run counter to expectations, he can be fired or counseled in his decisions by the City Manager.

The City Manager? He has the direct responsibility for police administration. It is his belief that the shooting occurred within a framework of duty. But even he is subject to higher authority.

The City Council? The City Council is the policy-making body for all branches of city government. It is clear that they made no policy decisions that would prevent the shooting of Bruce Williams. These decision-makers were elected by Evanston citizens and must reflect the views of their constituents to remain in office.

The Citizens of Evanston? Evanston citizens as a whole have not demonstrated dissastisfaction by demanding a review of the police policy, or participation in determining that policy. Expressions of outrage at the implications of police policy for Bruce Williams have come only from Evanston's Black citizens. Evanston's white citizens have not been similarly aroused. There is nowhere else to place responsibility—the citizens of Evanston must assume it.[11]

Attempts by Newly Emerged Groups
to Affect Policy

The sharp rise in political dissent and the rapid change in values and customs in the past decade placed the police in contact with a number of new groups, most of whose members had little prior contact with the police. Among these people were those who, for example, took to the streets in demonstrations against government policies; those who experimented with narcotics and other dangerous drugs; and those whose life-style subjected them to frequent inquiry because of the conditioned tendency of the police to be alert to deviations from the community norm. Unlike blacks and other racial minorities who are only now obtaining a voice for themselves in community affairs, individuals in these groups, since they came from the majority community, had been accustomed to immediate response to their grievances. When they clashed with the police, they moved much more rapidly to attempt to influence police functioning through established channels. Finding—as minority groups did before them—that these channels were often blocked, they began to clamor for new ways in which the citizenry could have more of a say in determining the operating policies of police agencies.

Illustrative of this reaction is the statement of a Madison, Wisconsin, alderman after a police action that resulted in the arrest of eighty persons on drug-related charges.

If we are to defuse the issues raised as a result of that raid, we must . . . be afforded the opportunity to explore the charges, the facts, the policies and the attitudes surrounding all of the issues involved. . . .
. . . The police administration and the mayor have been reluctant to establish any forum, to encourage any discussion, to promote any means by which the citizens of this community can review or investigate questions about police practices and policies. . . .
To remedy that basic communications gap, that essential element in re-establishing civilian control over police policies and practices, I have

introduced a resolution calling for the establishment of a five-member committee of aldermen to review police policies and practices. . . .

Were the no-knock, middle of the night tactics necessary? Were a number of people picked up in those raids and later released who had nothing at all to do with those not released? Was the way in which the raids were carried out, the timing and the targets arranged so as to terrorize the youth community? Is it the practice and the policy of the police department to deal differently with student and other minority groups than with the population as a whole? . . .

The only change in the policies of the police administration for which I call is the willingness on the part of the police administration to discuss the issues, to present their policies freely and openly. The police have nothing to lose and we all have much to gain from such an exchange. . . .[12]

Rebuffs of Mayors

Although most mayors have avoided controversial issues involving the police by deferring to the autonomy the police are commonly assumed to have, some have sympathized with criticism of the police and have sought to change police policies. Those who have moved aggressively in an effort to do so, however, have suffered serious setbacks. Among the most common issues that have drawn municipal chief executives into debates over police policies have been disagreements over the form of the police response to a disturbance, over the use made of deadly force, or over the manner in which a given law has been enforced. But the conflict almost invariably gets translated into a much more simplistic debate in which the conflicting parties are characterized as either overly tough or overly permissive. In such an atmosphere there is little opportunity to discuss issues rationally. And there is a tendency, especially by rank-and-file police, to claim that the chief executive's effort to influence police operations constitutes the very kind of political interference from which the police should be shielded.

Rank-and-file personnel have demonstrated in these conflicts that they can be a formidable political force in the community.[13] In New York City in 1966 the police soundly defeated the city administration's effort to establish a civilian review board by arranging to have the issue submitted to the voters in a referendum and by then carrying out an intensive campaign that resulted in the overwhelming defeat of the proposal at the polls.[14] In Cleveland, when the city turned down police requests for pay increases, the police took their case to the people through a referendum. They conducted an energetic campaign that resulted in the adoption in 1967 of a charter amendment that requires the city to pay its policemen 3 percent above police salaries being paid in any other city with a population of more than 50,000 in the state.[15] In several large cities (Minneapolis and Philadelphia, for example) the political power of the police and the support they have been able to enlist have resulted in police personnel being elected mayor.

Commenting on the demonstrated capacity of the police to exert political "muscle," former Mayor Carl B. Stokes of Cleveland is quoted as having said:

> There is simply no question of the political power of the police in any city. They can make all kinds of appeals to the people for support, and they can eventually ruin almost any politician.
>
> In most of the big cities, if there is some friction between political leaders and the police, you would probably find a great portion of the people siding with the police, and simplifying all the issues terribly. There is a great danger in this situation to the very order of society.[16]

In 1975 Mayor Coleman A. Young of Detroit, speaking on the same subject, drew attention to the need for reasserting civilian control over a department that he viewed as dominated by its internal establishment.

> Other mayors have tried it and failed, but I tell you, we're not going to turn this city around, and have a united city, until we deal with the Police Department.[17]

Many people believe it is good that mayors and other political figures cannot influence police policies. They see this as proof that the system developed over the years to shield the police from improper political influences is working effectively. Others argue that those conflicts that have been taken to the voters have been resolved in the most democratic fashion. But both of these positions fail to acknowledge the complexity of the problem. The kind of influences from which the police have been successfully shielded are often precisely those to which the police in a democracy should be subjected. And majority votes on issues and candidates are not the ultimate test of the appropriateness of police policies. On the contrary—and herein lies the heart of the problem—the real test of a police force in a democracy is the degree to which it responds to the legitimate demands of minorities, whether the minorities be racial, religious, political, geographical, or even criminal. That minorities have experienced difficulty in pressing their claims and that elected officials have been rebuffed in their efforts to represent them should be cause for grave concern. And when, to this state of affairs, is added the great political power of rank-and-file police personnel, the situation is troubling indeed.

COMMON ERRORS IN ATTEMPTING TO REESTABLISH ACCOUNTABILITY

A number of suggestions have been made in recent years to correct the great discrepancy that now exists between the commitment to citizen control of the police and the absence of effective means for exerting such control. Present arrangements, and the public opinion that supports them, are partly a result of public misconceptions about the police. Quite naturally the suggestions for change often reflect similar misconceptions, resulting in confusion over what should be done and unrealistic assessments of the likely consequences in adopting specific proposals. Some of the most common errors in the proposals for change and in the criticism of these proposals are examined here.

Failure to Acknowledge the True Nature of the Police Function

Existing systems of accountability were constructed on the assumption that the chief concern of the police is law enforcement. As long as people continue to believe this, they will support the concept of insulating the police from the citizenry on the supposition that only people who are trying to get around the law would want to influence the police. It need not be pointed out again how fallacious the underlying assumption is.

The insistence that the police task is a ministerial one further lulls the public into assuming they should have no role in directing police operations. It carries with it the notion that the police have no discretion—that all necessary guidance is provided by existing legislation. Naturally, if there are no decisions to be made, there need be little concern about affording citizens the opportunity to participate in making them.

A further common misconception accounting for present difficulties is that the police function is apolitical. But city government is political and, of necessity, police functioning is political. The wide range of discretionary decisions discussed in chapter 5 that involve the setting of policies are political decisions. The idea that the police are apolitical stems, in part, from confusion between the political decision-making process in its broadest sense and narrow partisan politics. Geoffrey Marshall speaks to this point in his insightful work on the accountability of the police in England, where problems have arisen not unlike those in the United States:

> Many decisions are made "politically" in the sense that they have an impact on society and are made according to some discretionary policy rather than by fixed rules, but they need not thereby be either partisan in the party sense or biased against individuals. When we say that the police must be impartial we mean that they must apply rules of law without exceptions or favours for particular individuals or parties. . . . In so far as there are clear rules of action everybody must be impartial. In so far as there is discretion to act or discretion as to the manner of acting or applying rules, then everybody's judgment, including that of the police, is political or policy judgment.[18]

Marshall observes that the failure to provide an effective means for challenging police policies appeals to a normal and optimistic assumption that the concept of law and order is "nonpolitical"; that the application of the law is an automatic process for which no one need take responsibility:

> Legal machinery, we like to feel, is both a part of and yet separate from the machinery of politics and government. This, in some ways peculiar, belief rests upon the existence of a constitution and a stable society and it most obviously tends to break down when the law is put into operation to enforce policies which are the subject of strong moral or political disagreements within society. The suffragette movement, fascist public meetings and nuclear disarmament demonstrations provide examples.[19]

His observation is illustrated by our recent experiences in the United States. Relatively small and homogeneous communities have not had to deal with the tough issues that larger cities have had to face. The challenges of police practice have occurred in those communities that have felt the brunt of social change—where demonstrations are common, where racial conflict has erupted, and where the heterogeneity of the population gives rise to sharp differences of opinion on the investigative and enforcement practices of the police.

Confusion Between Citizen Involvement in Policy Decisions and Citizen Review of Individual Police Actions

Demands for a greater citizen voice in determining police operating policies have been attacked by those who, in the past, have vigorously campaigned against demands for an increased role for citizens in the investigation and review of complaints filed against individual police officers. But the new demands are quite different, so it does not follow that opposition to civilian review of complaints requires, as a matter of consistency, opposition to citizen participation in policy-making as well.

The primary objective in proposals for the creation of a civilian review board or another form of civilian review of police actions is to judge the legality and propriety of police action in an *individual* case *after* an action has been taken. In contrast, citizen participation in policy determinations has nothing to do with sitting in judgment on events that have already transpired, nor is it concerned with police action in a given case. Rather, it is a matter of citizens setting priorities and choosing from among alternative policies so that the future actions of the police will be in accord with the desires of the community. Civilian review is a negative form of control over police activity. Involvement of citizens in policy determinations, by contrast, has a positive character.

Citizens on a review panel might, for example, sit in judgment on a complaint charging a specific officer with having acted improperly when taking an intoxicated person into custody. Citizens helping determine policy would decide whether police officers should be instructed to make use of alternatives to arrest in the case of intoxicated persons and, if so, what criteria the police should employ in selecting from among available forms of action.

Confusion Between Accountability and Responsiveness

Accountability and responsiveness are often used as if the terms are synonymous, with the result that an important distinction between the two concepts is lost.

In many of the criticisms made of the police in recent years it was claimed that they were unresponsive to the community. In rebuttal the police have claimed that they enjoyed overwhelming public support for their actions. And some police administrators who have been charged with being most unresponsive have demonstrated the popularity of their policies by remaining in office and, when they chose to run for elective office, by winning at the polls. This comes as a shock to critics of the police, who often err in attributing to the total community the concerns of a minority that feels its interests or rights have been violated or ignored. But the police also err in suggesting that the support of the majority is to be interpreted as proof that their actions are correct.

The police should not be responsive in an unlimited sense to either the entire community or minority interests in the community. In many situations it is essential that the police act independent of local community interests, responding instead to state or federal laws that preempt local legislation and override local preferences. It is precisely because we require a system that will insulate the police from some pressures while subjecting them to others that the task of achieving a proper form of citizen control over the police is so complex.

But, although the police should not always be responsive to the community in their actions and their policies, they must always be accountable to the community for whatever they do. So while there is likely to be considerable disagreement over police actions and policies, there ought not to be any ambiguity over who is accountable for them. It is far more important that a citizen know who is accountable for a specific decision than that the decision meet with his or her approval. With accountability clear, citizen differences are more likely to be resolved through the support or opposition given responsible officials.

Overreliance upon Formal Systems

Citizens concerned over either the accountability or responsiveness of the police tend to react by proposing a change in the formal organizational arrangements that determine the body or official to whom the police are responsible. The history of the police in this country reflects a constant shifting from one arrangement to another in what seems to be an endless search for the ideal system. When it was concluded that the police were overly responsive to improper influences, the most frequent reaction was to create an independent board to administer the police agency or switch to a police administrator appointed to a term independent of the elected mayor. When it was concluded that the accountability of the police should be increased, the police administrator was made directly responsible to an elected mayor. In some respects recent proposals for establishing community control or neighborhood control over the police are a continuation of this same tendency to resort to redefining formal lines of responsibility as the principal means for achieving accountability.

Altering the administrative structure would make sense if the results of each alternative were clearly predictable and likely to be uniform over an extended period of time. But such is not the case. Organizational arrangements (such as independent boards or state control) have not, in most instances, accomplished what they were designed to achieve. Arrangements that have worked well in some communities have failed in others. And many schemes, heralded as successful soon after their implementation, have subsequently been condemned.

In 1931 the Wickersham Commission singled out the city of Milwaukee for having established a police and fire commission to control appointments and promotions and for having insulated the chief by giving him permanent tenure. The commission reported that it was refreshing to observe that, as a result, politicians did not control the department and added: "There is no charge in Milwaukee . . . that the head of the police department is autocratic excepting perhaps by evil doers who in transgressing the law have contacted with law enforcement officials of that city."[20] In December of 1972 a report of the Wisconsin State Committee to the United States Commission on Civil Rights concluded:

> Almost all of the major deficiencies of the Milwaukee Police Department enumerated in this report are attributable to the isolated condition of the department in relation to the citizenry it serves. The responsibility for law enforcement policymaking and implementation is concentrated in an office whose incumbent is directly accountable to no one. . . . The preeminent national position which Milwaukee once enjoyed among police departments has eroded seriously over the years. It is the belief of this Committee that the erosion is due not so much to any personal inadequacy of the police chiefs who ruled during this time, but rather to the department's structure, which has insulated the entire organization from, and rendered it ill-equipped to cope with, significant changes in Milwaukee neighborhoods.[21]

Unrecognized in this groping for the ideal system is the fact that purely structural arrangements for achieving accountability do not, on their own, reach the problems citizens want most to reach. Situations that prompt demands for greater responsiveness, or for isolation and autonomy, are not usually administrative practices subject to correction by reorganization, but rather are substantive policy decisions of the kind described in chapter 5 that are rarely articulated.

If these decisions are not structured and controlled, mere changes in designating who is responsible to whom will not have the effect that their proponents anticipate.

Underestimating the Need for Delegating Administrative Responsibility

The several proposals that have been made for more direct citizen control of police agencies have usually called for citizens to take on greater responsibility for purely administrative matters—matters that do not require value judgments and that, under any circumstances, might best be left to professional administrators. Thus, for example, had the proposal for community control of the Berkeley, California, Police Department been adopted, the civilians responsible for running the agency would undoubtedly have been so overwhelmed with minutiae that they would have had little time for important policy matters.[22] Those who argue that it is essential that citizens have direct control over the administration and personnel of a police agency in order to control its policies underestimate the complexity of running a police agency on a daily basis and overestimate the extent to which such control can be used to affect policies.

It may well be that the purchase of a piece of equipment, the assignment of a given officer, and the establishment of a specific reporting requirement involve some political judgment. But it is an invitation to chaos to require that such decisions be subject to the review of a group of citizens prior to being implemented. Indeed, the average police chief finds that he himself must delegate many of these decisions to subordinates to be carried out in accordance with broad policies to which he gives his approval. If a specific action in the day-to-day administration of the police agency poses policy questions, the issues involved should be isolated and dealt with rather than the specifics of a given case that may have called attention to the issues.

And yet important as it is to give police administrators sufficient room to carry out their responsibilities, it is difficult to establish where their authority should end. Some will be tempted to resurrect the dichotomy that existed for many years in the public administration field between policy-making and administration. Under the city-manager plan of local government, for example, it was long held that city councils formulated the policies of city government and that the city manager carried out the policies as a professional administrator. But recent events have made it obvious that this was a rather sterile concept; much of administration is policy-making.

Efforts to make similar distinctions in the police field have been rendered equally futile by changes in the social and political climate. A decade ago, for example, the recruitment and selection of police officers were viewed as rather routine tasks to be carried out almost exclusively by administrative personnel. Today, setting standards, designing examinations, and processing applicants call for judgments in which concerned citizens have a vital interest. Likewise, the form that patrol takes, previously considered exclusively the prerogative of the police administrator, is now a difficult policy question which cannot be resolved solely on the basis of an administrator's concern for efficiency and effectiveness. The old distinction between policy-making and administration will be further blurred if substantive policies are initially formulated by police administrators through the rule-making process suggested in chapter 5.

Overestimating the Potential of Citizen Involvement

In their enthusiasm to compensate for the insulation of the past, advocates of greater citizen involvement are apt to misjudge both the feasibility of achieving greater citizen involvement and the contribution that can be realized. They tend to define expectations unrealistically and to overlook predictable problems. It is extremely difficult to organize and sustain groups at the grass-roots level that are truly representative of a cross section of the community. Limited experience with the use of advisory groups indicates that it is often difficult to achieve a consensus, that interest soon fades, and that persons representing special interests, such as the business community, become the strongest voices through the default of others. My own observations of informal efforts to encourage greater citizen involvement at the neighborhood level in large cities leave me with the impression that, absent vigorous representation of the people affected, persons attracted to membership on such a body are inclined to encourage and support some of the very police practices to which the advocates of decentralized decision-making are most strongly opposed. The results might differ if citizens had formally established roles and were vested with specific authority to determine certain policies.

ESSENTIAL ELEMENTS FOR ACHIEVING
GREATER ACCOUNTABILITY

It is quite natural that those who are concerned with achieving greater accountability by the police and more citizen input into decision-making, on recognizing the weakness of recent proposals, should continue their search for an ideal plan that could be applied universally to solve all existing problems without producing any negative results. But no single model is available, nor is it likely that one will evolve in the near future. There are simply too many variables from one community to another. Moreover, our experience in attempting to elicit greater community involvement at the neighborhood level in large cities and in structuring police discretion—which are two important components of any system of accountability—is extremely limited, so there is little to build on. It appears, therefore, that the next several decades will be a period of experimentation in which the dynamics and needs of different municipalities will lead to a variety of arrangements aimed at improving the process by which citizens can influence and exert appropriate control over police operations.

Although no single model can be recommended, recent attempts to provide a clearer form of accountability suggest that some minimal elements are essential if the system is to work.

Including All Aspects of Police Functioning
The most obvious requirement is that the system be sufficiently broad and comprehensive to encompass all aspects of police operations. This means that it must extend far beyond the apparatus of the criminal justice system, which provides for accountability with regard to but a portion of police business. Channels must be opened for consideration of citizen opinion in setting priorities relative to the multiple functions police perform and in choosing from among the various methods available to the police for carrying out these functions (see chapter 2).

Tying into Systems for Structuring Discretion
Before much more in the way of accountability can be achieved, some structure must be given to the mass of important decisions in policing that are now made in a disorganized, unarticulated, and therefore unreviewable manner. This entails not only recognizing the vast amount of discretion exercised by the police, but also acknowledging that the multifarious nature of the police function requires that different policy questions be resolved in a variety of different ways at different levels of government (see chapter 5). Increased use must be made of those decision-making processes (legislation, budgeting, administrative rule-making, and so on) that give visibility to policies, making them subject to public scrutiny and review; that afford the opportunity for citizen reaction in their formulation; and that produce guidelines in the form of statutes, ordinances, rules, or policies to which the actions of the police can then be related.

Thus, in the controversial area of narcotics enforcement, a police agency might initiate a move toward greater accountability by articulating its enforcement priorities (as between different types of drugs and as between users and sellers, for example), by drawing up guidelines on the use to be made of informants, and by setting forth its policies for conducting searches and making arrests. Citizen comment might be solicited by special request or by publication as part of a rule-making process; or the proposed policies might be submitted for approval to some superior authority, be it the elected chief executive of the community or the local legislative body. And once guidelines were adopted the police would be expected to conform to them in practice.

Decentralizing to the Maximum Degree
It is only natural that the frustrations of community groups who failed to change police operating policies should have produced demands in the large cities for absolute neighborhood control of the police. The movement reflects the common tendency to solve the problem of most immediate concern without full regard for the impact that the solution will have in other areas. In many re-

spects the reaction is similar—in its extreme character—to the earlier reactions to the destructive effects of partisan politics, which resulted in insulating police agencies from legitimate influences as well.[23]

But the problems likely to be created by total decentralization of the police function ought not to blind us to the desirability of establishing new channels by which residents of a small area within a larger community can—when there is no compelling reason to apply a policy uniformly throughout a city—have a voice in determining the policies affecting service in their neighborhood. There is a far greater difference in the makeup and character of selected neighborhoods within a large city than there is in the makeup of smaller cities located within the same state. And yet a large-city police department is usually committed, at least formally, to providing a uniform style of police service to all neighborhoods, whereas the form of police service in smaller communities differs significantly in accord with the wishes of local residents.

That independently organized police agencies are more effective than the larger city-wide departments in meeting the demands of citizens residing in their communities is the major point made in a study reported by Elinor Ostrom and Gordon Whitaker.[24] They based their conclusions on measurements of such factors as the rate of victimization of residents; the amount of assistance rendered citizens; the promptness with which police responded to calls for help; and citizens' assessment of police-community relations and the kind of job they thought the police were doing.[25] A major problem with such inquiries is that measures of police responsiveness and citizen satisfaction are not always indicative of the quality of police service. A police agency may be very responsive to citizen demands and be rated highly by the people it serves, but when its actions are measured against standards of legality and propriety the quality of the service may be poor.

The residents of neighborhoods within large cities would in all probability realize a higher degree of satisfaction if police services were under their direct control, but this might be at the cost of a deterioration in the quality of the service a person traveling through the neighborhood would receive. The challenge in the larger cities is in trying to achieve some of the benefits of neighborhood-oriented policing without sacrificing the commitment that the larger jurisdiction must maintain toward providing a high level of service to citizens moving between areas—including those who enter the larger jurisdiction from the smaller communities.

This poses some fundamental questions. What decisions can be left to a neighborhood or some other subdivision of a larger municipality? It is unlikely that anyone would seriously suggest that state statutes prohibiting homicide or rape should be enforced differently in different areas of a city or even in different sections of a state. But a strong case could be made for adopting different operating policies for resolving conflict in order to acknowledge different cultural practices and preferences. How does one decide what an appropriate subdivision of a large community would be for purposes of determining these police policies and practices? By what mechanisms can a community arrive at its position? Are local elected boards desirable? Should these be institutionalized or should they be maintained on an ad hoc basis? Would they provide the degree of accountability that is required for decision-making? And what status should their decisions have? Would they be binding or simply advisory?

The suggestion that some substantive decisions concerning the form of police service be made at a level lower than that of municipal government is probably the most controversial of all the proposals for achieving greater police accountability. The idea runs contrary to the whole movement of recent years, in which emphasis was placed on achieving uniformity, objectivity, and equal enforcement of the law within a jurisdiction. But it deserves serious consideration, given our new awareness of the degree to which the quality of police service is influenced by police acknowledgment of variations in the life-styles of different neighborhoods.

Meeting the Continuing Need for Insulation

Given the history of domination of police agencies by partisan political interests, it is clearly essential that the system of political accountability be designed to minimize the likelihood that political parties will be in a position to manipulate the police to their advantage. Moreover, police administrators and police officers must be free to enforce the law without fear that the person or class of offenders against whom they take action has the power to retaliate against the enforcing officers. Obvious as this should be, it is nevertheless important to stress that much of what the police do—whether it be issuing a summons for speeding or prosecuting a case against organized criminals—places them in an adverse relationship with members of the community. Persons without police experience do not realize the magnitude of this problem and the extremes to which individuals will go to "get even" with the police. It would make for an intolerable situation if such individuals, properly and legally proceeded against and afforded an opportunity for judicial review of the charges against them, were able to use the channels for citizen direction of the police as a means of revenge.

Beyond these concerns, proper police functioning, as was previously noted, requires that the police act in a number of different circumstances without regard to the interests and demands of the community that they are serving and the citizens who may in fact be paying their salaries. They must be insulated from local pressures when fulfilling a responsibility that is theirs by virtue of legislation or other form of direction promulgated at a level higher than that of the municipal government, be it a provision of the United States Constitution or a state statute. The citizens of a given neighborhood, for example, should not be allowed to interfere with police action designed to protect the right of an individual to move into the neighborhood. The police should be free to provide adequate protection to a person speaking on behalf of an unpopular cause, however strong the objection within the community might be to the speaker. The police should be insulated from community pressures that demand they use their authority and their coercive power to proceed improperly and illegally against individuals whose actions have offended broad segments of the community. And the police should be sufficiently insulated to enable them to guarantee the constitutional rights of individuals taken into custody.

Police administrators also require independence and flexibility in order to administer an agency within the policies established by the appropriate bodies. Citizen groups should provide guidance on direction and priorities, but they ought not become involved in developing detailed instructions on how policies are to be implemented. A chief's day-to-day control over personnel, equipment, and resources cannot be reduced without seriously detracting from his ability to manage.

The results of various administrative arrangements to provide needed insulation in the past make it appear unwise to resort, once again, to the creation of independent boards and commissions to serve as buffers between the police and the community. Nor does it seem desirable, given recent experience, to give police administrators ironclad tenure. Yet some security in office is essential. Without it a chief would be too vulnerable to the numerous pressures exerted on him. Aside from being subject to outside pressures, an administrator would find it extremely difficult to maintain control over personnel. Many subordinates will not cooperate fully with a chief who does not have tenure and who appears in danger of being fired because of his actions or the positions he takes—especially if the subordinates themselves are tenured. If every administrative decision has the potential of becoming a test of the chief's capacity to stay in office, qualified candidates will not apply for the chief's job in the first place.

One method for providing needed tenure without sacrificing accountability to the public appears to have considerable merit, but has not been widely employed. It calls for appointment of the chief to a set term of office, with the provisions of his employment established by contract. The length of service could be sufficiently long to enable a chief to gain a foothold in the first years, when the pressures are likely to be greatest and when conflict-producing changes must be carried out. By contract, a community could commit itself to providing financial security in the form of salary for the full length of the term while reserving the right to terminate the service of a chief before the term expires. The financial obligation that would be incurred if the contract were terminated before the incumbent's term expired would serve as some protection against frivolous dismissals. Yet the cost involved in "buying out a contract," especially after several years had passed, would not be an unreasonable price to pay if a community concluded that its desires and the policies of its chief were irreconcilable.

Pinpointing Responsibility

Even though police actions derive from policies formulated by a range of officials and legislative bodies, the police should be accountable to a single public official and through that official to the citizenry for the manner in which these policies are carried out. The logical official is the mayor or appointed chief executive of a municipality who is responsible to either the electorate or the city council. This provides the clearest and most direct means for achieving political accountability. It is consistent with the concept, advanced in chapter 2, that the police should be viewed primarily as an agency of municipal government in which is housed a whole range of functions. And it supports prevalent feeling that, in order to bring about a more coordinated response to the complex problems of urban areas, the authority of municipal chief executives to supervise municipal government should be strengthened. It has the additional advantage of being in line with public expectations, for although most municipal chief executives have very limited control over city government, citizens tend to look to the mayor or city manager as the official in overall charge.

Holding the municipal chief executive responsible for police functioning in this manner does not mean that he or she would make all the decisions or exercise unlimited supervision. On the contrary, a major responsibility would be to see to it that the police agency conformed with legislation and policies established at a higher level of government. Likewise, it would be the municipal chief executive's job to assure that the agency carried out its responsibilities to consult community groups in formulating policies. If increased use were made of administrative rule-making as a way of structuring discretion, the mayor or city manager would be expected to oversee this process personally and participate in the formulation of new policies.

It follows that on occasion the municipal chief executive, in accounting to the community for a specific police action or practice, will have to point out that what the police were doing was in conformity with constitutional requirements, or legislative mandate, or the wishes of the city council. It will be an improvement over current arrangements in many jurisdictions if there is a single official who, even if he cannot act on citizen requests and complaints, can, with some authority, advise citizens where they should go in order to alter policies and practices to which they object.

Accepting the Costs of Subjecting Decisions to the Political Process

The suggestion that police agencies be directly supervised by elected municipal executives conjures up the image of police administrators beholden to various interests—including criminal elements—on whose continued support the elected mayor, their boss, may depend. It implies a system in which the professional judgments of police administrators may be overridden and supplanted by the judgments of amateurs.

As to the first of these concerns—opening the door to improper influences—the feared consequences need not necessarily follow. In many jurisdictions police chiefs who are directly responsible to elected officials have nevertheless managed to remain free from improper influences. Indeed, a reduction in the autonomy of the chief and greater involvement of the mayor may, in some situations, actually reduce the amount of improper influence brought to bear upon police operations. In the long run the potential for minimizing improper influences depends upon the local situation and, most especially, upon the operating philosophy, commitments, and integrity of the individuals involved.

But even if the worst consequences feared by police administrators were to materialize, is this not one of the costs of operating under our system of government? It may, indeed, be preferable to operate under a system in which political decisions, however bad, are plainly visible, than under a system in which partisan pressures are covertly exerted.

Doubtless many of the decisions reached by amateurs through increased resort to the political process would be "bad" by some criteria. But it is a mistake to assume that there is a "right" way and a "wrong" way to resolve the many important policy questions relating to the police. Although a combination of police experience and research makes it possible for the police to make some judgments in some areas with considerable confidence, many similar judgments made several years ago with equal confidence have since been discredited. But, beyond this, a number of the judgments that must be made involve a weighing of competing values to which different people attach different importance at different times.

The practice of labeling decisions "bad" assumes that there is merit in imposing upon a community professional policy judgments which the community may not support. What is preferable? To create and seek to maintain a form of police service that lacks community support? Or to afford a community the opportunity to make "mistakes" on the assumption that, providing there is clear accountability for the errors, these will eventually lead to the creation of a more solid base of community support for what is considered to be "right"?

Greater involvement of elected officials in decision-making affecting police operations means that both the police and the community must be prepared to accept decisions that are not to their liking. It is inconsistent to condemn the mayor of Chicago for interfering in police operations at the Democratic Convention of 1968 (if he did so) because one disagrees with the consequences of his directions, and to praise the mayor of New York for interfering with police operations because one concurs with his position. Rather than criticize the relationship between the mayor and the police, displeased citizens must seek to influence the mayor through traditional political means.

When the instructions issued to the police are adopted through the established decision-making process, and when they are legal, the police administrator's job is obviously to implement them to the best of his ability, even though he may disagree with them. One of the marks of a truly professional administrator is his ability to adjust police operations to meet the formally expressed desires of the community.

But what happens if, for example, the police administrator is of the opinion that the instructions of his mayor are in conflict with state law or the federal Constitution and that he, as police chief, must abide by these higher authorities? Should a police chief, for example, order the arrest of demonstrators upon order of the mayor, even if he believes that no legal basis exists for making such arrests? Should he prohibit a march or ban a speech on orders from his boss, the mayor, even if he feels the right to march and the right to speak are constitutionally protected?

What about the lesser situation where there may be a legal basis for police action, but the chief feels it is either unfair or unwise to take action? Should a police chief upon orders from the mayor press the arrest of petty street gamblers in the inner core of a large city even though the chief feels such arrests are unjustified in light of the department's policy of ignoring petty gambling in other areas of the city? Should a police chief withdraw police officers from a riot situation upon orders from the mayor, even though he is convinced it is unwise to do so from a tactical standpoint? Should a police chief, at the mayor's instigation, instruct his personnel to make wholesale arrests of marijuana smokers at a rock festival even though he is convinced that the making of such arrests will cause a riot that he will not be able to control?

In the past, with the lines of responsibility unclearly drawn, police administrators either followed without question the instructions of those they considered their superiors or—in the exceptional case where the incumbent found that course unconscionable—resigned without articulating the reasons for doing so. Neither of these alternatives contributes toward tightening accountability and improving police operations.

Disagreements over basic policies between police administrators and their superiors should be public. If a mayor chooses to override the advice of the chief, the mayor should be prepared to go on record as doing so. Likewise, if a chief takes exception to a policy or program imposed upon him, he should have the opportunity to express his disagreement openly. Such a public record introduces a stronger element of accountability and responsibility into the decision-making process. The mishandling of many of the large-scale confrontations between citizens and the police that occurred in recent years was attributable, in large measure, to the fact that the most critical decisions were made by individuals who were not required to acknowledge responsibility for them.

In most fields, dismissals and resignations—costly as they may be to the progress of an agency and disruptive as they may be to the lives of the individuals involved—are recognized as powerful vehicles for highlighting conflicts over policies, for clarifying directions, and for generally sharpening accountability in government. The awareness that a professional administrator is likely to resign if ordered to do something illegal, unjust, or unwise, and may state publicly the reasons for resigning, is in itself a most effective deterrent against the issuing of such orders by elected officials.

But how realistic is it, in the present climate, to expect a police administrator to take such a stand? A police chief, unlike others in equivalent positions of responsibility, is not free to quit his job with confidence that he can obtain employment in a community that is more in accord with his concepts and operating policies. A decision to resign means, for him, returning to a subordinate position in the same agency, retiring, or seeking employment outside the police field. Absent a contractual arrangement such as was suggested earlier, he may also suffer a substantial financial loss. Boxed in in this manner, many chiefs surrender to the pressures brought to bear upon them.

The community also gets boxed in. Because a police chief cannot be relieved without great personal loss, city fathers are reluctant to change administrators; so they perpetuate, by their failure to act, policies and practices that they may recognize are out of tune with community desires.

Achieving greater accountability, therefore, requires, among other things, more widespread acceptance of lateral movement for police administrators. One of the most compelling reasons to support the concept of lateral movement is that it maximizes the possibility that the chief and local citizens will be in accord on matters of basic policy.

NOTES

1. President's Commission on Law Enforcement and Administration of Justice, *Task Force Report: The Police* (Washington, D.C.: Government Printing Office, 1967), p. 7. Some have used a smaller figure. A survey by LEAA in 1970 found that there were 208 enforcement agencies at the state level, 4,800 at the county level, and 14,603 at the local level—but this survey did not include agencies of municipalities with a population of less than 1,000. See United States Department of Justice, Law Enforcement Assistance Administration, *Criminal Justice Agencies in the United States: Summary Report, 1970* (Washington, D.C.: Government Printing Office, 1971), pp. 11–13. Whatever differences there may be in calculating the exact total, it is clear that a large number of police agencies exist in this country, and almost all of them are organized at the local level of government.

2. For a recent review of the efforts that have been made to consolidate police agencies, see National Advisory Commission on Criminal Justice Standards and Goals, *Police* (Washington, D.C.: Government Printing Office, 1973), pp. 108–117.

3. There are many detailed accounts of the sordid conditions created by the alliance between the police and political-party organizations in this period and up to the present. See, for example, Raymond B. Fosdick, *American Police Systems* (1920; reprint ed., Montclair, N.J.: Patterson Smith, 1969); Leonhard F. Fuld, *Police Administration* (1909; reprint ed., Montclair, N.J.: Patterson Smith, 1971); National Commission on Law Observance and Enforcement, *Report on Police* (Washington, D.C.: Government Printing Office, 1931; reprint ed., Mont-

clair, N.J.: Patterson Smith, 1968); Lincoln Steffens, *The Shame of the Cities* (New York: McClure-Phillips, 1904). For an account of a contemporary situation, see John A. Gardiner, *The Politics of Corruption* (New York: Russell Sage Foundation, 1970).

4. The most comprehensive summary of the various systems employed in an effort to achieve effective control of the police in this country—up to 1920—is contained in Fosdick, *American Police Systems*, pp. 58–187.

5. National Commission on Law Observance and Enforcement, *Report on Police*, p. 51.

6. Ibid., pp. 49 and 52.

7. International City Management Association, *The Municipal Yearbook* (Washington, D.C.: International City Management Association, 1972), p. 276.

8. Wallace S. Sayre and Herbert Kaufman, *Governing New York City* (New York: Russell Sage Foundation, 1960), p. 290.

9. Ibid., p. 292.

10. Most recently there has been much greater concern with the accountability of enforcement agencies at the federal level, as debates have taken place over the practices of the FBI, and IRS, and the CIA. In a classic restatement of the problem the FBI has been attacked for being too responsive to political direction (in helping, as some allege, to cover up the Watergate incident) and too immune from citizen control (as, for example, in adopting a policy of infiltrating anti-war groups). The first complaint leads to urgings that the Bureau be more tightly insulated from the influence of politicians; the second leads to demands that it be made more susceptible to political control. So far this has resulted in suggestions for limiting the tenure of the director and creation of a congressional committee to oversee FBI operations. In what may appear to some as a contradictory development, the Director of the FBI promised that there will be no presidential interference in the functioning of the Bureau. "Kelley, With Nixon at Side, Pledges Integrity of F.B.I.," *New York Times*, 10 July 1973. To whom is the FBI responsible? As an agency of the executive branch it is formally accountable to the attorney general and, through him, to the president. But the ambiguity surrounding this arrangement mirrors the confused situation that exists at the local level of government.

11. *Community, Police, and Policy, The Report Emerging from the Bruce Williams Case by the Police Hearing Board of the Evanston Human Relations Commission* (Evanston, Illinois: Evanston Human Relations Commission, 1969), pp. 8–9.

12. "Birkley Tells Optimists: 'Drug Furor Proves Police Review Need,'" *Madison (Wis.) Capital Times*, 31 January 1972.

13. For an interesting study of three large jurisdictions, see Leonard Ruchelman, *Police Politics: A Comparative Study of Three Cities* (Cambridge, Mass.: Ballinger Publishing Co., 1974).

14. In addition to Ruchelman, *Police Politics*, see David W. Abbott, Louis H. Gold, and Edward T. Rogowsky, *Police, Politics and Race: The New York City Referendum on Civilian Review* (New York: American Jewish Committee, 1969).

15. See Hervey A. Juris and Peter Feuille, *Police Unionism* (Lexington, Mass.: Lexington Books, D. C. Heath, 1973), p. 120.

16. Mayor Carl B. Stokes as quoted by D. J. R. Bruckner in "Stokes Target of Bitter Battle," *Madison (Wis.) Capital Times*, 29 October 1968.

17. Mayor Coleman A. Young as quoted by William Stevens in "High Goals of Detroit's Black Mayor Foiled by Recession," *New York Times*, 22 January 1975. For an interesting analysis of the problems of the mayors of several large cities who sought to more actively direct police operations, see the series of articles entitled "Insight: Blue Power," that appeared in the *Washington Post* starting 15 December 1968.

18. Geoffrey Marshall, *Police and Government* (London: Methven and Co., 1965), p. 76.

19. Marshall, *Police and Government*, pp. 112–113.

20. National Commission on Law Observance and Enforcement, *Report on Police*, pp. 43 and 50.

21. Wisconsin State Committee, United States Commission on Civil Rights, *Police Isolation and Community Needs* (Washington, D.C.: Government Printing Office, 1972), pp. 114–115.

22. The proposal called for five commissioners, to be selected by citizen councils, to direct police operations in the three separate departments into which the existing department was to be divided. These commissioners would have become responsible for much of the detail of running the agency and it seems likely that the councils themselves would also have become involved. Berkeley, California, Charter Amendment No. 1, voted down at the general municipal election on April 6, 1971.

23. For a discussion of some of the problems in implementing neighborhood control of the police, see James Q. Wilson, *Varieties of Police Behavior* (Cambridge, Mass.: Harvard University Press, 1968), pp. 284–299; and Albert J. Reiss, Jr., *The Police and the Public* (New Haven: Yale University Press, 1971), pp. 207–212.

24. Elinor Ostrom and Gordon Whitaker, "Does Local Community Control of Police Make a Difference? Some Preliminary Findings," *American Journal of Political Science* 17 (1973): 48–76. See also Elinor Ostrom et al., *Community Organization and the Provision of Police Services* (Beverly Hills, Calif.: Sage Publications, 1973).

25. Ostrom and Whitaker, "Does Local Community Control of Police Make a Difference?" pp. 61–74.

Chapter 7

Controlling and Reviewing Police–Citizen Contacts

Up to this point we have been discussing but one aspect of accountability—the process by which major policy decisions are made or simply evolve in the running of a police agency and the problems in pinpointing responsibility for them. If clear directions, whatever their source, are in fact given to the police, there is then need to assure compliance and, beyond this, to afford citizens an opportunity for redress if, in their view, the police have acted improperly. So we continue in this chapter to dwell on achieving accountability on the part of the police, but focus now on the complex considerations involved in controlling and reviewing the actions of individual police officers in their contacts with citizens at the street level.

PLACING CONTROL AND REVIEW IN CONTEXT

Complaints arising from police–citizen contacts account for much of the attention police receive. Many proposals have been made in the last twenty years for improving the methods by which allegations of police misconduct are investigated. These proposals have evoked such strong reaction from the police, however, that most discussions and writings on the subject now reflect only the polarization that has occurred. Before one can begin to deal with the issue of how to control and review police actions, one must put these passionate and extremely divergent positions in proper perspective.

Interest in the control of police conduct first began to accelerate in the 1950s. The United States Supreme Court and other courts throughout the country, as part of the "due process revolution," became highly critical of police practices revealed in the cases that came before them. It was largely in response to this concern that the Supreme Court in 1961 imposed on the state courts the requirement that evidence obtained through an illegal search or seizure be excluded from a criminal prosecution—a decision generally accepted as an effort to provide judges with more effective control over police conduct.[1] Also starting in the 1950s, various citizen groups—contending that existing means for seeking redress were ineffective—began to demand some form of civilian review of complaints filed against police officers. A widespread movement developed to establish civilian review boards that would be empowered to receive, investigate, and hold hearings on complaints filed with them.[2] Interest in control over the police peaked in the late 1960s when the police dealt first with urban rioting and then with massive political protest. Participants in these confrontations who were aggrieved by police actions added their voices to those who had previously been calling for new, more effective mechanisms for airing their complaints.

Because minority groups and political dissidents were among those complaining most vigorously about police conduct, the debate over control and review mechanisms became entangled with strong and often bitter feelings on political and racial matters. The referendum on a civilian review board in New York City in 1966 was converted into a rather crude tabulation of public attitudes on the racial conflict in that city.[3] But even where such tensions were absent, the debate over control of the police generated strong antagonisms.

The police saw much of the criticism directed at them coming from groups and individuals against whom they were required to take action—alleged criminal offenders and disruptive protesters. They feared that the proposed review mechanisms would be used by these groups to retaliate against them. Officers in agencies which did not engage in the practices most commonly criticized resented the wholesale distrust implied both in the criticism directed at them and in the proposals that were made. They were offended by the notion that their actions would be judged by individuals removed from the situations they confronted. And they claimed such review would eliminate much of the initiative and aggressiveness on which—they believed—police work heavily depends. Less commonly articulated, but of no small concern, was police recognition that the patchwork nature of policing did indeed make the police terribly vulnerable to an outside review if such review were to be based upon formal concepts and criteria rather than the realities of police work. It was understandable, too, that the police should tire of the continued emphasis on abuses, feeling that quality police performance deserved a proportionate share of public attention. Together, all of these concerns produced a solid wall of resistance to the whole notion of civilian review. In fairness it must be recognized that many of the objections of the police were not unlike those expressed by other occupations and professional groups when faced with proposals for review of their activities by individuals outside their field.

The proponents of more effective civilian review, however, had ample basis for concern. Case after case and study after study have documented situations in which police authority has been abused and in which citizens were left without an effective avenue for redress. Many of these accounts were compiled by groups such as the American Civil Liberties Union and other champions of civil liberties and minority rights whose business it is to draw attention to such concerns.[4]

The fact that the studies were conducted and published by groups viewed as inherently antagonistic to the police was often used by the police to discredit the claims that were made. But criticism came from more neutral sources as well.[5] As recently as 1973, for example, the *Chicago Tribune*, which in the past had taken strong editorial positions defending the police from censure by civil libertarians, published the results of an investigation which was highly critical of Chicago police practices.[6] A team of reporters persuasively documented incidents of wrongdoing by officers and the failure of the department to investigate effectively the complaints that had been filed about them.

If one looks objectively at the anguish, humiliation, loss of income, and physical suffering experienced by those who have been wronged by the police (through false imprisonment, false prosecution, or beating) and who have unsuccessfully sought redress through established channels, one can appreciate the intensity of the feelings that underlie demands for more effective control of police conduct. And one can understand, too, how these feelings get translated into sweeping proposals that do not always communicate clearly the primary source of concern.

In order to bring the problem back into perspective, both the police and citizen critics of the police must be jarred from their extreme positions. The police can ill afford to bury their heads in the sand and maintain that there are simply no problems. Nor can they, under a system of government that attaches so high a value to protection from improper action by its agents, continue to resist in blanket fashion all efforts to provide aggrieved citizens adequate opportunities to air their grievances. Critics of the police, on the other hand, have an obligation to recognize the realities and complexities of police work, the handicaps under which the police function, and the difficulty in achieving effective control in a police operation. They must recognize, too, that many of the specific wrongs upon which they focus, though inexcusable, nevertheless are symptomatic of more basic problems that will be solved only if citizen interest extends to matters beyond control and review.

This brings us, then, to two factors that must be recognized in restoring a more balanced perspective in the quest to control police conduct. First, we have seriously erred in placing so heavy a burden on control mechanisms as a way of solving long-standing problems in the police field. Second, we have erred, too, in viewing control almost exclusively in terms of identifying and taking action against wrongdoing.

It is inevitable that people who take an interest in police matters because they have suffered some abuse will concentrate on creating methods for controlling police behavior. But there are serious limits to what one can do, through this essentially negative procedure, to change police performance. However well designed a system of control and redress might be, it is not likely to have a significant impact on police conduct in an agency that is in a state of disarray—that suffers from lack of clarity as to its function, from lack of clear direction, from internal conflicts, and, in addition, is often poorly organized, poorly administered, poorly staffed, and poorly trained.

The police field would have profited greatly if the energies devoted to both advocating and resisting new forms of control in recent years had instead been applied, for example, to better defining the police task; to providing police with needed alternatives for carrying out their duties; or to improving the recruitment and screening of police personnel, their training, and especially their leadership. Leadership is of special importance, for a competent police administrator has much greater potential for achieving a higher quality of police service than can ever be realized by others attempting to control a poorly administered organization from the outside.

The second failing of proposals for control—the narrow concentration on wrongdoing—commits the police to waiting for complaints to be filed. It commits them to focusing their attention on investigations, disciplinary procedures, and sanctions. Both the police and the public become so preoccupied with identifying wrongdoing and taking disciplinary action against errant officers that they lose sight of the primary objective of control, which is to achieve maximum conformity with legal requirements, established policies, and prevailing standards of propriety. This objective is far more likely to be attained by fostering an atmosphere in which the police conform because they want to conform, rather than out of fear of the consequences if they do not.

FACTORS COMPLICATING
CONTROL AND REVIEW

Although new positive approaches to achieving control would reduce the need to concentrate on wrongdoing, it would nevertheless be necessary, under the best of circumstances, for police administrators to maintain and perfect procedures for identifying improper conduct, reviewing police actions, and imposing sanctions. Many factors inherent in the police function make this task extremely complex and at times almost impossible.

The Adversary Nature of the Police Function

Tensions and hostility are a part of policing. Police officers must, as part of their job, issue orders to people, catch them in violation of laws, deprive them of their freedom, and bring charges that may lead to the imposition of severe punishment. Contacts between officers and citizens are often initiated under conditions that are emotionally charged, such as immediately after a fight or other disturbance, or following the commission of a crime. Even the person getting a traffic ticket frequently becomes indignant. However scrupulous the police may be in carrying out their responsibilities, they are bound to incur the wrath of some of those against whom they must proceed. This hostility manifests itself in various forms—sometimes immediately, by verbal abuse or physical resistance to the police; sometimes later, by alleging that the officer's actions were improper or illegal. Under such circumstances an officer must be able to count on support for actions taken in the line of duty. As was noted in the preceding chapter, the police officer expects and indeed needs some insulation from the community being served. But insulation can serve as a shield for the officer who is not so scrupulous—who in fact acts improperly.

The most difficult cases to review are those alleging improper use of force or verbal abuse, for it is often impossible to establish, in the rapid escalation that characterizes such encounters, who provoked whom, recognizing of course that the officer is under an obligation to exercise restraint and not respond in kind. To this must be added the fact that most police encounters occur under isolated conditions. Police usually apprehend criminals in such places as closed commercial establishments, residential areas in the early hours of the morning, and areas closed to the public after dark, where the absence of witnesses makes it likely that a crime will be committed. But even the giving of a traffic citation on a crowded street is often unobserved.

That otherwise honorable citizens resort to lying as a defense against police is well established. It is also clear that some police officers lie to justify action they have taken. The task of getting at the truth is further complicated because many of the people with whom the police have contact are unscrupulous individuals. Hard-core criminal offenders do not hesitate to make a false allegation if they think it might help to cloud the issue of their own guilt. People in organized crime also use this technique to discourage the police from taking action against them.

The frequency with which such allegations are made and the degree to which investigation shows them to be unfounded lead some police supervisors to discredit all complaints from known criminals. But these people are especially vulnerable to police abuse. A violence-prone officer, for example, may conclude that an offender's reputation is such that his word would not be trusted in any subsequent review. Thus complaints filed by the most discredited people require the most careful investigation.

The Insensitivity that Stems from Dealing Routinely with Crises

For the individuals involved, the events that lead to contact with a police officer (and the contact itself, as previously noted), may be quite traumatic. This is especially true of complainants and victims who never previously had occasion to call the police. They often have high expectations as to what they will receive in the way of a response.

By contrast, what citizens view as crises may seem trivial to the police, who are in the business of handling such matters routinely. At the start of his career, an officer may respond with some urgency to such incidents as a family squabble, a traffic accident, a typical home burglary, or a drunk causing a disturbance. But after handling a hundred domestic disturbances, a hundred accidents, a hundred burglaries, or a hundred drunks, the officer understandably may not display the same degree of concern and inquisitiveness. Moreover, there are often depart-ment pressures on the officer to take shortcuts in disposing of such cases. And the full resources of the department, such as technicians equipped to search for physical evidence, are generally not available for assignment in minor cases. In large-city departments, where high volume results in some forms of crime being handled by special units, the members of these units may develop an insensitiv-ity over such serious matters as rapes, robberies, and aggravated assaults.

The sharp contrast between the state of mind of the officer in these cases and that of the complainant, victim, or arrestee is a common source of conflict and dissatisfaction.

The Absence of Adequate Guidelines

Outrageous as an incident may seem to a citizen, the action about which he or she complains is quite often within the limits of the officer's legal authority. And relatively few departmental regulations or policies establish narrow stan-dards of conduct for those sensitive actions about which complaints are most commonly received. The question, then, becomes not whether the officer acted illegally or in violation of departmental rules, but whether the officer acted improperly. And in making that judgment everything depends upon whose stan-dard of propriety is employed. Many police agencies follow a practice of vindi-cating officers unless their actions can be classified as illegal. This is a convenient way of disposing of cases for a police administrator who is—from the outset—inclined to react adversely to citizen complaints. For the police administrator who concludes the behavior was improper and who wants to take corrective action, the absence of a specifically applicable standard or rule makes it difficult or even impossible for him to do so. (Civilian review boards, during their brief life in some cities, found themselves in the same predicament.)

Occasionally a police chief may attempt to deal with such a situation by taking action based on some peripheral element in the case, such as the fact that the officer may have been off his beat when the alleged misconduct occurred. This explains why so many disciplinary actions taken against police officers appear to be for violation of trivial or obscure administrative regulations. There was a time, too, when an administrator could simply bring a charge of conduct unbecoming a police officer, but recent litigation in some jurisdictions has estab-lished that an officer is entitled to know in specific terms what he is charged with, and beyond this, is entitled to know in advance the specific definition of conduct that will subject him to discipline.[7]

This situation adds support to the proposals made in the preceding chapters for structuring police discretion. The most elaborate apparatus for reviewing police conduct will not succeed unless explicit rules and policies are established to which police officers can then be held.

Department-wide Practices that
Are Themselves Questionable

A citizen's complaint alleging wrongdoing by an officer may in effect challenge a practice that is common throughout the agency. Police officers are frequently accused of having acted improperly despite the fact that their actions were in accord with their instructions from their supervisors, in harmony with the actions of fellow officers, and in conformity with long-standing practice.

Thus, for example, a citizen may complain that an officer stopped his car, ordered him out of it, and frisked him without adequate grounds for doing so. But in many departments officers are encouraged to do precisely this without being held to strict legal guidelines on when such action can be taken. When this is the case an agency can hardly penalize the accused officer, nor can it offer effective redress to the citizen. Likewise, an agency is not likely to discipline an officer against whom a complaint is filed because the officer ordered street-walking prostitutes to move on, or seized a weapon in an illegal search, or arrested a petty gambler without adequate evidence, if personnel are instructed and sometimes even rewarded for doing these very things.

For the progressive administrator, citizen complaints are often the best indicators of long-standing practices in need of correction. They bring to light police procedures that are often more traditional than necessary. A woman taken into custody for a traffic violation, for example, may accuse a police-woman of a gross indignity for subjecting her to a complete body search. But inquiry may reveal that all women who are detained, whatever the charge, are searched in this manner. Given the offensive nature of the procedure, the number of occasions on which it must be followed could be greatly reduced by such steps as eliminating the need for jailing minor offenders; refining the standard operating procedure regarding the search of prisoners to specify when body searches are necessary; and housing unsearched prisoners separate from those who have been searched.

Where, however, the administrator supports continuation of a procedure considered offensive by some, a form of control and review is needed that gets at the practice rather than just the action of one officer. This has implications for the design of systems for citizen redress that will be examined later.

Atmosphere of Duplicity and Hypocrisy

Effective control requires honesty in dealing with subordinates. Ideally a police administrator should be in a position to mean what he says. But the great inconsistencies between articulated policies and actual practices often require a police administrator to play a hypocritical role. The police are told they enforce all laws equally, but are expected to be highly selective in their enforcement practices. They are told they have no discretion, but are constantly expected to use discretion. If a discretionary action results in a complaint being filed, however, they know their performance will be judged by the formal requirements of the law. They are told they are responsible for all crime, but know their potential for preventing crime is limited. The net result of this hypocrisy is that, understandably, officers do not take seriously what they are told. This has a devastating effect on the capacity of the administration to control their conduct. The situation is so serious in some agencies that the administrator who desires total compliance with a specific order has to send a special message through informal channels making it clear that he really means, in this particular case, what the formal promulgation says.

The problem surfaces time and again in reviewing police conduct. The police often act in violation of the law on the grounds they are acting in the public interest—as, for example, in arresting inebriates for their own safekeeping. They do so with the support of the community, the police administrator, and the vast majority of police officers. Along comes an officer who, without adequate legal grounds, breaks into several private homes in search of a person responsible for a brutal attack on a small child. He argues that his violation of the law also was in the public interest. Can the administrator contend that one violation is to be condemned, while the other is justified? How does one weigh the relative seriousness of one illegality compared with another?

This dilemma of being expected to operate illegally in some situations is almost certainly what police officers have in mind when they contend that laymen do not have the kind of understanding required to review police conduct; that police behavior should be judged by those who have themselves been police officers. Interpreted, this plea means that police want their conduct measured by the informal code by which they operate rather than the formal criteria that define their function and authority.

Fear of Incurring Tort Liability

Still another bind in which the police administrator is caught stems from the liability of subordinates or of the municipality to civil suit. The success of the city attorney or corporation counsel in defending officers and the department against civil actions is measured in some degree by an ability to avoid judgments against the city and its employees.[8] This official is, as a result, constantly enlisting the aid of the police in the defense of actions brought against them as well as in the defense of actions brought against other city agencies. This makes the police sensitive to the possibility of civil action and especially to the adversary nature of such a proceeding.

It follows that, whenever it appears that there is the slightest possibility that the agency or officers may be sued in connection with a complaint filed with the department, the police begin to think in terms of defending the action. And as soon as a civil action is filed or the city attorney learns of the possibility of a suit from some other source, interest in defending the case usually takes precedence over the agency's interest in establishing the facts and especially in assessing blame.

The classic example of this dilemma is found in police efforts to promote safe driving on the part of their officers. Elaborate programs are frequently set up to review accidents involving departmental vehicles in order to establish the cause. If it is concluded the accident was avoidable, the officer may be required to take a driver-improvement course. And if the officer is adjudged guilty of careless or reckless driving, he may be punished. When, however, the accident causes serious injury or death, the process is likely to be stopped short on orders of the city attorney because of the high probability that a suit will be filed. So in the most serious accidents the officer is for all purposes exempt from immediate disciplinary action and, especially in large jurisdictions where the litigation may extend over several years, may never be called to account, even if eventually found to have been responsible for the accident.

Ideally the interests of a city attorney would transcend the possible liability incurred in single cases and extend to correcting the practices that give rise to suits by full and immediate implementation of existing administrative controls and by development of new guidelines as suggested in chapter 5. As noted there, this should produce a gradual decrease in the number of suits filed and, in addition, a gradual improvement in the quality of police service. But as a practical matter, short-termed city attorneys are generally unwilling to incur the immediate costs inherent in so long-range a proposal, and as a result the dilemma continues.[9]

The Blue Curtain

Those most likely to witness police actions are other police officers. It follows that review of a specific incident often is heavily dependent upon the testimony of other officers. But police will rarely incriminate a fellow officer.[10] They will either support the officer's actions or deny knowledge of the incident. This attitude has come to be referred to in police circles as the blue curtain.

Of course unwillingness to testify against a co-worker is not a characteristic unique to the police. Many other occupations and some of the most highly regarded professions, such as the legal and medical professions, protect themselves in the same manner. While there is no basis for making precise comparisons on this score between professional and occupational groups, those who work in the police field say that the code of secrecy among police officers is tighter and more absolute than in other fields. A number of factors, which also contribute to the police subculture, may account for this situation: (1) The police see themselves as members of a group aligned against common enemies. An attack upon any one of their members is considered an attack on the group. (2) Officers are greatly dependent upon one another for help in difficult situations. If an officer wants to count on fellow officers when his own life is endangered, he cannot afford to develop a reputation for "ratting." (3) The police are vulnerable to false allegations. An officer can easily imagine himself accused of wrongdoing in a difficult-to-review incident. He hopes that his defense of fellow officers when so accused will result in their willingness to assist him should their situations be reversed. (4) Police officers are as aware as their administrators of the disparity between formal policy and actual practice. The feeling emerges that it is necessary to cover up wrongdoing because practices that have developed which the police have rationalized as serving the public interest will not stand up to scrutiny. (5) An officer has no occupational mobility. He must anticipate continuing to work in the same place with the same people. He cannot ordinarily avoid an uncomfortable situation by transferring to another agency. He may even have to work, at some time in the future, under the supervision of an officer whose wrongdoing he observed.

Under these conditions it is not surprising that an officer at the bottom rung in an organization, concerned about such pragmatic things as supporting a family, will maintain the blue curtain. It is the easier alternative; he avoids subjecting himself to the harassment and anguish he may suffer on being ostracized by his fellow workers. For the police administrator the challenge is in attempting to create the kind of administrative atmosphere and arrangements that will enable the most principled among his subordinates to put integrity above loyalty to their peers. But his potential for achieving such an atmosphere is seriously limited unless steps are taken to reduce drastically or eliminate the underlying problems of policing in this country, which buffet officers between conflicting pressures and make their actions so vulnerable to criticism, if not prosecution, that they must depend on one another for protection.

Dealing with Abuse While Building Morale

Police at the operating level would like their leaders to subscribe to the same informal code that dictates relationships among themselves. Specifically they want supervisors and a police chief who will defend their agency from outside criticism. This is why police personnel usually prefer a chief selected from their own ranks. It is why they support a candidate who has a reputation for having been "one of the guys."

How subordinates view their leaders is important in a police agency, for it has a major influence upon morale. And morale, it is usually argued, is of central concern in an agency where much of the work is frustrating, routine, and seemingly endless; where its quality depends on the initiative of the individual; and where the authority and capacity of operating personnel are so often challenged. Moreover, if police leaders are to carry out new programs, they can do so only with the respect and support of their subordinates.

Can a police chief support his subordinates without committing himself to defend everything they do? For some chiefs this presents no problem, for they place a much higher value on maintaining a good relationship with their subordinates than upon being responsive to public criticism. Many are prepared to defend the actions of their officers, however illegal or improper they may have been; or, as a minimum, resolve all questionable cases in favor of their personnel. The chief who attempts to balance, in a judicious manner, the interests of his men with the public's interest undertakes the more difficult chore, for he must be prepared to incur the wrath of his subordinates or the public or, in borderline cases, both. His conclusions may lead to his punishing an officer who has a reputation for many accomplishments and acts of bravery. To cite a specific case, an officer had become a local hero of sorts for his daring exploits in apprehending street robbers. But behind the cover of his reputation, he had engaged in some brutal attacks on disrespectful teen-agers. Despite overwhelming evidence supporting the charges of wrongdoing, the disciplinary action brought against him by the administration was unsuccessful, primarily because of the tremendous amount of support for the officer expressed by the police themselves and by the mass media, whose hero the officer had become. The reverse is also true. A chief finds it extremely difficult, on weighing the evidence, to dismiss charges against an officer who was at the center of an incident about which there was an outpouring of public criticism.

Ideally a chief with a reputation for fairness in the investigation and review of alleged wrongdoing will gradually alter the prevailing code somewhat, making it clear that he can indeed be counted on to support those whose behavior is proper. But it takes time to establish such a reputation, and the tensions in most large police agencies today simply do not afford such an opportunity. The rank and file typically are quick to criticize disciplinary actions resulting from citizen complaints. Well-intentioned administrators committed to open and fair investigation of citizen complaints are especially vulnerable to allegations that morale, under their leadership, has declined. Important as morale may be, it is not an objective to be pursued independently at any cost.[11] Yet large segments of the public—uninformed on the dynamics of police operations—tend to view an allegation of poor morale as an especially serious indictment of a police chief's ability to run an agency. So a police administrator who wants to take appropriate action against wrongdoing must not only be concerned with the impact that those actions will have on the attitudes of subordinates toward their work; the administrator must also be prepared to do battle in the public forum in response to the charge that personnel are unhappy and morale is low.

OPPORTUNITIES FOR IMPROVEMENT THROUGH CHANGES IN ADMINISTRATIVE PRACTICES

Making Maximum Use of Positive Approaches

Police administrators can do much of a positive nature to achieve conformity with desired standards of conduct. Some of these opportunities were described in earlier chapters. Structuring discretion is perhaps the most obvious, for there is no more logical way to avoid wrongdoing than by giving police officers clearer and more positive directions on what is expected of them. One can shake one's head in dismay over the bizarre and perhaps offensive manner in which an officer handles a given incident, only to be pulled up short by the realization that no one ever told the officer to handle it differently.

A new system of incentives and rewards should be designed to elicit desired conduct. The present system, described and denounced with increasing frequency, is absurd. Police officers are rewarded in various ways for the number of arrests they make, for the tidiness of their uniforms, for their promptness in reporting for work, and for the neatness with which they maintain their notes in training programs. Police units are rewarded for the number of traffic citations issued, for the cleanliness of their facilities, and for their performance in target practice. Some or all of these measures may be important, but few directly affect the nature of the service rendered the public. An officer can register exceptionally well on all of them and still, in the eyes of the public, perform shabbily. New factors must be found that measure directly the quality of police services actually delivered.[12]

Perhaps more important than these administrative devices, however, is the need for aggressive advocacy by police leaders of a quality of police service that is more responsive to the diverse needs of the community, that is more sensitive to humanitarian concerns, and that reflects a full awareness of the delicate nature of the police function in a democracy. A skillful administrator who sincerely stands for these things and who manifests his values in everything he does—especially in the numerous opportunities he has for communicating both with his community and with his personnel—has tremendous potential for eliciting support for his values from his subordinates. Some of the most significant and often-cited differences between the police in the United States and in England are attributable to the fact that the police leadership in that country has, through hard work and long tradition, succeeded in instilling in police officers a commitment to a high set of values that guide them in their conduct even when specific direction is lacking. The prevailing character of police operations in England makes wrongdoing of the kind and magnitude that occurs in this country unthinkable.

It will take at least as much hard work and long tradition for police leadership in this country to change the values and priorities of individual officers, who are pressured by their peers into a police subculture that is greatly resistant to change. In pursuing this objective an administrator must make use of a variety of measures—some of a very positive nature and some which, of necessity, involve the use of traditional discipline and sanctions—in seeking to accelerate the process whereby the behavior of the police is brought into line with the law and with the standards of the community.

Viewing Individual Wrongdoing as an Agency Problem

If alleged wrongdoing is verified, police tend to defend the reputation of their agency by characterizing the wrongdoing as an isolated phenomenon not representative of their operations. This traditional response has contributed, perhaps unwittingly, to a prevalent attitude within police departments that wrongdoing is exclusively the responsibility of the wrongdoers; that the agency itself is exempt from any responsibility for the misconduct. It follows that, while sergeants, lieutenants, captains, and higher-ranking officers are held to strict account for investigating wrongdoing, they are rarely held to account for having failed to prevent the alleged misconduct in the first place or for having failed to uncover it on their own. Thus, preoccupied with defending themselves in the community, police administrators in many jurisdictions have forfeited one of the oldest and potentially most effective means for achieving conformity with legislative and administrative promulgations—the simple process of creating through traditional administrative devices an agency-wide sense of responsibility for the prevention of misconduct.

A factor that may contribute to this lack of responsibility for the wrongdoing of others is that—aside from the negative publicity—the agency incurs no direct liability or other costs when wrongdoing is proved. This is in sharp contrast with the effects on an agency when its officers have automobile accidents. Damage to vehicles and personnel means direct costs in the form of budget expenditures for repairs and replacements; injuries may result in loss of manpower; and sizable claims may be filed against the city which are made known to the department because the funds for them are generally quite limited and closely watched. Confronted with these problems, most large police agencies and many smaller ones develop, as was previously noted, elaborate programs aimed at preventing accidents. Accidents are carefully reviewed. Drivers with a propensity for having accidents are identified, counseled, schooled, and, in the most serious cases, grounded. Safe-driving campaigns are launched within the agency. Refresher courses in defensive driving are offered to all personnel. The most common causes of accidents are described and analyzed in training programs and in safety campaigns. And awards are given to the department unit having the best safety record.[13] Departments with such programs have accepted the responsibility for preventing automobile accidents. If administrators applied these same techniques to police wrongdoing, they could eliminate many current abuses.

Accepting the responsibility for achieving conformity requires, specifically, that an administrator inculcate an administrative philosophy that holds supervisory officers responsible for the actions of their subordinates. Enough pressure should be exerted on a precinct commander, for example, to result in his viewing an overly aggressive police officer who is constantly offending citizens as a major administrative problem, rather than—as is often the case—an extremely valuable employee who frequently gets in trouble. Each captain, each lieutenant, and each sergeant should be made to feel as responsible for an officer's conduct in relating to citizens as they do for assuring that an officer appears for work on time. This would make the task of controlling police conduct far more manageable than it is today.[14]

**Measuring Performance and Identifying
Patterns of Wrongdoing**

If police agencies were profit-making institutions whose success depended on the marketability of their end product, they would take the initiative in conducting research to determine how their product was received. They would not simply wait for complaints. Those that were filed, however, would be carefully analyzed, not just to establish their veracity but to learn what it was about police operations that antagonized people.

Most police agencies have some form of internal administrative audit. In some an inspections unit conducts exhaustive checks of the various sections of the agency to assure compliance with standard operating procedures. But these inspections—like the systems of incentives and rewards for individual officers— dwell on matters unrelated to the quality of services rendered the public. They deal with the completeness of records, the cleanliness of facilities, the presence of required equipment in vehicles, and the appearance of personnel at roll call.[15] Occasionally an effort is made to time the response of vehicles to calls for assistance and to interview citizens who frequently need police service. But this is the closest the traditional inspection comes to evaluating the quality of police service, and the measurements employed do not assure accurate and objective results.

Techniques are available to provide police with more accurate feedback on the effects of their programs and policies. Carefully developed surveys have been used to great advantage in recent years to establish the actual incidence of crime (by identifying the victims of crime), to measure citizen attitudes toward the police, and to measure citizen satisfaction with police service.[16] Practically all of these efforts, however, have been initiated by individuals outside police agencies. Two notable exceptions were studies conducted by the police departments in Kansas City, Missouri, and San Diego. These efforts demonstrated that the police can, by contract with established survey research organizations, employ recently developed survey techniques to get more reliable feedback on their efforts and especially on the effects of new programs. An agency that is truly committed to improving the quality of its performance could, on its own and through proper design of the survey instrument, pinpoint the areas of functioning in need of improvement. Such information would go a long way toward filling in the police administrator on what is happening "out there" and would be an extremely valuable tool for achieving greater conformity with administrative policies. It might even be used as a basis for rewarding officers for appropriate conduct.

Inspection techniques that test performance, especially if they are surreptitious, understandably rankle employees, who consider them demeaning and offensive. The techniques are particularly offensive if disciplinary action for failure to conform with established policies is automatically taken. An experiment in New York City, for example, in which the police department itself arranged for a number of wallets to be turned in to police officers with the request that they be properly processed, caused a furor among the rank and file and unfavorable comment from the public as well.[17] But it does not follow that a police administrator who takes on the rather elementary, but often needed, chore of assuring that a call to the police department is answered quickly should be denied the opportunity to place test calls in order to measure how quickly they are answered. In many areas auditing of performance affords the clearest and most precise measurement of conformity with department policies and aspirations. If the testing offends operating personnel, it may be worthwhile to forgo disciplinary action in order to obtain a more accurate measure of actual operating conditions in the agency. Employed in this fashion, testing can be used in a positive way to support departmental conformance rather than as a means for getting at individual wrongdoing.

Identifying Officers with a Propensity for Wrongdoing

In city after city situations arise in which a few officers acquire a reputation for being physically abusive and riding roughshod over the rights and dignity of citizens. Such officers are well known to their supervisors, to the top administrators, to their peers, and to the residents of the areas in which they work. And yet little is done to alter their conduct.

In Pittsburgh recently, residents who had been the victims of one such officer contacted each other, compared experiences, gathered witnesses, and filed a lawsuit with the United States District Court for Western Pennsylvania seeking relief for the entire class of law-abiding citizens desiring to use the city's sidewalks and streets. The court, finding against the defendant, issued a preliminary injunction enjoining the officer from continuing his abusive practices.[18]

Why should it take a court action to put an end to a pattern of conduct that was so obviously wrong and so well known? Many factors account for—but do not justify—the situation, including the fact that such officers often build up a large following of people who feel better protected because of the officer's aggressiveness.

In a positive program aimed at controlling police conduct, abusive behavior would be identified and corrected long before it reached these proportions. And the purpose in early identification would not be to discipline or dismiss the officer (although this may be necessary in some especially difficult cases), but to assist him in overcoming what, from the standpoint of both administrators and fellow officers, should be considered a serious handicap.

Several of the more advanced police departments in the country have recently been experimenting with programs to deal with this problem. In Oakland, under the direction of Professor Hans Toch, officers with a record of violent involvements were enlisted in a program of research and training aimed at preventing violence—their own as well as that of fellow officers.[19] The Kansas City, Missouri, Police Department, building on the Oakland program, experimented with a peer review program in which panels of experienced and specially trained officers counseled those officers whose records or requests for help indicated they were having trouble. But a review of the Kansas City experiment concluded that the manner in which it was conducted made an assessment of its value extremely difficult; that there were, in fact, no discernible results.[20] The review called for more rigorous tests of the concept, which is still viewed as having considerable potential as a way of reducing violence and altering conduct that offends the public.

Training Specifically Aimed at Preventing Improper Conduct

In addition to working with officers whose conduct needs correcting, police training programs must do a more effective job in anticipating the situations that create the greatest stress and challenge for a police officer, and they must devise ways in which an officer can meet them. It is, for example, in the nature of police work that some people will resist arrest. Likewise, it is to be anticipated that officers will often be in situations in which they are taunted, provoked, and defied in various ways. How an officer handles such a situation will depend in large measure upon how he perceives it. If he sees the opposition and hostility, however expressed, as an attack upon him as an individual, he will probably react in kind. If instead he develops some understanding of the factors that produce such attacks on the police, he will be more capable of responding in a cool and dispassionate manner. Of course when the police must deal with persons who have no respect for the law or the police—and this is frequently the case—the most strenuous effort to be tactful and persuasive will not work. In these situations the training an officer receives in using minimal force becomes extremely important.

Meeting stress with calm is counter to natural inclinations; it is certainly in conflict with the stereotype of how the police are expected to function. The young person going into police work most likely believes that one should stand up to a challenge, and this attitude is often reinforced by seasoned police officers.[21] As an officer, he must be convinced that the height of maturity and prowess is to deal with challenges to his authority in a calm, unemotional, and somewhat detached manner. He must rise above the emotions of those with whom he is dealing, even at the risk of appearing cowardly. Restrained dispassionate conduct on the part of police in hostile confrontations has won a great deal of respect for them and has, at the same time, provided some clear and dramatic lessons for the community on the true nature of the police role in our society. My own impression is that officers who develop a reputation for being unflappable receive less resistance to their actions and to their authority.

Some training programs have experimented with ways to teach police to function under stress. But, on the whole, in the keen competition for available training time, this problem has not received the priority it deserves.[22]

If improvement in the quality of police service is the primary objective of a training program, those engaged in training police should take a special interest in citizen complaints. The situations that prompt a citizen to complain—no matter who is subsequently determined to be at fault—provide an excellent indication of areas to which training time might profitably be devoted, for even if a complaint stems from a misunderstanding, it is important that police learn to avoid such misunderstandings. Appropriate and often-repeated training could, for example, reduce substantially the frequency with which police are accused of verbal abuse. It could also remind officers, in an effort to keep them from appearing callous, that the situations that are routine for them are emotionally charged for others.

All of these comments about training, of course, are made with full awareness that a high percentage of current training is negated by the working environment in which the officer is subsequently placed. The most sophisticated training techniques will obviously be of little value if they are not reinforced by a form of administration that succeeds in eliciting conformity at the street level.

Investigating Complaints

In order to adequately investigate citizen complaints, agencies must employ procedures that meet some basic criteria. Although these have been set forth and elaborated upon in many studies, some police agencies have been slow to recognize just how essential they are.[23]

The first thing the police must do is to create an atmosphere that affords people who feel they have been wronged easy access to the complaint process. Since the police are so often the target of criticism, it is sometimes difficult for them to realize that many citizens are afraid to lodge complaints about them. The problem has recently been aggravated by the practice, initiated by some police associations, of threatening to file a defamation suit against a complainant if his allegation is proved to be without foundation. [24] The concern of police personnel over frivolous complaints is understandable. The better solution, however, is a system of investigations that is scrupulously objective. Police administrators must, therefore, despite this most recent development, work to create a situation in which complainants are not, from the outset, confronted by a challenge to their veracity. Furthermore, it is essential that all complaints be investigated; that the complainant be kept informed on the progress of the investigation; that it be conducted speedily; and that the complainant be informed of the outcome. It is, of course, equally important that officers against whom allegations are made be provided with a full opportunity to defend themselves; that all of their rights be adequately protected; and that they be kept informed about the processing of the complaint. (The rights of the officer are discussed in chapter 10.)

Adoption of elaborate procedures to receive and investigate allegations of police wrongdoing does not, however, in itself assure that the task will be carried out effectively. All administrative devices inevitably depend for their effectiveness on the commitment of those making use of them.

Internal investigations tend to take on the character of an adversary proceeding that pits a complainant against an officer. This leaves little room for flexibility and possible negotiation. Investigators feel pressed to find for or against the officer, even though the circumstances may indicate that both parties erred. As a consequence, in the difficult-to-settle case the officer feels put upon if labeled the guilty party; and the citizen feels offended if told his or her allegation was unfounded. For a large number of complaints alleging relatively minor misconduct, police might profitably consider mediation as an alternative form of disposition. This would, however, require a greater willingness than police have demonstrated in the past to acknowledge, on occasion, that a mistake was made. Many minor disputes could be settled satisfactorily with a letter of apology.

PROVIDING CITIZEN REDRESS

Whether there ought to be some form of civilian review of police conduct is not really an issue. The need to provide means for aggrieved citizens to obtain redress—which must entail some form of review from outside the agency—is an essential element in the policing of a free society. The issue, rather, is the form such review and opportunity for redress should take.

Any arrangement for review and redress must first provide relief for the aggrieved citizen. Beyond this, however, it is of the utmost importance that the arrangement work in such a way that it strengthens and supports the traditional system for controlling police conduct—the process whereby the chief supervises his personnel and is held accountable for their performance.

Why is this point so important? Given the decentralized and dispersed nature of police organizations, it is utterly hopeless to attempt to control police conduct other than by making the administrative system work. No court or specially constituted civilian body, based outside the police agency, can possibly provide the kind of day-to-day direction that is essential if the behavior of police officers at the operating level is to be effectively controlled. This means that even in the most acute situations, when administrators and supervisors are either unwilling or incapable of asserting themselves, there is simply no way to work around them. They must be replaced or forced to function properly. To attempt to compensate by giving agencies outside the police department the responsibility to carry out some control functions that are usually a part of management invites still further abdication by administrators and supervisors—the very people who have the greatest potential for achieving maximum control. And it seriously weakens the ability of a well-intentioned administrator who already has enough difficulties in achieving conformity to his standards.

If the administration is to be held responsible for the conduct of its personnel, it follows that it must be given an opportunity to look into allegations of wrongdoing—to conduct the initial investigation and, if it concludes that its personnel erred, to take appropriate corrective or disciplinary action. In some cases the agency may conclude that it incurred some liability and may even wish to take the initiative in recommending that damages be paid the complainant. The more effective and open a job the police do in managing their internal investigations, the less likely it is that there will be need for external review.

When police conduct is reviewed from outside the police agency, the focus should be on the agency rather than the individual officer. Admittedly the question involved in a given case may revolve around a specific officer's use of authority. But if the agency has had the opportunity to review the case and chooses to support (and perhaps even defend) the officer's actions, then, quite appropriately, the agency's policies and judgments are at issue rather than just those of the officer. Today, civil actions can be brought against police officers without any implication that the police administrator was responsible for the behavior. And, as mentioned earlier, the city attorney routinely defends such cases vigorously in order to minimize the judgments against the municipality. This process, like the proposed civilian review boards, is dysfunctional; it may provide some form of citizen redress, but at the cost of seriously weakening the administrative apparatus upon which effective control of the police depends in the long run.

If primary dependence is placed upon the administrator and the agency for achieving conformity, it follows that any system for citizen review and redress must cope with two distinct situations: (1) the public must have the opportunity to appeal from a decision reached by the internal investigative processes of a police agency on conclusion of its investigation of a complaint filed against a specific officer or group of officers; and (2) the public must have the opportunity to deal with the more difficult situation when an agency tolerates widespread abuse, fails to establish effective internal investigation procedures, and fails to establish sufficiently specific rules governing police conduct.

This distinction is important in examining and designing redress procedures, for a process that may be effective in achieving one objective may be of little use in achieving the other. Indeed, failure of efforts in recent years to control police conduct is a result, to a great extent, of not distinguishing between these two quite different needs.

Appeals from Administrative Decisions on Specific Complaints of Officer Wrongdoing

Even under the best circumstances, when a police agency demonstrates a strong commitment to conformity with the law and established policies and to self-policing, there are bound to be situations in which a citizen is convinced that the agency reached the wrong conclusion in its investigation of a complaint. Whether the disagreement reflects an understandable difference of opinion in evaluating a difficult-to-judge incident or—at the other end of the spectrum—

citizen outrage that the agency could dismiss a complaint in light of the evidence presented, how can one best provide for an appeal from the agency's decision?

A citizen who is displeased with the results of a police inquiry into a complaint filed with the agency currently has a few avenues to pursue, though none is wholly satisfactory. If the complaint alleged that an officer violated a law, whether it be the prohibition against false imprisonment or some more common offense, the complainant can turn to the local prosecutor in an effort to have the officer prosecuted. But prosecutors tend to be as reluctant to bring charges against police officers, on whom they so heavily depend as a group, as are police administrators. They are generally under less pressure to take action and traditionally have enjoyed great latitude in deciding whether or not to initiate a prosecution. If the aggrieved citizen had alleged a violation of constitutional rights, such as being deprived of liberty without due process of law, he can seek to institute a prosecution in the federal courts under the criminal section of the federal Civil Rights Act.[25] But the statute has been narrowly construed to require proof that the officer was motivated by a specific intent to deprive the complainant of constitutional rights.[26] And initiating a prosecution requires the cooperation of federal prosecutors, who are often as reluctant to place themselves in an adversary position with local police as are the local prosecutors. While the federal prosecutors receive numerous complaints of police misconduct, few cases are tried and in only a third of these are convictions obtained.[27]

Also at the federal level, if the complaint alleged a violation of constitutional rights, the citizen can resort to a civil action under the federal Civil Rights Act,[28] which avoids any dependence upon the federal prosecutor and which can be instituted without first exhausting state remedies.[29] But the availability of a defense based on "probable cause and good faith" and limitations on the law of damages in the federal act result in such proceedings holding the potential for redress only in the case of individuals severely injured by outrageous instances of police illegality.[30] Bringing such action, needless to say, can be an expensive and difficult undertaking.

By far the most common alternative is for the complainant to seek damages by instituting a civil action under state law. There would usually be a basis for doing so if the original complaint alleged false arrest, false imprisonment, malicious prosecution, or assault and battery.[31] The number of such suits has skyrocketed in some jurisdictions, but—except when the violation is unusually flagrant—there continues to be only a slight chance for adequate recovery.[32] The problems in pursuing this avenue have frequently been cataloged: the cost of hiring a lawyer; the delays before the case is tried; the fact that the plaintiff often was engaged in criminal activity, was an alcoholic or mentally ill or possessed other characteristics that make the case less than convincing to a jury; the difficulty in establishing damages; and the full or partial immunity of the jurisdiction from damages. And even if the plaintiff should obtain a substantial verdict, the officer's financial condition or the manner in which his assets are held usually makes collection unlikely.

Considerable emphasis has recently been placed upon the possibility of making greater use of the tort remedy. The standards set forth in *The Urban Police Function*, for example, approved by the American Bar Association and the Board of Officers of the International Association of Chiefs of Police, urged: "In order to strengthen the effectiveness of the tort remedy for improper police activities, governmental immunity, where it still exists, should be eliminated, and legislation should be enacted providing that governmental subdivisions shall be fully liable for the actions of police officers who are acting within the scope of their employment."[33] Specific proposals have been advanced by, among others, Chief Justice Warren Burger[34] and the District of Columbia government, the latter with the support of the Metropolitan Police Department.[35] If the city and, through budget arrangements, the police agency become responsible for damages incurred, the tort remedy may create the leverage that will force the police to take the necessary administrative steps to eliminate misconduct that results in suits being filed.

Important as these efforts are, it must be borne in mind that the tort remedy, in its potentially most effective form, nevertheless would be available for but a very limited range of wrongdoing. Many actions, though less damaging, are serious intrusions on the dignity and privacy of citizens and therefore warrant some form of appeal from an administrative investigation of them. Currently no effective method exists to provide for such a review.

The creation of a specially constituted appeals panel has not been seriously advocated in recent years in this country because it sounds too much like another civilian review board.[36] But in England, Sir Robert Mark, Commissioner of the Metropolitan Police, urged establishment of an independent board to review cases where complainants were dissatisfied with the results of a police force's own inquiry. He stressed that he wanted to continue the present system whereby Scotland Yard conducts its own investigations of alleged wrongdoing, but he felt public anxiety would be lessened if it were known that the Yard's findings would always be available for examination by persons other than policemen. He suggested that the review body consist of a prominent public figure and a number of assistants, including one with professional knowledge of police procedure and another entirely divorced from police administration and law.[37]

This proposal is significant for the elements it contains: it recognizes the distinct need for an appeal process, it is intended to augment rather than supplant the internal investigation procedure, and it is expected to serve a positive function by building public confidence in internal investigations. Implied is the assumption that the mere existence of such a form of review will aid the administrator in maintaining the objectivity and integrity of the internal investigation apparatus.

In many respects the concept of an ombudsman—so often advocated in recent years—is essentially a system for affording citizens the opportunity to appeal from administrative decisions. It contains many of the same elements embodied in the English proposal, except that it is typically not limited to the police. Where it is established, in the Scandinavian countries and in New Zealand, agency heads are expected to investigate allegations of wrongdoing and to take appropriate action. The ombudsman becomes involved only when there is reason to believe that a complaint alleging wrongdoing has been inadequately dealt with by administrative officials or when it appears that the policies and practices to which a complaint relates ought to be reviewed and possibly modified.[38]

The mere presence of a detached independent critic supports a police administrator desirous of making the right choice when confronted with strong pressures that move him in the other direction. Because the ombudsman concept applies to all agencies of the government employing the ombudsman, the police are not being singled out for special treatment. And the attention typically given by the ombudsman to making constructive suggestions for change and improvement gives the appeal process positive value as a vehicle for strengthening administrative procedures and—in the end—the quality of services rendered the public.

Dealing with Pervasive Agency-Tolerated Wrongdoing

What happens, however, if a citizen or group of citizens concludes that certain practices or policies of a police agency are illegal or improper? Or that the agency has failed to establish a fair and effective system for investigating complaints filed against the agency or its personnel?

Citizens can, of course, pursue a specific case to obtain redress and thereby also illustrate their concern, but even if they succeed there is no assurance the practice or policy will be altered. They can, for example, challenge the legality of a search in the course of a criminal prosecution, with the result that the evidence, if judged to have been illegally obtained, is declared inadmissible. But the manner in which such rulings are made usually serves neither to influence the future behavior of the officer nor to influence the policies and practices of the police agency.[39] Or, in some instances, they can sue and—in the rare case—possibly even win a judgment against a police officer, but, as has been noted, a successful suit does not generally result in a reevaluation of department practices.

As another alternative, aggrieved citizens can turn to the political processes by which a police agency is—at least theoretically—directed. They can take their concerns to a mayor, city manager, city council, or special board having supervisory responsibilities over the police agency; and they may well receive a satisfactory response from these officials. But, as discussed in chapter 6, the responsibility of these officials to supervise and, more specifically, to correct police policies and practices, is often unclear and, even where clear, commonly shirked. On the other hand the political processes and channels may be wide open, and the responsible officials may accept their responsibility for directing police operations, but they may nonetheless support the policies and practices being protested. And they can do so with relative immunity if the group filing the complaint is but a small minority.

Ideally, clarification of the channels through which citizens are supposed to influence their police agency and adoption of additional systems for structuring police discretion, including administrative rule-making, will together provide the means for more effectively exposing and challenging questionable policies. Without such mechanisms a group that is aggrieved by police policies or by the lack of appropriate internal investigation procedures currently has no effective remedy available unless the alleged wrongdoing is a violation of some constitutional right. Where it is, there may be a basis for the use of the injunction authorized by the general remedy section of the federal Civil Rights Act.[40]

Federal courts have issued injunctions in widely varying circumstances.[41] In *Lankford* v. *Gelston* a group of neighbors in Baltimore obtained an injunction in 1966 to stop the police from indiscriminately searching private dwellings after the police had searched over 300 residences in an effort to locate the person responsible for killing one police officer and wounding another. The searches were made by heavily armed officers on the basis of anonymous tips, without search warrants and without the consent of the occupants.[42] Although the searches relating to this incident had obviously ceased, the court of appeals, finding that such searches were, on a smaller scale, routinely carried out by the police to apprehend persons accused of serious crimes, remanded the case for entry of a decree enjoining the department from searching any private house based only on an anonymous tip.

A number of individuals who have studied the control of police conduct have urged greater use of the injunction provisions of the Civil Rights Act as a way of forcing police agencies to articulate their policies (thereby exposing those which infringe constitutional rights) and as a way of requiring an agency to take steps—such as improved training—that might prevent patterns of behavior considered unconstitutional.[43] When used in this manner the process contains a number of the elements so seriously lacking in some of the most commonly proposed systems for controlling police conduct. It operates on the top police administrator, thereby applying pressure to the entire agency rather than to individual police officers. It focuses upon administratively tolerated and continuing patterns of police violations, rather than isolated incidents of wrongdoing. It is more concerned with preventing such violations in the future than in providing redress for the past. And it has the potential for contributing, in a very significant way, to stimulating police agencies to better control their personnel through the structuring of discretion by requiring that the agency itself produce explicit guidelines for police functioning in important areas. By depending on the agency to formulate the policy, the court may produce a much more workable operating code tailored to local needs than the court could ever prepare on its own.

The United States Supreme Court, however, in *Rizzo* v. *Goode*, has narrowed the availability of injunctive relief as applied to the police.[44] In 1973 the United States District Court for the Eastern District of Pennsylvania, on finding that violations of constitutional rights by Philadelphia police occurred in what the court described as an unacceptably high number of instances and that, in the absence of changes in procedures, such violations were likely to continue to occur, concluded that revision of the procedures for handling civilian complaints was a necessary first step in attempting to prevent abuses.[45] The court required the Philadelphia Police Department to formulate and submit to the court for approval a comprehensive program for dealing adequately with civilian complaints alleging police misconduct, and offered some specific guidelines for doing so. The decision was affirmed by the Court of Appeals for the Third Circuit.[46] On appeal, however, the Supreme Court reversed the decision, holding that the facts failed to establish a sufficient showing of controversy between the plaintiffs and the defendants to warrant the bringing of an action under the Civil Rights Act; that, in effect, there had been a failure to prove that the police chief and other city officials against whom the action was brought were responsible for the alleged violations and a failure to prove that the specific individuals seeking relief were likely to continue to be the target of such violations. The Court also concluded that the number of incidents cited did not constitute the pervasive pattern of violations that had been established in prior cases in which the use of the injunction had been upheld.

The Supreme Court distinguished the *Rizzo* case from the *Lankford* decision by pointing out that in the Baltimore case the pattern of abuse was clear and flagrant; had extended over a long period of time; was acknowledged as the routine practice of the department in serious cases; received the tacit approval of high-ranking officials of the department; and most likely would have continued in the future without judicial intervention. The majority concluded that these conditions had not been established as present in the *Rizzo* case.

The Supreme Court's holding in *Rizzo* gives new emphasis to the reluctance of the federal courts to intrude in local police matters absent extraordinary circumstances. Except in very clear-cut situations, such as existed in the *Lankford* case, a prolonged and difficult process of proof will be required to establish a record adequate to warrant injunctive relief. The difficulty arises, in particular, from the need to prove a sufficient number of violations to document that they are in fact pervasive; to prove the authorization and approval of top officials, which requires penetrating the bureaucratic shields with which some administrators protect themselves from being held accountable for operating practices of a questionable nature; and to prove the likelihood that the pattern of deprivations will affect the same individuals in a similar fashion in the future.

Although the Court concluded that the plaintiffs failed to meet the required standards of proof in the facts presented by the record in the *Rizzo* case, those familiar with police operations in large cities recognize that the situation the plaintiffs attempted to substantiate in *Rizzo* is a fairly common one: patterns of violations engaged in by numerous officers that continue over a period of time with either the support, awareness, or indifference of top administrators. Indeed, the district court, which had concluded that the facts warranted injunctive relief, found that the problems disclosed by the record were fairly typical of the problems afflicting police departments in major cities.[47]

One method of preserving the use of an action under the federal Civil Rights Act to provide injunctive relief—while avoiding the problems which concerned the Court in *Rizzo*—would be for the federal courts to make use of a device similar to that now being recommended for the handling of prisoner civil-rights cases, whereby the judge requests that the defendant prepare a special report giving the court "the benefit of detailed factual information that may be necessary to decide a case involving a constitutional challenge to an important, complicated correctional practice."[48] This procedure has the advantage of placing the responsibility for describing the existing practice upon the government (in this case, the police department whenever high-ranking administrators are the defendants). Certainly the department itself is best equipped to supply information regarding current practice, as well as factual data on department policy, training, and supervision, as these bear on conduct alleged to violate a plaintiff's civil rights. The mere act of responding to the judge's inquiry would itself constitute a departmental review of existing policies and practices. And assuming the department would produce an accurate and adequate report of the facts, the court could use it to determine whether there was a basis for ordering injunctive or other relief. The department could even be encouraged to take administrative action to change the challenged practice without a judicially imposed requirement to do so.

In setting forth the reasons for limiting access to the federal courts for injunctive relief, the Supreme Court in the *Rizzo* case reflected the belief that the control of the police is better left to state and local governments. This suggests, as still another alternative, that it may be desirable to cope with pervasive agency-tolerated wrongdoing through civil actions for injunctive and other forms of relief brought in the state rather than the federal courts.[49] Plaintiffs have usually shown a preference for federal courts, presumably on the grounds that federal judges are more sensitive to and supportive of the rights of citizens to be free of improper police practices than are state judges.[50] It is assumed that state judges, because they must be concerned about reelection, hesitate to condemn police practices that have been sustained over a prolonged period of time and that—whether lawful or unlawful—generally have the approval of a majority of the community. But this situation may be changing, particularly in those states where state courts are imposing stricter controls on police than are now supported by the United States Supreme Court.[51]

NOTES

1. *Mapp* v. *Ohio*, 367 U.S. 643 (1961). For a comprehensive study of the development, use, and effectiveness of the exclusionary rule, see Dallin H. Oaks,

"Studying the Exclusionary Rule in Search and Seizure," *University of Chicago Law Review* 37 (1970): 665– 757.

2. For a review of these developments, see James R. Hudson, "Police Review Boards and Police Accountability," *Law and Contemporary Problems* 36 (1971): 515–538; Harold Beral and Marcus Sisk, "The Administration of Complaints by Civilians Against the Police," *Harvard Law Review* 77 (1964): 499–519; Walter Gellhorn, *When Americans Complain* (Cambridge, Mass.: Harvard University Press, 1966).

3. For an analysis of the referendum and the events leading up to it, see David W. Abbott, Louis H. Gold, and Edward T. Rogowsky, *Police, Politics and Race* (New York: American Jewish Committee, 1969).

4. See, e.g., American Civil Liberties Union of Southern California, *Law Enforcement* (Los Angeles: Institute of Modern Legal Thought, 1969); and Paul Chevigny, *Police Power* (New York: Vintage Books, 1969).

5. See, e.g., National Advisory Commission on Civil Disorders, *Report of the National Advisory Commission on Civil Disorders* (Washington, D.C.: Government Printing Office, 1968), pp. 162–163; National Commission on the Causes and Prevention of Violence, *To Establish Justice, To Insure Domestic Tranquility*, Final Report (Washington, D.C.: Government Printing Office, 1969), pp. 145–149; Donald J. Black and Albert J. Reiss, Jr., "Patterns of Behavior in Police and Citizen Transactions," in *Studies in Crime and Law Enforcement in Major Metropolitan Areas*, Field Surveys III, vol. 2, Report of a Research Study Submitted to the President's Commission on Law Enforcement and Administration of Justice (Washington, D.C.: Government Printing Office, 1967).

6. George Bliss et al., *Police Brutality*, pamphlet (Chicago: Chicago Tribune, 1973).

7. See, e.g., *Bence* v. *Breier*, 501 F.2d 1185 (7th Cir. 1974); *Perea* v. *Fales*, 114 Cal. Rptr. 808 (1974). For a general analysis of due process requirements vis-à-vis government agency regulations, see *Parker* v. *Levy*, 417 U.S. 733 (1974).

8. According to a survey by the IACP covering 1967–1971, it was estimated that 75 percent of all suits filed against the police were defended by the city attorney or other public legal officer. Counsel for insurance agencies defended 23 percent of the cases, and 2 percent were represented by attorneys for police associations. Wayne W. Schmidt, *Survey of Police Misconduct Litigation 1967– 1971* (Evanston, Ill.: Americans for Effective Law Enforcement, Inc., 1974), p. 8.

9. One method of dealing with the problem has been proposed in the form of legislation in both Michigan and California that would amend the rules of evidence in those states so that written policies, procedures, rules, guidelines, orders, or directives of a law enforcement agency concerning the discharge of duties by its officers would not be admissible as evidence of a standard of care or negligence in any civil action other than the disciplinary proceedings between the agency and its officers. See, e.g., Senate Bill No. 899 proposed in Michigan, October 17, 1973.

10. An exception to this pattern is so unusual that it receives widespread publicity when it occurs. See, e.g., "A Station House Divided: Police Debate Officers' Indictment," *New York Times*, 31 October 1975, in which it is reported that the

testimony of fellow police officers resulted in the indictment of one officer on a charge of murdering a prisoner who was in custody at a station house; three others on assault; and a police sergeant on a charge of perjury.

11. Actually the relationship between morale and productivity is not clear by any means. See, e.g., Charles Perrow, *Complex Organizations: A Critical Essay* (Glenview, Ill.: Scott, Foresman & Co., 1972), pp. 104–105, in which he concludes that a happy worker is not necessarily a good worker.

12. This need is discussed in American Bar Association, *The Urban Police Function*, Approved Draft (Chicago: American Bar Association, 1973), pp. 277–292. Some efforts to develop new measures are under way. See, especially, Gary T. Marx, "Alternative Measures of Police Performance," Innovative Resource Planning Project, Working Paper WP-12-74, MIT Operations Research Center, mimeographed (Cambridge, Mass., 1974); and Gary T. Marx, "An Application of Some Alternative Measures: Validation of the 1972 Massachusetts Police Selection Exam," Innovative Resource Planning Project, Working Paper WP-13-74, MIT Operations Research Center, mimeographed (Cambridge, Mass., 1974).

13. See, e.g., National Safety Council, *Guidelines for Developing an Injury and Damage Reduction Program in Municipal Police Departments* (Washington, D.C.: Government Printing Office, 1973).

14. This point has frequently been made by those who have delved into the problems of handling citizen grievances and controlling police conduct. See, e.g., Gellhorn, *When Americans Complain*, p. 182; and Fred M. Broadaway, "Police Misconduct: Positive Alternatives," *Journal of Police Science and Administration* 2 (1974): 215.

15. For an example of an inspection report in a large police agency, see O. W. Wilson, *Police Administration,* 2d ed. (New York: McGraw Hill, 1963), pp. 494–508.

16. On victimization studies, see Albert Biderman, "Surveys of Population Samples for Estimating Crime Incidence," *The Annals* 374 (Nov. 1967): 16–33; Phillip H. Ennis, *Criminal Victimization: A Report of a National Survey*, National Opinion Research Center, for the President's Commission on Law Enforcement and Administration of Justice (Washington, D.C.: Government Printing Office, 1967); United States Department of Justice, *Criminal Victimization Surveys in the Nation's Five Largest Cities: National Crime Panel Surveys of Chicago, Detroit, Los Angeles, New York, and Philadelphia* (Washington, D.C.: Government Printing Office, 1975); and United States Department of Justice, *Crime in Eight American Cities: National Crime Panel Surveys of Atlanta, Baltimore, Cleveland, Dallas, Denver, Newark, Portland, and St. Louis*, advance report (Washington, D.C.: Government Printing Office, 1974). On measuring citizen attitudes and satisfaction with police services, see, e.g., Gene E. Carte, "Changes in Public Attitudes Toward the Police: A Comparison of 1938 and 1971 Surveys," *Journal of Police Science and Administration* 1 (1973): 182; Frank F. Furstenberg and Charles F. Wellford, "Calling the Police," *Law and Society Review* 7 (1973): 393–406; and Victor Cizanckas and Fritzi Feist, "A Community's Response to Police Change," *Journal of Police Science and Administration* 3 (1975): 284–291. For one of the latest examples of the use made of such survey techniques in getting feedback on police performance, see George

L. Kelling et al., *The Kansas City Preventive Patrol Experiment: A Technical Report* (Washington, D.C.: Police Foundation, 1974).

17. "15 Policemen Keep Money 'Lost' in Test," *New York Times*, 17 November 1973.

18. *Wecht* v. *Marsteller*, 363 F. Supp. 1183 (W.D.Pa. 1973).

19. Hans Toch, "Change Through Participation (And Vice Versa)," *Journal of Research in Crime and Delinquency* 7 (1970): 198–206. For the final report on this project, see Hans Toch, J. Douglas Grant, and Raymond T. Galvin, *Agents of Change* (New York: John Wiley and Sons, 1975).

20. The project, as initially conceived, is described in Broadaway, "Police Misconduct: Positive Alternatives," pp. 210–218. For its evaluation, see Tony Pate et al., *Kansas City Peer Review Panel* (Washington, D.C.: Police Foundation, 1976).

21. See, e.g., John Van Maanen, "Working the Street: A Developmental View of Police Behavior," in *The Potential for Reform of Criminal Justice*, ed. Herbert Jacob (Beverly Hills, Calif.: Sage Publications, 1974), pp. 116–120.

22. Under a grant from the Police Foundation the International Conference of Police Associations has launched a major study of the causes of stress in the police occupation. One of the objectives of this study is to find effective ways in which police training programs can aid officers to deal with stress.

23. For the most recent set of detailed recommendations for police agency processing of citizen complaints, see the National Advisory Commission on Criminal Justice Standards and Goals, *Police* (Washington, D.C.: Government Printing Office, 1973), pp. 469–491.

24. See, e.g.., "Police Protective League Is Filing Defamation Suits," *Los Angeles Daily Journal*, 30 January 1975.

25. 18 *U.S.C.* §242 (1970).

26. *Screws* v. *United States*, 325 U.S. 91, 107 (1945).

27. The Criminal Section, Civil Rights Division of the Attorney General's Office, reports 7,000 complaints of alleged criminal interference with the civil rights of citizens during 1973 (most of which were police misconduct). Only 61 defendants were tried during 1973, of which only 19 were convicted. *Annual Report of the Attorney General of the United States: 1973* (Washington, D.C.: Government Printing Office, 1974), p. 73.

28. 42 *U.S.C.* §1983 (1970).

29. See *Monroe* v. *Pape*, 365 U.S. 167, 183 (1961); *McNeese* v. *Board of Education for Community School District No. 187*, 373 U.S. 668, 671 (1963); *Preiser* v. *Rodriguez*, 411 U.S. 475 (1973).

30. For a discussion of these limitations, see National Commission on the Causes and Prevention of Violence, Task Force on Law and Law Enforcement, *Law and Order Reconsidered* (Washington, D.C.: Government Printing Office, 1969), pp. 376–378.

31. Although now somewhat dated, Caleb Foote, "Tort Remedies for Police Violations of Individual Rights," *Minnesota Law Review* 39 (1955): 493–516, continues to be one of the most helpful treatments of this subject. See also National Commission on the Causes and Prevention of Violence, Task Force on Law and Law Enforcement, *Law and Order Reconsidered*, pp. 370–375; and

Joyce Blalock, *Civil Liability of Law Enforcement Officers* (Springfield, Ill.: Charles C. Thomas, 1974).

32. Based upon a survey of litigation in the period from 1967–1971, the IACP estimates that, whereas there were 1,741 suits filed in police jurisdictions having ten or more officers in 1967, 3,894 such suits were filed in 1971. In the period 1967–1971 the plaintiffs were successful in only 18.5 percent of the cases that went to trial. Schmidt, *Survey of Police Misconduct Litigation 1967–1971*, pp. 5–6.

33. American Bar Association, *The Urban Police Function*, supplement p. 11.

34. *Bivens* v. *Six Unknown Named Agents of Federal Bureau of Narcotics*, 403 U.S. 388, 422–424 (1971).

35. District of Columbia Law Enforcement Liability and Legal Assistance Act of 1971 (proposed legislation).

36. Actually, there are now a number of jurisdictions where a civilian body with some general superintending responsibility over the police force is authorized to hear citizen complaints—both initially and on appeal. See, e.g., Mark Berger, "Law Enforcement Control: Checks and Balances for the Police System," *Connecticut Law Review* 4 (1971/72): 492; and Matthew Flynn, "Police Accountability in Wisconsin," *Wisconsin Law Review* 1974: 1166.

37. For a summary of proposals made for the review of citizen complaints in England, and for reactions to these proposals, see *The Handling of Complaints Against the Police: Report of the Working Group for England and Wales* (London: Her Majesty's Stationery Office, 1974). Sir Robert Mark's comments appear on pp. 49–52.

38. For an exploration of the ombudsman concept, see Walter Gellhorn, *Ombudsmen and Others* (Cambridge, Mass.: Harvard University Press, 1966); Stephan Hurwitz, "Denmark's Ombudsmand," *Wisconsin Law Review* 1961: 169–199; Donald C. Rowat, ed., *The Ombudsman*, 2d ed. (Toronto: University of Toronto Press, 1968); Stanley V. Anderson and John C. Moore, *Establishing Ombudsman Offices* (Berkeley, Calif.: Institute of Governmental Studies, 1972).

39. See, e.g., Wayne R. LaFave and Frank J. Remington, "Controlling the Police: The Judge's Role in Making and Reviewing Law Enforcement Decisions," *Michigan Law Review* 63 (1965): 987–1012; and Herman Goldstein, "Trial Judges and the Police," *Crime and Delinquency* 14 (1968): 18–19.

40. See "The Federal Injunction as a Remedy for Unconstitutional Police Conduct," *Yale Law Journal* 78 (1968): 143–155; George J. Siedel III, "Injunctive Relief for Police Misconduct in the United States," *Journal of Urban Law* 50 (1973): 681–699; and "Injunctive Relief for Violations of Constitutional Rights by the Police," *University of Colorado Law Review* 45 (1973): 91–129.

41. See Siedel, "Injunctive Relief for Police Misconduct," pp. 681–682. The case cited earlier in this chapter, *Wecht* v. *Marsteller*, is another example.

42. *Lankford* v. *Gelston*, 364 F.2d 197 (4th Cir. 1966).

43. See, e.g., Anthony Amsterdam, "The Supreme Court and the Rights of Suspects in Criminal Cases," *New York University Law Review* 45 (1970): 814; and "The Federal Injunction as a Remedy for Unconstitutional Police Conduct," p. 149.

44. *Rizzo* v. *Goode,* 18 CrL 3041 (1976), rev'g 506 F.2d 542 (3d Cir. 1974).

45. *Council of Organizations* v. *Rizzo,* 357 F. Supp. 1289 (E.D.Pa. 1973).

46. *Goode* v. *Rizzo,* 506 F.2d 542 (3d Cir. 1974).

47. *Council of Organizations* v. *Rizzo,* 357 F. Supp. 1289, 1318 (E.D.Pa. 1973).

48. Federal Judicial Center, *Recommended Procedures for Handling Prisoner Civil Rights Cases in the Federal Courts,* Tentative Report (Washington, D.C.: Government Printing Office, 1976).

49. Most state courts have been reluctant to enforce 42 *U.S.C.* §1983, although they clearly have authority to do so. If they do not use the federal Civil Rights Act, it is uncertain whether an alternative is available to them.

50. Also, because courts have held that a state decision precludes a subsequent litigation of the issues in federal court (*res judicata*), plaintiffs have been reluctant to have the door to the federal court closed. See, e.g., *Spence* v. *Latting,* 512 F.2d 93 (10th Cir. 1975); "Constitutional Law—Civil Rights—Section 1983—Res Judicata/Collateral Estoppel," *Wisconsin Law Review* 1974: 1180.

51. See Donald E. Wilkes, Jr., "The New Federalism in Criminal Procedure: State Court Evasion of the Burger Court," *Kentucky Law Journal* 62 (1974): 421–451; and "State Constitutional Requirements—Divergence from U.S. Supreme Court Opinions," 18 *Criminal Law Reporter* 2507–2508 (1976).

Chapter 8

The Corruption Problem

Corruption is examined separately here for three reasons. First, unlike other forms of wrongdoing, corruption is to a great extent initiated and sustained by the community. There is seldom a clearly identifiable victim or a complainant. Second, corruption has a systemic character to it. Once it gets started it tends to spread through an organization, affecting all of its parts. Third, it has a preemptive quality. If it exists to any substantial degree, police leaders are prevented from exercising effective control over their personnel. Corruption thus not only weakens the capacity of the agency to deal with police wrongdoing of the kind described in chapter 7; it greatly curtails the potential for dealing with the full range of problems related to improving the quality of police service.

Until recently it was almost impossible to generate open discussion of corruption by police themselves. They felt they were being made scapegoats; that because they were responsible for policing the conduct of others, some segments of the community delighted in alleging police corruption. They argued that certain elements of the community, by seizing every opportunity to paint the police as corrupt, hoped to convince themselves that their own corruption was less serious. It understandably angered the police to be aware that institutions and professions which enjoyed more prestige than they did were as corrupt and yet seldom singled out for blame. What we now know in this Watergate era about corruption in government supports these feelings.

If corruption was discussed by the police at all, the discussions usually took place among officers who knew and trusted one another. Corruption was seldom

The material in this chapter appeared, in somewhat modified form, in a separate monograph, *Police Corruption: A Perspective on Its Nature and Control* (Washington, D.C.: Police Foundation, 1975).

referred to in police administration and law enforcement texts. It was rarely covered in police training programs. Nor was it discussed at meetings of police administrators. Most strikingly, the chiefs of some of the most corrupt agencies publicly denied its existence. And when confronted with evidence that some of their personnel were indeed corrupt, they typically proceeded quickly against those who were implicated, claiming that, by removing the few rotten apples expeditiously, they were saving the barrel.

Today there is a greater willingness to discuss the problem. The session on police corruption at the 1973 meeting of the International Association of Chiefs of Police was among the most heavily attended of the entire conference. Articles on the subject are appearing in police journals. Several conferences have recently been held for the specific purpose of encouraging more open concern. But even at these meetings, called to discuss the problem, some participants try to divert attention from police corruption by insisting that it should be seen as only a part of the problem of corruption in the criminal justice system and society.

THE SCOPE OF THE PROBLEM

Defining Corruption

There is considerable disagreement about what constitutes police corruption. Sometimes it is defined so broadly as to include all forms of police wrongdoing from brutality to the pettiest forms of questionable behavior. Then again it may be defined so narrowly that patterns of behavior with all the characteristics and consequences of corrupt acts are excluded.

The term "police corruption" is used in this chapter to describe the misuse of authority by a police officer in a manner designed to produce personal gain for the officer or for others. Excluded from consideration are the various forms of police misconduct, discussed in the preceding chapter, where authority may have been abused but where there is no indication the abuse was motivated by a desire for personal gain. Many would argue that such actions should be seen as part of the corruption problem, involving a corruption of power. Admittedly the line is not a clear one. Corruption and physical abuse are sometimes inseparable. Police have, for example, been known to use force or the threat of force to obtain payoffs. But most of the complaints alleging improper use of force do not include charges of corruption for personal gain.

The term "bribery" is commonly used to describe all forms of police corruption, but this is technically incorrect. All police bribery is corruption, but not all police corruption is bribery. In the criminal offense of bribery, the officer must have solicited, received, retained, or agreed to accept something of value or personal advantage which he or she was not authorized to accept. The officer must also have known the bribe was offered with the intention of influencing official actions. Many patterns of police corruption lack these elements. They may, however, involve other criminal offenses, such as official misconduct, perjury, extortion, or theft.

While most forms of police corruption are criminal, and should be viewed in criminal terms, it does not always follow that all crime involving police officers is corruption. Police are occasionally charged with committing crimes such as petty theft, burglary, or robbery—behavior referred to as police criminality.[1] In most communities such incidents are regarded as the ultimate form of corruption, as blatant violations by those entrusted with preventing criminal activity and enforcing the law. This view is reinforced because such activities usually occur in agencies known to have a high tolerance for corruption. Many of the same conditions that allow corruption to thrive make it possible for police to commit these offenses. The officer who uses his authority, along with the camouflage, information, and access to premises that it provides, in order to steal or rob is very much a part of the corruption problem.

But the officer who commits a burglary without making use of his authority is no more a part of the corruption problem than the officer who murders his wife. In the police community, as in the larger community, one can expect a certain percentage of the population to engage in deviant conduct.[2] To ignore the possibility that such incidents will occur reflects more faith in the ability to identify persons likely to commit crimes than is justified by current knowledge. Crimes committed by police will probably continue to be seen as a form of corruption. But without the misuse of authority, which is the defining element of corruption, crime by police presents a problem which differs little from the problem of crime in the larger community.

Probably the most difficult decision in defining police corruption is whether to include only acts resulting in significant gain or to extend the definition to include *any* favor or *any* gift.

Many would argue that there is nothing wrong with accepting small gratuities under certain conditions. And it is probably natural for a police administrator struggling to cope with gross forms of corruption to feel irritated when pressed to turn attention to the officer who accepts free cups of coffee. Yet those who argue that small favors and gifts are first inroads into police integrity and objectivity have much to support their position. The important questions of *whether* a line should be drawn and, if so, *where*, are discussed later in this chapter.

Police corruption is not limited to monetary gain. Gains may be made in the form of services received, status, influence, prestige, or future support for the officer or someone else. For example, an officer who agrees to tolerate criminal activity by a local politician may believe this will lead to a promotion. An officer who grants immunity to certain violators may simply be executing an agreement made by his superiors in exchange for political support.

The most prevalent forms of police corruption prior to the 1940s were part of the web of corrupt practices that pervaded municipal government. The primary benefit for the officer was the opportunity to continue working for the agency; in many jurisdictions participation in corrupt practices was a condition of employment. Civil service, which provided job security, helped to sever the tie between local political corruption and police corruption, although there were some obvious exceptions where civil service itself fell under political control. But it also afforded corrupt officers an opportunity to profit more directly and personally, since they were no longer in debt to local politicians for their jobs.

Some agencies are still dominated by local politicians who, in a covert manner, use their control to serve their own political objectives. But even in the many agencies where partisan influences have been largely eliminated, remnants of previous practices can be found. The continued existence of these practices requires their inclusion in an exploration of the corruption problem.

The Impact of Corruption

What specifically are the costs of corruption? The existence of corruption clearly impairs an agency's credibility in enforcing the law. As previously noted, police commonly work to build their image as law enforcers. They frequently make appeals to citizens to be law-abiding, and they point out the need for widespread respect for the law. Yet corrupt practices are usually serious violations of the criminal code. If legislative provisions for punishment are indicative, bribery is as serious an offense as aggravated assault, major theft, or simple robbery.

The police officer who accepts payoffs is obviously doing what he is paid by the taxpayers to prevent. He is like a fireman setting fires or a physician spreading disease. The enormity of his offense is compounded when his activity contributes to the spread of serious antisocial behavior; for example, when he tolerates the sale of hard narcotics or engages in sales himself. But his activities are rarely recognized as contradicting everything he is supposed to uphold. The president of an association of police officers in New York City stated a common position when he said, "Corruption is not the No. 1 priority of the Police Commissioner. His job is to enforce the law and fight crime."[3]

Because corruption is not equated with other forms of criminal activity, police officers sometimes proceed with indignation against some minor offenders while prepared to leave them alone for a payoff. This absurdity is not lost on those who live where petty offenses are common. Black citizens in particular consistently rate the integrity of police officers much lower than whites do and react with understandable disdain when urged to have greater respect for the law by officers whom they know to be corrupt.[4]

Where police officers are controlled by payoffs from outside parties, the formal administrative control structure of the agency becomes increasingly ineffective.[5] Rules and operating procedures promulgated by the administrator are held in contempt. As a *Life* magazine article once put it, "You can't expect police on the take to take orders."[6]

This problem is aggravated when the administrator is committed to changing the orientation and operating philosophy of the agency. If his personnel are corrupt, it becomes extremely difficult to develop greater sensitivity in them to the culture and interests of minority groups, to elicit a stronger commitment to due process, or to encourage more effective responses to domestic quarrels. The values that the corrupt officer develops are in many ways the opposite of those for which the administrator seeks support. The officer who routinely profits by exploiting narcotics addicts and peddlers is not likely to take seriously a request to act with greater respect for minority interests and individual rights. His response, at best, is likely to be minimal compliance.

Effecting change almost always requires altering the way personnel are organized. If corruption is pervasive, its patterns are generally related to the organization of the department. Indeed, one of the objectives of a police administrator in reorganizing may be to reduce corruption. Altering the organizational structure, however, is likely to be seen as a threat to the arrangements from which corrupt officers profit. Corrupt subordinates will resist such changes and may even actively work to sabotage them.

The effect on administrative control is especially devastating if supervisory personnel are corrupt. A large-city precinct commander who routinely accepts bribes may lose control over his subordinates. In order to carry on his illegal activities, it may be necessary for him to do or refrain from doing things that will eventually reveal his corruption to subordinates. If the commander shares his profits with his officers or openly tolerates their own corrupt practices, he still may continue to exercise reasonably effective supervision. If he does not, the fact that his subordinates know about his illegal activities renders the commander impotent and gives the officers license to operate without regard for departmental regulations and procedures. Without effective supervision, police officers typically respond more slowly to calls for assistance, avoid assigned duties, sleep on the job, and perform poorly in situations requiring discipline and organization.[7]

These inadequacies become apparent to the public, but their relationship to corruption may not be equally apparent. People tend to say they are willing to live with police corruption as long as the police keep the streets reasonably safe, failing to recognize that corrupt police officers may do little police work.[8] They are unlikely to take seriously requirements that they check the security of various premises, that they investigate suspicious circumstances, or that they respond speedily to calls for assistance. In extreme cases, they may even see such requirements as intrusions on their time. If their supervisors are also corrupt, it becomes even more likely they will ignore these responsibilities.

The prevalence of corruption also affects the overall atmosphere in the agency. With the disclosure of any pattern of corruption there is an expectation the administrator will, in addition to proceeding against the guilty officers, take steps to deal with the corrupt practices that are exposed. This frequently takes the form of a new procedure or prohibition intended to prevent similar incidents. The ineffectiveness of such hastily drawn remedies is often so apparent that it suggests either intentional efforts to deceive the public or incredible naiveté about the value of administrative procedures. Moreover, the new regulations often create more problems than they solve.

For example, when an arrested person is found to have paid off a police officer to arrange for release, the police often overreact by prohibiting the release of any arrested individuals except on court-authorized bail, thereby requiring all arrested persons to be taken to court. It then becomes impossible for a police officer to release someone legally arrested when information proving innocence is acquired. Instead the person must be told that while the police made a mistake (and perhaps regret it) they are without authority to correct their error immediately; the person must sit in jail and await a court appearance.

After a few years so many prohibitions accumulate that the agency's written orders and regulations provide little positive guidance and consist instead of a long series of negative precepts, starting with "A member of this department will not, under any circumstances. . . ." It is disconcerting to realize that the agency's overall direction and control have been dictated not by a desire to do an effective job, but rather by disclosures of corrupt practices. This emphasis upon negative guidance creates an atmosphere of distrust that is demoralizing to honest and well-intentioned police officers.

Variations in Magnitude

It would be helpful if there were some way to accurately measure corruption. This would avoid the distortions which have marked much of the public discussions of the issue. Unfortunately the very nature of corruption makes it impossible to quantify. If we spoke only of allegations resulting in convictions, we would be grossly underestimating the problem. It is therefore necessary to lean heavily on the results of public investigations and the experience of those who have dealt with corruption from within a police agency.[9]

Although it is not possible to make meaningful comparisons, it is obvious to close observers that there is wide variation in the reputations of police agencies. In agencies which enjoy a national reputation of high integrity it is very unusual for an officer to become involved in corrupt behavior. Within other agencies corruption is limited to so-called clean graft, such as acceptance of tokens of appreciation for services rendered. In some agencies corrupt practices are limited to petty offenses, such as accepting bribes from a traffic violator or vice operator. In still other agencies, especially in larger cities, corruption pervades the entire organization.

An agency's reputation can vary over time. A number of cities where wholesale corruption once existed have succeeded in reversing their image. Los Angeles, Oakland, and Kansas City, Missouri, for example, were once plagued by corruption but now maintain a reputation in police circles for high integrity. New York City has had periods of reduced corruption, but that department's history is marked by a series of major public investigations suggesting that gains were short-lived. The Lexow Hearings of 1894, the Curran Committee investigations of 1913, the Seabury Investigation of 1930, the investigation into the Harry Gross scandal in 1950, and the Knapp Commission investigations of 1971 are instructive signposts in that history. All these investigations revealed practices and problems that have remained remarkably unchanged. The recurrence of corruption can be documented in many other large cities as well.

It is a common impression that the extent of corruption in a police agency is heavily influenced by the moral climate of the community.[10] A community where business and governmental affairs are conducted honestly is likely to have a high level of integrity in police operations. In contrast, it is unrealistic to expect police to adhere to high standards of integrity in a community where bribery of public officials and payments for special favors in the private sector are common. Such a contrast exists between the neighboring states of Illinois and Wisconsin. In Illinois, exposures of corruption at all levels of government are routine. Corruption among police has generally been accepted as a fact of life. Wisconsin, on the other hand, has honest government at all levels and no tolerance of corruption. Isolated incidents that surface in Wisconsin are minor compared to those in Illinois, and they are usually exposed by government agencies having the responsibility for dealing with them. Bribery among Wisconsin police is rare. In Illinois the citizenry no longer seems shocked by revelations; in Wisconsin the documentation of a minor corrupt act leads to public outrage.

Along with variations among jurisdictions, it is important to note the variations in the practices of different units within the same agency and of individual officers within those units. Where corruption is under control, incidents that surface will usually involve only a small number of people in the agency, and the corruption in which they engage will often be petty. But even in departments permeated by corruption the behavior of individuals varies a great deal. This was summed up well in the recent Knapp Commission report on New York City:

> Corruption, although widespread, is by no means uniform in degree. Corrupt policemen have been described as falling into two basic categories: "meat-eaters" and "grass-eaters." As the names might suggest, the meat-eaters are those policemen who . . . aggressively misuse their police powers for personal gain. The grass-eaters simply accept the payoffs that the happenstances of police work throw their way. Although the meat-eaters get the huge payoffs that make the headlines, they represent a small percentage of all corrupt policemen. The truth is, the vast majority of policemen on the take don't deal in huge amounts of graft.[11]

The grass-eaters may not, in a corruption-dominated department, be acting out of free choice. As the Knapp Commission noted:

> One strong impetus encouraging grass-eaters to continue to accept relatively petty graft is, ironically, their feeling of loyalty to their fellow officers. Accepting payoff money is one way for an officer to prove that he is one of the boys and that he can be trusted.[12]

The commission reported that officers who made a point of refusing small payoffs were not fully accepted into police fellowship.

THE NUMEROUS FORMS OF CORRUPTION

Corruption takes many varied forms. It is most commonly associated with the police role in enforcing laws relating to gambling, prostitution, homosexuality, narcotics, and alcoholic beverages.[13] But in a department riddled with corruption, corrupt practices extend to many other areas. The circumstances surrounding all arrests, for example, create a high potential for profit. "Collars make dollars" is the way it is expressed by some police officers. One of the most amazing things about police graft is the endless variety of schemes that come to light. Opportunities for personal profit in a corrupt agency seem to be limited only by the imagination and aggressiveness of those intent on realizing private gain.[14]

Vulnerable Areas

Listed below are some of the most common corrupt practices in which police have been known to engage in their dealings with citizens. The list is by no means exhaustive, but it indicates the major areas where a police agency is vulnerable.

1. Failing to arrest and prosecute those the officer knows have violated the law. Examples are: motorists parked overtime or illegally; traffic violators, including drunk drivers; gamblers, prostitutes, narcotics users, homosexuals; violators of minor regulatory ordinances, such as those regulating business hours; violators of the conditions of a license administered by the police agency; juvenile offenders; and more serious offenders, such as burglars and persons engaged in organized crime.
2. Agreeing to drop an investigation prematurely by not pursuing leads which would produce evidence supporting a criminal charge.
3. Agreeing not to inspect locations or premises where violations are known to occur and where an officer's presence might curtail the illegal activity—such as taverns in which prostitution or gambling flourishes and probably contributes to the volume of business.
4. Refraining from making arrests on licensed premises where an arrest results in license review that could lead to revocation. This includes taverns, night clubs, dance halls, and motion picture theaters.
5. Reducing the seriousness of a charge against an offender.
6. Agreeing to alter testimony at trial or to provide less than the full amount of evidence available.
7. Providing more police protection or presence than is required by standard operating procedures. Examples are: more frequent and intensive checks of

the security of private premises; more frequent presence in a store or other commercial establishment, such as a hotel, club, or restaurant where the officer's presence benefits the owner by keeping out "undesirables"; observation of parked cars while owners attend a social gathering or meeting in an area where cars are commonly stolen or damaged; and escorting businessmen making bank deposits.

8. Influencing departmental recommendations regarding the granting of licenses, for example, by recommending for or against continuance of a liquor or amusement license by either giving or suppressing derogatory information.

9. Arranging access to confidential departmental records or agreeing to alter such records.

10. Referring individuals caught in a new and stressful situation to persons who can assist them and who stand to profit from the referral. Police can get paid for making referrals to bondsmen or defense attorneys; placing accident victims in contact with physicians or attorneys specializing in the filing of personal injury claims; arranging for delivery of bodies to a funeral home; and selecting the ambulance or tow truck summoned to the scene of an accident or an illegally parked car.

11. Appropriating for personal use or disposal items of value acquired on the job, such as jewelry and goods from the scene of a burglary; narcotics confiscated from users or peddlers; funds used in gambling; items found at the scene of a fire; private property of a drunk or a deceased person; and confiscated weapons.

It is clear from these examples that many segments of the public, including organized criminals, legitimate business interests, private citizens, and the pettiest of offenders, stand to gain by influencing the decisions a police officer makes. Some act under threat of criminal prosecution, but many are not—except for their corrupt acts—violating any law. The latter include those who wish to buy extra police services or benefit from information and situations to which police have access.

People threatened with prosecution have quite different motives for offering money to police. Some are primarily concerned with being able to continue their illegal activities (for example, the professional burglar, the dealer in stolen merchandise, the gambler, the narcotics peddler, and the street prostitute). Others are anxious to avoid the inconvenience of arrest, fines, or other consequences of conviction (such as the motorist who fears loss of his license). Those facing arrest are especially likely to offer payoffs if their livelihoods are threatened (salesmen, taxi drivers, truck drivers, or tavern keepers). Some may be primarily interested in not having their situation given any publicity (an errant spouse or homosexual). This diversity should be a warning against the more simplistic remedies offered as solutions to corruption.

Internal Corruption

When officers on the street are realizing financial profit in their relationships with citizens, officers with positions in station houses or at headquarters, who do not have such contacts, tend to devise ways to supplement their own incomes. They may do this by exacting payments from street officers in exchange for the services which so-called inside men are in a unique position to provide or withhold. Investigations of police corruption in several large cities have described such practices as street officers paying inside men for falsifying attendance records, influencing the choice of vacations and days off, reporting them on duty when they were not, providing them with records faster than usual, arranging for them to be called at the beginning of a court session, and giving them passing grades in training programs. Of special importance is the practice of paying superiors or other police personnel to influence assignments. Certain assignments are much more desirable for the corruption-prone officer, a point made with great clarity by the Knapp Commission.[15]

Occasionally police officers working inside can develop their own direct relationships with special interests, for instance, by offering to check the files for private employers to determine if job applicants have arrest records.

Degrees of Organization

There is great variation from one community to another (and within the same community at different times) in the extent to which corruption becomes organized. For example, a single officer may enter into an agreement with businessmen to tolerate illegal parking in a designated area. A sergeant may enter the agreement, sharing whatever funds he receives with his personnel; or a lieutenant may make the arrangement, sharing payments with sergeants and patrolmen. There even have been frequent allegations that police commanders establish systems for the routine collection of payments from businessmen, tavern keepers, vice operators, and others, with the funds being distributed to some or all members of the police unit serving the area.[16]

The initiative for an organized system of corruption may come from organized criminal interests. Those in charge of a large gambling operation, for example, may seek out the commander of the area where they operate and offer a payoff for immunity, with the understanding that the commander will distribute appropriate portions to subordinates.

Occasional discovery of collection records, such as a "bagman's little black book," has provided a picture of the type of organization police construct to collect and distribute graft in a routine manner. Only a few major inquiries into corruption, however, have succeeded in documenting the full extent to which corruption is organized. The Knapp Commission gives an indication of how large and complex the organization can be in describing the pad—a system for distributing payoffs received for tolerating gambling in New York City:

In a highly systematized pattern, described to the Commission by numerous sources and verified during our investigation, plainclothesmen collected regular biweekly or monthly payoffs from gamblers on the first and fifteenth of each month, often at a meeting place some distance from the gambling spot and outside the immediate police precinct or division. The pad money was picked up at designated locations by one or more bagmen who were most often police officers but who occasionally were ex-policemen or civilians. The proceeds were then pooled and divided up among all or virtually all of the division's plainclothesmen, with each plainclothes patrolman receiving an equal share. Supervisory lieutenants who were on the pad customarily received a share and a half and, although the Commission was unable to document particular instances, any commanding officer who participated reportedly received two full shares. In addition, the bagman received a larger cut, often an extra share, to compensate him for the risk involved in making his collections. . . .[17]

Investigators have suspected the existence of similar arrangements in other jurisdictions involving criminality other than gambling, but it is understandably difficult to acquire solid proof.[18]

The widespread assumption that corruption, where it is common, is highly organized creates an atmosphere in which many nefarious practices can thrive. This occurs in large measure because of the secrecy surrounding the arrangements police have established and the public's ignorance of what a single officer can deliver. An individual officer, for example, can command a very high price when promising immunity to a large vice operator. The amount, he may explain, is necessary to take care of all his supervisors and the special units established to check on vice enforcement. This may in fact be the case; but more likely the officer pockets the full amount knowing from his experience that there is little likelihood that even the most incorruptible supervisors and investigating units will interfere with the operation. If they do he can apologize to the operator, or even go so far as to refund the payoff, explaining that things did not work out right. This practice, not at all uncommon, creates the impression that police corruption is much more pervasive and organized than it is. Without adequate means for establishing the facts, both the public and police administrators are left guessing whether such cases illustrate the unusual greediness and audacity of a single officer or the wholesale purchase of an agency. Nor can they know how often and for how much the unscrupulous officers have sold immunity which they were not in a position to deliver.

CONTRIBUTING FACTORS

Commonly Cited Factors

Several factors contributing to corruption are fairly obvious and have been mentioned frequently. They include unenforceable laws, organized criminal interests, and improper political influence. Because legislatures continue to prohibit conduct in which large numbers of people are engaged, nonenforcement is inevitable, and this in turn provides many opportunities for the public to buy immunity and for police to take or withhold action in exchange for payoffs. Organized criminals—those who engage in crime as a business—are a common source of corruption because their survival and profits often depend on their ability to buy freedom from interference. Politicians and political parties attempt to control the police in order to build their power and their support.

All three factors often are inextricably interrelated, with each feeding on the others. Much organized crime, for example, involves violations of unenforceable laws, such as those pertaining to gambling, prostitution, and narcotics. Political pressure on the police often has as one objective the tolerance of organized criminal interests and vice. The impact and interrelationship of these factors have been extensively documented in numerous investigations; in the literature on overcriminalization, organized crime, local government, and police corruption; and in accounts by police administrators.[19]

The importance of these factors may, however, have been overstated. Changes that have been proposed would be limited in their effect. It is, for instance, a gross oversimplification to argue that decriminalization will eliminate corruption. Even the most ardent supporters of decriminalization agree that some form of regulation would necessarily remain. It follows that opportunities for corruption also would remain and might even increase in areas that continue to be regulated. Elimination of the prohibition against the use of liquor may have ended or reduced some forms of corruption, but any knowledgeable police administrator would point out that much current corruption stems from liquor consumption and sale.[20]

The direct link between partisan politics and the police has been broken in most cities. But the introduction of civil service, merit-based promotions, and purchasing through competitive bidding, for example, has not eliminated corruption. Corruption-prone police can find areas unaffected by these reforms in which to operate.

Political influence in the past has been narrowly and somewhat naively defined in terms of pressure from machine-type politicians. But the most professional of city governments is still, hopefully, political. Otherwise it would have no accountability to the public. So long as this is true, opportunities will remain for corrupt practices where political decisions affect police operations.

Coming to grips with overcriminalization, organized crime, and improper influences on police would substantially reduce corruption. It would not be eliminated, however, and it is therefore important to acknowledge briefly some of the less frequently cited factors contributing to its existence.

The Nature of Police Work

The extent to which the day-to-day nature of police work contributes to corruption has not been adequately recognized. The average officer—especially in a large city—sees the worst side of humanity and is exposed to a steady diet of wrongdoing. In the course of this exposure, the officer discovers that dishonesty and corruption are not restricted to those the community sees as criminal; many individuals of good reputation engage in practices equally dishonest and corrupt. Almost any officer can cite specific instances of reputable citizens defrauding insurance agencies by false claims, hiding earnings to avoid taxes, or obtaining services or merchandise without payment. He often develops a cynical attitude in which he views corruption as a game in which every person is out to get a share.[21]

Given the temptations for additional income, it is easy to see how corrupt police rationalize their behavior and minimize its gravity. Whether accurate or not, the impression that corruption pervades society leads an officer to reflect on his own plight. Police compensation rates have not kept pace with rates in other occupational groups. Despite dramatic improvements in many larger and some smaller cities, low pay continues to be a problem.

Furthermore, many individuals who try to bribe police are themselves engaged in professional criminal activity. Corrupt police reason that, if a hard-working officer takes money from a criminal, it is not as if the criminal were being deprived of something that was legitimately his.

Prosecutors and Courts

Police officers are close observers of the operations of prosecutors and courts. An officer who sees the processing of hundreds of petty offenders through a city's minor courts cannot help but be struck by the futility of the procedure— the lack of justice, the lack of dignity, and the ineffectiveness of the criminal process in dealing with the behavioral problems which bring defendants to court. The same impression is generated by the processing of those accused of more serious offenses. In agreeing not to make an arrest or to drop a charge in exchange for a payoff, an officer may justify such an action by claiming that further processing would produce no more effective or just disposition.

This reasoning is greatly reinforced when the prosecutor's office and the courts are also corrupt. Through their daily contacts with prosecutors, judges, and other court personnel, police become very aware of wrongdoing. The honest officer understandably resents delivering cases to persons who, shielded by the high prestige of the prosecutor's office or the bench, extract monetary payments in exchange for favors. When this happens the officer usually cannot register any objection because corrupt prosecutors and judges deliver on agreements by using discretion that is officially theirs. A prosecutor need not account for a decision not to prosecute, nor must a judge justify a decision to dismiss. Many officers, after having successfully resisted temptations, have felt that the subversion of justice in the rest of the system made their own integrity completely pointless and have succumbed. The rationale then goes something like this: "If my efforts put cash into the hands of corrupt prosecutors, court clerks, and judges, I'm a fool for not taking it myself."

Police Discretion

The common assumption that the police have no authority to exercise discretion aggravates the corruption problem in several ways.

First, it enables a corruption-prone officer to make use of the unbridled discretion which he does in fact have in ways that will produce profits for himself— without having to account for his actions.

Second, because each officer is vulnerable to charges of illegality or impropriety for discretionary acts, he becomes dependent on fellow officers to support him, and this support readily extends to protection from allegations of any nature, including corruption.

Third, the atmosphere of duplicity and hypocrisy, which makes it so difficult for police administrators to exert control over their personnel, is an ideal setting for corruption. Police who are constantly being informally told they must bend, ignore, or violate laws and rules may understandably conclude that similar flexibility exists with regard to corrupt behavior.

The Addictive Element

Once an officer has agreed to accept the profits of corruption, he usually becomes addicted to the system. He comes to depend on the additional income, expanding his personal budget by the amount of graft he anticipates. This expansion often takes the form of payments on a new car, home, or other major purchase. Under these conditions, any possibility that illegal income may be cut off or reduced poses a threat similar to the possibility of a sizable salary cut for the honest employee. Thus the pressures from an officer's peers to engage in corruption are augmented and may eventually be overshadowed by self-generated financial pressures.[22]

If a corrupt officer goes further and seeks to build his financial holdings through investments or gambling, his attitude may become exploitative and predatory to the extreme. This pattern is sometimes revealed when officers are charged with extortion.

ADMINISTRATIVE DILEMMAS

Citizens frequently boast about bribing a police officer. They casually discuss among themselves the corrupt practices of police personnel. Occasionally they may even report such activities anonymously to the local police administration. Almost invariably the inference drawn by citizens is that these conditions could not exist without the knowledge and possible involvement of superior officers and the police administrator. In some localities where corruption is pervasive, inside knowledge about the patterns of corrupt practices may well confirm these inferences. Evidence of corruption at the bottom, however, does not always mean corruption at the top. Several incredibly complex problems confront the administrator who attempts to eradicate corruption, problems that prevent him from dealing effectively with the kinds of violations that may seem so conspicuous to the citizenry.

Drawing the Line

When a police administrator declares himself against corruption, he is confronted by questions about his exact position. Does he mean an officer should not accept a free cup of coffee? How about a meal? What about a Christmas gift? What about a reward sincerely offered for meritorious service? And what about the tip offered by a visiting dignitary to the officer who served as his bodyguard? These are clearly on the periphery of the corruption problem. They are not usually the practices which prompted the administrator to speak out against corruption, nor are they likely to be of central concern to those most troubled by the existence of corruption.[23]

They cannot, however, be ignored, for they raise several more fundamental questions. Should police be subject to a substantially higher standard of conduct than those in other government agencies, the business community, and the private sector generally? Is it preferable to have a department policy absolutely prohibiting the acceptance of any gratuity? Or is it desirable to have what some would characterize as a more realistic policy which permits officers to accept minor gratuities offered not to corrupt but in sincere appreciation for a job well done?

Most administrators, at the risk of sounding fanatical, have chosen the first alternative. The late O. W. Wilson always maintained that a police officer should not be allowed to accept any gratuity, not even a free cup of coffee. Patrick Murphy more recently stated: "Except for your paycheck, there is no such thing as a clean buck."[24] These men would argue that the smallest offerings have a corrupting influence and that accepting them lowers the officer's resistance to other temptations. Free coffee doubtlessly is used to get officers into places which commonly experience trouble and to induce the officers to look more kindly on the giver. It is a small step to the next stage where officers provide different service to those who offer coffee and those who do not. If it is permissible to accept free coffee, what about a modest lunch? And if free lunches are permissible, what about more elaborate meals? If acceptance of the latter for the officer is tolerated, what about bringing along family or friends? Those who advocate an absolute ban on gratuities argue that it is impossible to draw up standards that both accommodate expressions of sincere gratitude and assure that an officer will not do something he should not do in exchange.

An opposing viewpoint, less often expressed, is that absolute prohibitions are so unrealistic that they undermine efforts to get at more serious forms of corruption. The argument is that the probability of stamping out free coffee and meals is so remote that such a ban conveys the impression that the administrator does not really intend to do very much about corruption. Holders of this view say the administrator should establish guidelines permitting the acceptance of small offers of appreciation, thereby enabling him to be much more absolute and effective in dealing with more serious forms of corruption.

Several other lines must be drawn. Should police be permitted to sell tickets to an event sponsored by a police association? In police agencies that might otherwise be corruption-free, police regularly sell tickets to an annual ball or police-sponsored sporting event, often during working hours. Advertisements are solicited for program books distributed at these events. Because these solicitations are conducted openly and a ticket of admission or an advertisement is offered in exchange, they are not considered a form of corruption. But are they so different? Ticket buyers frequently do not attend the event. They make the purchase because they feel that the police service they will receive in the future will depend on their response to the solicitation. A variation on this practice is the sale of stickers that merchants, homeowners, and car owners display in their windows indicating they support the police association.

Should police be permitted to do indirectly what they are prohibited from doing directly? For example, if solicitations are banned, what about the police association that hires private solicitors to sell the tickets or stickers and fill the ad books? What about the privately published but official-sounding magazine catering to police interests that is distributed to all police personnel, its contents often consisting largely of advertisements placed by establishments subject to police licensing and regulation?[25]

Should publicly announced rewards be viewed as a form of corruption? There was a time when most criminals were apprehended by bounty hunters.[26] Today, rewards are sometimes prohibited, along with gifts and gratuities.[27] But victims of crimes often post a reward for information leading to the arrest of the offender. Bail bond companies offer rewards for the arrest of those who jump bail. If police officers are among those eligible to receive these rewards, as they are in many jurisdictions, these cases often receive extra attention. Time is taken away from equally serious matters involving victims unable to offer rewards. In many respects a system of privately sponsored rewards is much like some forms of corruption, but such systems frequently exist in conjunction with vigorous anti-corruption programs.

Acquiring the Evidence

There is no more formidable barrier to eliminating corruption than the blue curtain—the conspiracy of silence among police. Just as an officer will not report police abuse of authority, he will not disclose the corrupt behavior of a fellow officer. It is extremely unlikely that he will testify in support of allegations of corruption made by persons outside the agency. It is unusual for a police intelligence unit, assigned to gather information on criminal activity, to discover and report evidence of corruption, though one would expect their inquiries to lead inevitably to such discoveries. For the police administrator the situation is like the one he faces in dealing with organized crime. There is almost no way the curtain can be penetrated.

The procedure most commonly employed for investigating corruption in a police agency depends for its initiation upon a citizen's complaint. Given the consensual nature of most corrupt behavior and the fear citizens have of informing against police, this procedure obviously brings only a small percentage of existing corruption to the attention of an administrator. Complainants may include a wife annoyed because her husband uses limited family funds to pay the police, an out-of-towner behaving in line with the noncorrupt norms of his community, an idealistic person confronted with his first bribe solicitation, or a person angered by an officer who violates an agreement for which he has been paid. Another complainant could be someone who stands to gain if a specific form of corruption is ended, such as a tavern keeper competing with an illegal liquor distributor whose continued operation is made possible by payments to the police.

The value of these complaints is limited because most are submitted anonymously. It remains for the police to acquire the evidence needed to prosecute or to bring department charges against the officers involved. When a complainant does identify himself, there are often other problems. If he is an out-of-towner, it is expensive to bring him back to the community for the subsequent proceedings. Furthermore, while his sense of duty may extend to reporting the corrupt act, it is unlikely to extend to being inconvenienced for long periods of time. Counsel defending a police officer have been known to seek delays in such cases, confident that the key witness will tire of appearing at court trials or civil service proceedings. Of the complainants who live in the community, the value of many as witnesses is diminished because they have extensive criminal records or are of questionable emotional stability.[28]

In view of all these limitations, why do police administrators wait for complaints instead of instigating investigations on their own? They have available all the techniques police use in investigating serious criminal activity—surveillance, undercover operations, paid informants, the exchange of immunity for information, and the staging of situations that encourage corrupt police officers to violate the laws (but do not constitute entrapment).

All these techniques can be used legally, but pressures from within the department and the community can combine to prevent the reform-minded administrator from employing them. Their use typically raises the charge of gross unfairness from the police association. This in turn draws surprisingly strong support from the larger community. There is a certain irony in the association's position, for it is rank-and-file personnel who most steadfastly defend use of these techniques to control other forms of crime. The explanation for this inconsistency, aside from the self-interest of the corrupt officer, apparently lies in a refusal to see corruption as a form of criminal conduct. Public response must be attributed to the citizens' desires to preserve their own interests in being able to pay off police, to their ignorance of the magnitude and seriousness of corruption, or simply to their tendency to defend the police. The result is that relatively few administrators aggressively try to ferret out wrongdoing, and many of those who do soon dilute or abandon their efforts because of the opposition they encounter.

There have been a few occasions when an officer has reported corruption in an agency in which corruption is widespread. Where the report was made internally, it sometimes was discounted by supervisors or the administrator.[29] Where it was made to another agency and publicized, the report on occasion led to full-scale public inquiry. If, however, a testifying officer is motivated by the desire to obtain immunity from prosecution for his own acts, the impact of his testimony is limited because his credibility is subject to question.[30]

The Risks of Speaking Out

To be effective in coping with corruption the administrator must publicly acknowledge the problem and must mount an aggressive program to attempt to control it in a manner that receives full public exposure. This is true for several reasons.

First, he will have no public support for the punitive actions he must take unless the public is aware of the magnitude and consequences of corruption.

Second, despite the secrecy surrounding many aspects of police work, corruption cannot be dealt with privately. It requires procedures traditionally subject to public scrutiny and the involvement of officials outside the agency, such as civil service personnel, prosecutors, and judges.

Third, the administrator must communicate with those who offer as well as those who accept payoffs. The greatest potential a police administrator has for reducing corruption may lie in convincing the citizenry not to make illegal propositions to police and threatening criminal prosecution of persons who continue to do so.[31]

Important as it is for the administrator to speak forthrightly, however, ventilation of the problem impugns the reputation of the honest officer, who understandably resents having people view him as dishonest and who has no easy way to distinguish himself from those implicated.[32] A somewhat similar situation occurs when, in a sincere effort to educate the public, investigating commissions make public the testimony of police officers and ex-offenders who have alleged widespread corruption. However inclined one may be to weigh such testimony, innocent officers are left defenseless.

Public acknowledgment of corruption has an even greater impact on police morale than do vigorous efforts to deal with the various forms of wrongdoing discussed in chapter 7. Allegations of corruption are viewed by the police as much more damaging than allegations that they have used excessive force or otherwise exceeded their authority. Corruption is a selfish endeavor, engaged in for private gain, which is considered morally wrong by the community even though some contribute to it. Police excesses are commonly justified as being in the community's interest, and the officer accused of engaging in them often receives widespread community approval.

Many administrators who dealt aggressively with corruption in the past found that a combination of internal and external pressures made it impossible for them to continue in their jobs. In contrast, those who developed an uncanny ability to publicly deny or minimize corruption while presiding over thoroughly corrupt agencies earned unwavering support from their personnel. The cover they provided guaranteed their security in office.

Against this background it is understandable why public pronouncements on corruption by many responsible police administrators are carefully guarded and appear at times to be defensive. A chief may recognize the existence of corruption, but is likely to attempt to minimize the problem by maintaining that it involves only a small percentage of the force. He may combine an attack on corruption with praise for the courage of police personnel. Or he may seek to place police wrongdoing in perspective by pointing out that the public shares responsibility for the problem. The public and operating police officers are left to judge for themselves whether such statements are offered as excuses or whether they are simply a reflection of the administrator's difficult position.

Measuring Integrity

Among the major factors contributing to the anxiety of police administrators is their uncertainty in assessing the magnitude of corruption and in evaluating the integrity of those they most heavily depend on for its control.

Some signs of corruption are obvious. Large numbers of cars routinely parked illegally in an area covered by an officer given clear responsibility for parking enforcement invite investigation. Licensed premises open after hours point to the likelihood that arrangements have been made with officers responsible for enforcing closing hours. Unfortunately these high-visibility indicators are rare. Most forms of police corruption carry few visible signs, and those which do exist become less visible as efforts to deal with corruption intensify.

Knowledge about the exact nature of corruption is important not only to cope with the problem but also to assess the integrity of those in key administrative positions. Rewarding a dishonest officer through promotion or placement in a key position can have devastating effects. It tells the rank and file who know the man is dishonest that administrative efforts to deal with corruption are either inadequate or insincere.

The measurement problem is complicated when corrupt officers float rumors impugning the integrity of those fighting corruption. This may result in the administrator making a special effort to support his subordinates. How far should the administrator go, however, in denying the allegations when he has no adequate means for investigation? False charges of corruption, extremely difficult to deal with, have ruined the careers of some excellent police officers. Such charges are a powerful weapon in the hands of irresponsible individuals.

An administrator will occasionally receive information that throws a cloud over his entire assault on corruption. For example, having made what appears to be substantial progress in cleaning up gambling corruption, it is disconcerting for him to learn that a newly appointed supervisory officer has been offered a large amount of money to continue the corrupt relationship that existed with his predecessor, who maintained an image of high integrity. How does one evaluate such information? Are the corrupters hoping to work out an arrangement with the new commander which they did not in fact enjoy with his predecessor? Was the previous commander really corrupt? If he entered into an arrangement behind his facade of integrity, how common is the practice in other areas of the department? What does this say about the success of other anti-corruption efforts?

Some use has been made of financial questionnaires to investigate allegations of corruption and to defend police officials against false charges. But proposals that the questionnaires be made mandatory have been met by complaints that they are an unwarranted intrusion into the personal affairs of an officer. Their use has generally not been pressed over these objections, primarily because there is no reason to believe a corrupt official would complete a questionnaire honestly. There have also been efforts to require that ranking officers submit to polygraph examinations. These suggestions have been met by similar objections, together with expressions of concern over the reliability of the tests.

COMMON SOLUTIONS: THEIR STRENGTHS
AND WEAKNESSES

It is common sport to predict that an honest administrator appointed to run a corrupt agency will be either co-opted or totally frustrated in his new position. The prediction often proves true. The history of reform provides many illustrations of elaborate attempts to eliminate dishonesty followed by rapid reversion to prior practices.

It is difficult for an administrator to do all that has to be done, even in a corruption-free agency, in order to maintain a constant alert for corruption. It is irksome and time-consuming to have to deal with an occasional outbreak of corrupt practices. Relatively speaking, however, these tasks seem minor when compared with the formidable task of coping with corruption in an agency where the problem has reached epidemic proportions. The pervasive nature of the problem, the deep roots of existing practices, the unlimited opportunities for developing new practices as old ones are controlled, and the extent to which a department's moral climate is dependent on that of the criminal justice system and the community as a whole are major obstacles to success.

Yet in the face of these limitations and failures, some corrupt agencies have been transformed into honest ones. From the experiences of the past we can draw some impressions of the strengths and weaknesses of the most commonly proposed methods for dealing with corruption. Many of these solutions, of course, will be recognized as having been proposed for dealing with other police problems as well, including control of the kinds of wrongdoing discussed in the preceding chapter. They are examined here with specific focus upon their application to the corruption problem.

Changes in Existing Laws

Elimination of certain criminal sanctions would obviously reduce the amount of police work which lends itself so readily to corruption. Decriminalization would eliminate much of the activity that accustoms officers to accepting bribes and makes them targets for corruption related to more serious offenses.[33] In the absence of any significant reduction in the use of criminal sanctions other than those associated with Prohibition, however, there is little basis for measuring the exact impact of such a change. Many questions remain unanswered.

Will corrupt police simply move to other areas as the unenforceable laws are repealed? As was previously noted, even the most ambitious effort to eliminate regulation of private morality will probably retain prohibitions against behavior that is nonconsensual, that involves children, or that constitutes a nuisance to others. To what extent would police corruption concentrate in these areas? How does the corruption currently tied to the regulation of liquor, for example, compare with the amount of corruption that prevailed during Prohibition? Is there a tendency for new patterns of corruption to emerge, as is alleged to have occurred where gambling has been legalized? None of these queries is intended to rebut arguments about the desirability of modifying the large number of unenforceable laws now on the books. There are, in many instances, sufficiently strong reasons for doing so on other grounds.

Among the factors previously noted as contributing to corruption is the widespread belief that police are supposed to enforce all laws; that they do not exercise discretion (see chapter 5). The opportunity to threaten prosecution of all laws is what makes solicitation of bribes possible. If legislatures were to recognize the existence of police discretion and provide methods for administrators to control it, a further positive consequence, beyond those mentioned in earlier chapters, would be that the power of the corrupt officer would be greatly undermined. Also directly relevant to the corruption problem are the suggestions made earlier that legislatures should give police properly restricted authority to fulfill their actual responsibilities, provide alternatives to the criminal process, and make needed resources available. By reducing the frequency with which police must bend the criminal process in order to carry out their duties, legislatures could create a healthier atmosphere in police agencies, an atmosphere in which appeals for integrity and adherence to the law would not be subverted by a shared awareness of a need to function with questionable legality.

Educating the Public

Large segments of the public do not realize how detrimental their bribing or otherwise corrupting an officer is to the overall effectiveness of the police. Each sees his or her act as an isolated one with limited consequences. Since a citizen's offer is frequently made in sincere appreciation for a service rendered, the benevolence of the act is commonly thought to overshadow whatever taint of wrongfulness it might carry.

While police administrators have a general responsibility to educate the public on the problem of corruption, they have a particular responsibility to make citizens aware of how their individual actions affect the quality of police service. A significant element in each community would respond affirmatively to this information and to a request to stop practices previously assumed to be harmless.

An appeal of this kind seems especially appropriate when the corrupters are a special category of citizens such as restaurant owners, hotel keepers, construction firms, or taxicab drivers. The fear of the consequences of not offering a bribe while competitors do results in wholesale conformity with the pattern. If an entire category of businessmen agreed to simultaneously abandon corrupt practices, the pattern would be effectively terminated. Such an agreement requires intensive efforts by the police administration, usually in collaboration with an association serving as an umbrella for the businessmen involved. In some jurisdictions an effort of this kind would be naive and futile, while in others it might work.

Stance of the Administrator

The factor most clearly distinguishing the relatively few successful efforts to deal with corruption has been the unequivocal stance against it taken by those leading the effort. Operating personnel do not judge the administrator's stance simply on the basis of his public pronouncements. They measure it by everything he does—communications on the subject of corruption within the agency, investigation of allegations, disciplining of corrupt officers, and promotions made. They have learned from past experience that publicly stated positions do not necessarily describe real intentions, but may actually be a cover to protect prevailing practices. It becomes critically important, therefore, that the message from a police administrator, however conveyed, reflects an unwavering commitment to dealing with corrupt behavior directly, quickly, and decisively.

But the necessity for a strong stance against corruption should not be equated with waging a war on corruption. There is an element of phoniness about most such efforts very much like that in the frequently declared wars against crime. Such a declaration suggests a goal of total elimination and victory, which is as unrealistic for corruption as it is for crime. An administrator must guard, too, against becoming a fanatic. Corruption sometimes arouses an emotional involvement that can be dysfunctional. Important as it is to address corruption, concern with it must be related to the magnitude of the problem in the given community and be balanced by concern with other problems.

If corruption rages uncontrolled, however, there is little chance of solving other problems in the community. Under such conditions, is it better for a progressive chief to speak out on corruption, risking the possibility that he will alienate his subordinates to the point that he is driven from office, or for him to attempt to deal with the problem in a less aggressive manner? Some people say the second approach is more mature. But those who have equivocated in their public pronouncements on the corruption issue, hoping to deal with it within the confines of the department, have not had much success. When they left office their agencies were in much worse condition than when they took office. If corruption is a serious problem, it seems preferable—ideally—for a progressive chief to speak out even if it means the loss of his job. It is far better to draw the attention of the community to the inability of an honest administrator to control an agency than it is to lull the citizens into believing that, because they trust the head of the agency, the honesty of the personnel is assured. But is it realistic to expect chiefs to sacrifice their jobs in hopes that this will bring corruption to light, when the only certain result is that their own careers will be permanently terminated?

The administrator who is committed to dealing with the problem and who also wants to remain in office must, to maximize his potential for success, attempt to make it clear that his attack upon corruption is not an attack upon his personnel. He must be able to get the department and the community to see his anti-corruption program as a way of backing the honest, hard-working, dedicated, and heroic police officer. Every effort aimed at dealing with corruption must carry with it this affirmation of support.

Tenure of the Administrator

For many years, granting a police chief tenure was seen as the necessary first step in combating corruption.[34] It was generally assumed that administrators without tenure were vulnerable to improper political pressures and corrupt influences while those with tenure would resist such pressures. Guaranteed tenure has not always produced corruption-free administrations. Too much faith may have been placed in this single reform. Few efforts to control corruption have succeeded, however, without some guarantee of tenure for the top man. If the administrator's stance on corruption is critical, it obviously follows that he must speak from a position of strength. The chief's strength is heavily influenced by the degree of job security he enjoys.

Actual longevity in office, made possible in part by tenure, may be of even greater importance than tenure in bringing about lasting change. However committed and secure a police chief may be, it still takes time to carry out reforms. Significantly, those corrupt agencies which have since acquired reputations for integrity were directed by one person for an extended period of time.

How the continuing need for tenure can be reconciled with the need for greater accountability of police chiefs is discussed in chapter 6.

Improved Administration

The preoccupation of some police reformers with greater operating efficiency has drawn much criticism recently. As a result of this criticism the emphasis previously given to organizational improvement has been played down. In addressing police corruption, however, some minimum standards of administration must be met. Corruption thrives best in poorly run organizations where lines of authority are vague and supervision is minimal.

Before he can attack corruption, a police chief must place his house in order. For some departments this means implementing elementary improvements that were adopted years ago in others. It means utilizing modern management techniques such as have been outlined in most police reorganization efforts in recent years: clarifying the organization; establishing clear lines of supervision; streamlining operating procedures; providing adequate equipment and facilities; improving record-keeping procedures; and updating the application of newly available technology to all aspects of police work. To get at corruption an administrator must be able to account for all personnel, be clear on their responsibilities, and have some basic systems for holding them accountable for carrying out their assignments.

There is, however, always the danger that too heavy a dependence will be placed upon administrative procedures. Some departments, for example, establish elaborate procedures to keep track of police activities in those areas where officers commonly accept bribes on the assumption that this is one way to control corruption. Monthly, weekly, and even daily reports may be required on arrests made for gambling, prostitution, narcotics, and violations of liquor laws. But arrests obviously do not provide an accurate measure of corruption. The pressure to make them can be easily satisfied by arresting petty offenders operating independently of larger protected operations, by arresting offenders in a way which assures the charge will be dropped, or even by arresting innocent persons, knowing that charges cannot be proved. Among the many additional ways to satisfy pressures for arrests is an arrangement with the corrupting party to routinely deliver people to the corrupt officer so that he can fill his arrest quota.

The point, very simply, is that corrupt personnel demonstrate a remarkable capacity to accommodate themselves to some of the traditional methods for improving the administration of a police agency; that while efficient administration makes it possible to deal more effectively with corruption, an agency can achieve an outward appearance of efficiency while harboring corrupt practices.

Recruit Training

One of the most common recommendations for dealing with corruption is that it be realistically covered in recruit training. Most police training programs avoid discussion of corruption, often on the rather naive grounds that it is undesirable to draw attention to wrongdoing. There seems to be a fear that open discussion might invite rather than prevent corrupt behavior.[35] Yet subsequent discovery by new officers of the true dimensions of corruption is among the major factors discrediting the value of recruit training.

Where corruption has been discussed in training, the usual procedure has been to review ethical codes, laws relating to bribery, and departmental procedures for dealing with corrupt conduct. Often the training has consisted of lectures delivered by chaplains or warnings by supervisory officers of the consequences of corrupt acts. It is doubtful that these measures work.

If recruit training is to have any impact on corruption, it must explore fully and realistically all the dimensions of the problem, including specific examples of corruption known to exist or to have existed in the department. The more realistically training deals with corruption as a hazard of police work, the more credibility the staff is likely to have and the greater the probability that the recruit will take warnings seriously. Training should be designed not simply to make it clear corruption is prohibited. It should provide an officer with an understanding of the problem that enables him to avoid involvement.[36] It should seek to instill in an officer a desire to protect his integrity, not out of fear of apprehension, but because corruption is wrong.

Internal Investigation Units

Giving supervisory personnel absolute responsibility for investigating all forms of wrongdoing in their agencies is fraught with danger if they themselves are corrupt. It is obviously futile to refer complaints to a command officer who is profiting from the practices about which complaints are filed, or who, because of his own illegal activities, dares not crack down on other forms of wrongdoing. Where corruption is pervasive, complaints regarding corruption are used by corrupt supervisors as a means of identifying "leaks" in their system.

In responding to the need to deal with corruption as well as other forms of wrongdoing, many departments have chosen to concentrate responsibility by creating special units to conduct internal investigations. In a small department the responsibility might be given to a single officer. In a large agency the unit may be of substantial size.

The value of such units depends upon the level of integrity established in the agency. In departments that have succeeded in controlling corruption, internal investigation units appear to contribute significantly not only toward maintaining the integrity of the force, but toward achieving conformity with other standards as well. The unit then mirrors, in effect, the prevailing standards of the department. But just as problems arise in leaving control in the hands of a supervisor who is corrupt, problems arise in using an internal investigation unit as the primary means for bringing corruption under control in a corrupt department. And still more problems arise when such a unit is established in a department in which no serious effort is being made to control corruption.

In some large cities having a serious corruption problem there are several levels of investigators. Those at the top check the integrity of those assigned to check the integrity of those at the bottom—a situation contributing to the paranoia that often pervades an agency. Beyond this the proliferation of levels dissipates responsibility to the point where no one except the top administrator feels totally responsible for ferreting out corruption. Creation of the units may also serve to increase the amount of a payoff, since a corrupt officer may extract a sum sufficient to take care of both himself and those nominally responsible for overseeing his integrity. Where there is no serious effort to combat corruption, the units often become the chief apologists for the agency.

Various compromise procedures have been developed, but none is completely satisfactory. The most common holds each command officer responsible for corruption in his unit. To support this responsibility he is given all information received about corruption on the assumption he will act to correct the problem. At the same time a special "bird-dog" unit is created to audit conditions in each command and to make its own investigations in response to citizen complaints. Exposure of corruption by the bird-dog unit is commonly interpreted as prima facie evidence of the failure of the accused officer's superior to control corruption. Theoretically, establishing two independent checks in this manner assures the integrity of both. In corrupt departments, however, it may be extremely difficult to maintain the integrity of the bird-dog unit. Because of its exceptional powers, its members are offered far larger payoffs than those offered at lower levels. If the integrity of this unit is undermined the entire system collapses.

The greatest weakness of special investigative units is one seldom acknowledged by police. It is absolutely unrealistic to expect officers on special assignment, however honest and dedicated, to investigate zealously the activities of fellow officers who may one day be their partners or superiors. It has been suggested that this problem can be overcome, especially in larger departments, by permanent assignments to the investigative units. But this may intensify the difficulty in maintaining the unit's integrity. And it can be argued that officers assigned to investigating corruption over a long period of time, like those permanently assigned to vice investigations, eventually cease to be fair and objective investigators.

Where corruption is widespread, the difficulty in maintaining an investigative unit of unimpeachable integrity is so great that serious consideration should be given to obtaining investigative assistance from outside the agency, a possibility examined later.

Investigations and Prosecutions

In those communities in which corruption is not of epidemic proportions and where, as a result, an internal investigation unit is unlikely to become corrupt, the effectiveness of the unit will depend heavily on the program it develops for itself.

In fashioning a comprehensive plan to attack corruption, police would do well to review what they themselves do in coping with other forms of crime. Admittedly, questions are constantly raised regarding the value of criminal prosecution and punishment as a deterrent to crime. In the absence of any better alternative, however, society continues to lean heavily on the criminal justice system. Similarly, with the same doubts, the police must continue to lean heavily on the criminal justice process in seeking to deter corruption. Police themselves consistently argue that, if the deterrent value of the system in regard to criminals is to be maximized, the probability of apprehension and conviction must be high, the certainty of punishment clear, and the process must function without unreasonable delay.

Apprehension is not very likely if police limit their anti-corruption efforts to investigating complaints. Despite the difficulties noted earlier, a strong case can be made for police utilization of all legal means available for ferreting out corruption.

Granting immunity from prosecution to an officer willing to testify against fellow officers—repugnant as this may be to some—is as justified in a corruption proceeding as it is in a proceeding against other forms of crime. This technique, which has come to be known as "turning corrupt officers around," was considered unthinkable in the past. Police administrators argued that it would be intolerable to retain, but to forgo prosecuting, an officer who admitted to having been involved in corruption. It is difficult to separate this concern from an awareness that "turning" a corrupt police officer requires that the agency be prepared to subject itself to publicity that can be markedly damaging to its reputation. Nevertheless, since the Knapp investigation the New York City department has made extensive use of "turned-around" officers to great advantage in its effort to combat corruption.[37]

Using undercover men can be justified if an administrator is willing to share with the public the problems resulting from their employment. Actors have posed as drunks to apprehend officers who remove valuables from a drunk's pocket; accidents have been staged to obtain firsthand evidence of an officer's practice of making referrals to doctors and lawyers; and gambling operations have been simulated to acquire evidence of payoffs in exchange for freedom to operate. Pressures resulting from disclosure of these undercover practices have dissuaded agencies from continuing their use, but the techniques did effectively apprehend guilty officers and serve as a deterrent. The public and police sensed an increased likelihood that the corrupt—be they citizens or police—would be identified and prosecuted.

Many chiefs argue that the extent to which the public and corrupt police fear apprehension is the factor most directly influencing the level of corruption. They further argue that this fear can be greatly increased and the amount of corruption reduced by a single well-publicized investigative effort initiated by the agency in a community where efforts have never been made before. Unfortunately, hard data are unavailable to prove these claims. Sociologists will quickly point out that the relationship between fear of detection and deterrence is much more complex, that corrupt officers and citizens, like other criminal offenders, will respond in varying ways. Yet it is with deterrence in mind rather than the expectation of eliminating corruption that agencies periodically carry out campaigns against various forms of police wrongdoing.

Those who planned the effort to reduce corruption in Chicago in the early 1960s recognized that bribes were commonly offered and accepted for ignoring traffic violations. Some officers obviously were not involved, but although they did not accept bribes they rarely arrested the party offering one. Therefore all personnel were instructed to arrest anyone offering a bribe and to file a special report. A small number of officers immediately complied. The arrests and resulting prosecutions were highly publicized. At the same time the public was urged to report any officer soliciting bribes. A few responded and immediate action was taken.

The mere fact that a relative handful of officers arrested those who offered a bribe and that a few citizens reported bribe solicitations introduced such a high degree of uncertainty into the practice that many people thought it had been greatly reduced. The benefits of this uncertainty were short-lived, however. They gradually diminished as officers and the public probed the effectiveness of the system and concocted methods of avoiding detection.

In the case of the common traffic bribe, the citizen may, through conversation prior to offering a bribe, try to determine if the officer is likely to accept it. Corrupt officers have a variety of gambits. They may restrict solicitation to out-of-town drivers, who are not likely to be aware of current administrative attitudes toward corruption and would be least likely to remain for investigation and prosecution. They may also restrict solicitation to those who depend on their drivers' licenses for their livelihood, knowing that such people have a much greater stake in continuing to drive than in contributing to the integrity of the police force.

All of these considerations make it clear that aggressive action in ferreting out corrupt practices is essential, but that such action will lose its effectiveness unless two conditions are met: (1) enough evidence must be uncovered to remind both police and citizens that action is being taken; and (2) a continuous and aggressive effort must be made to identify new patterns of corruption and the offenders involved in them.

Over a prolonged period of time, deterrent value depends on the certainty that involved citizens and officers will be prosecuted and punished. If a corrupt officer finds the consequences of being caught are minor, or that there is a high probability he can avoid prosecution and disciplinary action, he will have little reason to be deterred.

Speaking of the support a community must provide to police for an effective attack on corruption, Whitman Knapp, the head of the commission appointed to investigate corruption in New York City in 1970, observed:

A police officer who—totally alone and unobserved—is placed in a position where the mere acceptance of a proffered bribe may produce more wealth than an entire year's salary, or in the more usual position where the pressures are more subtle, is entitled to at least three elements of support to fall back upon:

(1) The officer in such situations should be entitled to feel confident that society is so organized that if a bribe be refused and the matter reported to superior officers, there is a reasonable chance that the corruptor will land in jail; on the other hand,

(2) such officer should feel that if he or she yields to temptation there is a reasonable chance that he or she—and any other officer similarly situated—will be apprehended, separated from the force and subjected to criminal prosecution; and, finally and perhaps most importantly,

(3) such officer should be confident that a refusal of the bribe and a report of the corruptor would produce commendation—and not hostility—from his superiors and fellows.[38]

When criminal prosecutions are initiated the acquittal rate is usually high. If there is a finding of guilty, the widespread impression is that penalties tend to be low. Failure to convict or the imposition of modest penalties may be proper dispositions in some cases. They often result, however, from the poor quality of the cases being presented, reluctance to press a prosecution vigorously, or, most serious, corruption of the prosecutors and court. Prosecutors and judges who are themselves corrupt are understandably uncomfortable punishing an officer whose criminal conduct may be less serious than their own. It is in their interest to establish a precedent for treating corruption as an insignificant matter.

Many departments prefer departmental disciplinary procedures to criminal prosecution. Internal action lessens the likelihood of adverse publicity. The standard of proof required in the past has generally been lower than that required in a criminal prosecution. Most important, it avoids the possibility of acquittal in a criminal prosecution, which may be used by the officer as a defense against dismissal. The disciplinary process in many departments, however, suffers problems similar to the criminal process. It is slow, cumbersome, and complex.

External Investigations

In coping with various forms of police wrongdoing other than corruption, the existence of a complainant provides some external pressure. And, as was set forth in the last chapter, so long as some basis and means exist for demanding that an agency conduct an appropriate investigation and provide adequate redress, it is preferable to press the agency into developing its investigative apparatus rather than attempt to do the job for it. The situation relative to corruption, however, differs significantly in that in the most aggravated situations, where corruption is widespread and deeply imbedded, it often takes some form of external investigation to surface enough evidence to pressure an agency to take any action on its own. That is why there appears to be growing support for anti-corruption investigative efforts based outside the police agency.

These investigations have taken four forms: (1) those conducted by specially constituted groups such as the Knapp Commission in New York City and the Pennsylvania Crime Commission in Philadelphia; (2) those conducted by state agencies, such as the state police or the attorney general's office; (3) those conducted by the United States Department of Justice; and (4) those conducted by specially appointed prosecutors such as the one in New York City assigned to ferret out corruption in the entire criminal justice system.

The increased involvement of the federal government is based upon two developments: a broadened interpretation of the Hobbs Anti-Racketeering Act,[39] which prohibits interference with interstate commerce and which has been used to indict police officers who have extorted payoffs from liquor dealers; and enactment of the Organized Crime Control Act of 1970 which, among other things, makes it a federal crime for a state or local official to conspire with another to obstruct the enforcement of the criminal laws of the state or local jurisdiction with intent to facilitate illegal gambling.[40]

Investigations by the federal government and by a specially appointed prosecutor tend to be more acceptable to rank-and-file police personnel than other arrangements because they do not single out the police, but are concerned with a broader segment of governmental activity. (The special commissions need not have been—but were—restricted to investigating the police.) Federal prosecutors in several cities and the special prosecutor in New York City have taken action against local prosecutors and judges as well as the police. These moves against other areas of corruption meet many of the objections police have expressed to external investigative efforts, though, in the case of New York City, they—along with the personality and style of the incumbent—have made the office the center of continuing controversy.

Beyond this factor it is increasingly apparent that an outside agency provides a place where officers can turn if they know their superiors are corrupt or if they have been frustrated by corrupt prosecutors and judges. Honest officers have been much more willing to cooperate with such investigations. That they can often read newspaper accounts of developments that grew out of information they provided adds to the credibility of the agency and reinforces their confidence in it.[41]

External investigations also have proved to be valuable to the police administrator. By airing the true magnitude of the corruption problem in a community, they have helped to create an atmosphere which has justified aggressive action on his part that he may not have been able to take without such disclosures. The pressure generated by these investigations has offset, to some degree, the tendency of police personnel and large segments of the community to characterize the anti-corruption efforts of a police chief as unwarranted attacks upon the reputation and integrity of his subordinates.

It has been argued that there is no need for a special external investigation if the local prosecuting attorney is doing an adequate job. But nationwide experience makes it clear that, because prosecutors are so dependent upon police cooperation in carrying out their daily responsibilities, they cannot afford to offend the police by bringing a prosecution against them in matters relating to corruption any more than they can when faced with evidence of other forms of police wrongdoing.[42] It is only under the most extraordinary circumstances that a prosecutor will aggressively undertake to investigate the police.

Growing recognition of the value of external investigations raises questions as to whether such units should be institutionalized. Should a permanent agency be created at the level of state or local government that would have a continuing responsibility for investigating corruption in criminal justice agencies? Those who oppose such a development argue that much of the effectiveness of recent external investigations has stemmed from their temporary character; that the atrophy that so often accompanies permanent status would make the formally established organization much less effective.

A separate need exists for external investigations designed to serve the limited objective of providing police administrators with a more accurate measure of agency corruption. It would be convenient if such a measure could be taken by survey techniques of the kind discussed in chapter 7, but it is generally assumed that citizens who have direct knowledge of police corruption are not likely to acknowledge its existence in a survey lest they implicate themselves. The most one could expect from a survey would be an indication of the community's perception of the corruption problem, which may be of value in its own right, but which would not disclose the actual incidence of corruption. Thus one is left to resort to actual investigations conducted by people knowledgeable in recognizing the presence and the symptoms of corruption. Such investigations need not acquire the kind of evidence necessary for criminal prosecution. Nor need they be surreptitious.

There are various ways in which the integrity of an agency can be audited by observation and inquiry in the community. A specially developed service could take the form of a state, regional, or national organization staffed by personnel whose advancement depended entirely on their effectiveness and who had no connections with a police agency. Few police administrators are in a sufficiently strong position to request such a service. There is reason to believe, however, that many would subscribe if it were urged upon them—especially if a subscription came to be viewed as a form of certification of the agency's commitment to integrity.

Rewarding the Honest Officer

The honest officer who survives in a corrupt atmosphere is usually quite lonely.[43] The pressures for conformity make it impossible for him to take any action against corruption without recognizing that such action may eventually force him to resign. If an officer does risk being ostracized for reporting corrupt practices, what assurance does he have that his actions will be looked on favorably by his superiors? Will the administrator protect him from the acts of retaliation he can anticipate? What will his position be when top administrators and supervisory staff change? Many competent officers have found that to have reported corruption even once had the effect of permanently impairing their careers. The facts of the situation become obscured over time, but the reputation of having been disloyal remains.

There have been proposals for a system of awards to encourage and recognize a high level of integrity. But formal recognition in an agency riddled with corruption only compounds problems. The honest officer would appreciate most an opportunity to report corruption in a way that does *not* require his testimony or identification. An administrator can make good use of these reports, employing independent forms of investigation to disprove or verify the allegations. An aggressive follow-up will encourage the honest officer and demonstrate the administrator's sincerity. If these leads are pursued vigorously and other efforts aimed at reducing corruption are stressed, the current imbalance that rewards those who are corrupt or remain silent could be significantly altered. Once this occurs it would be much more feasible to introduce a system of awards designed to recognize contributions toward increasing departmental integrity.

REALISTIC GOALS

Corruption is endemic to policing. The very nature of the police function is bound to subject officers to tempting offers. If corruption spreads through an agency it overshadows all other problems as personnel become preoccupied with pursuing personal gain and as the leadership tries to cope with the problem. Solutions, so far, seem inadequate and certainly are not likely to produce permanent results.

Some consider the problem of corruption unsolvable. Given corruption's complexity and the extent to which it is tied to the even larger complexities of human behavior and social disorganization, it is tempting to adopt this posture. Observers who have reviewed past efforts to deal with corruption and who have assessed the situation across the country over a span of years may well be justified in concluding that it is more sensible—and certainly more realistic—to recognize corruption as a problem to be lived with rather than one that can be eradicated.

Police administrators, however, cannot afford the luxury of such a detached viewpoint. Difficult as it has been to stamp out all corruption, it is clear that it can be reduced and, in some specific situations, eliminated. Moreover, it is important that our view of the problem not be restricted to the failures. Many police agencies have had a great deal of success in maintaining the integrity of their personnel.

It follows that police leadership has an obligation to work aggressively toward controlling corruption, however awesome and frustrating the task. The skilled administrator must come to see the problem not as unmentionable, but rather as a natural and expected challenge to his administrative ability. He must explore the feasibility of applying elements of the various solutions that have been proposed, selecting that blend which seems most likely to contribute toward a reduction in corruption in his community.

An essential first step for the administrator is to explore the problem thoroughly, both independently and with fellow administrators. A much more open exchange of views, experiences, and ideas is greatly needed. Such an exchange could result in the development of more effective techniques for coping with the problem. It could result in the development of new forms of support for the administrator who must deal with it. It could also result in the launching of new research efforts and experiments aimed at gaining greater insight into the problem than is currently available.

NOTES

1. See James Q. Wilson, "The Police and Their Problems: A Theory," *Public Policy* 12 (1963): 189.

2. It is sometimes helpful to recognize that if the members of a medium-sized or large police agency and their families lived in a community of their own, the community would surely experience some crime and have need for its own police force.

3. "P.B.A. Head Says Murphy Is Destroying Police Force," *New York Times*, 3 September 1971.

4. President's Commission on Law Enforcement and Administration of Justice, *Task Force Report: The Police* (Washington, D.C.: Government Printing Office, 1967), p. 148.

5. An exception, of course, is where the administrator is himself corrupt, in which case he may exert unusually tight control over departmental operations in order to avoid detection and assure continuance of his ability to deliver on corrupt agreements.

6. Sandy Smith, "You Can't Expect Police on the Take to Take Orders," *Life*, 6 December 1968, p. 40.

7. The last point, however, has been questioned by some. It is often pointed out that some of the most corrupt agencies did the best job when called upon to handle large-scale disorders and massive crowds in recent years. A number of suggestions have been made to account for this seeming paradox: an overestimate of the importance that organization, discipline, and supervision play in the handling of such incidents; the practice of some agencies to organize new units that quickly develop an esprit de corps that compensates for weaknesses in the larger organization and provides the needed unity and coordination; or the possibility that police officers rise to the challenge of public disorders to redeem themselves in the eyes of a public which suspects them of corruption.

8. Frank Serpico, the corruption-fighting New York policeman, observed

that the corrupt officers he knew were often first-class investigators who would have been highly effective in coping with crime if they had spent their time doing police work instead of pursuing graft. Peter Maas, *Serpico* (New York: Viking Press, 1973), p. 169.

9. In 1973 the Police Foundation arranged to receive clippings of newspaper articles about police corruption from across the country. In a period of two months, clippings were received from thirty states. They reported on alleged corruption in small cities, sheriffs' offices, state police forces, and suburban departments. The reports reflected the full range of corrupt practices discussed in this chapter.

10. Virtually every study of police corruption has reached this conclusion. See William F. Whyte, *Street Corner Society* (Chicago: University of Chicago Press, 1943), p. 138; John A. Gardiner, *The Politics of Corruption* (New York: Russell Sage Foundation, 1970); New York City Commission to Investigate Allegations of Police Corruption and the City's Anti-Corruption Procedures, *Commission Report* (Whitman Knapp, Chairman) (New York: Bar Press, 1972) (hereafter cited as *Knapp Commission Report*); James F. Richardson, *The New York Police* (New York: Oxford University Press, 1970). These studies fail, however, to account for the situation where a police agency has been notably upgraded while the general community atmosphere and political structure have remained ostensibly unchanged. Why reform has succeeded in some cities, but not in others, has not been adequately studied.

11. *Knapp Commission Report*, p. 4.

12. Ibid., p. 65.

13. For an analysis of the relationship between corruption and the responsibility of the police for the enforcement of laws against vice in the history of policing in this country, see Lincoln Steffens, *The Shame of the Cities* (New York: McClure-Phillips, 1904); Arthur Woods, *Policeman and Public* (1919; reprint ed., New York: Arno Press, 1971), pp. 110–134; August Vollmer, *The Police and Modern Society* (1936; reprint ed., Montclair, N.J.: Patterson Smith, 1971), pp. 81–118; Albert Deutsch, *The Trouble with Cops* (New York: Crown Publishers, 1955), pp. 75–95; Jonathan Rubinstein, *City Police* (New York: Farrar, Straus and Giroux, 1973), pp. 372–433.

14. There have recently been several interesting efforts to categorize the various forms of police corruption. See, e.g., Julian B. Roebuck and Thomas Barker, "A Typology of Police Corruption," *Social Problems* 21 (1974): 423–437.

15. *Knapp Commission Report*, pp. 67–68; Rubinstein, *City Police*, pp. 394–398.

16. Such a system was recently documented in the federal prosecution of two district commanders in the Chicago Police Department. It was established that $275,000 was collected from thirty tavern owners in a period of four years. "Fired Cop Pleads Guilty to Payoffs," *Chicago Tribune*, 5 February 1974. And in New York City the special prosecutor investigating police corruption, with the cooperation of the New York City Police Department, recently indicted a club of ten sergeants who were alleged to have collected more than $250,000 in a decade. "10 Police Sergeants Held As Graft 'Club' Members," *New York Times*, 9 August 1974. Later in the same year the commissioner of police in New York dismissed nineteen officers who shared in $240,000 in annual payoffs for pro-

tecting a multimillion-dollar-a-year gambling operation. "Codd Dismisses 19 as Bribe-Takers," *New York Times*, 19 November 1974.

17. *Knapp Commission Report*, p. 74.

18. For a journalistic treatment of similar systems outside of New York City, see Ralph Smith, *The Tarnished Badge* (New York: Thomas Y. Crowell, 1965); and Robert H. Williams, *Vice Squad* (New York: Thomas Y. Crowell, 1973).

19. On overcriminalization, see notably Herbert L. Packer, *The Limits of the Criminal Sanction* (Palo Alto, Calif.: Stanford University Press, 1968), and Williams, *Vice Squad*. On organized crime, see Gardiner, *The Politics of Corruption*; Donald R. Cressey, *Theft of the Nation* (New York: Harper & Row, 1969), pp. 187–195. On local government, see Gardiner, *The Politics of Corruption*; Arnold J. Heidenheimer, ed., *Political Corruption: Readings in Comparative Analysis* (New York: Holt, Rinehart and Winston, 1970). For the personal accounts of police administrators, see, e.g., James C. Parsons, "A Candid Analysis of Police Corruption," *Police Chief*, March 1973, p. 20; Patrick V. Murphy, "Address [Police Corruption]," in *The Police Yearbook: Papers and Proceedings of the Eightieth Annual Conference of the International Association of Chiefs of Police, Inc.* (Gaithersburg, Md.: International Association of Chiefs of Police, Inc., 1974), pp. 28–32.

20. For a description of liquor-related corruption in Philadelphia, see Pennsylvania Crime Commission, *Report on Police Corruption and the Quality of Law Enforcement in Philadelphia* (Saint Davids, Pa.: Pennsylvania Crime Commission, 1974); and Rubinstein, *City Police*, pp. 419–429.

21. Rubinstein, in his observations of police operations in Philadelphia, claims policemen see themselves as "operating in a world where 'notes' are constantly floating about, and only the stupid, the naive, and the fainthearted are unwilling to allow some of them to stick to their fingers." Rubinstein, *City Police*, p. 400.

22. Sherman describes another dimension of this addiction, a gradual escalation to more serious forms of corruption as officers make the psychological adjustment by which they rationalize their behavior. See Lawrence W. Sherman, "Becoming Bent: Moral Careers of Corrupt Policemen," in *Police Corruption*, ed. Lawrence W. Sherman (Garden City, N.Y.: Anchor Press, 1974), pp. 191–208.

23. Ironically, however, some agencies tend to concentrate on these minor offenses to the exclusion of more serious forms of corruption. This may be attributable to a desire to demonstrate anti-corruption activity without actually interfering with the more profitable forms of corruption.

24. "Police Aides Told to Rid Commands of All Dishonesty," *New York Times*, 29 October 1970.

25. For an interesting journalistic investigation of this common problem, see a series of articles in the *Milwaukee Journal*, August 18 through August 22, 1974, about methods used to sell advertising for magazines published in the name of various law enforcement and firemen's groups.

26. Leon Radzinowitz, *A History of English Criminal Law and Its Administration from 1750*, 4 vols. (New York: Macmillan, 1956), 2: 57–138, 239–244.

27. See, e.g., the regulations of the Oakland, California, Police Department cited in President's Commission on Law Enforcement and Administration of Justice, *Task Force Report: The Police*, p. 213.

28. For a journalistic account of the reluctance of a jury to believe a prosti-

tute who had been subjected to extortion by a vice officer, see Nicholas Pileggi and Mike Pearl, "What Happens When Cops Get Caught?" *New York Magazine*, 23 July 1973, pp. 23–29.

29. The most famous case in recent years involves officers Frank Serpico and David Durk of the New York City Police Department, who could get no one to investigate their allegations of corruption except the news media. See *Knapp Commission Report*, pp. 196–204.

30. Officer William Phillips, a turn-around witness for the Knapp Commission, was branded a "rogue cop" by the police commissioner.

31. A campaign launched by Commissioner Patrick Murphy in New York City to arrest those attempting to bribe police officers resulted in increasing the number of arrests from 56 in 1969 to 670 in 1972.

32. Wilson, "The Police and Their Problems," p. 204, points out that this phenomenon shows the extent to which the public perceives policemen as an organization rather than a profession. The misconduct of one policeman is often sufficient to bring the entire department under suspicion. The misconduct of one doctor rarely discredits others in the medical profession.

33. See *Knapp Commission Report*, pp. 132 and 263; and Sherman, "Becoming Bent," pp. 185–203.

34. See Raymond B. Fosdick, *American Police Systems* (1920; reprint ed., Montclair, N.J.: Patterson Smith, 1969), pp. 249–267, for one of the early statements of a theme that has become one of the basic tenets of the professional movement among police.

35. For an account of the consideration given to corruption in training programs, see Arthur Niederhoffer, *Behind the Shield* (Garden City, N.J.: Doubleday & Co., 1967), pp. 43–54; and William A. Westley, *Violence and the Police* (Cambridge, Mass.: MIT Press, 1970), p. 155.

36. New training methods, such as role playing, are now being employed by the Oakland, California, and New York City departments to give recruits a better sense of the temptations and pressures to which they will be subjected. For a description of an "integrity workshop," see Edward Doyle and George Olivet, "An Invitation to Understanding: Workshop in Law Enforcement Integrity," *Police Chief*, May 1972, p. 34.

37. See "Bribe-Taking Policemen Help Catch Officers," *New York Times*, 28 October 1973.

38. *Knapp Commission Report*, p. 278.

39. 18 *U.S.C.* § 1951.

40. 18 *U.S.C.* § 1511. In addition, the 1970 act provides for the establishment of special grand juries to investigate misconduct, malfeasance, or misfeasance involving organized criminal activity by an appointed public officer or employee and establishes certain reporting procedures when such misconduct is discovered. 18 *U.S.C.* § 3333. For a detailed and comprehensive examination of the legal basis for the rapidly increasing role of the federal government in the investigation of local police corruption, see Herbert Beigel, "The Investigation and Prosecution of Police Corruption," *Journal of Criminal Law and Criminology* 65 (1974): 135–156.

41. For an interesting case study of a situation in which many of the benefits of an external investigation were achieved by a team of newspaper reporters aided by twenty-eight police officers, see the *Indianapolis Star*, starting with the issue of February 24, 1974.

42. The Pennsylvania Crime Commission is the most recent group to reach this conclusion. For their analysis of the district attorney's conflict of interests, see Pennsylvania Crime Commission, *Report on Police Corruption*, pp. 807–819.

43. For a classic case, see Maas, *Serpico*.

Chapter 9

Developing Critically Needed Leadership

Recognition of the full magnitude and complexity of police functioning and the many conflicts inherent in it requires rethinking many of the traditional recommendations for improving police operations. In this and the following two chapters, three areas on which recommendations have concentrated will be examined: strengthening the leadership of the field, upgrading the quality of police personnel, and, as it relates to both leadership and personnel, higher education. New programs in these areas will be fruitful only if they acknowledge the realities of police work and confront the problems that have been discussed in the preceding chapters.

THE DEMANDS OF LEADERSHIP

The police administrator is a much more important figure in the overall structure of government than is commonly recognized. He is constantly being called upon to formulate policies that require the balancing of fundamental and often conflicting values. His decisions directly affect the quality of life in his community. Moreover, it is the police administrator upon whom we depend most heavily to take the initiative in solving the many problems that plague the police and that reduce their capacity to provide quality services to the public. Responsible leadership of the highest caliber is essential if needed change is to be carried out.

Until recently, relatively little effort has been made to define the qualities deemed essential for a police leader. Developing such a definition is complicated by that fact that "police leadership" includes people with widely differing responsibilities. Police agencies range in size from those having a few part-time employees to those having thousands of officers. Yet the head of each is considered a leader. When police chiefs from all over the country assemble, the convention is commonly referred to as a gathering of the country's police leadership. But in many respects the captain or lieutenant of police in a big city who has a large number of subordinates and a sizable community to police carries a much heavier responsibility than the chief of an agency having five or ten employees. Those filling middle-management positions in large police agencies are very much a part of the police leadership in this country. This is not to say that leading a small agency is a simple task. Small agencies have problems that differ in kind as well as magnitude from those of larger agencies.

Even among jurisdictions of equal size, however, widely different criteria have been employed in assessing police leadership. To some, police leadership connotes the ability to lead a group of officers under dangerous circumstances. A police commander who bravely takes charge of his subordinates and, under threat of gunfire, rescues an individual being held hostage often is viewed as epitomizing the highest leadership qualities. Such ability has in fact been a major factor in the selection of police chiefs in this country, although there is no reason to think that because a person possesses physical courage he also has the capacity to take on the burdensome and intellectually demanding tasks that the chief's job usually entails.

To others, leadership connotes the ability to achieve a high level of operating efficiency. Police agencies have long suffered from grossly inefficient management. This condition is in large measure a result of incompetent leadership. So it is understandable that many communities have sought police administrators who are skilled in management—in the ability to reorganize a police agency, streamline procedures, reallocate manpower, reduce paperwork, and improve facilities and equipment.

The most ambitious and most formal effort to establish key factors to be considered in the hiring of a police leader is the study completed in 1976 by the Los Angeles Police Department for a committee of the International Association of Chiefs of Police under a grant from LEAA. Opinions were solicited from 1,665 individuals who are currently chief executives of police agencies and from 806 individuals to whom these executives report. The firmest conclusions of the study were also the broadest: all candidates for a top position in an agency should have personal integrity, honesty, good judgment, and common sense. With less consensus, the study recommended that an appointing authority consider such qualities as "flexibility and openmindedness, alertness and intelligence, patience and self-control, energy and initiative, and courage and self-confidence." In assessing past performance, the study recommended that consideration be given to the candidate's demonstrated ability to "motivate personnel; develop subordinates into effective teams; relate to the community; organize personnel and their functions effectively; administer internal discipline; and establish and communicate objectives and priorities."[1]

The emphasis placed on administrative skills draws attention to the fact that administration is commonly equated with leadership. But in reality, the ability to administer well is just a first step toward achieving a broader concept of leadership. In his classic work on leadership, Philip Selznick captures well the situation commonly found in the police field in which good management has become an end in itself and the ultimate objective of the police chief:

> There is a strong tendency not only in administrative life but in all social action to divorce means and ends by overemphasizing one or the other. The cult of efficiency in administrative theory and practice is a modern way of overstressing means and neglecting ends. This it does in two ways. First, by fixing attention on maintaining a smooth-running machine, it slights the more basic and more difficult problem of defining and safeguarding the ends of an enterprise. Second, the cult of efficiency tends to stress techniques of organization that are essentially neutral, and therefore available for any goals, rather than methods peculiarly adapted to a distinctive type of organization or stage of development.
>
> Efficiency as an operating ideal presumes that goals are settled and the main resources and methods for achieving them are available. The problem is then one of joining available means to known ends. This order of decision-making, we have called *routine*, distinguishing it from the realm of *critical* decision. The latter, because it involves choices that affect the basic character of the enterprise, is the true province of leadership as distinct from administrative management. . . .[2]

Selznick defines responsible leadership as a blend of commitment, understanding, and determination; as requiring, among other things, setting goals which prevent the institution from drifting; enunciating governing principles; and developing stable relationships with the community of which the organization is a part.[3]

As applied to the police field, this means that a police administrator must be fully aware of the sensitive and delicate nature of the police function. It means that he must attach a high value to protecting constitutional guarantees of free speech, due process, and freedom from unreasonable search and seizure. He must fully appreciate the need for various systems to assure accountability on the part of the police to the body politic. He must be knowledgeable regarding the legislative process, the functioning of the criminal justice system, and the operation of the various other systems which the police employ. He must be well informed about different categories of deviant conduct, the range of behavioral problems of concern to the police, and the dynamics of the various political and social movements in our society. And he must be conversant with the major issues of current public interest that involve the police and be articulate in discussing them in the public forum.

Beyond these basic requirements, a leader in the police field is often expected to rescue an agency that has been drifting without clear objectives and principles for years. He is the central figure in any attempts to effect significant changes in the organization and staffing of the agency and in the form of services it provides. This requires a great deal more than traditional managerial skill. He must be aware of the need for change and committed to achieving it. He must be open, challenging, curious, and innovative. He must be sufficiently confident of his capacity and sufficiently secure in his position to take risks and to conduct experiments. He must be unflagging in his determination. And he must have a masterful capacity to relate well to the various elements that comprise his community so as to win support for his programs, and an equally effective ability to relate to his own personnel, eliciting their best performance and coordinating their efforts toward his preestablished goals.

And if this were not enough, the field itself—beyond simply the agencies—requires new forms of leadership which quite naturally become the responsibility of its top administrators. Ideally the combined leadership of the police field would contribute toward developing a "theory of policing" by taking an active role in addressing some of the complex issues discussed in the earlier chapters. What should be the position of the police with regard to their function? With regard to the uses made of the criminal law? With regard to the recognition of discretion? What should their posture be on such issues as achieving political accountability and effective control of police conduct? Strong leadership would address these issues; would take the initiative in conducting research; would encourage innovation and experimentation; and would acknowledge the need for some risk-taking. Put most simply, the police field must—in developing its leadership—develop its own thinkers as well.

INADEQUACIES IN POLICE LEADERSHIP

The record of this country in providing the police with qualified leaders is, on the whole, a poor one. In the conclusion to his study of the police in 1920, Raymond Fosdick reported that he found "a shifting leadership of mediocre calibre—varied now and then by flashes of real ability which are snuffed out when the political wheel turns."[4] In 1931 the Wickersham Commission pointed to incompetent leadership as the primary cause of inefficient policing.[5]

Writing in 1949, Bruce Smith reached similar conclusions, but he observed that a mere handful of able administrators had, over the prior twenty years, put police service on a new basis.[6] Leaning heavily on their performance, he optimistically heralded a new era in police administration. Much of this progress was attributable to the efforts of one man, August Vollmer, and to the economic depression in the early thirties which attracted an unusually high number of competent people into police employment. Many of the existing strengths in the police field can be traced back to this period.

A new kind of police administrator did emerge from the Vollmer era who brought to the police field a high level of managerial skill. These men created the professional model which has been upheld until recently as the solution to all the problems of the police. Police agencies were reorganized and their operating efficiency was vastly improved. Some of these administrators succeeded in eliminating wholesale corruption. Under their guidance subordinates were groomed who possessed many of the same managerial abilities. Where these men differed from August Vollmer was in their rather narrow perspective. Vollmer himself was as comfortable and as confident exploring the role of the police in our society as he was in setting out the most detailed police operating procedure; as interested and conversant in the theories of criminality as he was in investigating the activities of an alleged pickpocket; and as desirous of discussing the value of the criminal sanction as a control over victimless crime as he was in contributing toward the development of an improved system for counting crimes.[7]

It took the events and especially the turbulence of the past decade to focus attention on the need for police officials with Vollmer's ability, who would understand and be capable of dealing with much more than the intricacies of good management, who would understand the dynamics of social conflict, the basic principles of democratic government, and the contradictory pressures which the police must somehow balance in their operations.

Given the absence of any concerted effort to prepare police leadership for this role, the really amazing thing—as noted in chapter 1—is that so many police administrators responded so well to the crises that occurred. Some of them demonstrated far more sensitivity and understanding of current social problems than did many mayors, university and school administrators, and other public officials. Admittedly they were often motivated by a very pragmatic concern for dealing with threatening conditions, but a number of these men exhibited a strong commitment to the principles of equality and freedom of expression that were often at stake. They undertook a variety of ambitious programs, often in the face of great resistance and under emergency-like conditions, to prevent further violence, to facilitate legitimate protest, and to rectify weaknesses in their agencies. Unfortunately some of those who accomplished the most and won national recognition for their enlightened leadership of the police field also suffered so much in the crossfire of criticism from the community and from their own personnel that they either resigned or took an early retirement.

This situation draws attention to the precipitous drop often found in the quality of leadership within an agency. It is rare to find an enlightened police leader whose immediate subordinates approach him in competence. This lack of depth in the quality of leadership supports the contention that the most highly qualified police administrators are "accidents" rather than the natural products of the system by which they came into office. If the system were working effectively, there would not be so big a gap. Competent subordinates would not only be available to advance into more responsible positions, their presence would also enable the top administrator to implement his policies with a greater chance of success.

Another consequence of the recent pressures on the police has been the emergence of a still newer kind of police administrator, one who is particularly cognizant of the issues of the day but who is noticeably lacking in managerial skills. This failing would not, by itself, be fatal if such leaders had staff who were equipped to fill the vacuum. But since managerial skill is usually in short supply, the innovative potential of such chiefs has been severely limited. Their concepts are not effectively translated into programs.

There has been no systematic effort to assess the quality of police leadership in recent years, and most critics of the police have been extremely guarded in their comments on the subject. The President's Commission on Law Enforcement and Administration of Justice criticized promotion procedures and observed that numerous studies had found that police forces were, with some notable exceptions, poorly organized and managed.[8] The National Advisory Commission on Criminal Justice Standards and Goals placed all of its emphasis upon the need for programs to improve leadership, from which we can only infer that they concluded current leadership is inadequate.[9] Patrick V. Murphy recently stated that "the police, to improve, will require better leadership than is currently provided by closed civil service systems."[10] James F. Ahern, the former chief of police of New Haven, observed:

> Officers who have worked their way up through police-department ranks to become assistant chiefs, chief inspectors, and captains find themselves in middle-management positions in multimillion-dollar enterprises without the training, and often without the inclination, to handle management and planning problems. In most police departments ranking officers have become clerks or petty bureaucrats by default.[11]

And in arguing that the police are unusually vulnerable to political influence, he noted: "Above the cop on the beat there is a vacuum of true leadership that exists in few other professions."[12] A. C. Germann is most blunt. He asserts:

> Police leadership decisions, today, tend to preserve the status quo and enshrine the archaic. Somehow, in the police establishment, leadership must be developed that is open, willing to listen, willing to question, willing to experiment, and willing to change even the most revered attitude or practice. Most current police leadership does not have the breadth of vision, perspective or motivation to do what must be done. . . .[13]

The costs of having made inadequate provision for police leadership are plainly apparent as one views the overall status of policing in the United States. Many police agencies tend to drift from day to day. They respond excessively to outside pressures; they resort to temporary expedients; they take comfort in technical achievements over substantive accomplishments; their internal procedures become stagnant, cumbersome, and inefficient; and they seem incapable of responding innovatively to new demands and new requirements. But perhaps the greatest cost is the strikingly defensive posture that police leaders, operating under these conditions, commonly assume.

Because of the problems that have accrued and have grown more complicated for lack of adequate attention, top police administrators must spend much of their time defending the agency from attack. The ability to do so has become a valued skill in its own right. Thus a segment of current police leadership has been selected in part because of its special ability to defend the agency, rather than to lead it.

Few things are quite so inimical to improvement in the police field as the personable, attractive, articulate, and perhaps colorful police official whose strongest qualification for heading a police agency consists in his ability to fend off all attacks made upon it. Behind him, untouched by his administration, one can usually find all of the complicated problems common to policing— not only festering from lack of attention, but aggravated by the negative and regressive administrative style that a defensive chief tends to employ.

In its most institutionalized and worst form, a defensive posture results in subordinate administrators and supervisors also being selected with an eye to their loyalty to the agency and their ability to defend the agency from outside attack. This includes the ability to cover up mistakes; to suppress evidence of wrongdoing; to placate complainants and pressure groups without necessarily solving underlying problems; and to devise various informal accommodations and adjustments in operating procedures in order to meet the most pressing needs of the moment. The rewards in such an organization are reserved for those who "don't rock the boat" and who stay out of trouble. And the most vigorous discipline tends to be directed against those members whose actions subject the agency to criticism from the outside.

FACTORS ACCOUNTING FOR THE LACK
OF ADEQUATE LEADERS

There is no need to dig deeply for an explanation of our failure to develop a reservoir of competent leadership in the police field. This country has tenaciously clung to the concept that leadership of a police agency should be drawn not only from within the police field, but from within the agency, and yet no provisions have been made to assure that police agencies systematically produce people with the requisite qualifications for leadership. Worse still, the citizenry and the police together have stubbornly adhered to provisions governing recruitment and promotion of police personnel that appear to have the opposite effect. These provisions stymie the natural processes that contribute to the development of competent leadership. And they discourage highly qualified people from entering police service, with the result that the police field has failed to obtain anything approaching its proper share of intelligent, imaginative, and dedicated individuals. Indeed, if one set out to design a system to prevent and discourage the police from developing their own leadership capability, it would be difficult to come up with a more sure-fire scheme than that which currently exists.

Leadership Potential Not a Factor
in Initial Recruitment

Any agency that restricts itself to selecting its leaders from within faces a basic dilemma. The criteria used in hiring and in promotion—if they are carefully related to the specific duties to be performed—may exclude those people who possess the characteristics most needed at the head of the agency. Police agencies in this country do not recruit with an eye to attracting personnel who have the potential for leadership. Recruiting efforts are generally geared to locating and attracting people who, according to the standards of the particular agency, will function well at the entry level. It follows, therefore, that whatever capacity these people may have for leadership is purely fortuitous. Yet it is from these recruits that the chiefs and their immediate subordinates are drawn.

One can argue that there is probably as much latent leadership ability in a group of police recruits as there is in a cross section of the population. But many individuals who possess characteristics most needed in police leaders are dissuaded from entering the field because they conclude, on brief inquiry, that their chances for making use of their potential are extremely limited. Moreover, the criteria commonly employed in the selection of new officers from among those who do apply often screen out those who have leadership qualities. In many jurisdictions the applicant who appears to be thoughtful and imaginative, for example, and who questions the performance of the police in the past, will be passed over in favor of the applicant who demonstrates a willingness to conform with and support the existing police structure. As a consequence the reservoir from which the community and the police administrator can draw when filling key positions is not as large as it could be. Nevertheless, the police ranks are not devoid of individuals with the capacity for leadership; but we do not do enough to identify these individuals and afford them an opportunity to use their ability before they lose their incentive to lead or become discouraged and leave the service for some other occupation.

Ineffective and Cumbersome Promotion Procedures

How we go about identifying and grooming the limited number of officers at the bottom who have the potential to rise to the top can be seen in the procedures for promoting personnel: in the criteria that are employed, the selection system itself, and the training provided for those assuming broader responsibilities.[14]

Personnel officers in the past relied heavily on examinations based on textbooks covering various aspects of policing. They apparently did so on the assumption that these were authoritative sources for the best administrative practices and policies. In some jurisdictions officers were actually given a list of the books on which an examination would be based. And in order to grade examinations objectively, the examiners tended to solicit specific answers provided in the texts. Indeed, because of the frequency with which grading practices were challenged, some examiners cited in their questions the source to which they would turn for the correct answer. The whole process was further restricted because the examiner's selection of topics to be covered was heavily influenced by a stereotyped notion of policing, rather than an intimate familiarity with the nature of the police function and, specifically, with the requirements for leadership in a police agency.

Under these circumstances the ability of an officer to score on the examination depended upon his reading of the texts. And the officer who could cite from such sources by rote clearly had an advantage. The system has given rise to several sizable businesses that sell materials—in the form of questions and answers based on specific texts—designed to coach officers preparing for examinations. Although much can be criticized in the police field, few practices seem more abhorrent and wasteful of human effort than requiring police officers to commit to memory vast amounts of minutiae regarding functions, policies, and procedures that are often foreign to their work and have little relevance to the job to which they aspire.

Another serious limitation of the examination process has been the tendency to measure past performance rather than attempt to assess future potential. The examination for sergeant, for example, was much more likely to measure an officer's performance as an officer than his capacity to assume the responsibilities of a sergeant. So, perhaps unwittingly, many police agencies and civil service systems have used the promotion system primarily to reward what they conceived to be good performance rather than as a means for identifying those who are capable of performing at a higher level in the organization. While past performance is obviously a strong indicator of future capabilities, it is by no means the exclusive measure. A person may make an excellent officer, but a very poor sergeant. Each level of responsibility in a police agency requires a new set of qualifications. This is essentially the same point Fosdick made some fifty-five years ago when, in commenting on the qualifications for a police chief, he observed:

> The officer who has walked his beat as a patrolman, investigated crime as a detective, and managed the technical routine of stationhouse activity as lieutenant or captain, is not fitted by this experience to administer the complex affairs of a large police department.[15]

The practices cited here are still commonly employed. Recently, however, under pressure generated by court suits claiming past examinations were racially biased, a major effort has been made to ensure that examinations are more job related. This has forced abandonment of some of the worst practices of the past, but it has posed even more clearly the dilemma created when an examination for patrol officer or for sergeant also determines who shall be the future captains, inspectors, and chiefs of police. While a well-designed job-related examination is an enormous improvement over those used in the past, it could be so narrowly constructed that it would screen out individuals with leadership ability. The person with such ability may not excel, for example, in mastering the detailed operating procedures that a sergeant—as the first-line supervisor—must know.

Objective written examinations, past and current, test the capacity of a police officer to repeat knowledge and principles developed by others. They reveal little about the officer himself: how he views the nature of the police function, how he relates to others, and the degree to which he is familiar with the major problems and issues in the field. Yet these are probably the most important areas to be explored in screening for new leadership. Such information can only be obtained by evaluating written answers to open-ended questions, through interview, or by observation, all of which are highly subjective processes. Yet in most police departments, open-ended questions are not used on written tests and only a small percentage of the score on promotion examinations has been based upon interviews or performance ratings. And where interviews and performance ratings are used, the quality of both leaves much to be desired.

Performance rating, like most subjective evaluation, is a two-edged sword. It provides greater opportunity for appraising important qualifications, but its value depends on the individuals making the judgments. And since these are usually the officer's immediate superiors, it should come as no surprise that the highest scores go to those who most closely mirror the qualifications and orientation of the existing leadership. So where the process works in this manner and where the results of the subjective evaluation have a significant bearing upon final scores, the quality of existing leadership is almost automatically perpetuated. And, sadly, the officer with real promise of leadership may go unrecognized. Because the interview process and the performance-rating system are often so poor, there is pressure to abandon them in favor of testing exclusively by objective written examination, when in fact they should be improved and given greater weight. Admittedly, this is no easy chore. Those who have been attempting to develop techniques for evaluating leadership potential have found it extremely difficult to design a system that accurately measures this quality and at the same time guards against favoritism and is free of cultural bias.

Further complicating the promotion process in many cities is the practice of awarding grade points for seniority in the agency, seniority in rank, and veteran's preference. Thus, even if the examination procedure itself results in a ranking of candidates based upon their leadership qualifications, the ranking is subsequently revised as a result of factors that may be irrelevant or weighted out of proportion to their importance. The problem is particularly acute in large agencies where the cumulative score of one candidate may differ from another by only hundredths of a point, so that tacked-on points for such reasons as seniority determine who is promoted and who is not.

All the defects of the promotion system are further compounded because it frequently operates at an incredibly slow pace. The aspiring officer must first await the creation of vacancies through deaths or retirements. Even with vacancies, years may elapse between examinations, and those who take them may have to wait a long time for the results. Legal battles over the validity of the scoring process and over the ranking of those who took the examination have tied up the entire system in some cities—accounting for still further delays. Under such conditions it can readily be seen why competent and highly motivated police officers become discouraged. They tend to leave police service while they still have time to start another career, or they simply resign themselves to remaining at their existing rank in the organization. The net result is that the already limited reservoir of leadership potential is reduced still further.

Lack of Training for New Responsibilities

In 1919, Arthur Woods, police commissioner of New York City, said:

> In American cities there is no special course of training for officers of higher grades. They have all been patrolmen, have all risen from the ranks, and they are given no special preparation for the duty of the higher rank. All they know of it is what they have observed from below. A patrolman who is promoted to sergeant, for instance, has never had training in the duties of the sergeant, as distinguished from those of the patrolmen. He has never been taught how to get the best out of men under his command, how to lead, to control, to inspire. He knows nothing of the higher job except what he has observed while, as patrolman, he came in more or less frequent contact with sergeants,—and the principal thing he learned about the sergeant was how to avoid him. . . .[16]

In 1968, some fifty years later, the International Association of Chiefs of Police reported that only 21 percent of 276 agencies surveyed had mandatory training for all officers promoted to higher responsibilities, and this ranged from programs lasting for 2 hours to programs lasting 160 hours—the length of the programs being of significance only as an indication of their variety and not their quality.[17] Most of these programs were devoted to refreshing the officer's knowledge of the fundamental elements of policing. And almost all were offered after, rather than before, an officer assumed his new responsibilities.

The situation has improved since the IACP survey. Ten states and some individual agencies now require training prior to promotion or within one year of promotion.[18] And the summary of personnel-development activities compiled by the National Advisory Commission on Criminal Justice Standards and Goals contains an impressive list of programs implemented by police agencies.[19] These efforts, however, are often seriously limited by available funds and currently reach but a very small percentage of the total number of people who need training. Such department-initiated programs are, moreover, still very much in the exploration and development stages. Few programs come near—in their size, length, and content—to covering what is necessary to equip an officer for the responsibilities of leadership in an agency and in the field.

In the absence of effective programs, many agencies have sent selected members of their staffs to one or more of the established police training schools, such as the FBI National Academy, the Northwestern Traffic Institute, and the Southern Police Institute. These institutions have made major changes in their programs in recent years. The FBI National Academy, for example, used to dwell on subject matter that, in the opinion of many, was more suitable for recruit training. The academy has broadened its course offerings, dropped much of its technical training, and strengthened its faculty.

One can of course take issue with the orientation of these schools, with the manner in which material is covered, and with the format that often results in uniform instruction being given to personnel drawn from large agencies and small, state and municipal, rural and urban. And yet it must be recognized that in the many years in which the police field itself did almost nothing to develop its own leadership, these schools sought to provide training for police administrators. Their sponsors, who can see and count their graduates, understandably take pride in their claims about the contributions their programs have made in improving the quality of police leadership. But even these programs, in their content, duration, and number of students enrolled, have filled but a small portion of the total need.

It is partly in response to the sensed need for additional training and education for those going into leadership positions that police agencies have increasingly turned to the nation's colleges. This development and its potential impact are examined in chapter 11.

Limitations on Lateral Movement
Of all the factors that have stifled the development of police leadership, none has had as devastating an impact as the laws and traditions that restrict the movement of an officer from one agency into a position of increased responsibility in another.[20] The President's Commission on Law Enforcement and Administration of Justice noted:

> Under existing police structures, nearly all local enforcement agencies restrict advanced appointments to personnel within the department. The only exception to this restriction is that some departments exempt the position of chief administrator from Civil Service, and it is possible for persons who are not in the department to compete for this position. A consequence is that America's police personnel are virtually frozen into the departments in which they started.[21]

Relatively few of the communities that have the right to do so select police chiefs from outside their police departments. Community sentiments for appointment from within are generally strong even though the overall record of achievement of police administrators brought in from outside is an impressive one.

This limitation on lateral movement has had far-reaching consequences for the police field. It has contributed, in one way or another, to each of the major problems discussed in chapters 6, 7, and 8 of this book. The most direct impact of the limitation, however, has been on the quality of police leadership.

First, as was indicated earlier, the competent officer who does not attain a position of leadership is denied the opportunity to market his talents elsewhere. His failure to progress in his own agency may result from a style and from principles that are inimical to his superiors or to the particular community. Or it may result from ineffective promotion procedures or a surplus of talent. The officer in a small agency is especially limited even though his capacity for leadership may equal or exceed that of men in responsible positions in larger agencies. Given the scarcity of administrative talent, it is tragic that experienced police personnel who demonstrate leadership potential cannot be placed in positions where they can make use of their abilities. Despite all that has been said about the absence of adequate leadership in the police field, there exists a substantial cadre of police personnel who have exceptional qualifications, but who simply have not had an adequate opportunity to make use of their abilities. Additionally, many highly qualified individuals who have contemplated a career in the police field and have been willing to enter at the lowest level have been discouraged from doing so by the realization that their potential for advancement would be limited to the agency in which they were initially employed.

Second, the municipality that desires to increase the competence of its police leadership is denied the most obvious method for doing so. Although municipal officials may conclude that their police agency does not have a single officer qualified to fill the top position, or a chief may conclude that none of his subordinates is capable of filling the positions directly under him, the municipality often must select from among the unqualified. The best-intentioned administrator cannot elicit desperately needed leadership and administrative performance from subordinates who, through perhaps no fault of their own, can neither lead nor administer.

Third, the absence of opportunities for lateral movement stifles innovation and creativity and builds a low ceiling above which the quality of police leadership rarely rises. We have ample indications in other professions and occupational groups that competition in an open job market rewards competence and results in steadily increasing levels of performance. The administrator who does well in one situation is invited to take on heavier responsibilities. And if a job restricts his opportunities for development and growth he need not stagnate with it; he can seek another position. It is interesting to reflect on what the status of the fields of education and public health might be today if superintendents of schools and directors of public health were drawn almost exclusively from their respective systems and if they were foreclosed from moving to other communities.

The lack of mobility means that an administrator cannot afford to be too ambitious, too creative, or too daring in experimenting with new methods and procedures lest the support of superiors, subordinates, or the community be lost. As was noted in earlier chapters, he is often reluctant to take a tough stand on important issues for the very practical reason that doing so may cost him his job, and relatively few attractive employment opportunities are available for ex-police chiefs who wish to continue to work in the police field.

The same considerations smother initiative, creativity, and self-criticism on the part of supervisory personnel. Sergeants, lieutenants, captains, and officers of higher rank are inhibited in everything they do by their awareness that they must live out their careers in the agency. This means a command officer sometimes withholds support from programs of which he may privately approve to avoid conflict with his colleagues. He may not endorse changes he recognizes as needed—and may even join in resisting them—unless they have close to unanimous approval from the rank and file. And he typically refrains from criticizing associates and even subordinates lest they someday become his superiors.

Finally, the restrictions on lateral movement make it highly unlikely that the thousands of self-contained systems (and nonsystems) for the production of police leadership—equal in number to the police agencies in the country—will ever improve at a sufficiently rapid rate to meet the critical need for executive talent. These systems themselves require new leaders who will introduce the best practices developed elsewhere and who will then go on to improve these. The whole process is slowed if each agency is sealed off from the competence, the experience, and the impetus that would be available to it through the movement of administrators between agencies.

PROPOSALS FOR DEVELOPING LEADERSHIP

Among the most common suggestions that have been made for supplying effective leadership in the police field are: increased reliance on higher education; in-service training in management techniques; career-development programs; restructuring the promotion system; a West Point for police; exchange programs; and greater lateral movement. Any one of these programs, by itself, is probably inadequate. And many of them, as proposed, are much too modest given the magnitude of the need. Indeed, the need is so great and so critical that a full-scale master plan to fill it might well incorporate all of these suggestions in one form or another.

The Need for a Comprehensive Program

Many people concerned with the problem are reluctant to propose a large-scale program for providing leadership, contending that the more ambitious the program, the less likely it is to be implemented. An alternative would be to undertake many different efforts, some large and some small. But these do not seem to materialize at the required rate; and, as noted, those that are launched usually have a very limited effect. It is becoming apparent that the lack of progress is due, in part, to the absence of a specific, identifiable, widely-agreed-upon program to develop police leadership to which smaller efforts might be related. One is compelled to conclude, therefore, that government authorities at all levels—federal, state, and local—must address, in an organized fashion and as a matter of urgent public concern, the question of how to provide leadership to the approximately 418,000 people employed full time by local governments in providing police service.[22] A strong, highly visible program is needed. And once there is agreement on the program there must be a bold commitment on the part of the citizenry and government bodies to carrying it out.

Other countries made such policy judgments and commitments long ago. The small country of Denmark, for example, chose to draw its top leadership from the legal profession and has invested tremendous time and effort in training those who enter the service as constables to equip them to assume positions of middle management. In the Netherlands, chief commissioners and commissioners are appointed by the Crown from outside the police service, often from other government positions. Command personnel from the rank of assistant inspector and above are specially recruited, trained for four years at the Police College at Hilversum, and subsequently assigned directly to command responsibilities. Those who enter the service at the bottom can rise to the position of adjutant, at which point they may undertake a program of private studies and then take the examination given at the end of the college course. If successful they can then move into the "commissioned" ranks.

Like us, the English place a high value upon local control of their police and are now fully committed to filling all positions—up to and including that of Commissioner of the Metropolitan Police—with individuals who enter the service as constables.[23] Having decided upon a system of appointment from within, however, the English have taken a number of significant steps to produce their own leadership.

The focal point of the English program is the Police College at Bramshill. The objective of the college is to provide appropriate training for the future leaders of the police service. It defines its aims as "enabling its students to broaden their outlook, to quicken their mental powers and to improve their professional skill and knowledge."[24] Students are selected on the basis of their aptitude for police work and the evidence they give of potential for assuming greater responsibility.

Approximately one-half of the course offerings at the college are in liberal studies. The balance relate to police functioning. Considerable emphasis is given to instruction in history, political science, and economics in an effort to provide the students with a better understanding of their country's political and social institutions. International problems and current world events are explored—all as a way of providing students with a better foundation for understanding the role of the police in the total scheme of government and in society.

Of the several programs operated at Bramshill, the "special course" seems most significant. Of one year's duration, it accelerates the movement of qualified personnel into leadership positions. Its students are young officers of outstanding promise, nominated because of their high rank in promotion examinations for sergeant and selected on the basis of interviews extending over three days. In both the examination and the three-day assessment, a special effort is made to measure the degree to which a constable is aware of the current issues and problems confronting the police. A constable may qualify for the special course before the end of his fourth year of service. He is promoted to sergeant at the completion of the course and to inspector twelve months after the course is ended—a rank which he may reach at the age of twenty-four. The most qualified members of the accelerated course can compete for the privilege of undertaking full-time studies at one of the major English universities. If selected, they are given their full pay and are provided with living quarters, tuition, and book costs.

In addition to the Bramshill program, which includes a senior command course as well, there are other important elements in the English system for grooming leadership. Constables and officers are free to move about the country by applying for transfer. A positive value is attached to transfer as a means of broadening a man's experience. It is required that a candidate for appointment to chief constable have served with more than one force.

One can certainly quibble with some aspects of the Bramshill programs. One can question their depth. One can argue about the processes used to select the students. And one might object to the arrangement for rapid promotion of young personnel on the grounds that it unwisely reduces the opportunities for promotion of those who are slower in developing leadership abilities. But the basic outline of a sound program is there. The English, faced with the need for producing police leadership from within the police field, have, as a matter of government policy, establishing a program to supply it. Reflective of the government's commitment is this comment contained in a White Paper presented to Parliament in 1961:

> It is therefore important, if the Service is to produce enough leaders of the right calibre, that training of the right sort should be made available to those who have demonstrated that they are suitable for higher rank. It is also important that the Service should be seen to offer attractive prospects for the recruit of good quality and that he should feel that he will be given the opportunity to use his talents to the best advantage. The working out of the new schemes outlined above will have to be carefully watched; but it is believed that they will improve the ability of the Police Service to attract and train its own leaders, and enable the Police College to make an even greater contribution than at present to the efficiency of the Service.[25]

In drawing on the British experience it is of course important to acknowledge that the police forces of that country, while local in character, are integrated in various ways and subject to some forms of national direction and control. Applying any elements of the British model to the development of police leadership in this country is complicated by the multiplicity and diversity of police agencies here.

Determining Priorities

In contemplating the form that a comprehensive program for developing leadership might take, the tendency is to turn first to educational programs—the creation of a Bramshill or a West Point or the requirement of college education for police personnel. The assumption is that educated officers will differ from police leaders of the past in that they will have a broader and more sophisticated approach to policing; they will be more sensitive to the delicate nature of the police role; and they will be more confident in handling their leadership responsibilities and in taking on the complex problems that have been ignored for so long.

That this does not necessarily follow is a point explored in chapter 11. And even if educational programs were guaranteed to achieve these objectives, the insular character of police agencies in this country greatly limits the potential of the officer who does acquire the broader outlook. He will usually return to work in an agency in which there is little support or appreciation for his new-found values. He may rise to a higher position in that agency, but he will be unable to affect the quality of police service unless the atmosphere within the agency changes, and this is not likely to occur until the community itself redefines what it expects of its police.

When a community begins to pressure for a new concept of the police function, these more sophisticated officers may be tapped to carry out new programs. Or, if no such officers can be found within the agency, the community can, if it has the legal authority to recruit from outside, break with tradition and look elsewhere. Among the multiplicity of independent police agencies, some are bound to produce more highly qualified leaders, and communities should be able to draw from these agencies. That is why lateral movement is so crucial to the substantive development of policing in this country. Until broad opportunities are opened up for movement among agencies—both at the top level and in positions of middle management—one cannot begin to expect anything approaching full return on the investment in educational programs for police personnel. The Bramshill program would be of little value if its students were selected by and returned to agencies whose development had been stunted through inbreeding—agencies that had not benefited from the uplifting effect of new and varied leadership and the unlimited nationwide competition to excel.

Some will say that the importance of lateral movement has been overstated here; that even if lateral movement were practiced, 80 or 90 percent of all administrative positions would be filled from within the agency. This may be so, but if personnel within an agency must compete with outsiders for vacant positions, they will strive much harder to meet the top administrator's criteria for filling supervisory positions. Thus, although the opportunity for lateral movement may not result in as much mobility as some anticipate, the very potential for movement is beneficial; the top administrator can use it to elicit support for his policies, programs, and administrative style.

Breaking the Barriers to Lateral Movement

The first and most obvious step that must be taken to promote mobility among police agencies is to repeal state statutes and local ordinances that presently require applicants for the job of police chief in some jurisdictions to have been local residents or to have had prior service in the local agency. Preferably such requirements for the lesser supervisory positions should be eliminated at the same time. This is of course more easily said than done.

Resistance to such a move has in the past come from police personnel who understandably would like to reserve for themselves opportunities for upward movement in their own organizations, and from police, public officials, and local citizenry who—often simply as a matter of local pride—have felt that "importing" police leadership was demeaning to the community. There were indications several years ago that this resistance was diminishing, but the realization that the police must be more understanding of the culture and interests of local communities has revived some of the opposition to opening recruitment, promotions, and the appointment of chiefs to outside candidates. The present trend within large cities, for example, is to avoid a situation in which the commander of a police precinct is drawn from some distant neighborhood of the city. If black supervisory personnel are available, they are likely to be assigned to areas having large numbers of blacks. Given the general consensus that these are troubled times, moreover, communities tend to attach a high value to police personnel who know—in intimate detail based on their long associations—the dynamics of a community, feeling that this will equip them to deal with difficult situations that may arise.

In some localities the value in utilizing police personnel indigenous to an area may well be more important, given today's problems, than the impact this practice has on the long-range development of police leadership. It must be recognized, however, that residency requirements, uniformly applied, deny a municipality the opportunity to hire an outsider when it feels it simply does not have anyone in its ranks sufficiently sensitive to the problems of social change or does not have adequate numbers of officers representative of minority interests. Job mobility might well make police leaders available who have qualities that would more than offset any handicaps resulting from their lack of familiarity with a given area.

Greater resort to lateral movement is obviously going to require increased initiative from appointing authorities. More important, however, it will require strong support from within the police field itself. Such support is commonly voiced by individual police officers. A survey conducted in 1966 in California, where some interdepartmental movement is possible, found that almost 70 percent of the responding officers of all ranks felt that such an opportunity would benefit individual officers, and 82 percent felt it would benefit policing in the state.[26] Much less clear is the position of rank-and-file police personnel throughout the country, as reflected through their associations. Hervey Juris, in his study of police unions published in 1973, found no union that had actively worked for lateral entry, and found two that had actively opposed it.[27] The consensus among persons active on the national scene in police associations is that the present leadership of the associations would, if polled, be strongly opposed to lateral movement. But police unions are undergoing a rapid metamorphosis, as discussed in chapter 12, and it is entirely possible that they will, in the interest of their members, make an about-face in the next decade and become a strong force supporting lateral movement. In many foreign countries the associations of police personnel work vigorously to protect and expand opportunities for mobility within the field.

The fact that pensions cannot be transferred has often been cited as a major barrier to lateral movement. The importance of this factor has been questioned with regard to public service employees generally.[28] But a study sponsored by the National Institute of Law Enforcement and Criminal Justice in 1971 and conducted by Geoffrey N. Calvert concluded that: (1) pension rights and expectations, and the fear of losing pension credits already accrued, were indeed among the most serious impediments to lateral movement; and (2) removal of the impediments would immediately stimulate police officers to acquire new skills and specialized knowledge, resulting in better overall performance, greater professionalism, greater competition for senior positions, and, in the end, an improved capacity to cope with crime.[29] As one might expect, however, the motivation of police officers seeking lateral movement was primarily to improve their financial condition and only secondarily to take on increased responsibility and a bigger challenge.[30]

In order to overcome the problem created by the multiplicity of independent police pension systems, the Calvert study recommended that initially each state establish a single unified system so that transfers of employment within the state would not affect benefits. It recommended as a second step that reciprocity then be established between the state systems, making transfers across state lines possible. The federal government could aid such a development by encouraging the states to centralize their systems and by providing some financial inducement, such as by covering some of the reserves that might be required in a move from one state to another or by covering the administrative costs of the reciprocity arrangement. The allocation of funds by all levels of government for programs to promote lateral movement—such as by providing some salary guarantee in the first few years after a move or by covering such seemingly simple matters as moving expenses—could conceivably produce far more improvement in the overall capacity of the police in this country than many of the expenditures that have already been made.

Proposals of this kind always raise the specter in some people's minds of a movement toward nationalization of our police forces, the implication being that the federal government would come to control the individuals who benefit from programs financed out of federal funds. This is obviously a danger. But support could be structured in ways that would reinforce the control local governments exercise over the police. The role of the federal government could be restricted to recognizing the need for such programs and to providing the funds with which to finance some aspects of them. The danger, in any event, would be no greater than that created by charging the FBI with the training of local police personnel, by providing financial support to enable police officers to pursue college studies, or by the kind of program funding in which the Law Enforcement Assistance Administration has engaged.

Preparation for Leadership

If lateral movement becomes a standard practice, those who bring a first-rate education to their police jobs will have greater opportunities to utilize their capabilities. And police personnel themselves will have added incentive to pursue an education. Ideally the educational component—along with related research—would be the elevating force in a comprehensive program to improve police leadership. It should serve to raise the intellectual horizons of the future leaders, thereby building into the field a steadily increasing capacity to come to grips with its own problems.

With so many police officers and those aspiring to work in the police field presently enrolled in community colleges and four-year college programs in police science or criminal justice administration, some would argue that this need is already being met. But, as discussed in chapter 11, few of these programs are, in their present form, effectively broadening police perspectives, reorienting police leadership, or training new leadership in a systematic fashion.

It may be, as some have suggested, that the need for leadership can best be met by establishing a single institution. A number of factors, however, might combine to give such an institution an insular character that could defeat the very purpose in creating it. The police establishment would exert tremendous pressure for instruction designed to meet needs as they are currently defined by the field, such as training to combat terrorism, to apply computer technology to police work, or to develop more sophisticated records systems. A new institution, to be of value, would have to be sufficiently independent to offer courses of broad content aimed at changing the nature of police leadership without having to fend off charges that its instruction was either disrespectful of police dogma or irrelevant. Moreover, it would seem that much of the value of interchange that occurs in an educational process in which people of various backgrounds participate would be lost in a program designed exclusively for police. Yet such an institution could have great positive impact. It could concentrate the limited human resources currently studying the problems of the police; it could quickly become the recognized national center for developing police leadership, itself providing a model for similar efforts organized on a regional or statewide basis. Perhaps most important, such an institution would at least assure that a major effort was being expended toward producing police leadership. Its program would be highly visible and easily subject to evaluation.

An alternative is to create several centers within existing institutions of higher education that would specialize in grooming leaders. If the institutions are themselves strong, there will already be built into them the resources that make it possible to fill the most critical need for a broadening education, and they will also have the capacity to insulate themselves from pressures from the police establishment.

Given the tremendous magnitude of the need, perhaps all of these approaches should be tried simultaneously: the further development of such existing institutions as the FBI Academy; the establishment of a new national academy to specialize in the development of leadership for municipal police agencies; and the creation of specialized centers for the same purpose in well-established institutions of higher learning. Each might even carve out a specialty for itself, based on the region served, the different levels of leadership, or the size of police agencies in which officers are to function when their training is completed. Lest there be concern about a proliferation of efforts, it is helpful to bear in mind that each of the European countries—some of which are smaller in population than some of our states—has its own institution for training its police leadership. How well off we would be in this country if each state had assumed similar responsibility!

Selection for Leadership

It now appears that recent court challenges of the validity and fairness of police promotion procedures will provide the impetus for much-needed change in this area. As agencies, their personnel consultants, and their lawyers struggle to validate their promotion criteria, they will no doubt feel that they are being forced to move backward. Formal requirements such as the college degree, for example, are bound to be questioned and, in some instances, may even be invalidated because of existing stereotypes of what policing entails and lack of adequate documentation of the value of higher education. It is likely, however, that this process will, in the long run, bring about a more realistic definition and articulation of the requirements of the various ranks of police leadership. And this will inevitably lead to more widespread recognition of the complexity and importance of the jobs of the police supervisor and administrator.

Initially this should result in better examinations and grading procedures. It should result in weighing more relevant factors more heavily. It may eventually lead to much more sophisticated methods for selecting the top leadership in the police field. Of special interest is the current experimentation with efforts to assess the management capabilities of police personnel in a more comprehensive manner. The experience of the London Metropolitan Police in assessing their personnel has frequently been cited.[31] In a procedure extending over several days, they make use of intensive interviews and various exercises that place the candidate in situations similar to those likely to be experienced on the job. The New York City Police Department has been using a management-assessment center to screen candidates for promotion to noncivil-service status above the rank of captain. The process consists of a series of exercises designed to test the capacity of a candidate to handle a high-level position in that agency.[32] While use of the process has spread rapidly among police agencies, some have cautioned that it rewards those capable of a certain form of gamesmanship; that its value in selecting able leaders has not yet been validated.[33]

In removing restraints on individuals with the potential for leadership, it is vital to make it possible for the qualified officer to nominate himself not only for promotion within his department, but for educational opportunities and for appointment to a position of responsibility in another agency. This means that educational programs designed to develop police leadership, whether under the auspices of a college or a government-financed institution or program, should not limit their admissions to agency-nominated personnel; some positions should be reserved for those who apply directly to the program and who are selected by the educational institution rather than the agency in which they are employed. Indeed, some educational programs might restrict themselves to such admissions. The obvious purpose in urging a provision of this kind is to enable qualified personnel to bypass agency leadership that adheres to outdated criteria in the selection of subordinates. Ideally, increased lateral movement would afford such individuals an opportunity for placement upon completion of the educational program. This is another situation in which federal support in the form of fellowships, to provide both an education and some mobility, could greatly benefit the field.

Internships and Apprenticeships

A few isolated programs have been set up to enable supervisory officers from one agency to observe or work for another agency. The Police Foundation in 1975 experimented with a program in which six police agencies in the San Francisco Bay area exchanged officers, with the visiting officer serving as a staff assistant to the chief of the host department for six months.[34] Extremely limited as these programs are, the participants and those close to them are enthusiastic about the results. In some programs of a quite different nature, undergraduates work in an agency for a semester or quarter, but the students are often given simple chores that do not challenge their ability, and therefore these programs have questionable educational value.

Properly managed, a vastly expanded program that uses internships and apprenticeships at much higher levels in police organizations holds tremendous promise for helping to break down the insular character of the field. In such a program the most qualified personnel in the field would have to assume a teaching role as part of their regular responsibilities. The internship would continue for a year or more. And an apprentice would be expected to assume responsibilities, be productive for the agency, and learn in the process. A qualified apprentice might provide more assistance to a police chief than his regular subordinates do, especially if the apprentice has just completed an educational program that acquainted him with the most recent developments in the police field and that equipped him to apply basic research tools to police problems. Thus an apprenticeship program can provide not only a rich experience for the apprentice, but also an improvement in the agency's performance. And it could demonstrate the value in bringing fresh talent into an agency that suffers from a dearth of competent leadership but nevertheless resists appointments from the outside.

We tend to think of internships as restricted to students just out of college. As outlined here, however, they are primarily an advanced form of training for the officer who already has some police experience. An extended internship may be the best way to round out the training of officers selected to participate in special educational programs because of their leadership potential. Conceivably, a young lieutenant from City A may, after completing an educational program, intern with the chief of police in City B for two years, after which he may, unless he has commitments to City A, be an excellent candidate for the job of chief in City C. Internships could be more extensively used, also, by departments in their own leadership-development programs. Arrangements could be made for a lieutenant in City Y to spend a year with the research staff of the police department in City Z, after which he would return to City Y.

In a variation of this arrangement it would be profitable for police in middle-management positions to work temporarily in other departments of city government, thereby acquiring a different form of administrative experience, while at the same time becoming familiar with an agency to which the police must relate. In exchange, middle-management personnel from other city agencies, during their assigned term at the police department, would provide the police with the benefit of assistance and criticism from people with different professional perspectives who shared an interest in administration and in the improvement of municipal services.

The Alternative of Civilian Leadership

Periodically the suggestion is made that in the absence of qualified leaders communities should appoint laymen as police administrators. This was common practice in the early part of the century. As Bruce Smith observed, many people felt that the police administrator drawn directly from civilian life was more closely in touch with public attitudes, more sensitive to popular needs, and therefore better adapted to the purposes and requirements of popular control. He is more likely to have enjoyed the advantages of broad interests and wide experience than is the man risen from the ranks, who has been subjected throughout his career to the deadening and narrowing effects of official routine.[35]

Cities also turned to lay leadership in hopes of correcting the worst inadequacies in the operations of police agencies, but with little success:

Every occupation and profession has been drawn upon to produce a Moses to lead the police out of the wilderness. One of our late ex-Presidents made little or no impression during the several years he served as commissioner of one of our large police departments. . . . Editors, lawyers, doctors, all have been tried; all have failed, with but few exceptions.[36]

A combination of factors accounted for the failures: short tenure; lack of technical knowledge; absence of adequate staff assistance; the resistance of the rank and file; and susceptibility to local political influences. In a few notable exceptions a blend of personal competence, useful experience, and local circumstances resulted in successful administrations. Today, however, there are only a few jurisdictions (excluding counties having elected sheriffs) in which the operating head of the police agency is without prior police experience. Several large cities have a position with the title of police commissioner or director of public safety to which a layman may be appointed, but the positions are usually filled by individuals who have come up through the ranks or, in a limited number of cases, have had police experience in some other agency.

Would lay leadership fail with equal frequency in today's environment? Some say that since the problems of police administration have grown even more complex, the need is even greater for individuals experienced in the technicalities of police work. Others argue that the nature of the police administrator's job has changed; that running a police agency is now like running a large business enterprise or any other large government agency; that the top administrator must be concerned with matters of broad public policy that do not necessarily require intimate familiarity with day-to-day operations; and that today's problems require that the highest priority be placed on characteristics often lacking in those who have risen in the ranks.

It seems significant that, although civilian control over police agencies has been discussed frequently in recent years, the suggestion that the head of the agency be a civilian is rarely made. It appears to be tacitly recognized that civilian status, in itself, is no assurance of greater accountability to the electorate. And although a civilian may have a more balanced view of policy issues by virtue of not having spent a career in the police service, this is by no means guaranteed. But so long as the selection of the top administrator is restricted to personnel within a single agency, the blunt fact is that there are agencies so devoid of capable personnel that some laymen would, by comparison, be better. Thus, unless something is done very soon to increase dramatically the capacity of the police field to produce its own leadership, we may see a revival of the practice of appointing lay people to head police agencies.

FACILITATING LEADERSHIP

The task of selecting a properly qualified police administrator is often so difficult that, when appointing authorities conclude that a good choice was made, they are apt to assume that their job is done and that the police problems will now be solved. It should be obvious, however, that if the new appointee, however qualified, is going to meet expectations, he must have certain minimal forms of support. The most important are some degree of security in his job; freedom to select and appoint immediate subordinates and staff; and backing from his superiors and from the community when his efforts to make changes begin to cause turmoil.

Security in Office

The need for tenure was discussed earlier as it relates to both political accountability (chapter 6) and corruption (chapter 8). Tenure was first advocated as protection from political pressures. The incredibly fast turnover of police administrators in the early part of the century created an intolerable condition, described graphically by Woods:

> When commissioners are mere birds of passage, as they have been at times in some cities, and when they fly so fast and remain on the perilous perch for so short a time that their species can hardly be determined, is it any wonder that the men mark time, lie low, do nothing that can be avoided, until they find out just where they stand and what is expected?[37]

His observations accurately describe a condition that continues to exist in many police agencies today. The contributing factors, however, have changed somewhat. Civil service has afforded to many chiefs protection from partisan political pressures. The strongest pressures now come from conflicting segments of the community, from persons holding different concepts of the police function, and—perhaps most important—from a chief's own personnel.

To resist these pressures, job security does not really seem enough. The administrator with tenure can, if he wishes, dig in, comfortable in the knowledge that he cannot be fired except for cause. But the constant stress, the harassment, the demands on his time, and the frustration in not being able to accomplish what he wants take their toll; so the chief often retires early or takes a job outside the field.

Job security in today's environment is a minimum protection. It insulates the chief from only the simpler pressures. It does not protect him from the more intense pressures that are generated when he takes a position—as he must do—on controversial issues. He must, for example, defend minority interests. He must act aggressively against wrongdoing on his force. And he must make the painful changes that are so long overdue in the operations of police agencies.

The pressures that arise in the process of effecting change in a police agency make it imperative that both the administrator and the employing authority are committed to a term of office that spans more than a few years. If subordinates are to be expected to abandon the old in support of the new, to take risks and make enemies, they must have assurance that the movement to which they attach themselves will not be short-lived. Many recent changes in police organizations have been temporary ones, discontinued because of the resignation or retirement of the chief or because further financing was unavailable. The discerning police officer learns to be cautious in supporting such programs. Recalcitrant subordinates possessed of enough patience to sit out the period of reform have in many instances emerged as the "victors," to relegate those who joined in the effort to bring about change to the least attractive assignments in the organization.

These considerations make it clear why it is so important that efforts to achieve greater accountability through more direct popular control of police administrators take cognizance of the need for security as well. Several ways in which these conflicting needs might be reconciled were discussed in chapter 6.

Freedom to Select Immediate Subordinates

In a large bureaucracy that has a long-established life of its own, it is the height of naiveté to assume that one individual, appointed to head the agency, can single-handedly bring about significant change. This is especially so if the appointment reflects a conscious effort on the part of the appointing authority to alter the agency. And yet public recognition of the need for new leadership rarely extends to recognizing that the head of an agency must be free to select key subordinates, to reassign personnel, and to bring new talent into the organization.

Chiefs have been appointed to some of the largest police departments without the authority to bring a single person—not even a secretary—into the organization with them. Civil service provisions often make it impossible to demote or reassign personnel. Where the opportunity does exist, a decision to alter the status of a high-ranking officer, however incompetent the officer may be, frequently results in widespread resentment toward the new chief. And when the chief hires staff assistants from outside the agency, both he and the assistants tend to become the target of attack.

Imagine taking on the responsibility to head a large agency only to find that it is difficult to acquire the most basic information about how the organization functions, that no one is available to conduct a simple study, and that instructions issued to subordinates are not carried out. Yet this is precisely the situation in which many police administrators are placed. If the immediate subordinates enjoy security in their positions as a result of either civil service or strong public support, they can easily cripple the new chief's efforts. They may well have seen new administrators come and go and have little reason to believe their newest boss will have any more effect than did his predecessors. Hostile to their superior, many of them see their primary objective as defending their own subordinates from his influence. At the same time they strive to strengthen their relationships with their subordinates, thereby building their own power base within the organization.

Naturally these problems are most acute when the police chief is appointed from outside the agency and has no immediate power base. But the problems also arise in somewhat milder form where the new appointee is selected from within.

A chief faced with this situation may simply resign himself to it, making the limitations of his staff his own. He then becomes a leader in name only, having no significant impact on the organization, its operations, or its policies. Or the chief may become totally frustrated and leave. Between these extremes there have been a number of efforts to "do something" about the problem which are worth noting.

The crudest and least satisfactory response is also probably the most common—"benching" key personnel by assigning them to responsibilities other than those they normally would have. A deputy chief of police, for example, may be given work usually performed by a person of much lower rank, which carries no supervisory duties. The objective, of course, is to limit the negative effect that the indifferent, obstinate, or openly hostile command officer has upon the agency, and at the same time to make it possible to put in key positions personnel who are more helpful to the administrator. Aside from the wastefulness and humiliation inherent in this practice, the administrator of an agency that is bankrupt of qualified leadership very quickly runs out of suitable "benches." Moreover, the benched officers, unless they resign or retire, serve as daily reminders of wounds that the new administrator has inflicted on the agency and may use their idle time to attempt to undermine administrative changes. The cost of such a practice, therefore, is high.

In some cities key administrative positions are exempt from civil service, subject to appointment by the agency head. In New York City, for example, the police commissioner is free to remove incumbents and make new appointments to all positions above the rank of captain. But until recently there was great reluctance to remove or reassign an officer once appointed. Much the same situation exists in Boston, where the reluctance to remove a high-ranking officer remains strong. In Chicago, by contrast, the superintendent not only has the authority to fill all positions above the rank of captain, but makes extensive use of it, and the propriety of his doing so is accepted by the police and the community.[38] In most situations in which the head of the agency is free to appoint top administrators, he can draw them from outside the agency. But the pressures from within the organization result in the choice almost always being limited to those currently within the ranks, though not necessarily having the highest civil service standing.

This concept of "exempt" positions in a police agency—positions exempt from civil service—not only makes great sense; it is vital to the development and support of new leadership. It becomes essential, therefore, that such a system be established where none now exists. And it is essential that a police administrator make full use of it to remove the hostile and incompetent; to take advantage of the best available talent within the agency regardless of current rank; and to bring in outsiders when it is necessary. An individual drawn from the department by this system retains his civil service tenure in his previous position and reverts to it if he is relieved of his higher post. Thus the top positions can be viewed as special assignments, with a widespread understanding—as is true at the cabinet level in the federal government and in some state and local governments—that all appointments to them are of a temporary nature and at the discretion of the chief. With such an understanding an administrator's action in dropping an individual back to his civil service rank becomes part of a normal process rather than an extraordinary measure equivalent to being demoted or fired. The financial hardship on being reduced in rank, which often becomes a major impediment to taking such action, can be relieved somewhat by an arrangement whereby the person affected continues to receive the same salary or a gradual reduction in salary over several years. The cost incurred is a relatively small one to pay for the difference between a competent and loyal staff and a staff whose allegiance is elsewhere.

Support of the Community and of the
Municipality's Chief Executive

The suggestion that efforts be made to win community support for competent police leadership has a somewhat hollow ring to it; appeals for public support and for the education of the public often turn out to be simplistic when relied upon as solutions to complex problems. And yet it is unrealistic to seek to elevate the quality of police leadership without recognizing the need to create an environment that will support that leadership. The need is not for slogans or for advertising campaigns, but for a better understanding within the community of the intricacies of police work that, in turn, produces more intelligent and more constructive criticism of the actions and policy decisions of police administrators.

Changing a police agency—which is usually the prime objective of those who seek new leadership—is a highly complex business. Actions that a police chief must take are not easily comprehended by the general community. They are often at odds with stereotyped notions of policing. Familiar practices must be altered. Heroes must be reassigned. Resistance must be overcome. If the actions of a new chief are judged on the basis of a simplistic and perhaps mythical concept of policing, public support will be quickly eroded. Some groups in the typical community work for just such a result.

Under these conditions a newly appointed police administrator frequently becomes embroiled in a community-wide dispute over what appears to be a relatively minor issue. He may, for example, be confronted by the customary demands for establishing foot patrols as a way of responding to the concern over street crimes, which he must usually resist lest his limited manpower be quickly dissipated. He may be pressured, as the new chief, to clamp down on long-tolerated conditions—morally offensive to some segments of the community—to which he personally, in any event, would attach a low priority. And he may be pressured to continue practices he stopped because he believed them to be illegal. In each instance the administrator who resists demands for the traditional response runs the risk of appearing insensitive to community needs. And a number of chiefs who have stood by their basic convictions in handling such matters have found themselves, as time went on, without the community support required for them to remain effective in office.

The police leader can do much to solve this problem. He can substitute alternatives that have broad acceptance for traditional responses. He can, in time, become a major force in reeducating the community about the complexities of the police function and the inadequacies of some of the traditional responses. His ability to do so will depend in large measure on the effort he invests in establishing contact with various community leaders and organizations and in building a positive relationship with the mass media. In some situations in which the stakes are limited he may decide to respond in the expected stereotyped manner. His choice of issues on which to take a stand is, in itself, an important measure of his capacity as a police leader.

But the police chief cannot, nor should he have to, stand alone in interpreting his actions to the community. As discussed in chapter 6, the mayor or appointed chief executive to whom a police leader is responsible provides the channel through which citizens influence police actions. This is obviously not, however, an unfiltered channel. The chief executive of the municipality has a responsibility to defend the police chief from undue criticism incurred as a result of efforts to implement agreed-upon policies. A mayor, in particular, as an elected official, can contribute a great deal toward effective implementation of police programs by using his prestige as a political leader to interpret specific changes as they are carried out. Mayoral support on the controversial matters that arise in effecting change in a police agency, if it is based upon a full awareness of the intricacies of such change, may be the most important factor in determining the success or failure of a new chief. Without such backing, it is unlikely that police administrators will be able to accomplish any of their goals.

NOTES

1. Police Chief Executive Committee of the International Association of Chiefs of Police, *The Police Chief Executive Report* (Washington, D.C.: Government Printing Office, 1976), p. 17.

2. Philip Selznick, *Leadership in Administration* (New York: Row, Peterson and Co., 1957), p. 135.

3. Ibid., pp. 142–154.

4. Raymond B. Fosdick, *American Police Systems* (1920; reprint ed., Montclair, N.J.: Patterson Smith, 1969), p. 380.

5. National Commission on Law Observance and Enforcement, *Report on Police* (1931; reprint ed., Montclair, N.J.: Patterson Smith, 1968), p. 3.

6. Bruce Smith, *Police Systems in the United States*, 2d rev. ed. (New York: Harper & Row, 1960), p. 14.

7. See August Vollmer, *The Police and Modern Society* (1936; reprint ed., Montclair, N.J.: Patterson Smith, 1971).

8. President's Commission on Law Enforcement and Administration of Justice, *The Challenge of Crime in a Free Society* (Washington, D.C.: Government Printing Office, 1967), pp. 111–113.

9. National Advisory Commission on Criminal Justice Standards and Goals, *Police* (Washington, D.C.: Government Printing Office, 1973), pp. 421–441.

10. Patrick V. Murphy, *A Decade of Urban Police Problems*, Sixteenth Annual Wherrett Lecture on Local Government (Pittsburgh: Institute for Urban Policy and Administration, Graduate School of Public and International Affairs, University of Pittsburgh, 1974), p. 4.

11. James F. Ahern, *Police in Trouble* (New York: Hawthorn Books, 1972), p. 78.

12. Ibid., p. 119.

13. A. C. Germann, "Changing the Police—The Impossible Dream?" *Journal of Criminal Law, Criminology and Police Science* 62 (1971): 417.

14. For a description of promotion procedures in fifteen large jurisdictions, see Richard G. Kohlan, "Police Promotional Procedures in Fifteen Jurisdictions," *Public Personnel Management*, May/June 1973, pp. 167–170.

15. Fosdick, *American Police Systems*, p. 220.

16. Arthur Woods, *Policeman and Public* (1919; reprint ed., New York: Arno Press, 1971), pp. 149–150.

17. Cited in Charles B. Saunders, Jr., *Upgrading the American Police* (Washington, D.C.: The Brookings Institution, 1970), p. 137.

18. The ten states identified as having such programs as of January 1, 1975, in a survey by the National Association of Directors of Law Enforcement Training, varied a great deal in their requirements. California, for example, required 20 hours of training for advanced officers, 100 hours for middle management, and 80 hours for supervisors. Massachusetts and Minnesota, by contrast, required only 40 hours of training for supervisors. For a short account of some of the existing training programs offered before promotion, see National Advisory Commission on Criminal Justice Standards and Goals, *Police*, p. 399.

19. See ibid., pp. 426–432.

20. California has established procedures to facilitate entry into a higher position in another agency, but only a limited number of such transfers occur. See William L. Tafoya, "Lateral Entry," *Police Chief*, April 1974, pp. 60–62.

21. President's Commission on Law Enforcement and Administration of Justice, *Task Force Report: The Police* (Washington, D.C.: Government Printing Office, 1967), p. 142.

22. Actually, 470,258 individuals were employed by counties and municipalities in the provision of police service in October, 1973, but this included part-time employees. Of the 418,385 full-time employees, 77,132 were employed by counties and 341,253 were employed by municipalities. Law Enforcement Assistance Administration and the Bureau of the Census, *Expenditure and Employment Data for the Criminal Justice System: 1972-73* (Washington, D.C.: Government Printing Office, 1975), p. 42.

23. It should, however, be noted that such has not always been the case in England. See, e.g., Smith, *Police Systems in the United States*, pp. 195–198.

24. *Bramshill, The Police College*, pamphlet (Bramshill, England: Bramshill College, n.d.), p. 1.

25. Secretary of State for the Home Department, *Police Training in England and Wales* (London: Her Majesty's Stationery Office, 1961) pp. 3-4.

26. As reported in Geoffrey N. Calvert, *Portable Police Pensions—Improving Inter-Agency Transfers* (Washington, D.C.: Government Printing Office, 1971), p. 2.

27. Hervey A. Juris and Peter Feuille, *Police Unionism* (Lexington, Mass.: Lexington Books, D. C. Heath, 1973), p. 113.

28. See, e.g., Harold Rubin, *Pensions and Employee Mobility in the Public Service* (New York: Twentieth Century Fund, 1965).

29. Calvert, *Portable Police Pensions*, p. 6.

30. Ibid., p. 4.

31. See O. Glenn Stahl and Richard A. Staufenberger, eds., *Police Personnel Administration* (Washington, D.C.: Police Foundation, 1974), pp. 119–122.

32. See P. F. D'Arcy, "Assessment Center Program Helps to Test Managerial Competence," *Police Chief*, December 1974, pp. 52–53. The Kansas City, Missouri, Police Department and the Rochester, New York, Police Department are among the other agencies that have experimented with the assessment-center concept.

33. For a discussion of the methodology employed in assessment centers that acknowledges the limited experience in the use of this technique and that recognizes the need to study its value, see James F. Galvin and John W. Hamilton, "Selecting Police Using Assessment Center Methodology," *Journal of Police Science and Administration* 3 (1975): 166–176.

34. William J. Baer, *Police Personnel Exchange Programs: The Bay Area Experience* (Washington, D.C.: Police Foundation, 1976).

35. Smith, *Police Systems in the United States*, p. 191.

36. National Commission on Law Observance and Enforcement, *Report on Police*, p. 21.

37. Woods, *Policeman and Public*, p. 147. See also National Commission on Law Observance and Enforcement, *Report on Police*, pp. 46–48; and Smith, *Police Systems in the United States*, pp. 198–202.

38. Chicago recently expanded the number of positions the superintendent can fill. Under a new system of personnel administration a department head can, with the approval of the mayor, exempt additional positions from the career service (those filled by competitive examination) to ensure that they be filled by employees who will aid him in the implementation of policy. City of Chicago Ordinance 25.1–3 (10) passed by Chicago City Council, 24 October 1975 (recorded in *Journal–City Council–Chicago*, 24 October 1975, p. 1444).

Chapter 10

Upgrading Police Personnel

One of the basic tenets of police reformers is that raising the quality of personnel is the key to improved police functioning.[1] Many of the efforts to modernize police agencies have, as a result, concentrated on personnel matters: recruitment, selection standards, promotion procedures, training, and, most recently, education.

In their efforts to implement changes in personnel practices, police administrators have often been frustrated by local and state civil service systems that have seemed, at times, to be more concerned with achieving fairness in hiring, promotion, and disciplinary procedures than in improving the caliber of the police. More recently, complaints about civil service have been overshadowed by complaints regarding the police unions. Personnel practices previously established by civil service and department policy are increasingly being defined by contract, negotiated as part of the collective-bargaining agreement. Many police administrators see this development as further curtailing their capacity to make decisions on personnel matters and thereby seriously restricting their ability to deliver improved police services.

This concern would seem plausible if the relationship between personnel reforms and the quality of police service were clear. It is not. A large number of police agencies that have succeeded in carrying out most of the standard suggestions for upgrading their personnel have nevertheless not achieved the kind of overall improvement in the quality of their service that it had been assumed would automatically follow. It seems timely, therefore, rather than add still another voice in general support of these measures and rather than concern ourselves here with the effects of civil service and police unions, that we examine the potential that personnel reforms have for improving police service and inquire into what might be going awry in their application.

FACTORS LIMITING THE VALUE OF PAST
PERSONNEL REFORMS

Lack of Agreement on Specific Objectives

Inherent in the various programs designed to improve the caliber of police personnel is the assumption that the personnel who are recruited, selected, and trained according to the recommended procedures will be different from those who have entered police service in the past. But the nature of this difference is rarely articulated. And if it is, it is usually set forth in such general terms (e.g., individuals with a higher level of intelligence) that people can agree in supporting the new programs although they may disagree if pressed to define the objectives they have in mind. Many people in police service, for example, have the limited objective of using personnel reforms to realize greater prestige, better public relations, and improved salaries. They have no desire to alter the form of police service. Others—police personnel and citizens alike—see personnel reforms as a way of perfecting police performance, but they mean by this the realization of prevailing standards of good performance. Still others—including especially those outside police agencies who advocate police reform—see improvements in personnel administration as a way of bringing about a radical change in policing. They propose to achieve such change by attracting and promoting officers who have different values and different attitudes toward their jobs and toward the communities they serve.

One of the consequences of this lack of agreement on specific objectives is that advocated programs are frequently subverted when implemented, because those who carry them out tend, intentionally or unintentionally, to substitute their own objectives for the goals of those who initially supported them. Emphasis is often shifted from content to form. Thus, for example, administrators frequently cite as evidence of successful implementation of personnel reforms the large number of applicants rejected by an elaborate screening process, the number of hours added to training programs, and the number of employees who are college graduates. Lost in this preoccupation with numbers is the concern over substantive matters—over the criteria employed in screening applicants, the content and quality of instruction in training programs, and the usefulness of a college-educated employee.

This subversion is not necessarily an aggressive overt effort to undercut the objectives of reformers. More likely it results from the passivity and limited horizons of those in administrative positions combined with the incredible naiveté of those—both within and outside police agencies—who commonly overestimate what can be achieved by personnel reforms alone.

Failure to Recognize that Personnel Reform is But
One Aspect of a Complex Problem

The personnel reforms which have been advanced as solutions to basic problems in the police field and the experience in implementing these reforms demonstrate the futility in attempting to effect change without taking adequate note of the intricacies and dynamics of police operations. What are some of the most common oversights?

Changes in policies relating to personnel have often failed to achieve the expressed goal because they were based on an inaccurate assessment of the police function. An aggressive recruitment effort, for example, no matter how impressive, will be ineffective in producing needed change if it seeks individuals judged capable of performing tasks related to the stereotyped mythical concept of policing, rather than the actual duties police are called upon to handle. Such an effort may even be counterproductive, as police officers, expecting one sort of job and receiving another, feel deluded and become dissatisfied. In adopting programs to upgrade police personnel, it is imperative that there be increased recognition of the realities of police work—of the multiplicity of functions assigned to the police, the limited need for combat-like activities, the use police make of various alternatives, the discretion that must be exercised at the lowest levels in the organization, and the high value attached to restraint and accountability for one's actions—in other words, all of the dimensions of the police job that were explored in chapters 2 through 7.

Another common problem is that personnel reforms do not take into account the key role that police administrators play in effecting change and the resistance of traditional administrators to new policies and procedures. Prescriptive packages have been recommended and often adopted without any meaningful involvement on the part of the agency's administration, with the result that not only is needed support lacking, but opposition is intensified.

Ignored, too, has been the police subculture, with its emphasis upon mutual protection, secrecy, and resistance to external influence. Officers who become part of this subculture develop an uncanny ability to subvert the starry-eyed efforts of individuals they view as temporary intruders into their closed society.

Among the factors contributing to the police subculture are the working environment of the officer in the community and the working environment within the organization. The first is not easily altered, but the environment in the agency can be modified by change in leadership and in administrative policies. If a different sort of person is to be attracted into the police service, change must occur not merely in recruitment, selection, and training programs, but in the organizational environment as well. Otherwise new personnel have little chance of surviving within the organization. The pressures for conformity are so strong that the new officer will either be forced into the police subculture, with the values and orientation of the larger group replacing his own, or his life will be made so unpleasant that he will decide to resign.

The importance of this point brings into question the frequent assertion that personnel reforms deserve the highest priority. It may well be, in this chicken-and-egg dilemma, that one must first change the environment into which a different kind of officer is to be drawn. Indeed, existing problems in the organizational environment of police agencies are such a serious impediment to improving police personnel that they warrant detailed examination in the context of this chapter on personnel.

Effect of the Organization on Its Personnel

Policing is essentially a civilian job carried out in a civilian environment, and yet police agencies are organized in a pyramidal military fashion that can be extremely demoralizing to the officer at the lowest level, the person who has to make the most important and difficult decisions.

From the time a new officer enters recruit training there is a conscious effort to depersonalize him—most dramatically symbolized, perhaps, by the number assigned to him and the uniform he must wear. He is required to suppress individual opinions and forms of conduct and is encouraged, instead, to take on what is essentially a uniform personality molded by the department. Once on the job he is rewarded for conformity and for nonthinking compliance with department directives and may be severely disciplined for minor infractions of petty rules. He may be shifted about, often at great personal inconvenience, to meet the needs of the agency. He is often used in ways that suggest all officers are interchangeable and that their physical presence is more important than any distinctive skills or abilities they bring to the job. His superiors tend to maintain an aloofness that greatly inhibits open communication outside the chain of command. He is frequently kept in the dark on matters that directly involve him. And he is confronted with the realization that he, like many of the people around him, might well spend his entire career at the entry level—a fate some view as akin to spending an entire army career as a private. He must grab at straws for recognition. A complimentary letter from a citizen takes on a value far in excess of what it should be worth. I recall the spectacle of mature police officers competing vigorously for the honor of being selected as the most neatly uniformed officers of their respective units. With management policies that so destroy an officer's concept of his own importance as an individual, it should be clear why changes in recruitment and selection procedures, by themselves, are not enough.

Some would argue that the problems cited here have been met to a large degree by police agencies that have made a special effort to care for the off-duty needs of their personnel, such as for recreation, medical service, financial and family counseling, and special assistance at times of personal emergency. Such services are presented as proof of management's concern for the welfare of employees as human beings. Commendable as these services are, they are no substitute for more meaningful involvement in department affairs. On the contrary they are an extension of the military model, imitative of the paternalistic services traditionally offered in the military—in part as a way of compensating for the hardships of living in an authoritarian environment.

Until recently police were commonly prohibited from participating in any political activity, from criticizing police operations in the public forum, from joining various groups, including unions, and from associating with certain kinds of people, such as those who had been convicted of a crime. Many of these prohibitions have been successfully challenged in the courts by individual officers and by their unions. Despite this clear trend, however, prohibitions of this kind continue to exist in many police agencies. For those on whom we so heavily depend for the protection of basic constitutional rights to be deprived of their own rights in so sweeping a manner is—to put it mildly—a poor way of preparing the police to carry out their responsibilities.

It is little wonder, in retrospect, that many police officers failed to understand what motivated the numerous political and racial protests of the past decade. If the police are to be expected to take abuse and even, on occasion, risk their lives to protect those who are alleged to have committed crimes and those who protest government policies or express unpopular views, it follows that they —above all others—must have a clear understanding of the reluctance with which a democratic society places any restrictions on freedom of expression and association. Rather than contradict democratic values, the organization and administrative policies of a police agency should be consonant with and lend support to the values which the police are expected to uphold in the larger community.

The rigid military structure of police agencies is not only demoralizing to the officers and dysfunctional in its lack of support for democratic values. It is also wasteful in preventing administrators from taking maximum advantage of the best talent in the agency. If highly qualified personnel are newly attracted to a police agency, they may be able to serve immediately and effectively in their contacts with citizens. But they will be unable to contribute to the agency in broader ways until they have risen through the ranks. Even if their approach to policing is in full accord with that of the top management, through whose efforts they may have been recruited and trained, they can be impeded in various ways from moving up by the supervisory personnel who stand between them and the top. Assuming they do not become discouraged and leave, there is the added risk that the passage of time and the pressure of their peers will divest them of much of the ability, potential, and enthusiasm they had on entering the agency. An administrator may tap an officer's skills and knowledge by placing him in a staff position, but this usually makes for an awkward situation because the officer is nevertheless continually treated as an underling simply by virtue of his rank.

The same is true of experienced officers who, by choice or because they cannot pass the required tests, remain at the entry level. Many of these officers possess great expertise, but are precluded from using it to benefit the organization and the community because of their status in the agency. One can frequently observe situations in which the most knowledgeable members of the agency are ignored because of their rank, while the higher-ups struggle with problems they know little about and have not experienced directly in years.

BRINGING A NEW KIND OF PERSONNEL INTO THE AGENCY

Deciding Who Makes a Good Police Officer

As previously noted the stated goal of current recruitment and selection procedures is to attract applicants of "high quality," which is usually defined in equally general terms as high intelligence, character, and ability.

The President's Crime Commission chose to define quality in such a way as to include not just applicants with better education, but also those who more accurately represented the area they were going to police. The National Advisory Commission on Criminal Justice Standards and Goals, the latest group to conduct a national study of the police, was no more specific in defining quality, but it went on to urge research to find out what abilities and personalities are necessary for the police officer's job and to develop procedures for validating the selection system.[2]

In order to meet this suggestion, which has been the requirement of some courts that have sought to end racial discrimination in testing, police agencies—to establish job-relatedness—will have to define more accurately what it is that police officers are presently expected to do and, to prove validity, will have to show evidence that the subsequent performance of the applicants selected by the testing instrument meets the established requirements. This will certainly be an advance over current practice that leans heavily on prevailing stereotypes about the job. But it is disturbing that this process apparently leaves no room to use the selection procedure to identify those capable of doing what an officer *should do* if the complex dynamics of the police function are more fully recognized.

The several recent studies in which attempts were made to identify predictors of police performance illustrate this problem. Although the objective of the studies was ostensibly to build a foundation upon which recruitment and selection could be more soundly based, they were restricted to establishing criteria and testing procedures to find who succeeds best in the traditional police departments. Thus, for example, in the often-cited study conducted in Chicago by Melany E. Baehr, John E. Furcon, and Ernest C. Froemel, the conclusions were based largely upon an analysis and testing of officers identified by the present organization as the best performers. To identify the best performers, the study relied heavily on a special rating of personnel by their supervisors and past performance ratings, also given by supervisors. Such other factors as the tenure of the officer, the number of complimentary letters and awards received, the number of complaints registered, the number of disciplinary actions, and the total number of arrests made were also taken into account.[3]

These measures would obviously serve to perpetuate a certain kind of organization. Attaching a positive value to the number of arrests made, for example, is traditional in older agencies, but newer concepts of policing actually call for avoiding arrests in many situations. The study's findings, therefore, give no indication of the traits an agency should seek in an officer if the objective is to attract individuals who differ from what the agency has defined as its best personnel in the past. Likewise, in the study by Bernard Cohen and Jan M. Chaiken in the New York City Police Department, the measures of performance were heavily influenced by the values and traditional orientation of the agency.[4]

It is, of course, helpful to predict more accurately the characteristics of police officers who, on the basis of existing standards, are likely to be promoted and singled out for awards. But it must be recognized, in the broader perspective of police reform, that success by these standards alone, which are themselves subject to serious question, is not an indication of the traits that will enable officers to perform differently and more effectively in the future.

What can be said about the qualities needed in police officers, based upon the analysis of police functioning set out in the preceding chapters? A high level of intelligence is obviously crucial. Those joining a police force must be capable of making complex decisions on their own that have a major impact upon the lives of others. If they are to contribute to the field they must have the sort of inquiring mind that questions prevailing practices and comes up with new ways to improve the quality of police service. They must have the capacity to shift easily from performing one function to performing another one that requires a different approach and a different state of mind.

With proper instruction, recruits should be able to understand the cosmopolitan nature of an urban area and appreciate differences between cultures. They must learn to tolerate unconventional behavior and respect divergent life-styles. They must be able to appreciate the meaning of freedom and be sensitive to the awesome consequences stemming from the unbridled use of authority. They must take on the commitment to protect constitutional guarantees. They must subscribe to the value our society attaches to limiting the use of force, and they must learn to appreciate the controls exercised over the use of police powers and the role of the community in directing and reviewing police conduct.

Further, in a job that consists chiefly of relating to people, officers must have the self-discipline and maturity to enable them to deal with others in a clinical manner without outward display of emotion, that will equip them to tolerate stress in any number of different situations, and that will cause them to take an intense interest in incidents which, though routine for them, are crises in the lives of others.

This list of qualities would doubtless elicit a great deal of debate from both police administrators and private citizens. But even if some consensus could be reached on what characteristics are most desirable in a police officer, the question remains whether screening procedures can be designed to measure them.

At the present time selection tests are a topic of major concern in the field. New requirements have been established to ensure that they are not discriminatory. In response to charges that tests used in the past were unfair, many police agencies are now using testing mechanisms which measure only minimal capacities—the ability of the applicant to comprehend simple instructions, to recognize detail, and to reason logically. Although these tests will prevent an agency from selecting its employees according to the patterns of the past, they may—if they are the principal screening device—also prevent police administrators from utilizing the selection process to bring a new sort of person into the police service.

Some characteristics needed in police officers—such as the capacity to relate to individuals, sensitivity to the problems of urban life, and flexibility in the face of change—are as important as, if not more important than, the characteristics that written examinations are intended to measure. It would be unfortunate indeed if the pressure for objective measurement precluded an opportunity to weigh these factors at some point in the selection process, difficult as it is to do so. The problem, of course, is that an opportunity for making subjective judgments is also an opportunity to undo the progress toward equity that validated job-related written tests reflect. In addition, the subjective portion of the examination—if carried out by subordinates who do not share the administrator's objectives—may be used to protect the values of the police subculture.[5]

One possible solution may be to require much greater visibility and accountability in the subjective parts of the examination procedure. Another is to make greater use of nonagency personnel to conduct interviews and background investigations. This could be achieved in varying degrees by delegating the task to municipal employees somewhat removed from police operations, by using police personnel from other agencies selected because of their approach to the police function, or by using persons drawn from the community who would judge applicants from a consumer's point of view. Some communities already make use of interview panelists drawn from outside the agency.[6]

Changing the Climate in the Agency

To retain a highly qualified officer it will be necessary to give him an entirely new role in the organization. He should be more involved in planning policies and methods of operation. He should, in particular, have more of a say in policies affecting his own role in the agency. He should have greater opportunities to realize his full potential in ways other than through promotion.

This does not mean that a police agency should be run as a democracy. Some situations will always require authoritarian management, such as when large numbers of officers must be mobilized to deal with an emergency. Nor does it mean that police administrators should commit themselves to participatory management, with the degree of employee involvement in decision-making that this somewhat nebulous concept implies. What is called for is not substitution of some radical new style of management but, instead, a gradual movement away from the extremely authoritarian climate that currently pervades police agencies toward a more democratic form of organization.

It would, for example, be a great step forward if operating personnel were consulted about the problems that arise in areas where they have acquired a great deal of expertise, and if their opinions were solicited about some of the issues relating to the management of the agency. Modifications of a more mundane nature in the day-to-day operation of the agency may be equally important. How essential is it, for example, that officers stand at attention each day for formal inspection? Or that officers adhere to the chain of command in all communication? Or that an officer be considered on duty at all times? Any objective assessment of specific practices would lead to abandoning many and greatly altering others.

A number of agencies have already changed their working atmosphere with startling results. Tremendous improvement in communication, for example, occurs by such a simple modification as holding a conference at the beginning of a shift rather than the formal roll call. This in turn has the potential for directly affecting the quality of service the officers deliver on the street.

Among the practices being reviewed is the traditional use of military uniforms. The most common argument for abandoning the uniform or making it less military is that such a change would reduce citizen hostility toward the police. Of equal importance, however, is the impact current practice has on the police officer's working environment. Does wearing a full military uniform make it less likely that an officer will be treated as an individual? Against these considerations one must weigh the value of a uniform as an expression of authority. It may be that an officer attired in military garb has less need to resort to using his arrest powers and force.

Another area that invites special attention is the internal system for handling complaints against police officers and administering discipline. As previously noted, officers base many of their attitudes toward policing the public on how they themselves are policed. A police administrator has an excellent opportunity to teach many of the most sensitive concepts that are at the very heart of policing in a free society by establishing internal investigation and discipline procedures that scrupulously assure due process to the officer—adequate notice, full hearing, access to counsel, the opportunity to confront his accusers, and review on appeal of any judgment adversely affecting him. The use of interrogations, the polygraph, and psychiatric examinations as part of internal investigations should also be carefully regulated.

Some special needs peculiar to the police function clearly exist in this area, as in all other aspects of policing. Under some conditions immediate action may be necessary which might be interpreted as punitive, such as suspending an officer (with pay) or placing him on a different assignment before any evidence is formally presented against him. But these are situations that can be anticipated and for which adequate provision can be made in a carefully constructed policy.

The failure of police administrators to establish suitable guidelines for internal investigations has resulted in the police unions pressing for legislation that would alter existing practices. Introduced in Congress and in many state legislatures, the proposals—each of which is commonly referred to as a bill of rights for police officers—usually include provisions that go beyond assuring due process.[7] The bill, as enacted in Florida, for example, provides that all members of the board established to review citizen complaints shall be law enforcement officers and that the accused officer shall have the right to select a certain proportion of the board himself.[8]

One of the most promising developments in policing has been experimentation with task forces of officers to develop department policies relating to a specific aspect of their operations (such as the handling of cases involving the mentally ill); or to develop internal procedures or regulations (such as those covering the use of department equipment). In the most radical departure from prevailing practice the task forces have been assigned to develop new ideas for improving police operations and to design ways in which their ideas might be tested. FBI Director Clarence M. Kelley, when he was chief of the Kansas City, Missouri, Police Department, established a number of task forces to identify problems in their areas of operation and to design programs to address these problems. Each group of officers, with financial and staff support made available by the Police Foundation, came up with a project—one of which evolved into the well-known preventive patrol experiment.[9] The fact that this novel project was the brainchild of a group of officers was an achievement that was equal in significance to the project itself.

It is encouraging to witness what usually happens when a group of officers who have never been asked for their comments on police operations are taken out of the chain of command and invited to discuss the policies and practices that so directly affect them. After an initial period of awkwardness, as rank is ignored and respect for individuals as individuals is demonstrated, there is typically an outpouring of pent-up feelings and, more important, the tapping of a reservoir of knowledge and ideas regarding the running of the department. If the process is carefully developed, the sincerity of the top administrators confirmed, and the participants given the opportunity to actually carry out their ideas, an exhilarating spirit may spread through the agency as individual officers, with newly developed self-respect, contribute enthusiastically to improving operations.

All efforts to involve officers in thinking about agency problems are not, of course, successful. Much depends on the nature of the project and its leadership. Some personnel who were perhaps initially attracted to the police field because of its highly structured military organization are exceedingly uncomfortable in a less formal atmosphere and may have great difficulty participating in the making of decisions that have previously been made for them. The presence of such officers requires that special attention be given to their needs as an agency undergoes change, lest they become casualties of the process.

Still another way of modifying the working environment is to afford an officer an opportunity for advancement in both pay and formal status without requiring that he move into a supervisory position. Many officers, interested in and good at delivering services to the public, have neither the inclination nor perhaps the ability to supervise other personnel or perform administrative tasks. It should be possible to recognize and reward such officers in the same manner as some jurisdictions now reward school teachers who are excellent in the classroom, but who have no desire to be school administrators. An agency can take the first steps toward such a policy by altering its job-classification system so that officers who excel in their work receive the same salary as first- or second-level supervisors. Ample safeguards must be established, of course, to prevent the arrangement from deteriorating into a system that fills the more highly paid positions on the basis of seniority.

Related to this alternative is the feasibility—especially in the larger departments—of recognizing to a much greater degree the special skills and talents of individual officers. This is already achieved to some extent in those departments where assignment (not requiring promotion) as a detective or as a youth officer is based upon an examination or some other form of evaluation of the skills required in these jobs. But an endless variety of skills is still needed in most agencies, given the multiplicity of functions that are performed. With some adjustments in the usual arrangements for deploying officers, many additional opportunities can be created to assign officers selectively, based upon their demonstrated skills and interests. This is essentially what is meant by the concept of a "generalist-specialist" officer, popularized by the family-crisis intervention projects.[10]

The point, very simply, is that some officers are especially good at handling domestic quarrels, while others seem uniquely equipped to respond to the needs of rape victims; some do well in handling those accused of shoplifting, and others are good at handling disturbances involving teen-agers. To send an officer to an incident who is challenged by it—rather than possibly repelled—makes so much sense that it hardly requires justification, so long as one does not build too much rigidity into the organization. To the extent that police knowledge and skill can be systematized and effectively applied by specialization, citizens benefit and officers derive much more satisfaction from their work.

New Personnel as a Force for Change

Although efforts to recruit and retain different kinds of individuals as police officers are dependent upon changes in the atmosphere within police organizations, they need not await the completion of such changes. On the contrary, new personnel can contribute to bringing about change. Much depends on the ability of the police administrator to coordinate the modifications in personnel practices and the organization so that they complement each other.

Several recent developments will strengthen the position of the change-oriented administrator and seem likely to bring enormous pressure to bear upon the chief who resists departures from traditional methods of operating. One is the increase in the number of employees drawn from minority groups, hired through the initiative of the agency or in response to pressure from affirmative-action programs. A second is the rapid increase in women employees, again as a result of civil-rights legislation and court orders. And a third is the entry into the police ranks of young people who have grown up in a period in which established institutions have been challenged and their relevance to the problems of the day questioned. Given the percentage that these three groups constitute in the total pool from which applicants are drawn, it is unlikely that the police will be able to select only those individuals who fit the traditional pattern.

It is also unlikely that the existing police subculture will be capable of totally negating the unique perspectives that recruits drawn from these groups will bring into the police service, for some of their values and commitments will be deeply ingrained. This is especially true of blacks and Spanish-speaking people who, in applying for police employment, see it as an opportunity to advance some of the very principles that resulted in a recognition—however belated—of their own underrepresentation in police ranks. We are already seeing increased activism from associations of black police officers who, much to the dismay of tradition-bound administrators, are putting important issues before the police and the public.[11]

The most radical proposal advanced in recent years to use personnel reform to bring about change is for the creation of a program whereby young people could serve as police for a temporary period.[12] As originally advocated, police service was to be an alternative to the military draft, with the avowed purpose of bringing more of a cross section of the population into police employment. One of the proposals was aimed specifically at attracting college graduates by linking a college education with an agreement to serve with the police for a set period of time.[13] In addition to destroying the insularity of the police, the proposals were thought to have the potential for increasing police status, creating a more favorable atmosphere for present officers, encouraging career officers to pursue their education, and increasing community understanding of police operations—thereby generating public support for needed change by having in the community a greater number of people who had worked with the police. With the end of an active draft, much of the initial impetus for the idea faded.

The notion of replacing the existing career service with a short-term service appears so radical to most police officers and to others as to sound ludicrous. But if these employees were used to assist career officers—the way paraprofessionals are being used in other areas—the plan might win the support of police personnel. Short-term employees could not, however, be assigned only those duties that are mundane and routine. It would be essential that their assignments expose them to the full range of police activities.

Many young people who would otherwise never consider police employment might be willing to put in several years with a police agency if they were not expected to commit themselves to policing as a career. A reduction in college costs would make the opportunity even more attractive. Such service might come to be viewed as a unique form of graduate training for a career in urban affairs.

The police would benefit in several ways. They would attract individuals with a level of competence they claim to be seeking unsuccessfully in their current recruitment efforts. They would have the services of highly motivated, energetic, diverse young people. And if some of the short-term employees became suffi-· ciently interested in policing to pursue careers in the field, the program could become a major source of recruitment for the career service. At a time of grow-ing needs and shrinking financial resources, short-term employees—assuming they would not be highly paid—could supply the increased manpower frequently demanded by both police administrators and the community. And, given the critical need for better understanding of the complex nature of the police func-tion, one cannot emphasize enough the potential value in having a large number of people sprinkled throughout a community—in legislative bodies, in admin-istrative positions in government, in the professions, in the business community, and in grass-roots neighborhood organizations—who have an intimate knowledge of the police and their problems and who will then be in a position to support much-needed change.

Obviously, use of short-term employees to augment rather than supplant the career service would not produce the rapid transformation in police agencies that the original proponents of the short-term draft had as their objective. And there is no question that the permanent officers, especially if hostile to short-term em-ployees, could so isolate themselves as to become impervious to any change, thereby defeating the prime objective of the undertaking. But properly intro-duced into some settings, the short-term employee could contribute to the growth and maturity of the agency and its present personnel.

Attracting Minorities

In the many studies conducted after the wave of urban violence in the 1960s, police agencies were severely criticized for the low proportion of minority mem-bers found in their ranks compared to their proportion in the general population, and especially for their infinitesimal representation in supervisory positions.[14] There were, as well, charges of outright discrimination against blacks in hiring practices.[15] This criticism, since augmented by the pressure of affirmative-action programs, has made the recruitment of minorities a major concern of police administrators. The motivation, of course, varies. It may be a sincere belief that a police force should be representative of the community being policed, or a pragmatic effort to reduce the hostility between the police and minority groups, or simply the need to comply with the law.

In fairness to the police it must be recognized that many departments were far ahead of other government agencies, private businesses, and educational insti-tutions in employing and promoting minorities. But for an organization inti-mately involved with problems in the minority community, and repeatedly called on to deal with racial strife, this progress was not adequate. While many jurisdictions have greatly increased the number of minority-group members employed, others have actually suffered a net loss.[16] And most have had difficulty attracting minority members to police employment.

Drives to attract minority applicants have made use of a variety of techniques, such as mobile recruitment units sent into the inner city, store-front offices, visits to community centers, presentations at schools and colleges, advertisements in minority news media, and the use of integrated recruitment teams. All of these aggressive steps are in sharp contrast with previous practices that required the applicant to take the initiative in seeking police employment. Commendable as they are, however, they do not get at the central problem, which is that many members of minority groups view the police as hostile to them and their interests.

Admittedly minority communities depend heavily upon the police and seek out their services. But this usage alone—which is not always a matter of choice—does not offset basic attitudes of distrust and outright animosity. Obvious as this explanation of recruitment failures should be, it is not recognized or at least not openly acknowledged by those police administrators who often register surprise when their extremely aggressive recruitment efforts do not produce qualified candidates. Blacks and other minority-group members enter police service for some of the same reasons that whites do, such as the security it offers. But the more qualified the minority-group members are, the more likely it is that they will be concerned about the working environment in the agency; the opportunities for advancement; and the motives of the agency in recruiting them. This last is of special importance, for if it appears that the sole objective of the agency is to comply with the law or to continue practices that are offensive to the minority community, but which might be considered less so if carried out by officers drawn from the community, it is highly unlikely that qualified minority members will apply.

The single most important step a police administrator can take toward recruiting more members of minority groups is to demonstrate in unequivocal terms that he is working vigorously to ensure that the personnel of his agency do not, in their daily contacts with members of the minority community, discriminate against them. He must further provide clear evidence that members of minority groups employed by the agency will have equal opportunities regarding assignments and promotion. Once credibility is established in this fashion, a straightforward recruitment drive that communicates to potential applicants that they are really wanted will have a much greater chance of succeeding.

While a police administrator must be convinced of the importance in attracting minority members into police work simply as a matter of fairness, there are indeed a number of other reasons for recruiting them. If a chief is of the view that the quality of police service depends on an officer's knowledge of the specific neighborhood he polices—its values and customs—it follows that he should have in his department individuals drawn from the racial and ethnic groups represented in the city. These minority members would serve a further, perhaps even more important, purpose. The presence of increased numbers of minority police officers on a police agency and the interrelationships which it fosters can be the most effective means the agency has for developing understanding, combating prejudices, and curbing practices offensive to minority groups. No training program can possibly work as well as this day-to-day contact among peers to break down the barriers and hostilities between different cultures.

For the traditional police administrator, who is insensitive to the complex problems in achieving racial equality, adopting the steps suggested here may appear to unnecessarily stir up tensions in the community and among his own personnel. He might also feel threatened—and justifiably so—by the possibility that an increase in the number of minority officers will result in a challenge of police practices to which he is strongly committed. The more enlightened administrator should see such movement as significant progress toward improving police services and, thereby, the quality of life in an urban area. This is not to say that such progress can be realized easily. On the contrary, it requires a great deal of managerial skill. Tensions will indeed increase—especially within a police agency—and if not properly handled can produce explosive situations. Fights have broken out between white and black police officers in several large cities.

Screening for Emotional Stability

In selecting recruits, police agencies are under some pressure to attempt to identify and reject individuals who lack the stability required to make proper use of their authority and to function under stress.[17] In case after case in which an officer engages in bizarre conduct or repeatedly uses excessive force, the question is raised whether his potential for such conduct could have been anticipated. Yet police agencies that have recognized the need for psychiatric and psychological screening have often been criticized for the use made of these procedures— and frequently on sound grounds. A combination of improper use of existing testing techniques and the inability of the most competent psychologists and psychiatrists to be precise in their judgments leaves the agency vulnerable to the charge that a person turned down for psychological reasons was unfairly rejected. This poses a problem not only for the police, but for various community organizations committed to safeguarding individual rights. They find themselves wanting to advocate such testing, yet leery of the testing procedures that are used.

Mental stability, as all seem to agree, is extremely important in policing. And to the degree that methods have been developed and validated for predicting stability, the police would seem obligated to make careful and discreet use of them. But because it requires competent personnel to administer and interpret such tests and because the instruments themselves have inadequacies, the dilemma confronted by the police administrator can often best be resolved by using such tests only as gross measures—rejecting extreme cases where rejection can often be supported by biographical information independently collected and admitting somewhat questionable applicants for a trial period during which their behavior is closely observed. The high cost of training an individual who is subsequently dismissed may simply be one of the prices police agencies must pay for a screening system that is both thorough and fair.

TRAINING RECRUITS

In the constant search for ways to improve police operations, reformers give high priority to the training of new recruits. People routinely look to training as a way to equip officers to perform in stricter accord with desired standards. But beyond this, recruit training is often seen as a vehicle for bringing about much-needed change in the police. It is the point at which some feel it might be most feasible to inject new values and ideas.

Although a change-oriented police administrator typically has great difficulty exerting control over the units and personnel in his agency, he does have full and direct control over the formal training effort. He can select its staff and dictate what is to be taught. Under these conditions it is commonly assumed that a high quality of recruit training should overcome—or, as a minimum, offset—the pressures to which the recruit is subjected by the organization and by his peers.

With the support of both those who see recruit training as a way of bringing new personnel quickly up to prevailing standards and those who see it as a way of establishing new, higher, and somewhat different standards, the attention given to the training of new officers has greatly increased in the past decade. But partly as a result of this investment of more resources and energy, there is growing doubt that training in its present form achieves the objectives its proponents hold out for it.

Haphazard Development of Programs

Putting differing orientations aside, the need for recruit training of some kind—to convey the most fundamental knowledge and skills required in police work to individuals new to the job—seems so obvious as to hardly require mention. And yet this country has been incredibly slow in recognizing the need. California stands out as an exception, having established statewide programs for police training starting in 1959.[18] Elsewhere in the country, many police agencies, including some of the largest, were without *any* systematic recruit training less than a score of years ago. This situation has changed dramatically, especially as other state legislatures have enacted minimum statewide training standards requiring a specified number of hours of training before a candidate can be certified as a police officer.[19]

Yet most police agencies still do not give a high priority to preparing new personnel for police service. Many of the smaller agencies provide no training.

Where programs exist, agencies often follow the practice of first assigning new personnel to the street and only subsequently bringing them into the training program. Perhaps few things speak as clearly regarding the current commitment to recruit training as the low budgetary priority it typically receives. Training is among the first operations to be cut back in a financial crunch. And recruits in training are often looked upon as a ready reservoir of available manpower to be assigned to regular police duties when necessary. So the training of new officers is still thought of as a luxury, to be undertaken if time, resources, and staff permit. It is not yet considered indispensable preparation for a complex and awesome job.

With limited hours available and so much to cover, expediency rules: large numbers of facts are crammed into short periods of time; lectures are used in the belief that they maximize coverage; and one class is held after another, filling an eight-hour workday. Moreover, since the number of recruits fluctuates along with the number of hours of training, there is no permanent training staff except in the largest departments. Instructors are drawn from the ranks as they are needed and rarely receive adequate preparation for their task.

The makeshift arrangements account for the common practice of booking guest lecturers into hourly slots without integrating their presentations with class discussions. And they account also for the dearth of persons who devote themselves full time to recruit training and who should be developing this critical aspect of police operations more rationally.

The success of a training program is commonly measured in terms of the number of hours of classroom work. Eight weeks is considered a 100 percent improvement over four weeks, though the longer program may be no more effective and far more boring.

Assessment of Current Programs

Against this background it should not be surprising that those who have analyzed the status of recruit training in recent years have found much that is wrong.[20] Extraordinarily heavy emphasis is placed on maintaining neat notebooks and on committing to memory large numbers of irrelevant facts. Technical subjects are emphasized over basic principles of law, democracy, and human relations. The military atmosphere and the prevailing teaching techniques make the training process a very passive one for the recruit. And the programs are structured to convey only one point of view on controversial matters in a manner intended to avoid open discussion.

Beyond these observations there is an unreal quality in the training programs—in the emphasis placed on military protocol, in their narrow concept of the police function, and in their according-to-the-book teaching of police operations. In addition to the emphasis on the police function relative to crime, they often dwell on specific topics of little practical value and ignore large areas to which officers devote most of their time. They create the impression that the highly structured organization of the police agency results in a highly structured work environment as well. And they tend to portray the police officer's job as a rigid one, largely dictated by law, ignoring the tremendous amount of discretion officers are required to exercise.

Several years ago I reviewed the manner in which recruits were being taught to exercise their discretion in a recruit training program in one of the more advanced police departments in the country. The exploration of discretion was restricted to a one-hour session which was devoted to a consideration of how officers might handle extraordinary circumstances. We discussed the need for recognizing the more common forms of discretion police exercised daily, and the suggestion was made that the discretionary aspects of the police task be considered throughout the course. The staff, however, concluded it was preferable to maintain that officers do not have any discretion, but agreed to include a segment at the end of the program that modified their position slightly.

In searching for an explanation of why recruit training has taken this form, one gets the impression that the responsible administrators and faculty want their programs to convey to recruits how they think police should operate under ideal circumstances—as if providing such training might move police toward this image. And they evidently assume that any compromise of the stereotyped model of policing—with its emphasis upon spit and polish, objectivity, and rigid discipline—will increase the speed with which the new recruit will turn to less desirable practices.

In attempting to mold police officers according to an unrealistic model that is tied to all of the myths of policing, the training programs fail to achieve the minimal goal of orienting a new employee to his new job. Indeed it could be persuasively argued that many of the present programs not only fail to supply the orientation, they actually deceive the recruit by providing an inaccurate picture of what he can expect on the job. The major lesson this kind of training teaches the new officer is that he cannot take seriously the formal structure and administrative direction of the agency; that, as between the formal instruction of his superiors and the informal guidance of his peers, the latter has much greater validity.

Related to this observation is the noticeable failure to equip officers to understand the built-in stresses of their job. They receive no preparation for dealing with the conflicts and contradictory pressures—reflecting all of the underlying problems of policing discussed in chapter 1—in which they will inevitably become involved. Officers are often simply instructed to do things: to be courteous and respectful to members of minority groups; to warn suspects that they may remain silent; to protect the right of the most radical speakers to speak; to exercise restraint in the use of force; to refuse even the most sincere offer of a gift; to arrest petty gamblers and marijuana users. Each such instruction results from an extremely important legislative, judicial, or administrative judgment that has a long history behind it and that often reflects a balancing of competing values and priorities. But the full background of such judgments is usually not shared with the recruits. And without this background, some of these instructions make little sense. They may even seem contradictory. It should not, therefore, be surprising if officers implement policies in a manner that reflects less than full understanding, or if they fail to implement them with any conviction.

With such terse instructions in these controversial areas, officers are left to discover on their own the binds in which society places them: attempt to be polite, courteous, and respectful in what is often a hostile environment; pursue criminals relentlessly, but safeguard their rights; develop rapport with the community, but remain sufficiently aloof to be objective in enforcing the law; stand committed to enforcing all laws, but refrain from enforcing some of them some of the time; be responsive to the community, but resist the pressures of the majority in order to protect minority interests. Officers work their way through this maze by making a personal adjustment to the conflicting pressures on them. We complain frequently about the adjustments that are made, as reflected in the actions of the officers. But, despite the tremendous amount of knowledge we have about the problems the police must handle and despite the rich insights we have acquired into the dynamics of police operations, we do little if anything to help a recruit in the incredibly complex task of gaining a better perspective of his role either in the agency in which he will be functioning or in the society he is expected to police.

Opportunities to Improve Recruit Training

It is tempting to contend that an investment in improved recruit training is not likely to produce worthwhile results until other more basic problems in policing are addressed: the ambiguity in the nature of the police function; the over-reliance on the criminal justice system; the overly authoritarian structure of the police organization; and the attitudes of traditional police leadership. Only then could one expect support for needed change and the creation of an organizational environment in which the new recruit would have a reasonable opportunity to build upon—rather than abandon—his training experience. But by now it should be apparent that progress in all aspects of policing is closely interrelated. Work must go forward in developing recruit training programs, but with a full awareness of the changes that are needed and are occurring elsewhere, so that innovations in training will be designed to support these changes.

As a minimum, programs that do more harm than good should be stripped of their worst elements or even abandoned. It is better to have no training than to have a training program that misleads the recruit and contributes to his subsequent disillusionment. For most recruit training programs it would be a gigantic advance if they were designed simply to equip an officer realistically to do those things he will have to do. Specifically, this means that a recruit should be acquainted with the multiplicity of police functions, should learn the methods (informal as well as formal) the police use for intervening in incidents and for disposing of their business, and should be instructed in how to use his discretion in choosing among them. It means, too, that problems on which the police spend most of their time should receive more attention. And it means that instruction cannot be given in a vacuum. It must be integrated with experience in the field in such a way that the recruit learns to apply his training to real incidents he encounters on the street. By closing the gap between actual police work and the concept of police work conveyed in training, the whole recruit training process would take on much greater credibility.

Certain basic technical material must always be covered in recruit training. Beyond this minimum a recruit must be given the background that enables him to understand the milieu in which he will function. He should learn enough about the nature of serious criminal conduct, for example, to see such conduct in the context of the larger problems of social disorganization. He should be made familiar with the struggle for racial equality in order to better understand his role in handling racial tensions. He should be taught enough about political dissent and about various social and political organizations to see these movements in the larger context of our political system and the processes of social change. And he should be made aware of the way in which the public perceives the police and the historical basis for current distrust. The purpose in giving a recruit a background for his job is not to change his ideology. Nor is it assumed, for example, that such knowledge, by itself, will enable an officer to accept personal abuse without reacting in an emotional manner. The goal is a more modest one: to reduce in magnitude some of the acute problems suffered by police officers—the anxiety, the defensiveness, and the stress—which stem from a lack of adequate understanding by the rank and file of just how perplexing the problems are that they will be called upon to handle.

Given the extensive use made of the criminal justice system, for example, recruits should be acquainted with the operations of that system. This should go beyond a study of the formal steps in the criminal process. It should include a review of the major issues that arise in the operation of the system. By way of illustration, how healthy it would be if police recruits had the opportunity to explore the array of problems in sentencing. Such exposure might reduce the frustration felt by police officers when it appears to them that the sentence imposed does not fit the crime. It might also reduce the distrust and friction between the police and the prosecutors and judges which stem, in large measure, from the police belief that a light sentence is an indication of lack of support for police work, or incompetence, or corruption. This is not to say that there is no basis for police criticism of sentencing policies and other practices. On the contrary, constructive criticism by the police of the operations of both the prosecutor and the courts is much needed. But police criticism is usually stated in such simplistic terms—expressed in what has come to be viewed as the traditional police stance—that it is not taken seriously.

New recruits might even be expected to explore and debate the opposing views on such controversial subjects as the use of the criminal sanction to control prostitution, gambling, and narcotics; eavesdropping and wiretapping; the use of informants; the possible prohibition or registration of firearms; political surveillance; capital punishment; sentencing practices; methods of controlling police corruption; and the various proposals for effecting change in police organizations. Again, the objective here would not be to convert recruits to a particular viewpoint, but to enable them to recognize that there are two sides to many of these issues and very little hard data upon which judgments can be made. Hopefully, people holding different viewpoints would then be less threatening to the police.

This whole process might establish a pattern of analysis that would, during the career of a police officer, result in his constructively criticizing all aspects of police functioning. This kind of openness, commitment to analytical thinking, and tolerance of opposing views is what I suspect writers have meant when they have spoken of the need for a form of training that would broaden police perspectives.

The same reasoning suggests that police recruits be given the benefit of the many insights recorded in the growing literature on the nature of police organizations, on their resistance to change, on the existence of a police subculture, and, most specifically, on the difficulties experienced by new officers entering a police organization. Frank discussion could reveal ways in which the recruit might more effectively cope with pressures from peers and superiors. It could reduce the shock and disillusionment of discovering the realities of police work, and it would certainly add to the credibility of the training program.

To achieve these various objectives will require the development of new training techniques and further experimentation with techniques that have recently been introduced in a small number of departments, including Boston; Dayton; Madison, Wisconsin; and Oakland, California.[21] Two forms of training with which there has been some limited experimentation hold considerable promise. The first consists of efforts to familiarize new recruits with the wide range of people with whom they will be working and, in the process, to sensitize them to the different cultures and life-styles of citizens. Arrangements have been made for officers to spend time in minority communities. Political activists have been brought in to discuss their methods and aims. And it has proved helpful, under appropriate conditions, to have a free open classroom discussion with such people as convicted felons, juvenile gang members, prostitutes, drug addicts, alcoholics, and those who are mentally ill. Some agencies have assigned recruits to emergency rooms of hospitals, clinics for alcoholics, psychiatric wards, and welfare offices to afford them an opportunity for contact with people in a context other than the usual police-citizen relationship. The officer also has the opportunity in these contacts to learn about the various services to which referrals will be made.

The second novel form of training consists of experiential projects that have the limited but important objective of sensitizing police to the authority they exercise. An officer is put in a situation in which he is processed by the police. He might, for example, be taken into custody without advance notice and detained in a jail cell overnight; or he might be placed on a skid row in a strange city and have to explain his presence there to patrolling police officers. While these programs have not been carefully evaluated, they have been praised by both their sponsors and those who have participated in them.[22]

It has often been observed that when an officer is accused of wrongdoing he very quickly develops a respect for constitutional provisions he might otherwise have considered mere technicalities in the way of effective law enforcement. Although not as threatening as a real situation, well-designed exercises that pit an officer against the police and that are fully integrated with classroom work apparently have equal potential as a training technique.

Some would contend that the depth of police training advocated here ignores the average level of competence of police recruits; that it would be extremely difficult to engage a typical class of police recruits in a discussion of controversial policy issues. I strongly disagree with this contention. Those responsible for police training have for too long underestimated the abilities and interests of new officers; much of what is offered in training is so elementary that it is both demeaning and boring. Admittedly the gradual increase in the variety of individuals coming into police service results in classes of recruits that vary greatly in their abilities. This creates a need, however, not for curtailing the depth with which subject matter is pursued, but for developing training devices that recognize the varying speeds and levels at which recruits learn.[23]

IN-SERVICE TRAINING

If recruit training is inadequate, in-service training is more so. Many departments have initiated programs to systematically provide a week or more of annual training for all personnel, but few have been able to maintain their programs. It is very costly, requiring sufficient personnel to replace the officers while they are training or funds to compensate them for attending classes during their off-duty hours. Beyond its high cost, its value is seriously questioned. Those who administer in-service training programs are frequently dissatisfied with the use made of the time that is available. Officers who are taken out of the tempo of daily police operations and placed in a classroom present a special challenge. They tend to be cynical about administrative directions and formal training. They are often poorly motivated. They are deeply imbued with the police subculture. Moreover, they frequently have more expertise regarding some of the problems discussed than both their instructors and their supervisors. Given these conditions it is simply not sufficient to schedule lectures, whether the objective is to provide officers in specialized assignments, such as detectives, with knowledge about their specialities, or to bring all officers up to date regarding recent changes in the law and in the operating procedures of the department.

One way in which to make more effective use of available time is to engage officers in a way that draws upon their expertise—the skills and knowledge they have acquired from their street experiences. The Boston Police Department, for example, found that their effort to learn how police officers handle difficult arrest-and-search situations—which is a part of a rule-making project—created a classroom situation in which a good deal of learning went on.[24] The officers articulated their own practices, subjecting them to the criticism of their peers, and had the opportunity to compare their practices to those that the group decided (with the guidance of an instructor) were the most appropriate responses under the circumstances.

It is an error to view in-service training as limited to the classroom. Some of the best training experiences have been a by-product of projects aimed at testing the value of existing police practices or designed to evaluate new approaches to policing. The officers who participated in San Diego's Community Profile Project, for example, had an extraordinarily rich experience, learning a great deal about the people residing in the areas to which they were assigned, the problems that citizens experienced, and the resources available for dealing with them.[25] They had the opportunity to reflect on the nature of the police function, to experiment with new self-devised strategies for improving police service, and to evaluate the results of their efforts. The obvious benefits derived from participation in such projects tell us something about what it will take to make in-service training a more meaningful experience.

The absence of a greater number of experiments aimed at improving in-service training should be a matter of some concern, for the financial burden of such training will require that there be demonstrable proof of its value before administrators will be willing to argue more aggressively for making it a permanent part of their agencies' operations. But the pressures for improving in-service training have actually diminished as police administrators and other responsible officials have placed most of their resources and almost all of their hopes for upgrading police personnel in college-level programs for the police—a development explored in the next chapter.

NOTES

1. This is a constantly recurring theme in the literature on the police, including the various national studies and especially the management studies of individual police agencies. It was set forth most recently by O. Glenn Stahl and Richard A. Staufenberger in their preface to *Police Personnel Administration* (Washington, D.C.: Police Foundation, 1974), p. iii.

2. National Advisory Commission on Criminal Justice Standards and Goals, *Police* (Washington, D.C.: Government Printing Office, 1973), pp. 337, 348–351.

3. Melany E. Baehr, John E. Furcon, and Ernest C. Froemel, *Psychological Assessment of Patrolman Qualifications in Relation to Field Performance* (Washington, D.C.: Government Printing Office, 1968), pp. 21, 34–37.

4. Bernard Cohen and Jan M. Chaiken, *Police Background Characteristics and Performance* (New York: Rand Institute, 1972), pp. 7–8.

5. See, e.g., Thomas C. Gray, "Selecting for a Police Subculture," in *Police in America*, edited by Jerome H. Skolnick and Thomas C. Gray (Boston: Educational Associates, Little, Brown and Co., 1975), pp. 46–54.

6. This process has not, however, to my knowledge, been evaluated to determine how the judgments of the nonpolice members differ from those of the police personnel.

7. For the most recent proposal submitted to Congress, see U.S., Congress, House, A Bill, H. R. 5476, 94th Cong., 1st sess., 25 March 1975.

8. *Florida Statutes* §112.532 (Supp. 1974).

9. George L. Kelling et al., *The Kansas City Preventive Patrol Experiment: A Technical Report* (Washington, D.C.: Police Foundation, 1974), pp. 23–25. For a more detailed discussion, see Thomas Sweeney, "A Report on the Use of Task Forces for Change in the Kansas City Police Department," in *Changing Police Organizations: Four Readings* (Washington, D.C.: National League of Cities and U.S. Conference of Mayors, 1973), pp. 13–27. For other examples of the use of task forces, see National Advisory Commission on Criminal Justice Standards and Goals, *Police*, pp. 448–450.

10. See Morton Bard, *Training Police as Specialists in Family Crisis Intervention* (Washington, D.C.: Government Printing Office, 1970), p. 13.

11. The beginnings of this movement are described in Hervey A. Juris and Peter Feuille, *Police Unionism* (Lexington, Mass.: Lexington Books, D. C. Heath, 1973), pp. 165–175. The most recent and most far-reaching action was the civil-rights suit brought by the Afro-American Patrolmen's League of Chicago against the Chicago Police Department. *United States* v. *City of Chicago*, 11 CCH Employment Practices Decisions ¶ 10,597 (N.D.Ill. 1976).

12. See Irving Piliavin, *Police-Community Alienation: Its Structural Roots and a Proposed Remedy*, Warner Modular Publications #14 (New York: M.S.S. Publications, 1973); Adam Walinsky, "Proposal for a Fundamental Restructuring of the Police," mimeographed, n.d. (copy on file in University of Wisconsin Law Library, Madison, Wisconsin); and Anthony M. Champagne and Beatriz Champagne, "An Analysis of an Alternative to the Present Method of Police Selection: Conscription of Police in Argentina," *Police*, March 1972, pp. 21–25.

13. Walinsky, "Proposal for a Fundamental Restructuring of the Police," p. 9.

14. National Advisory Commission on Civil Disorders, *Report of the National Advisory Commission on Civil Disorders* (Washington, D.C.: Government Printing Office, 1968), pp. 165–166, 169.

15. In New York City, a court suit resulted in a special study of the problem. See Jan M. Chaiken and Bernard Cohen, *Police Civil Service Selection Procedures in New York City* (New York: Rand Institute, 1973).

16. Chicago and Philadelphia are among the larger cities in which the percentage of minority police officers has declined from what was reported by the National Advisory Commission on Civil Disorders in 1968.

17. See Ralph Knoohuizen and William Bailey, *The Selection and Hiring of Chicago Policemen* (Evanston, Ill.: Chicago Law Enforcement Study Group,

1973), as an example of a recent study financed by groups with a strong civil-liberties orientation that is highly critical of the police for failing to make greater use of methods for screening out applicants with emotional deficiencies.

18. For a comprehensive description of the development of this program, see Brooks W. Wilson, "The Growth and Development of the California Commission on Peace Officer Standards and Training" (Master's Thesis, California State University, 1974).

19. A survey by the National Association of Directors of Law Enforcement Training revealed that as of January 1, 1975, 38 states had enacted mandatory training standards and 6 states had adopted standards with which they seek voluntary compliance.

20. See, e.g., Richard N. Harris, *The Police Academy* (New York: John Wiley and Sons, 1973); John H. McNamara, "Uncertainties in Police Work: The Relevance of Police Recruits' Backgrounds and Training," in David J. Bordua, ed., *The Police: Six Sociological Essays* (New York: John Wiley and Sons, 1967), pp. 163–252; Charles B. Saunders, Jr., *Upgrading the American Police* (Washington, D.C.: The Brookings Institution, 1970), pp. 120–132; and Stahl and Staufenberger, *Police Personnel Administration*, pp. 125–138.

21. For a description of some of these programs, see Robert Wasserman, Michael Paul Gardner, and Alana S. Cohen, *Improving Police/Community Relations* (Washington, D.C.: Government Printing Office, 1974), pp. 32–39; Stahl and Staufenberger, *Police Personnel Administration*, pp. 130–138; National Advisory Commission on Criminal Justice Standards and Goals, *Police*, pp. 394–395, 401–403; and Hans Toch, J. Douglas Grant, and Raymond T. Galvin, *Agents of Change* (New York: John Wiley and Sons, 1975), pp. 305–318.

22. For example, both the trainees and the trainers in the San Diego field interrogation project ranked the experiential segments in the model training program designed for this project to be the "most meaningful and unifying components of the training curriculum." John E. Boydstun et al., *San Diego Field Interrogation: Final Report* (Washington, D.C.: Police Foundation, 1975), p. 11.

23. The Boston Police Department and the District of Columbia Metropolitan Police Department are among the agencies that have made the greatest progress toward designing training programs to meet the varying needs of individual officers.

24. The project was launched in April, 1975, by the Boston Police Department and the Boston University Law School Center for Criminal Justice with support from the National Institute of Law Enforcement and Criminal Justice.

25. For a full description of this project, see John E. Boydstun and Michael E. Sherry, *San Diego Community Profile: Final Report* (Washington, D.C.: Police Foundation, 1975).

Chapter 11

Higher Education and the Police

A major new relationship has evolved during the past decade between the police and institutions of higher education. Hundreds of colleges and universities have established programs of studies for police personnel, and thousands of police officers and those aspiring to a career in policing have enrolled in them. In addition the institutions of higher education are being expected to contribute toward developing the future leadership of the police field, as discussed in chapter 9, and to engage in research to assist the police in finding better responses to some of the problems they must routinely handle. These added dimensions, plus the sheer magnitude of the movement to increase the number of college graduates in police employment, warrant this separate examination of higher education as it relates to policing.

DEVELOPMENT OF THE CONCEPT OF THE COLLEGE-EDUCATED OFFICER

Few efforts to improve police operations in recent years have received such enthusiastic and widespread support as the general notion that police officers should be college educated. As a consequence tremendous resources have been invested in recruiting college graduates; in encouraging present employees to enroll in programs leading to a degree; and in the establishment of new college-level programs.

This support is all the more remarkable because it was so slow in coming. The first efforts to involve college-educated personnel in police work were made by August Vollmer in 1917, when he recruited University of California students as part-time police officers in Berkeley.[1] From the outset a college education was considered a major part of the professional movement associated with Vollmer's reforms. But few departments elsewhere in the country took any immediate steps to follow his lead. Vollmer's campaign gained some fortuitous support on the national scene in the 1930s when college graduates, lacking other opportunities, sought employment with the police, but this trend lasted only as long as the Depression.[2]

Vollmer did have a more direct influence in his own state of California, where the practice of hiring college graduates increased steadily, though slowly. With the end of the war in 1945, the number of graduates hired by California police agencies rose substantially, and already-employed officers in the state began working toward their degrees.

Elsewhere, however, rank-and-file officers strongly resisted the concept of college-level studies for the police, and the officer with a college education remained very much an exception—often referred to wryly as a "college cop." The term itself implied that there was something incongruous about an educated police officer. College graduates, despite their steadily increasing number in the general population, did not seek employment with the police. The old but lingering stereotype of the "dumb flatfoot," the prevalent concept of policing as a relatively simple task, the low pay, and the limitations on advancement—all of these factors made it appear that a college education would be wasted in such a job. And the tremendous difference between the social status accorded a college graduate and the status accorded an officer made an anomaly of the individual who was both.

Reluctant as some have been to accept the feasibility of requiring a college education for a police officer who might subsequently cover a beat, direct traffic, or serve as a detective, there has always been a greater readiness to endorse college training for the officer having administrative responsibilities.[3] The earliest college offerings devoted to police studies concentrated on administration and were commonly referred to as programs in police administration. They reflected the emphasis that police reformers placed on improved management as a solution to police problems. It was a constant source of embarrassment to those operating these programs that they were preparing college students to assume administrative positions in organizations that reserved their administrative positions for veteran employees.

While most of the progress in attracting college graduates to police service was limited to California, those concerned with police improvement throughout the country continued to place great emphasis on the desirability of a college education—to the point that college studies became a standard recommendation in all programs for improving the police. The goal seemed so inconceivable when related to prevailing recruitment standards that one gets the impression the supporters of the movement recognized that their recommendation, though perhaps unattainable, was an effective way to stress the need for intelligent people in the field and the need to raise the status of police work.

With a college education firmly established as a major element in proposals for improving the police, the President's Commission on Law Enforcement and Administration of Justice recommended in 1967 that the "ultimate aim of all police departments should be that all personnel with general enforcement powers have baccalaureate degrees."[4] It recommended, too, that police departments take immediate steps to establish a minimum requirement of a baccalaureate degree for all supervisory and executive positions. The commission apparently had the same faith in the uplifting effect of a college education as earlier reformers.

But the commission's endorsement was to have a much greater impact. In response to the commission's report the federal government has supplied large amounts of money to finance the college education of police personnel and those who desire to enter police service; hundreds of new educational programs have been established, primarily at the two-year colleges; police agencies have adopted incentive pay plans that provide increments in salary based upon educational achievement; some agencies have announced programs that will gradually increase educational standards both for initial appointment and for promotion; and a number of agencies already require a college degree. At the same time some of the largest police departments have been aggressively recruiting college graduates, aided by the slump in the economy that has produced a shortage of jobs for people trained for other occupations, such as teaching and social work.

An indication of the magnitude of this trend can be gleaned from the rapid increase in the number of colleges and universities offering two- and four-year courses especially designed for the police. In 1954 there were 22 such programs.[5] In 1966 there were 152 programs in community colleges and 39 in institutions that offered a baccalaureate in law enforcement. By 1975 the number of community-college programs had climbed to 729 and the number of four-year programs to 376.[6]

The Law Enforcement Education Program, under the Law Enforcement Assistance Administration, which since 1968 has been administering the program of federal support for criminal justice education, provided financial assistance for 20,602 students in the first year of its existence. In 1973 it aided 95,000 students.[7] Approximately 71 percent of those who have participated in the program since its inception either have been employed by or intended to seek employment with the police.[8] The budget for the past three years has been $40 million per year.

In 1973 the National Advisory Commission on Criminal Justice Standards and Goals, building on the recommendations of the president's commission of 1967, sought to speed up the drive for college-educated officers. It recommended, in order to "insure the selection of personnel with the qualifications to perform police duties properly," that specific deadlines be set for implementing the recommendation of the earlier commission, with two years of college to be required of all new recruits by 1975, three by 1978, and four by 1982.[9]

THE VALUE OF HIGHER EDUCATION
FOR THE POLICE

Arguments Supporting Higher Education

Many arguments have been offered in support of the general proposition that police should be college educated. They have been offered in various combinations and with varying intensity. They fall into two categories: (1) those that claim the police should draw their personnel from individuals who attend college whether or not it can be clearly demonstrated that a college education is of value for policing; and (2) those that contend, more specifically, that the college experience will produce a better police officer.

The reasoning of those in the first category is that the police must recruit college graduates if they are to acquire their share of the able, intelligent young people from each year's addition to the work force. Until recently the percentage of high school graduates who went on to college increased annually. It was claimed that the police, by recruiting from among those who did not, necessarily chose individuals lacking the intelligence or the motivation required for higher education. This situation has changed somewhat as the percentage of high school graduates enrolling in colleges has decreased. Nevertheless, in a society in which a college experience is so readily available and in which so high a value is placed on it, the vast majority of the most qualified high school graduates do go on to college. It follows that the pool from which the police recruit, if they do not attract the college graduate, is limited in both size and quality.

That police agencies, in recruiting officers, are recruiting their future leadership as well adds to this concern. The problem has never been expressed as strongly and as forthrightly here as it was in England in 1962, when the Royal Commission on the Police observed:

> We are extremely concerned that the conditions of entry and promotion prospects of the police service should be such as will attract a sufficient number of recruits who are likely to make good chief constables and other senior officers twelve, fifteen or twenty years hence. In the past, many men with distinguished careers lacked a university education, but this situation is rapidly changing: young men of ability now tend in increasing numbers to proceed to the universities. Consequently a system of police recruiting which shows no evidence of success in attracting a sufficient proportion of entrants of graduate standard endangers the future leadership of the service. Improvements in pay and new training arrangements will not by themselves cure this defect. The police play a vital part in our national life and well-being and it is deplorable that they, to a far greater extent than any of the other public services, law, commerce, industry or indeed any major branch of our national life, should for years have been failing to recruit anything like their proper share of able and well educated young men. We do not suggest that graduates are necessarily more likely

than others to make effective chief constables: our concern is simply that the police today are not securing a sufficient share of the better educated section of the community.[10]

Some contend that along with a greater share of intelligent young people, police departments, in requiring a college degree, would also attract a greater cross section of the population. It is assumed that young people who go to college are drawn from socioeconomic groups having a wide range of views regarding both the police function and the problems with which the police must deal. It is argued that these people would improve police operations by broadening the values to which police personnel subscribe.

Still others argue that making a college education a requirement for the job is perhaps the most dramatic way whereby the police can divest themselves of some of the persistent misconceptions attached to their work, such as the impression that it consists of simple tasks that can be carried out by anybody. Higher education is expected to bring much-needed respectability, dignity, and status to police service. It is argued that the degree-carrying officer whose education equals or exceeds that of most of the people he contacts tends to function with much greater confidence and in a much less defensive manner. The educational requirement is seen as an indication of what the agency—or the police field as a whole—thinks of itself.

Egon Bittner speaks to some of these points when he notes:

> We do not propose that education be made to matter in the sense that what is taught be specifically relevant to practice. Naturally this would be highly desirable; but because very little knowledge exists that could conceivably serve this purpose, the limitation would merely show that study does not really matter. Instead, we merely propose that the need for protracted and assiduous study be firmly associated with the occupation of policing. The main objective of the recommendation is to abolish permanently the idea that is all too prevalent in our society that if one does not want to take the trouble of becoming something worthwhile, he can always become a cop. . . .[11]

All of the preceding arguments support college education for police irrespective of what is learned. The second category of arguments reflects the position that police not only stand to gain by recruiting from among those who go on to college but, more specifically, that it is the substance of what is learned in college and in the college experience that will produce a better police officer. In support of this view some claim that a unique body of knowledge, directly relevant to police practice, can appropriately be taught at the college level. They point to the large number of college-level courses currently offered by both two-year and four-year colleges that have been developed specifically for those going into the police service or who are already employed.

Critics of these courses claim that most of them more properly belong in police training classes.[12] Yet they see specific value in a program of studies that is heavily weighted with the liberal arts—the humanities, the sciences, and the arts—on the grounds that such studies develop the ability of an individual to think, to be critical, and to be creative. They urge that students interested in policing major in sociology, psychology, or political science in their last two years of a four-year program and take courses on such subjects as urban government, constitutional law, systems of legal control (including the operations of the criminal justice system), minority groups, social conflict, deviant conduct, and research methodology. Knowledge of these areas would, presumably, put policing in its proper perspective and help an officer to cope more effectively with the problems and people he confronts. These arguments parallel those set forth in the previous chapter regarding the need for broader and more challenging training for new recruits. College studies, however, would make it possible for the student to delve into such areas in a much more intensive and comprehensive manner.

Still another position deemphasizes course coverage, dwelling instead on the value of living in a college atmosphere. The college-trained officer, it is claimed, benefits from his association with students of different races, cultures, and nationalities. He is exposed to many different viewpoints and grows accustomed to an environment in which viewpoints are freely expressed. He learns to cope with new people and new situations. He becomes more mature, more balanced, and much less parochial. Presumably this will make him a more flexible, thoughtful, and tolerant officer.

Recent Questioning of the Usefulness of Higher Education

As reflected in the most recent recommendations of the National Advisory Commission and in the continuing financial programs of the federal government, support for higher education for the police continues to be strong. In some quarters, however, there is a growing uneasiness with the movement—a feeling that a college education has been oversold as a panacea for the police.[13] Some believe that the program has diverted attention and scarce resources from other reforms that have equal or greater potential for improving police operations. Critics do not quibble with the basic notion that further education—of any kind—generally has some beneficial, if not quantifiable, results. It may benefit the individual, if not the agency or the field. The discomfort is with some of the assumptions behind the current campaign.

The contention that college graduates will be more tolerant and more sensitive in their contacts with citizens, for example, has not been proved. Future research may support it, but at the moment skeptics are increasingly seeking to disabuse us of the naive notion that college education guarantees any specific result. One recent study found that a group of largely middle-class college students, assigned to accompany police officers in the core precincts of a large city, developed a low tolerance for the kind of activity and treatment to which they were newly exposed.[14]

The most direct challenge of the college requirement has come from those who want to recruit more members of minority groups into police service. It has always been apparent that increased educational requirements would impede efforts to reach this objective. The dilemma was acknowledged by the President's Commission on Law Enforcement and Administration of Justice, which then went on to propose three levels of entry to police service, each with different assignments, educational requirements, and compensation, as a way of reconciling the need for minority representatives and college-trained personnel.[15] To enter at the highest level would require a college degree.

Critics of this proposal feared it would create new patterns of segregation; and some questioned why, without clear proof that a college education makes for a better police officer, such importance should be attached to higher education when there may be more persuasive evidence that the addition of minority members to a police force has greater potential for directly improving the quality of police service.

All of these issues recently came into focus in the litigation brought by a group of police officers in Arlington, Virginia, who challenged both the practice of paying college-educated police officers more than those without degrees and the policy of requiring that new officers have at least two years of college credit or the prospect of gaining that credit within a year's time.[16]

These challenges of the college requirement come at a time when society is beginning to question more broadly whether it has erred in requiring a college degree for entry into such a high percentage of the work force. As is true of many other aspects of their development, the rate of progress in policing is so slow that the police are often only beginning to implement concepts, procedures, and standards when others in both the public and private sectors, having used them for some time, are having second thoughts about their value. For many people who think policing is a simplistic job, the proposal that police be required to have a college degree is the ultimate absurdity. Understandably it seems ironic to those who have been advocating college education for police personnel that the police should now have to plead a case for education when they have been exhorted for so long to attract the college graduate and when, in other fields, a college education has been accepted on faith as highly desirable.

The factor that makes the whole movement toward college education for police personnel most vulnerable to attack is the emphasis which has been put upon the acquisition of college credentials without sufficient concern for what is to be learned. Given the multitude of colleges and the number of people who attend them, the degree itself reflects little about the value or relevance of the educational experience. That is why it is so difficult to react to proposals, such as that of the National Advisory Commission on Criminal Justice Standards and

Goals, requiring that new recruits have a college background. And that is why it is difficult for a local agency to determine what requirements, if any, ought to be established for formal education beyond the high school level. The range of college experiences available to high school graduates today is such that one can be for or against college education for police personnel without making any commitment as to what this might mean for the form and quality of police services.

Meager Substantiating Data

Given the massive investment in bringing higher education to the police, sufficient data should be available by now to enable us to judge whether the arguments supporting college education are being validated. But many problems complicate any attempt to make even a rough assessment.

First of all, despite the size of the program, not enough has been achieved to make it possible to examine these hypotheses. Consider, for example, the claim that recruitment from a greater cross section of the community, which would of necessity include those who chose to go on to college, will improve the quality of police service. Before this can be tested with any degree of preciseness, many more recruits must enter police service from the mainstream of college graduates than have so far been attracted. The same is true regarding the argument that a broad liberal arts college education and life in a college community will produce better officers. Relatively few individuals with this kind of background have come into police service.

In 1970 Charles Saunders gathered whatever evidence was then available to support the arguments for college-trained police. He found only a few isolated studies that in any way purported to measure the value of the college graduate in police work.[17] The National Advisory Commission on Criminal Justice Standards and Goals made a similar effort in 1973 with results that were equally meager.[18] But the commission chose to attach much greater weight to these findings, contending that it was no longer necessary to simply rely on a general faith in the value of higher education.

The major problem with the few studies that have been made is the one encountered in measuring qualification for promotion (see chapter 9) and in screening applicants for police service (see chapter 10). The measures used reflect a judgment of the goals and functions of the police about which there is considerable disagreement. One often-cited study, for example, related educational level to traditional self-reported measures of patrol performance, such as the number of parking tickets issued, concluding that productivity of officers declined as their years of college increased.[19] Several have relied heavily on the performance ratings of superiors, which are notorious for their inadequacies as measures of performance.[20] Moreover, the use of the performance rating implies that a supervisor's standard of desirable performance is also the standard of the agency and the community.

A number of recent efforts seem much more sophisticated, but the absence of clearly valid criteria for judging performance raises questions about their results. Bernard Cohen and Jan M. Chaiken concluded that officers on the New York City Police Department with at least one year of college education were very good performers and those with college degrees exhibited even better on-the-job performance.[21] But they based their conclusion primarily on the number of such officers who were promoted and the number of civilian complaints filed. Because of the inadequacy of promotion procedures, promotion is not a valid measure of quality of performance. High scores on a promotion examination may say little more than that the college-educated person is better at taking tests. So many factors influence the number of complaints citizens file against an officer that this measure, too, seems questionable. The absence of complaints may be a result of such varied factors as the officer's assignment, inactivity, or an aggressiveness that is so intimidating that it dissuades citizens from taking any action.

Frequent reference has been made to the series of studies conducted by Alexander B. Smith and his colleagues comparing measures of authoritarianism in police officers who enter or graduate from college and those who do not.[22] This series of studies lends support to the widely held belief that those who choose to take college courses tend to be less authoritarian than their brethren. But the authors make no claim that the college experience, by itself, affects the authoritarian attitude of the officer, nor do they attempt to assess the subsequent performance of the college graduate.

All of these observations point to the critical need for a carefully designed and carefully controlled study in which agreement is first reached on what constitutes improved performance, and in which an effort is then made over a period of time to compare the performance of various types of college graduates with the performance of police officers who have less education. Consideration should also be given to whether the value of a college education might differ, depending on the size of the agency, the character of the community served, and the specific nature of the duties performed. Is it as valuable, for example, for an officer assigned to street operations as it is for an officer having administrative responsibilities? Extremely difficult methodological problems are involved in developing such a study, but the tremendous investment that is being made at all levels of government to encourage college work—not to mention the time and effort of the people involved—would seem to warrant it.

DRAWBACKS OF THE CURRENT PROGRAMS

While any firm conclusions regarding the merit of present college programs for the police must await the compilation and analysis of additional data, it is possible to make some general observations regarding the direction that the programs have taken.

Education Without Change: Perpetuating
the Status Quo

Higher education has come to be viewed in this country as synonymous with a commitment to challenging, questioning, criticizing, and analyzing existing institutions, and as a way of instilling new values and broader perspectives. Many of those who have urged a closer relationship between the police and the institutions of higher education hoped this would result in a similar commitment within the police field. They sought to change the police—their values, their orientation, their policies, and the nature of the service they render the public. But, in an apparent effort to refrain from offending present police personnel, they have been reluctant to acknowledge that the desire for change is their prime objective. Instead the objective is usually stated in a more subtle manner, as if reformers want to seduce the police into higher education by announcing one set of goals while anticipating another. Their hedging makes it difficult to keep the movement on target. One can claim success based on lesser goals, such as increasing the number of college graduates in the police service, without having made any significant improvement in police functioning and in the quality of police service.

The ambiguity of the current situation is illustrated by the actions of many police administrators who support higher education for their personnel while successfully resisting those elements in it that lead to change. A chief, for example, may make an intensive effort to recruit college graduates, but systematically screen out those who give any evidence of independent thinking or who demonstrate an inclination to challenge police regimen. He may encourage an officer to undertake a program of graduate study, but be disturbed on learning that the officer criticizes the agency in a research project. And he may work hard to establish special college programs and offer extra compensation for college work completed, but then complain when instructors discuss such controversial subjects as police corruption, the legalization of prostitution and the use of drugs, civilian control of the police, or the effectiveness of local police operations. Many leaders in the police field have thus embraced the purely mechanical elements of college attendance while immunizing themselves from the disruptive effects that intelligent analysis could have on traditional policies and procedures.

This limited support is reflected, too, in the large gap between the professed desire to recruit the college graduate and the snail's pace at which police agencies have changed their policies to attract and retain the graduate. Administrators have not taken strong stands on such matters as residence requirements, lateral movement, and staffing changes to free officers from simplistic, boring, and unchallenging assignments. Many of the people in middle management positions in police agencies and a high percentage of the top administrators seem to be saying that if the college graduate is to be employed by the police, it is he or she who must change, not the agency. Thus they systematically reject the element of change inherent in the notion of recruiting the college graduate, just as they have frequently done in implementing other personnel reforms.

The Emphasis upon Post-Entry Studies

Support for education without change is demonstrated most clearly by the preference of the police establishment for educating the recruited rather than recruiting the educated. Although more college graduates are entering police agencies, their number is insignificant compared to the number of already-employed police officers who have enrolled in programs of college studies. Throughout the country the major response to the pressure for college-educated officers has taken the form of post-entry studies.

Several factors account for this situation. Most important is the LEEP policy that gives a higher priority to educating in-service students than to using federal funds to entice students from the mainstream of college graduates into police work. The program underwrites the cost of tuition up to $250 per quarter or $400 per semester for those already employed in criminal justice agencies who wish to enroll in part-time study. LEEP has also provided forgivable loans to both current employees and those planning to enter the criminal justice field who enroll in a program of full-time studies. But because in-service students receive highest priority and because the demands from them have been so great, the number of new awards made to college students interested in entering the field has been steadily declining. In fiscal 1973 more than 80 percent of the participants in LEEP were in-service students, and approximately 80 percent of these were police employees, the balance being employed by other agencies in the criminal justice system.[23]

Contributing to the emphasis upon post-entry studies and to the demand for LEEP funds are the incentive pay plans that have been adopted by many departments and the benefits to which veterans are entitled. Under the incentive programs the pay of a police officer goes up as he accumulates college credits. Under the benefits of the Veterans' Administration, an officer who has served in the armed forces and who, for example, has three dependents and undertakes a program of half-time studies will receive a cash payment of $193 per month. The amount increases with the number of credits and the number of dependents.

The unusually large number of police officers who have responded to these incentives by enrolling in college studies has had a profound effect upon the nature of the college programs that have developed. Employed officers must, of necessity, turn to a local institution (usually a community college) for their instruction—an institution that is equipped, by its proximity and its scheduling capacity, to meet the peculiar needs of persons working full time and often on rotating shifts. In setting up their programs such institutions have tended to respond as directly as possible to the needs of the police as the police have themselves articulated them. This has often resulted in narrowly oriented vocational training taught by part-time instructors who either are retired police officers or are drawn from local police agencies. The local colleges obviously do not have the resources of an independent school with a full-time diversified student body. The faculty members—except in unusual cases—are not likely to be actively engaged in research and other activities that contribute to their value as teachers.

And the concentration of officers from a single agency in a college-level program that they may be under some pressure to attend, plus the above-average age of many of those enrolled, makes for a radically different kind of classroom situation. With unusually competent faculty and other resources, some local colleges have risen above these handicaps and offer courses of high quality.

The community-college programs have received strong support from police administrators, partly because so many of them afford the tradition-bound administrator a convenient way to endorse college education while protecting himself from change. By recruiting noncollege personnel and training them in police work, and only then encouraging them to take college studies, the administrator can successfully sidestep any challenge to existing practices and policies. In many cities the local college program is a captive of the agency, servicing it in much the same manner as an in-house training program: the agency dictates the choice of subject matter, and the orientation and operating philosophy of the agency's administrators are mirrored in the orientation and philosophy of the teaching staff.

In fairness it must be recognized that many police personnel prefer practical courses because they are easier and because they are usually taught by people who are sympathetic to the officers and share an understanding of the complex environment in which the police work. The biases that many academic personnel have toward police are serious barriers to effective communication in a classroom.

Programs designed primarily for students already in police employ, although potentially valuable in their own right, nevertheless do not in their current form produce the benefits that proponents of higher education for the police have had in mind. The officers who are enrolled in them are still drawn from that portion of high school graduates who initially choose not to go on to college. The programs do not appear to bring a greater cross section of young people into police agencies. Nor do they give status to the officer who enrolls in them. By their very nature, they preclude the possibility of active participation in the life of a college campus. And by setting up special classes for officers, they segregate them from the rest of the student body. The tragedy in this situation is that the officer who wants to broaden his education often has no alternative but to attend college-sponsored courses of inferior quality that neither challenge his ability nor sustain his interest.

A comprehensive review of the various arrangements that have evolved to integrate college studies with police work reveals evidence of even more blatant efforts to subvert the original intents of those advocating higher education. In the various programs designed to provide additional pay for educational achievement, for example, officers have been credited for taking correspondence courses in electronics, for training in scuba diving and woodworking, and for typing classes. Awarding college credit for courses that are a part of traditional police training is another example. Such arrangements not only do not contribute toward elevating the quality of service, they support the arguments of those who question the propriety of requiring college education for police personnel.

Premature Specialization for Undergraduates

Of those who enter the police service with a college degree, the majority have either an associate degree from a community college in police science or criminal justice or a bachelor's degree from a four-year college with a similar concentration. In some instances these programs are the same programs in which police officers study part time, and they therefore suffer from the weaknesses already mentioned. But a number of four-year programs are designed primarily for regular full-time college students interested in pursuing studies in the criminal justice field.

The student who graduates from a four-year program in criminal justice, as most are titled, is much more likely to have some background in liberal arts than his counterpart in the community college. The curriculum is likely to be broader; the courses more issue-oriented; and the faculty of higher quality. In addition the student is much more likely to realize some of the benefits of intermixture on a college campus. Nevertheless, most of the four-year programs do not equip their students to become constructive critics of present-day policing.

The inadequacy of these programs raises a basic question. Is the current state of knowledge and academic research relating to the police and the whole criminal justice field developed enough to sustain independent programs of specialized study? Where it is possible to concentrate sparse resources, a viable program—usually at the graduate level—can be maintained. But at the undergraduate level at the moment, student demand far outstrips the capacity of most universities to respond. The number of faculty members with a specialization and continuing interest in criminal justice is extremely small. Staffing is a problem. Qualified faculty members in sociology, political science, and psychology are understandably reluctant to accept appointments that permanently commit them to teaching and research in an area that may represent but one of their interests. And the student demand itself is suspect, reflecting a search for relevancy that may be an escape from more rigorous and demanding courses of study. Together these conditions create the possibility of a seriously diluted program that cannot compete with the regular, more-established university courses and therefore tends to get relegated to second-class status.[24]

A related problem is the focus of the four-year programs on the total system of criminal justice. This has come to reflect a broader and more appropriate perspective for university coverage than police science or administration, for example. But criminal justice, for the reasons set forth in earlier chapters, is not sufficiently broad to encompass the many university-level studies that are relevant to the police. To the extent that the title implies an intention to study the police within the confines of the criminal justice system, this approach can be unduly restrictive.

REDIRECTING THE EFFORT

Whenever the value of a specific educational experience is questioned, a strong force pulls many people back to reasserting a basic faith in education—to claiming benefits that do not show up in an assessment of specific programs. No doubt most police personnel will have gained from the various programs in which they are now involved, though the gain may be small in many instances and not what it could have been in most. Under normal conditions one might be inclined to adopt a more patient attitude, with some confidence that a gradual upgrading in the quality of educational endeavors will take place. But the urgency to improve police services, the heavy dependence being placed upon college education in order to achieve this objective, and the vast amount of human and financial resources being invested in educational programs for the police compel a more aggressive critique and a rethinking of some of the judgments that have been made.

Relating Education More Directly to the Need for
Effecting Change in the Police
Basic to any rethinking of the application of college work to policing is the need to acknowledge forthrightly the hope that higher education will result in the police having in their ranks a greater number of people who have the breadth of understanding, the creativity, and the motivation to bring about changes in the orientation, policies, and operations of the typical police organization, and resolve the many conflicting pressures that currently hamper their effectiveness. This objective must be made explicit. Police personnel should recognize that when they embrace higher education, they must subject their operations to critical analysis.

Some have argued that a better relationship between higher education and the police requires prior agreement on a clearer, more precise definition of the police function, the implication being that universities could then develop more relevant offerings. But the police function is not likely to be redefined overnight. Any new definition will evolve over a long period of time and will be the result of many influences. And the college education of persons entering or currently in the police field is likely to be one of the major factors contributing to this process. It thus becomes clear that it is more important that college studies be related to the process of change; that the police be educated in ways that enable them to initiate and respond flexibly to change both in the police and, more broadly, in society.

Selecting Course Offerings
A program of selected studies within the liberal arts—while not guaranteed to produce specific results—has the greatest potential for equipping police to undertake constructive analysis of their functioning and to change in a changing society.[25] (This does not mean, as some interpret "liberal arts," that present or

future police officers should take any more courses in art, music, languages, and literature than do other college students.) To effect change the police are going to need the kind of understanding and perspective that might be developed by taking courses in history, economics, introductory sociology and psychology, and the development of political institutions and movements. They will have to develop a capacity to handle complex abstract issues; to function in an unstructured environment; and to live with ambiguities. Relevant courses might include political theory, philosophy, or jurisprudence. They will require analytical skills, as they move up through their organizations, for solving problems and choosing viable positions on major issues. Courses in research methodology, in mathematics, in statistics, and in reasoning and logic would aid them in their decision-making. And they must be thoroughly familiar with the setting in which they function and the problems with which they must deal, a need that might be met through such courses as criminology, social control, the problems of racial and ethnic minorities, urbanization, urban government and politics, and constitutional and administrative law.

Given the variety of courses that are available to teach people to deal creatively with the problems they will encounter in policing, it is difficult to understand why so much effort has been expended on specialized programs at the undergraduate level. Admittedly the interested undergraduate should have an opportunity to explore some of the specific issues confronting the police, and should have the opportunity to become familiar with the major issues that arise in the criminal justice system as well. But separate schools and departments need not be established to supply these courses. The most pressing needs for education within the police field can usually be met within the four-year university by simply routing students through already-existing programs. Special faculty and course offerings related directly to policing could be housed within existing disciplines (political science, sociology, psychology, or social work). Where there are many interested students, a program officer or counselor would be helpful.

Dependence on existing programs has several advantages. It puts emphasis on liberal arts studies in preparing people for a career with the police. It curbs the growing but erroneous impression that a university cannot contribute to the educational needs of the police without setting up a special program in police science or criminal justice. It maintains a highly flexible arrangement at a time of rapid development of a new interest. And it enriches the education of the students by affording them contacts with people in other fields of study.

Reasserting the Independence of the University in Making Educational Decisions

Responsible university or college officials often justify vocationally oriented programs by saying that they are responsive to the needs of the field as the police have defined those needs. Some colleges have created advisory groups of practitioners to review course offerings.

There is nothing wrong in a university attempting to respond to the expressed needs of an occupational group. Some of the professional schools have not done enough to relate their curricula to the needs of their students upon graduation and have been justly criticized on this score. But, at the other extreme, the university does a disservice to the field and, more broadly, to society if it merely puts together course offerings in response to practitioner-defined needs without making an independent judgment as to their value and without any assessment of what the university can contribute.

Universities can have a tremendous impact in fashioning the role of the police in our society. The public, through its elected representatives and especially its legislative bodies, is not likely, in bold fashion, to make major policy decisions regarding the police function, methods, and priorities. Nor is the police field itself likely to do so. In the absence of such decisions, the choices that are made in the format, coverage, orientation, and subject matter of educational programs for the police will, taken together, greatly influence the direction in which the field moves. If, for example, the prevalent view that the police function is a relatively simplistic task continues to receive support and if educational programs are designed from this point of view, the educational process itself becomes a major force in reinforcing traditional concepts—a much more powerful force than state legislatures, city councils, or neighborhood groups. If, on the other hand, the educational process challenges the premises upon which much current policing is based, it has the potential for contributing to a more enlightened and, in the long run, more effective form of police service. Thus the universities, in making decisions on the kind of educational opportunities to be provided police personnel, are being drawn into the growing debate over the role that the police should play in our society.

Given the strongly differing views on the appropriate role for the police, colleges and universities are bound to vary in their judgment on what is to be taught. Some will no doubt choose to supply the most traditional offerings. But whatever decision is made, it should be an informed one that is based upon a careful review of the needs of the field as seen from various perspectives and upon a painstaking assessment of the contribution universities and colleges can make toward improving the quality of police service.[26] Many large-scale programs have been established without benefit of such inquiry.

Making More Effective Use of the Community Colleges

The preceding discussion applies to the community colleges as well as the four-year institutions. The preservice student or the young police officer who turns to the community college for his education should be encouraged to study selected offerings in the liberal arts.

But it must be recognized that many police officers, either because of their age or simply because of their lack of interest, do not want to undertake an ambitious course of college-level studies. Those familiar with the current make-up of police agencies know how difficult it is to involve some personnel in a meaningful in-service training program of several hours' duration. It makes little sense to pressure a fifty-year-old officer into taking introductory courses in American government, in psychology, or in sociology. Nor does it make sense to force into a liberal arts program a police officer who may have joined the agency because he did not want further education after high school. Such officers might, however, be attracted into educational programs that are coordinated with in-service training and that are specifically designed to enable the officers to improve their competence on the job and to enable them to better understand the change taking place around them, inside and outside their departments. Their agencies will obviously benefit if appropriate courses are provided.

The community colleges are in a unique position to engage experienced officers in a program of studies by developing a special array of courses and, more important, by developing special teaching methods. The courses must be directly relevant to the problems police experience on the street, but they need not be technically oriented. Some community colleges have had good experiences in explaining to police personnel the reasoning behind court decisions; the causes of militancy in minority groups; and the nature of political dissent. Much more could be done to acquaint police officers with the issues surrounding their jobs so that they might better understand the complex environment in which they function and better comprehend the criticism, the antagonism, and the outright hostility to which they are commonly subject. Special offerings could also be designed to create greater receptivity to change in a police agency, affording a setting in which important current issues could be explored, such as those that relate to the nature of the police function, the development of alternatives to the criminal justice system, the exercise of discretion, and the control of police conduct.

Evaluating Individuals Rather than Credentials

The college degree or the successful completion of a designated number of years of college is no longer—if it ever was—a valid way of describing a uniform package of abilities and achievements. Rather than rely so heavily on the credential, for either hiring or advancement, the police will have to do more to examine each candidate individually in an effort to measure more directly the qualities and characteristics most needed in police service today. This need for individual assessment emphasizes the critical importance of current efforts, discussed in chapter 10, to devise adequate screening procedures, totally free of racial bias and sufficiently independent of agency influence, that will identify people whose talent the police field requires.

Whether or not college work is required prior to initial hiring, the police should undertake an aggressive program to encourage a cross section of college graduates to apply for police work. Until this is done, many of the advantages that are supposed to accrue from college graduates entering police work will not be realized.

As was acknowledged in chapter 10, the capacity of the police to attract such graduates will depend upon their ability to create a more receptive environment for the college graduate and to demonstrate a clear desire to change the nature of police operations. The current federal program of financial assistance that places so high a priority on educating those already employed by criminal justice agencies should be revised. Federal policies should strongly support programs designed to attract a greater variety of college graduates to police agencies.

If the police can bring into their ranks a true cross section of the community (college graduates and high school graduates, minority group members, and women), recruit training will become much more important as a leveling-out process during which the recruits can benefit from the variety of backgrounds, experiences, and diversified values held by individuals in the program.

THE POTENTIAL FOR ADDITIONAL
CONTRIBUTIONS BY THE UNIVERSITIES

The major focus of this chapter has been on the use of college education to upgrade police personnel. Colleges and universities obviously have an important role, as well, in conducting research relating to police problems. Indeed, their capacity to offer any instruction directly relevant to policing will depend, in large measure, on their research contributions.

But just as police agencies have been slow to make use of the college graduate, so academic people have been slow to interest themselves in the police and their problems. In retrospect it seems startling that this vast sector of governmental activity, which directly affects the quality of life in this country and raises such complicated issues, was neglected for so long by universities whose research, teaching, and services touch upon almost every aspect of our lives.

Among the factors accounting for this situation is the obvious conflict between the open and flexible character of the universities and the closed and rigid character of police organizations. Questioning in a university setting is routine and encouraged; in a police agency a much higher value is attached to unquestioning obedience. A further complication is the attitude that each group commonly has for the other. The police, through their actions and pronouncements, often sound anti-intellectual and suspicious of academics. University personnel often hold the police in contempt and treat them with condescension. The two attitudes feed on each other: the intellectual snobbery of the academics provides justification for the anti-intellectual attitude of the police, and the actions and pronouncements of the police provide continued justification for the contempt in which they are held.

Yet despite their differing outlooks, some police agencies and academically based people began, in the early 1960s, to collaborate in research projects.[27] This development received great impetus from the President's Commission on

Law Enforcement and Administration of Justice and from the several commissions that followed, since each had a range of immediate research needs that required a cooperative effort by academic and police personnel. Subsequently the gradual increase in federal funds for research stimulated many more joint endeavors.

Social scientists in particular have greatly increased their contacts with police agencies—so much so that a conference was recently held to explore the nature of the evolving relationship. The report of the proceedings of the conference provides an excellent summary of the numerous problems that have been encountered and the lessons that have been learned.[28] The chief complaint repeatedly registered by the police who have been involved in these new relationships is that they are studied as "animals in a zoo"; that academic studies have not been designed to assist them in solving specific problems. The police see the academicians as interested merely in new data and findings that will lead to publication and recognition in the academic world. They see themselves as harassed functionaries hungry for assistance in dealing with their overwhelming day-to-day problems, but not receiving it.

It is true, of course, that much of the research that has been undertaken has been intended to serve the limited interest and objectives of the researcher. Some of it, more broadly, has been designed to develop insights and greater knowledge on major issues in the police field—but issues in which the agency under study may have no particular interest. Problems have arisen because some researchers have been less than candid regarding the utility of their efforts to the agency. In order to gain access to needed data, they have promised results that either turn out to have no practical value or, in some cases, do not even materialize. Others have been explicit in disclaiming any direct "payoff" for the agency. Still others never claim that their work will produce immediate benefits, but since they do not spell out clearly what they are doing, expectations develop and disappointment often follows.

Poor communication creates other problems. Researchers, after making the initial arrangements for their research, often work independent of the agency, leaving the administration somewhat mystified and creating anxiety among those who are aware of their presence but unsure of their objectives. Academic researchers rarely involve the personnel of the agency in their research, which would by itself be an excellent training experience. Reports are frequently written in the jargon of the researcher, which is difficult for the practitioner to comprehend, and little effort is typically made to provide the agency with a concise summary of the implications that the research may have for agency operations.

The police have looked to the universities with the expectation that people more educated and more broadly grounded than themselves should have better solutions to police problems, only to find that these are not immediately available. They quickly discover that the universities are not simply storehouses of all knowledge and all solutions to current problems, capable of delivering at a moment's notice. They also discover that the quality of academic work varies greatly.[29] For the universities to be helpful to the police, the two interests must engage each other. They must build a relationship over a long period of time, defining problems and working jointly toward solutions. Academics must become intimately familiar with the police and their needs. They should associate directly with a police agency and its personnel. And they must be willing to engage in applied research. The police, on the other hand, must become familiar with the tools and the capacities of the academics.

A heavy responsibility for initiating this kind of relationship rests with the police. If they hope to gain anything from the universities they must begin by making a greater commitment within their respective agencies to inquiring into their own operations—their effectiveness as well as their efficiency. An interest in change and innovation pursued continuously and in sufficient depth will inevitably lead to the greater involvement of the universities.

As alliances between the police and academics develop, each partner will have to make allowances for the different problems that the other faces. Researchers who must meet specified conditions that restrict their inquiries or who fear that the asking of a question or the release of a finding will destroy their relationship with the agency will not wish to undertake such research. But likewise police administrators who sense that research will be conducted in ways that will interfere with their operations, or that the results may be used in ways that unnecessarily create problems, will understandably resist participating in it.

In a number of places a single faculty member in an established discipline or a small team of researchers has entered into a highly productive relationship with a police agency.[30] If initiative and support come from the police and if researchers from several disciplines are interested, such relationships can be expanded. A center within a university system could, by serving as a focal point, greatly facilitate interchange and stimulate additional work in the area. It could afford faculty the opportunity to work with police problems while maintaining a base in their home discipline. This would accommodate many academicians who have the potential for making a major contribution to the police field, but who do not want to devote their careers to work in this one area.

Aside from their potential for improving the effectiveness of the police through more research, universities—especially state universities—are uniquely equipped to disseminate research findings and general information to practitioners and others who might be concerned with police functioning. University extension services have aided many occupational groups to improve their capacity to function effectively and to keep abreast of the newest developments in their fields. In any overall scheme for maximizing the benefits to be realized from closer contacts between the police and higher education, the role of the extension services should not be overlooked.

THE RELATIONSHIP OF HIGHER EDUCATION
TO THE DEVELOPMENT OF NEW LEADERSHIP

At the beginning of this chapter it was noted that the earliest college offerings devoted to police studies concentrated on administration, with the avowed purpose of preparing students to assume administrative positions in police agencies. It is gradually being recognized that it makes little sense to train students exclusively for positions that are not available to them until they have served for years at the operating level in a police agency. It is also being recognized that future leaders have a greater need for a broad education that acquaints them with critical issues in the field than they have for courses in how to run a police agency. The biggest shift in point of view, however, is in acceptance of the idea that police personnel at the operating level should have higher education. This reflects increased recognition of the importance of the officer's job; that, even though he is at the bottom of a highly structured organizational pyramid and may never advance any further, he is, like the teacher and the social worker, an independent operative who relies more heavily upon his own qualities than upon directives communicated from above.

In the light of these developments, then, what special role, if any, should the universities play in grooming police leadership? For all of the reasons set forth in the earlier discussions it would seem that a future leader in the police field should, first and foremost, have the type of strong general liberal arts education previously described. Indeed, the stronger the education, the more likely it is that the officer will be equipped to fill a position of leadership. It follows that specialized training, relating to the issues in policing and the actual management of a police agency, should be built upon this base. Ideally, qualified practitioners—themselves college graduates—should have the opportunity to participate in full-time programs of advanced study of issues relative to policing, including the opportunity to become familiar with the techniques involved in carrying out research projects on specific problems. This could be accomplished by assigning students on an individual basis to study and work with faculty members having an interest in policing; by establishing university centers to study police problems, such as have been described; or by sending the students to one of the several graduate schools that the present state of knowledge and limited resources in the criminal justice and police fields can sustain. Detachment from the day-to-day pressures of police operations, the chance to critique the field, and direct familiarity with carefully structured inquiries into specific problems can afford the practitioner an invaluable opportunity to sharpen his ability to handle administrative tasks.

While this is an ideal arrangement toward which to strive, it obviously does not meet the immediate needs for leadership set forth in chapter 9. For some years to come leaders must be drawn from among officers who do not have a strong liberal arts experience upon which to build. Typically the effort to meet the crisis in leadership has taken the form of short courses in management and in leadership, developed within police agencies or by some of the established police training programs that draw officers from around the country. These programs understandably reflect a desire to respond as directly and as efficiently as possible to the urgent need. But one gets the impression that however intensive the effort, instructional programs in leadership and management have a rather sterile quality when many of the students lack any depth of understanding regarding the major substantive issues that are involved in the running of a police agency.

The universities could help to alleviate this problem by strengthening these programs. They could develop training materials on substantive issues and train instructors in their use. In this way, while not compensating for the lack of a general education, the colleges and universities could provide a better foundation for the more practically oriented management schooling. A thorough coverage of such issues as the nature of the police function, political accountability of the police, and the control of police conduct, for example, would sensitize future leaders to the factors that make the problems of directing a police agency distinct from those involved in running any other government agency or private business.

NOTES

1. Albert Deutsch, *The Trouble with Cops* (New York: Crown Publishers, 1955), p. 122.

2. In New York City, for example, more than half of the recruits appointed in June, 1940, had college degrees. For a summary of the experience in that city, see Arthur Niederhoffer, *Behind the Shield* (Garden City, N.J.: Doubleday & Co., 1967), pp. 16–17.

3. For example, in a survey of police chiefs conducted by the IACP in 1968, only 15 percent of the respondents thought fours years of college should be required for patrolmen. But 67 percent considered this an appropriate requirement for chiefs. Reported in Charles Tenney, *Higher Education Programs in Law Enforcement and Criminal Justice* (Washington, D.C.: Government Printing Office, 1971), pp. 87–88.

4. President's Commission on Law Enforcement and Administration of Justice, *The Challenge of Crime in a Free Society* (Washington, D.C.: Government Printing Office, 1967), p. 109.

5. As reported by Deutsch, *The Trouble with Cops*, p. 213.

6. *Law Enforcement and Criminal Justice Education: Directory 1975–76* (Gaithersburg, Md.: International Association of Chiefs of Police, 1975), p. 3.

7. Law Enforcement Assistance Administration, *5th Annual Report, Fiscal Year 1973* (Washington, D.C.: Government Printing Office, 1973), p. 119.

8. From a computer printout, "Participant File Analyzer and Profile," dated 3/21/75, provided by the Office of Academic Assistance, LEEP System, LEAA.

9. National Advisory Commission on Criminal Justice Standards and Goals, *Police* (Washington, D.C.: Government Printing Office, 1973), p. 369.

10. Royal Commission on the Police 1962, *Final Report* (London: Her Majesty's Stationery Office, 1962), p. 94.

11. Egon Bittner, *The Functions of the Police in Modern Society* (Chevy Chase, Md.: National Institute of Mental Health, 1970), p. 83.

12. See, e.g., Charles B. Saunders, Jr., *Upgrading the American Police* (Washington, D.C.: The Brookings Institution, 1970), pp. 101–110; President's Commission on Law Enforcement and Administration of Justice, *Task Force Report: The Police* (Washington, D.C.: Government Printing Office, 1967), pp. 127–128; and Tenney, *Higher Education Programs in Law Enforcement and Criminal Justice*, pp. 46–57.

13. See, e.g., Paul Chevigny, *Police Power* (New York: Vintage Books, 1969), pp. 272–273; Solomon Gross, "Higher Education and Police: Is There a Need for a Closer Look?" *Journal of Police Science and Administration* 1 (1973): 477–483; Norman L. Weiner, "The Effect of Education on Police Attitudes," *Journal of Criminal Justice* 2 (1974): 317–328; Dennis C. Smith and Elinor Ostrom, "The Effects of Training and Education on Police Performance: A Preliminary Analysis," in *The Potential for Reform of Criminal Justice*, ed. Herbert Jacob (Beverly Hills, Calif.: Sage Publications, 1974), pp. 45–81.

14. Robert E. Ford, James Meeker, and Richard Zeller, "Police, Students, and Racial Hostilities," *Journal of Police Science and Administration* 3 (1975): 9–14. See also, Weiner, "The Effect of Education on Police Attitudes." Recognizing that many of those who go to college study in vocationally oriented programs, he concludes that the educational level of police does not significantly affect their attitudes toward various ethnic groups.

15. President's Commission on Law Enforcement and Administration of Justice, *The Challenge of Crime in a Free Society*, pp. 107–109.

16. This case was filed in the United States District Court for the Eastern District of Virginia in 1974. The case was tried in April of 1975, but a decision has not yet been rendered.

17. Saunders, *Upgrading the American Police*, pp. 81–92.

18. National Advisory Commission on Criminal Justice Standards and Goals, *Police*, pp. 370–371.

19. Cited in Saunders, *Upgrading the American Police*, pp. 86–87.

20. An example is the Chicago study as cited by the National Advisory Commission on Criminal Justice Standards and Goals, *Police*, p. 371. Interestingly, in a recent Dallas study, officers receiving the lowest ratings were the more highly educated, M. C. Gottlieb and C. F. Baker, "Predicting Police Officer Effectiveness," *Journal of Forensic Psychology*, December 1974, pp. 35–46.

21. Bernard Cohen and Jan M. Chaiken, *Police Background Characteristics and Performance* (New York: Rand Institute, 1972), pp. 20–21.

22. Alexander B. Smith, Bernard Locke, and Abe Fenster, "Authoritarianism in Policemen Who Are College Graduates and Non-College Police," *Journal of Criminal Law, Criminology and Police Science* 61 (1970): 313–315; Alexander B. Smith, Bernard Locke, and William F. Walker, "Authoritarianism in College and Non-College Oriented Police," *Journal of Criminal Law, Criminol-*

ogy and Police Science 58 (1967): 128–132; Alexander B. Smith, Bernard Locke, and William F. Walker, "Authoritarianism in Police College Students and Non-College Students," *Journal of Criminal Law, Criminology and Police Science* 59 (1968): 440–443.

23. Law Enforcement Assistance Administration, *5th Annual Report, Fiscal Year 1973*, p. 119.

24. For a discussion of this problem, see Saunders, *Upgrading the American Police*, pp. 100–116.

25. For a sampling of recent arguments in support of this position, see American Bar Association, *The Urban Police Function*, Approved Draft (Chicago: American Bar Association, 1973), pp. 47–53; Lee P. Brown, "The Police and Higher Education: The Challenge of the Times," *Criminology* 12 (1974): 114–124; Weiner, "The Effect of Education on Police Attitudes," p. 325.

26. For an interesting case study of one university that methodically examined its appropriate role in providing education for the police, see Peter P. Lejins, *Introducing a Law Enforcement Curriculum at a State University* (Washington, D.C.: Government Printing Office, 1970).

27. For a summary of some of the major research efforts in this period, see Lawrence W. Sherman, "The Sociology and the Social Reform of the American Police: 1950–1973," *Journal of Police Science and Administration* 2 (1974): 256–258.

28. Terry Eisenberg, *Collaboration Between Law Enforcement Executives and Social Scientists* (San Jose, California: National Conference of Christians and Jews, Inc., 1975).

29. A major problem is the barrage of questionnaires that academicians send to police agencies. They are not only a tremendous imposition on police time, they are also frequently poorly constructed and reflect little awareness of the complexity of police operations. It is often obvious to police that the data being collected will, by its very nature, be meaningless when summarized. Since this is the only contact that many agencies have with academics, the police develop some strong and, in my view, justifiably negative impressions of academic research.

30. The work of Morton Bard in New York City and in Norfolk, Connecticut, and the work of Hans Toch in Oakland are excellent examples.

 *Chapter 12*

Effecting Change: An Overview

The ultimate objective of all efforts to improve the police is to increase their capacity to deliver high-quality services to the citizenry and to equip them to do so in ways that are consistent with and support democratic values. To accomplish this objective, attention must be given to long-neglected problems concerning the basic arrangements for policing in this country. Chapters 1 through 8 deal with the numerous changes that are required both in these arrangements and in our perceptions of the police function in order to align public expectations, legal requirements, and police capabilities in such a way that it will be possible for the police to perform their assigned tasks more effectively. While work is undertaken on fundamental problems, a more aggressive effort must also be made to fashion individual police agencies that are equipped—in their operating policies, in their leadership, in their staffing, and in their administration—to carry out the peculiar and complex responsibilities of policing in a free society. The changes that must be made in several of these areas are discussed in chapters 9 through 11. This concluding chapter focuses on how some of these changes might best be brought about.

THE PROCESS OF CHANGE

The rapid increase of public interest in the police that we have witnessed in the past decade has produced a plethora of proposals for change. Yet relatively little attention has been given to the actual process for effecting change—to the methods and techniques by which oft-repeated recommendations can be successfully implemented.[1]

Consistent with the focus of most reform efforts to date, the bulk of the experience we have had in actually carrying out major changes has involved the reorganization of police agencies. The individual efforts of such reform-oriented police executives as the late William H. Parker in Los Angeles and the late O. W. Wilson in Chicago have been widely publicized. Likewise, a number of accounts are available of the efforts of such chiefs as Robert J. diGrazia in Boston; Frank Dyson in Dallas; Charles R. Gain in Oakland and now in San Francisco; Bernard L. Garmire in Tucson and Miami; Robert M. Igleburger in Dayton; Clarence M. Kelley in Kansas City; Patrick V. Murphy in the four cities he served, including New York: and Donald D. Pomerleau in Baltimore. In the smaller communities, attention has been focused on the efforts of Victor I. Cizanckas in Menlo Park, California; David C. Couper in Madison, Wisconsin; and the late John Fabbri in Fremont, California. But no careful study has been made to integrate the experiences of these men and to analyze their successes and failures. A systematic review of their efforts would give us much insight on how to bring about change in the internal management of a police agency.

That we identify most reforms in police operations with the administrator who initiated them is, in itself, significant. It reflects the widely held belief that change in the police, to the extent it is likely to occur, is primarily the responsibility of the top police administrator. Important as it is to learn how internal change has been achieved by police chiefs, the limited impact of reform efforts in the past has alerted us to the need for examining the complex process of change in much broader terms. It is now increasingly clear that lasting change requires, in addition to the efforts of the administrator, the synchronized efforts of other forces in the agency, in the community, and in the country as a whole.

The role of these forces becomes even more important as we concern ourselves with the basic problems identified in this book, such as the need for clarifying the police function, developing alternatives to the criminal process, recognizing and structuring discretion, and improving systems for achieving political accountability and for controlling police conduct. Stimulating and carrying out fundamental changes in these areas will require that police management itself play a role somewhat different from what it has played in the past. The support of the police unions will be critical. And it will be essential that initiative be taken by a combination of forces external to police agencies—especially the legislatures; administrators in local, state, and federal government; the courts; and the media. The role that universities might play has already been discussed in chapter 11.

So the process of change is not simply a strategy to be followed by a police administrator within the confines of his organization, but more broadly it requires action by a number of major forces in society, of which the police themselves are but one, who have a vital interest in the police function. Each of these forces has a unique potential for contributing toward resolving the basic problems the police now face, and each must play a critical role if this crucial arm of government is to be reshaped to meet more effectively the needs of our times.

THE ROLE OF POLICE MANAGEMENT

While not the exclusive initiator of change, the police administrator remains a central figure in the process of change, for it is upon him and through him that both the internal and the external forces of change exert their pressure. If police leadership is weak or simply not tuned in to the process of change, a tremendous vacuum is created. To the extent that the agency is pressured for change from external forces and from rank-and-file personnel, it gets buffeted about without adequate attention being given to the long-term interests of the community that should be represented by police management.

In planning and directing change within the organization the police administrator must be somewhat like the conductor of an orchestra, blending the various elements of change in a manner that equips the total organization to perform more effectively. He will err if, for example, he becomes totally preoccupied with mechanical improvements to the point that substantive issues are ignored. But, likewise, even if new commitments and new orientations are the heart of his program, he will have to devote considerable time to technical areas that he may consider mundane. He must develop an atmosphere of change that permeates the entire organization, but which is managed in such a way that it is not disorienting or overly threatening. Change tends to be self-generating, with forward movement and evidence of progress in one area stimulating and supporting movement in others.

The police administrator must also be patient. A concomitant to recognizing the multifaceted nature of change is to acknowledge as well that change takes time. It is understandable that those committed to redirecting their agencies are often dissatisfied with the rate of progress and the resources and attention that have been applied to the task. But just as it is unrealistic to expect any lasting change by working in a single area, so it is unrealistic—after so many years of neglect—to expect quick results. When one considers how existing practices and orientations have developed and have been reinforced over the years, it is absurd to assume they can be immediately redirected. And yet large-scale national programs are expected to produce beneficial results in a year or two; specific projects are expected to produce results in six months to a year; and newly hired police chiefs are commonly expected to accomplish major improvements in equally short periods of time.

By its very nature, organizational change is a slow, difficult, and often painful process, some aspects of which cannot be artificially induced. It takes many years to change attitudes, to develop competence, to shape operating philosophies, and to win support for a new approach to performing old functions. Personnel must be hired, reassigned, and, in many instances, retired. New leadership must be identified, trained, and developed. Studies must be conducted, and the effect that any one change has on other aspects of department operations must be accommodated. And even when outward signs may suggest that change has been successfully accomplished, time must be allowed for the roots of new policies and orientations to take hold. The failure to allow a sufficient period of "incubation" explains why some of the most ambitious efforts to alter the operations of a police agency have failed over the long haul.

The capacity of an administrator to effect change will depend heavily on his ability to enlist the support of his personnel. Time after time in recent years, communities and the police field generally have rather naively had high expectations for a chief's administration, only to have a crisis of some kind reveal, often to the chief's surprise, just how limited his support was within the agency.

Clarence M. Kelley, who as police chief of Kansas City, Missouri, enjoyed the strong support of both the community and his personnel, gave a clue to his own success in effecting significant change in that agency when, in addressing the nation's police chiefs, he urged them to inculcate in their personnel, at all levels, "an attitude which encourages creative and innovative thinking. We need to encourage a perception of change as part of the thinking process of the officer as he carries out his daily assignments."[2] He added that specific changes, in his judgment, are not nearly as important as the efforts to build an organization capable of continuous change.

As discussed in an earlier chapter, rank-and-file police personnel whose functioning is to be changed must themselves be involved in the process of change. The administrator must, as a minimum, keep his personnel informed of the nature of contemplated change and provide them with the information on which management bases its key decisions. Ideally they should participate in the actual planning of change, for it is the rank and file of the organization who must actually carry out the procedures and policies that are altered. Their lives are often most directly affected by change. And their support is essential if the changes are to work and to endure.

Involving rank-and-file personnel in planning as well as execution is a difficult task, to be undertaken with great care lest people in positions of middle management see it as threatening their positions of authority in the organization. If personnel of all ranks are involved in bringing about change, much of the fear and tension associated with doing things in new ways can be relieved; trust, confidence, and respect can be developed. Moreover, operating personnel have the potential for making a major contribution to improving the quality of policy decisions, given their familiarity with the most important problems of the agency—those that arise in the actual delivery of service to the citizenry. The benefits seem particularly promising because communication regarding such matters has been so stifled in the past. The several projects previously cited that have involved police officers in planning department changes and in carrying out experiments appear to justify optimism (see chapter 10). Their significance extends far beyond their impact in the jurisdictions in which they were conducted.

In relating to the various external forces pressuring for change, the key role the police administrator must play is in articulating police needs. Police agencies have masses of information and vast experience which enable a chief to be among the best-informed and most-constructive critics of the almost unworkable arrangements society has made for policing and of the community's response to social problems. Unfortunately this information and experience have usually been used by chiefs in the past to support their own agencies, in rather crude fashion, in the traditional conflicts that erupt between municipal departments, the courts, and social agencies. Police management must use its resources to initiate legislation, to contribute to informed public discussion of critical issues, and to formulate proposals for correcting basic faults in the current arrangements for carrying out the police task.

The change-oriented administrator must have the opportunity to compare his experiences with those of other administrators who are similarly committed and who face similar problems. He needs to benefit from their successes and failures and to receive reinforcement for the basic convictions that motivate him. This does not by itself require a new organization or institution. Greater use of informal networks can put such administrators in contact with one another without the limitations of a formal organization.

THE ROLE OF THE POLICE UNIONS

Police employee organizations, after a long period of time in which they were relatively dormant, have recently emerged as a critically important force likely to have a major impact on the direction in which the police field develops. They add an entirely new dimension, the voices of those actually engaged in day-to-day policing, to the already complex configuration of pressure groups that determine the form and quality of police service.

The dramatic increase in the number of police unions[3] can be attributed to several factors: long-suppressed job dissatisfaction; the widespread feeling among police that they were imposed on in the confrontations of the 1960s; the first-hand observations by the police of numerous other employee and minority groups improving their position through collective action; and, as previously noted, the influx of young officers who have brought with them radically different attitudes toward authority and management.[4] As a result of these factors, previously existing prohibitions against unionization have fallen by the wayside, statutes authorizing police to engage in collective bargaining have been enacted, and employee associations have been voluntarily recognized in some jurisdictions as bargaining agents for their members.[5] An entirely new relationship has thus developed between the police and their employers.

As the union movement has gained momentum, some police administrators and commentators on the police have sounded an alarm out of fear that the police will abuse their new-found collective power. These voices often reflect many of the same concerns that had been for so long the basis of legal prohibitions against police unionization.[6] Others have concluded that unions are neither as threatening nor as powerful as they have been made out to be.[7] With regard to the impact unions are likely to have on the future development of the police, the division of opinion is equally sharp. Some see the unions as the natural enemies of needed change; as committed to protecting the hard-earned gains reflected in the status quo.[8] Others see the unions as a new and potentially dynamic force for positive change, especially as they press for a more democratic police organization.

Because the movement is so new, predicting the direction it will take is difficult. At the moment the situation seems very fluid, as both unions and management struggle to fashion a working relationship. The unions have gained a great deal of strength as they have concentrated their efforts on traditional areas—such as employee rights—where police management is extremely vulnerable because of the working conditions described in chapter 10.

Management has been slow in its response. A good deal of time was wasted initially in trying to avoid both collective bargaining and the need to recognize the unions. Most police administrators are now resigned to the existence of the unions, but they are often puzzled as to how to deal with them. Having come up through the ranks at a time when no unions existed, they have had no relevant experience. Accustomed to viewing the police agency as a sanctuary safe from the numerous controversies in which the police tend to become involved in the larger community, police chiefs now complain of having to contend with tumult in their organizations as well, and they often see their unions—a force within the force—as their major adversary.

The chiefs appear to be especially threatened by the extent to which unions might be driving a wedge between them and their personnel and are seeking to share in administrative decisions that have previously been management's exclusive prerogative. The net result is a radically redefined relationship that weakens many of the props on which chiefs leaned in the past and, at the same time, makes a variety of new demands on them.

In their comprehensive study of police unionism, Hervey A. Juris and Peter Feuille conclude that much of what the unions have actually accomplished to date has been to gain ground in meeting the traditional concerns of all unions for wages, hours, and improved working conditions. Broader issues of change in operating policies and procedures have been touched on only incidentally, where the concessions made by management relative to wages, hours, and working conditions have curtailed management's freedom to use financial resources and manpower in other ways. Juris and Feuille also found that there was a tremendous gap between what the unions said they would do and what they actually accomplished. And they found that most abuses that surfaced—where the unions appeared to command inordinate power—were a result of the tendency of unions to go outside the ordinary channels for collective bargaining (by turning to individual city council members, for example) because management had been unable to establish a more rational process.[9]

These findings caution against some of the totally negative assessments of the potential impact of the unions. And yet ample basis for concern remains. Substantive changes in the nature of police service are often heavily dependent on management's ability to change working conditions; so if a relatively minor change in working conditions is challenged by the union, a fundamental change in operating policies and procedures may be blocked. This means that management must sometimes negotiate with the union before changes can be effected. Furthermore, a union might take a strong stand regarding a whole range of important value-laden issues that are raised by substantive change, but which are not traditionally subject to the collective-bargaining process. These issues must be debated and eventually resolved in the larger political forum, but the union is likely to establish itself as a creditable adversary to police management and even to civilian authority in this forum.

Of course, any association of police officers, whether or not it is a union, can take a position on an issue like gun control or civilian review of police conduct. As Juris and Feuille point out, police rank and file would oppose certain policies even if unionism and collective bargaining were outlawed.[10] But the police position, when expressed through a union, is a more potent one. The strength a union derives from bargaining on bread-and-butter issues contributes to its strength as a voice on broad policy issues, and, in reverse, the strength the union acquires through its success on these broad issues reinforces its strength in bargaining. This is true not only in the eyes of the employees themselves, but also in the eyes of the legislators, city officials, and the public, whose opinions the union may seek to influence. This is an important distinction between unions and nonbargaining associations.

What specifically are some of the broad policy issues of concern in police reform upon which the unions are likely to take a stand? They will include the major issues raised in chapters 1 through 8 of this book. Police unions will almost certainly express themselves and attempt to exert major influence when a community, in one way or another, starts to define police objectives, to modify or expand the police function, and to create alternatives to the criminal justice system (see chapters 2–4). They are bound to become involved when police agencies move to structure the discretion of their personnel: such as the amount of force an officer may use; the conditions under which a specific law is to be enforced; the criteria for making a physical arrest as opposed to issuing a citation; or the manner in which demonstrations are to be handled (see chapter 5). And the unions will obviously play an active role as attempts are made to create more effective ways in which to direct, review, and control police conduct and to deal with police corruption (see chapters 6–8). Efforts to improve the caliber of both police leadership and police personnel through techniques such as lateral movement, standards to be employed in hiring and training new recruits, and programs for recruitment of minorities and for higher education will concern unions not only for their broad implications but for their specific relevance to wages, hours, and working conditions (see chapters 9–11).

As to all of these issues, the fear is commonly expressed that the unions will consistently adopt an ultraconservative position; that they will oppose all change in the direction that reformers have advocated. This is the basis of most current concern about the role of unions as it relates to police improvement. This concern is not unfounded, for indeed the union position almost always reflects a commitment to look out—first and foremost—for the short-term job-related interests of its members.[11] Sometimes this conservative position is magnified because the union also reflects the deeply held ideologies of the police subculture—the articulation of which helps police unions to win support.

The unions' efforts to protect the short-run interests of their members show up with special clarity in the position they have assumed toward procedures intended to increase the effectiveness of existing controls over police conduct. Stephen C. Halpern documents the intensive effort made by the police unions in Baltimore, Philadelphia, and Buffalo to shield policemen from effective review, noting that the unions in these cities have, as a consequence, further alienated the police from the citizenry.[12] And William P. McCarthy, former first deputy commissioner in New York City, describes the resistance of the unions to dealing aggressively with the problems of corruption.[13] Whereas the motivation of the unions in these situations is obviously one of protecting their membership, the position of union leadership on other issues may be motivated primarily by a strategy to deal with management or even their own members. It is in this context that these leaders make public statements that on the surface sometimes seem outlandish.

Will the prevailing positions of the police unions on the broader issues of police reform (that are not bargainable) solidify and grow stronger, or will they change? Some change may occur in the long run if management succeeds in altering recruitment standards and thereby changes the base from which the union draws its membership. But for the foreseeable future it is unrealistic to expect the union leadership to work actively for the kind of changes in the form and quality of police services advocated by those currently critical of police operations.

By the very nature of their job, union leaders, elected by their constituency to serve their needs, must be political. They must place the interests of their members above the goals of police reform. And while they may develop the capacity to influence the attitudes of their members on specific issues, they cannot—unless they develop enormous power—afford to stray far from representing the opinions of the majority of their members. So on matters of police reform the union leadership will almost always be reacting to management proposals. And the position a union will take will depend heavily on the ability of management to relate to the union and on management's own position regarding needed change. If management takes a consistently hard line toward the union, one can expect a more militant and less cooperative form of union leadership.

The police administrator committed to improving police services must, there-fore, communicate openly with the union; airing common grievances, obtaining feedback on administrative policies, and—while respecting the need of the union for independence—exploring ways in which union and management might work for common goals beneficial to both. He must not be afraid to consult the union and involve it in important department decisions, but he must retain for himself ultimate control and authority.

A cooperative attitude, however, ought not dilute the administrator's role as an initiator of change, for it is incumbent upon the chief, as a representative of community interests, to press hard in all of his relationships with the unions for an enlightened approach to policing. If he fails to do so, it is unclear who will. That is one reason why it is so essential that the chief be represented at the bar-gaining table, along with those representatives of municipal government who are primarily concerned with the financial aspects of bargaining. And that is why it is so important that the chief himself have as his foremost goal the development of a system of policing that is both fair and effective.

More opportunities exist for undertaking changes that would benefit both management and the unions than may initially appear to be the case. Many of the fundamental problems identified in the earlier chapters adversely affect not only the quality of police services but the individual officer as well. Alternatives to the criminal justice system, for example, could, if properly designed, result in a higher quality of police service, a reduction in the work load on the police of-ficer, and a greater sense of satisfaction for the officer in the results that are achieved. In like fashion, much of the stress currently built into policing could be reduced and other working conditions improved if the conflicting demands with which each officer must deal were even partially resolved—if, for example, the police function is clarified; the limitations under which officers operate are more widely acknowledged; specific grants of authority and additional resources are supplied; the discretion they must exercise is recognized; and if appropriate allowance is made for the risks they must occasionally take.

Individual officers stand to gain as well in prestige and monetary compensa-tion from the increased recognition of the importance and complexity of the officer's job that is bound to result from addressing the fundamental problems in the field. In 1975 the Patrolmen's Benevolent Association in New York City sought to break the pay parity of police officers and firemen and to increase further the existing 10 percent differential above sanitation workers. The arbitra-tion panel appointed to rule on the demand decided against the PBA, contending that the day-to-day work of the typical police officer in the city had remained generally the same in recent years. But the panel made some interesting observa-tions in suggesting circumstances under which a higher pay scale for police of-ficers would be appropriate:

Evidence before the Impasse Panel persuasively showed that the best qual-ified and most conscientious members of the modern big city police force may be called upon for a broad range of duties which demand not merely stamina, patience, and courage, but also an increasing measure of imaginative resourcefulness, sociological and psychological insights, and communications skills. If and when the police officers represented by the PBA are shown typically to be responsive to and reflective of these greater demands, the suitability of present salary scales may well be drawn into question.[14]

It follows from these observations that the unions do themselves a disservice when they take a position on administrative proposals that commits them to reinforcing and perpetuating the public's concept of the police job as a simple task requiring a minimum of knowledge, experience, and skills.

THE ROLE OF EXTERNAL FORCES

External pressures for change in the police can take various forms, from legislation and large-scale government programs down to expressions of opinion by the individual citizen on how police handle a specific incident. And they can vary in tone from the formal requirements of courts and legislatures and the militant demands of citizen groups to the persuasion, coaxing, encouragement, and assistance of government agencies, private foundations, research organizations, and, of course, the citizenry.

The Media

The media—radio, television, and the press—exert enormous influence over the form and quality of police service. Television probably impacts the most—not through its news coverage, but through the high percentage of its prime-time programming that is devoted to police shows. To the extent that these programs portray policing in an unrealistic manner—as consisting almost entirely of intriguing and invariably successful efforts to identify and apprehend dangerous offenders—they are probably most responsible for perpetuating the myths of policing and establishing expectations of police agencies that cannot possibly be realized.

With this steady diet of police shows being fed to the public, it is all the more incumbent on the media to cover actual events relating to the police in a balanced and intelligent manner. The public heavily depends on news reports—especially by the press—for their understanding of any issues relating to the police that may arise. Public attitudes and the pressures that the public bring to bear on the police are strongly influenced by media coverage.

The police are equally dependent on the media. They tend to respond directly and sometimes excessively to criticism from the media, whether explicit or implied. They do this because they realize that their image is largely determined by the manner in which they are represented to the community. It follows that if media coverage is sophisticated, reflecting an awareness of the importance and complexity of police operations, public understanding is increased and the pressures exerted on the police, both by the public and by the media, will support a more enlightened approach toward policing. But if the media lack this awareness they can be a major impediment to change.

In many situations an alert press, committed to fairness and integrity in government, has pressured aggressively for police reform. Much of what has been accomplished in modernizing police operations in this country is attributable to newspaper inquiries and coverage—to the work of investigative reporters who have described corruption, other forms of wrongdoing, and mismanagement of police agencies. The experience with corruption in New York City affords a good example. The city administration and the police department were forced, over great resistance, to endorse an intensive inquiry into corruption because of the pressure generated by the investigative reporting of David Burnham of the *New York Times.*[15] The Knapp Commission investigation, which followed, brought about major changes in the New York City Police Department, and the coverage given the investigation produced a wave of concern for corrupt practices in police agencies across the country.

Routine daily coverage of police business, by contrast, caters to a low common denominator of public understanding of policing. For the most part it focuses upon the more sensational incidents police handle, such as major crimes, violent disturbances, and emergencies. The police beat is often covered by the newest reporters as part of their training. Policy issues that arise in the running of a police agency are usually secondary to crime news, and it should not be surprising, therefore, that many issues are ignored and those that are covered are often reported inadequately. Simplistic stereotypes of the police role are constantly reinforced. It can be extremely frustrating for a police administrator to attempt to communicate with the public regarding complex changes in police operations if he must do so through a police reporter who views policing in a traditional way and whose only real interest is in the sensational or the technologically intriguing aspects of police operations.

The media could have a much more constructive influence on police functioning if they recognized, first of all, how potent a force they really are. To meet their heavy responsibility in reporting police business, they must appreciate that covering administrative issues requires a radically different approach from covering street events. Routine reporting of administrative actions, or disinterest in such actions, perpetuates police practices that perhaps should be questioned. And portraying much-needed but complicated changes in simplistic terms can make them sound unnecessary or even foolish, depriving them of public support and thus preventing them from being carried out. On the other hand, informed inquiry—in the best traditions of journalism—into such actions and changes can contribute immeasurably toward alerting the public to important policy issues. Improving the quality of coverage of police matters by the media holds tremendous potential for improving the police.

The Municipalities

Municipal officials—mayors, city managers, city council members, and police boards and commissions—come closest to being the formally designated watchdogs of police operations. They are also closest, in proximity, to the police and their problems. These factors together give them tremendous potential for influencing, for better or for worse, the directions in which the police develop. As detailed in chapter 6, they have, unfortunately, abdicated many aspects of this role, with the result that citizens have had to seek other means to reach the police. Chapter 6 sets forth various methods for correcting this situation and for giving new meaning to the concept of local control of police operations.

Recent events have forced mayors and city managers to take a much greater interest in police operations. Such organizations as the National League of Cities, the National Association of Counties, and the International City Management Association, in response to this interest, have operated training programs financed out of LEAA funds which, though modest, are designed to equip municipal executives to deal more effectively with the issues that arise in policing.

The impact that municipal government can have was recently illustrated in Los Angeles when, upon assuming office as mayor, Tom Bradley requested a newly appointed board of police commissioners to review the intelligence-gathering functions of the Los Angeles Police Department that relate to public disorders. The board met with key members of the police department for more than a year, reviewing all existing practices and focusing particularly on the criteria to be employed in determining the circumstances under which a record should be maintained of the activities of individuals and organizations.

The review resulted in the removal and destruction of 1.89 million cards that had been entered into the files since they were first established in the 1920s; it produced a drastic reorientation in operating policies in which the emphasis was shifted from a concern with people who held certain ideas to a concern with those who commit or threaten to commit criminally disruptive acts; and it resulted in adoption of detailed guidelines covering the collection, storage, and dissemination of intelligence information and a procedure for auditing compliance with them.[16] The police department then published its policies, inviting the public to comment on them at hearings called for the purpose.

The case offers a classic illustration of a situation in which citizen concern, expressed through a mayor and a board of police commissioners, along with an awareness of court actions initiated in other jurisdictions, pressured a police agency into reviewing long-standing practices in a highly sensitive area of their operations. It involved the department in confronting and balancing many conflicting interests. And it produced greatly refined procedures that are much more consonant with the role the police should play in a free society.

That these new procedures were subsequently shared with the community made the achievement even more significant. While some members of the agency may have been irritated—at least initially—by the intrusion into its operations, others may have welcomed the external pressure as a justification for doing what they wanted to do on their own, but could not attempt in the face of internal resistance. The net result sharpened the capacity of the Los Angeles Police Department to function in this area and provided the community with cause to have added confidence in its police.

The financial plight of local governments is now among the major factors accounting for greater involvement of local officials in police matters. The need to reduce expenditures has forced mayors, city managers, and city councils to examine more carefully the nature of police operations in order to make difficult choices in reducing services. Distasteful as it is for all parties, the process nevertheless can serve as an effective vehicle for reviewing old programs and practices and for setting priorities in areas in which none have previously been set.

As discussed in chapter 6, however, this greater involvement of local officials in police matters could have negative effects. It could put pressure on police administrators to engage in practices that are based upon simplistic notions of the police function. What happens will depend in large measure on the capability of the police administrator, and especially on his ability to acquaint city officials with some of the intricacies of police operations.

State Governments

State governments played a minimal role in matters affecting local policing until passage of the Omnibus Crime Control Act of 1968. As noted in chapter 6 there was a period when some local police agencies were actually placed under state control, and vestiges of this arrangement can still be found. A number of states had for some time provided several services to local policing, like the pooling of arrest and identification records, the collection and publication of crime and arrest data, and the provision of crime-laboratory services. Some also established minimum requirements for basic training, and a few actually furnished such training.[17]

With their new responsibility to serve as a conduit for federal funds added to their inherent authority to legislate in areas directly affecting local police, the states are now in a position to exert a much greater influence over municipal police agencies than they have exercised in the past. Should they be more active? And, if so, along what lines?

Admittedly the whole notion of greater state involvement in fashioning police service is complicated because there is usually so little that state governments can do, aside from using their legislative authority, to relieve the severe and unique problems from which the larger cities suffer. That is precisely why local governments have been assured, under the provisions of the Omnibus Crime Control Act, that they will receive an appropriate proportion of the funds that are available and that they will have a voice in determining how these funds are to be used.[18] This provision was intended to make progress possible in major urban centers that have the benefit of enlightened leadership, even though the state government is not equally enlightened. But the larger municipalities continue to complain that they do not receive their appropriate share of the funds and that the use of the funds they do receive is unduly restricted. Where state standards and goals are higher than those applied in the municipality, the pass-through arrangement—despite the complaints of the municipalities—seems to have prevented the states from improving local police by using their limited authority over spending.

When grappling with the complexities of state and local relations in police matters, it is instructive to note the seemingly smooth working relationship that has been developed in England over the years between the national government and local authorities. The police are essentially directed and controlled at the local level. But Parliament maintains a continuing and vital interest in the overall quality of police service. It investigates major problems that arise, defining its expectations by the very nature of its inquiries. And it provides, through the Home Office, a blend of controls, funding, and staff support that has contributed in many ways to upgrading police operations. It has, for example, established regional training facilities, created the Police College, facilitated lateral movement, and sponsored research of value to all local agencies. The arrangement also accommodates the unique problems of London by including the Metropolitan Police in some schemes and exempting them from others and by capitalizing on the size and capacities of the Metropolitan Police when they can be of service to smaller communities. To apply this model at the federal level in this country would entail many problems, but it is in some respects worthy of emulation within individual states.

Given the proliferation of small agencies in this country, the states are in a unique position to furnish services and forms of support of the sort that these agencies cannot provide for themselves, while encouraging them to vary according to the character and needs of their localities—thereby helping to make the concept of locally controlled police a more viable one. The current trend, made possible by newly available federal funds, to do much more to support and oversee training, to maintain records, to provide facilities for the analysis of physical evidence, to lend state-police personnel, and to provide legal counsel contributes to this end. It should be encouraged and expanded. The states, in collaboration with the larger cities, can take the initiative in working out arrangements whereby highly specialized police personnel (such as those assigned to the investigation of organized crime) can assist the smaller agencies when they must deal with problems they are not equipped to handle.

Beyond these services, however, many of which are now offered, the states could be much more aggressive in contributing to basic changes in the police. Elaborate programs have been established in the training area, but with primary emphasis upon their form and relatively little upon their content. The states would be justified, on the basis of appropriate citizen input, in using training as a vehicle for challenging traditional approaches to police functioning. And they could benefit a great deal from assuming more initiative in developing police leadership—by providing training and by facilitating, as suggested in chapter 9, the lateral movement of police officers within a state.

The states also have a role to play, though at a less ambitious level than the federal government, in sponsoring research and in planning new and better ways to improve the quality of police service. The small agencies do not have the in-house capacity to design experiments, the funds to finance them, or the know-how required to evaluate them. Yet there is frequently support for experimentation among the leadership and personnel of these agencies that one does not find in larger jurisdictions. And the middle-size communities in particular afford good laboratories for testing new approaches to old problems that might produce results applicable to large cities as well. The staffs of the various state planning agencies are currently involved in planning, but in a very limited fashion. Their involvement consists, for the most part, in developing annual spending priorities. It is then up to the local agencies to request funds, and the state staff typically devotes the rest of its time to processing these requests and, subsequently, to monitoring the approved expenditures.

The allocation of funds obviously affords an excellent opportunity to shape the overall development of not only the police, but the total criminal justice system. But under current practices these allocations are often made to finance the replication of existing programs of questionable value. If the state planning councils—or some other agency of state government—were to build a staff that could work in a very intensive fashion with those local agencies that want to experiment with new approaches to policing, the necessary expertise in research design could be developed over a period of time, various experimental projects could be conducted, and the results could then serve as a basis for more creative utilization of the federal funds channeled through the state.

Largely untapped is the inherent role that state legislatures can play in contributing to improved policing by reworking basic legislation relating to the police. Consider, for example, the potential impact of a statute—and the public debate that would most likely precede its enactment—that redefines police responsibilities; or the value of legislation that replaces the full-enforcement statutes with more realistically drawn provisions that recognize the need for police discretion and hold the police, as an administrative agency, responsible for the manner in which it is exercised; or the value of legislative inquiries that explore the desirability of various alternatives to the criminal justice system and the legislation that might be enacted to establish such alternatives. And, of course, legislatures can always contribute positively to police functioning by removing from the statute books, or by modifying, the many laws that are in their current form unenforceable.

As the states take an increasingly active role in matters affecting local policing, the great danger overall is that they may do so without giving serious attention to what specifically should be the nature of their contribution. The results could be negative if the states act in ways that reinforce and perpetuate the myths and questionable practices that now prevail. If the states raise all police agencies to some minimum standards, they will have made a contribution, but of a limited nature. State governments can contribute most effectively by marshaling support for a fuller recognition of the importance and complexity of the police function and translating this support into legislation and programs aimed at reducing the conflicts within the police task, thereby increasing the capacity of the police to meet their varied responsibilities.

The Federal Government

While most distant and purposely insulated from direct involvement, the federal government has had more of an influence on municipal police agencies than is generally recognized. The FBI has been, over the years, a potent force in shaping the form and orientation of local policing—through its training programs, the services it renders local police, and the information and services it elicits from them. Other federal law enforcement agencies have played a similar, though lesser, role. Events during the turbulence of the late 1960s demonstrated that the power of the United States attorney general can be enormous. When John Mitchell replaced Ramsey Clark in that office, for example, the signals that were sent out produced a dramatic shift in local policies for dealing with massive conflict.[19] With the creation of the Office of Law Enforcement Assistance in the Department of Justice in 1965, and its successor in 1968, the Law Enforcement Assistance Administration, the federal government—through a rapid expansion of support for research, training, and equipping police agencies—became much more formally and directly involved in matters affecting local police.[20]

The federal government's role has grown primarily out of a concern for crime.[21] In establishing LEAA, for example, Congress justified the legislation on the grounds that the "high incidence of crime in the United States threatens the peace, security and general welfare of the Nation and its citizens."[22] The FBI training programs have also been crime oriented, reflecting the concern of the sponsoring agency.

In practice, however, neither the LEAA nor the FBI has defined its program so narrowly. LEAA and the planning agencies responsible for administering LEAA funds at the state, regional, and local levels have funded many projects which, in isolation, appear to have little to do with serious crime. The program administrators are close enough to police functioning to realize that improving a police agency in almost any fashion has some potential impact on the capacity of the agency to cope with crime. But they are sensitive on this point, often taking extra care to show the relationship of a project to crime in the event that those judging the project will not recognize the interdependence of various aspects of police functioning. In its training programs for local police the FBI has recently been moving away from a narrow focus on crime, giving increasing attention to those aspects of the municipal police function that make municipal policing so radically different from policing at the federal level.

Should this movement be encouraged and given formal endorsement and support? Is the concern with crime the only justification for federal involvement in programs relating to municipal police? Or does the federal government have a broader role in improving the police as a critically important institution in our society?

In my own view the federal government does have a major responsibility to assist local and state governments in building a form of police service in this country that is locally controlled and uniquely equipped to meet the peculiar needs of our society. This type of commitment would not increase the authority of the federal government over local police matters. Nor would it reduce the federal government's present role in assisting local police in combating crime. It would simply place this function in a broader context. It would recognize that what local police do in coping with crime is only one of the tasks of the police; and that strengthening local agencies that are created to deal with crime is, in the long run, one of the most effective means by which to cope with crime. Independent of these considerations, however, the federal government has a very direct stake in helping to improve local police agencies because of the role that local police must play in upholding democratic values and in protecting our democratic system.

Such a stance has many practical implications. It would give a new sense of purpose and direction to some existing federal efforts, such as the program supporting college education of present and future police personnel. It would provide a firmer basis for federal involvement in new programs, such as that advocated in chapter 9 to facilitate lateral movement of police personnel. It would justify continuous—rather than one-shot—funding and the establishment of permanent programs to develop police leadership. And it would warrant a heavier and more explicit commitment to sponsoring research on all aspects of the police function.

Why these areas and not others? Because they are areas well beyond the capacity of almost all local jurisdictions and most states, in which concentrated high-quality work has the potential for producing results that will benefit the entire nation. For example, while it is important that police agencies develop their own capacity to conduct research and that their personnel participate in experiments, it is fairly obvious that all of the needs for research in the police field cannot be met by operating agencies. Some forms of research are simply too costly for a single jurisdiction to undertake. The expected return to the jurisdiction may not be sufficient to warrant funding out of tight operating budgets. If local funds are used, moreover, the agency is usually under tremendous pressure to produce positive results even though it is in the nature of true experimentation that some efforts will fail. Beyond this, for research to be of value, simultaneous projects must often be conducted in several different jurisdictions in order to compare results.

The Kansas City, Missouri, and the San Diego police departments would most likely not have been able to carry out the major experiments in which they have engaged in recent years were it not for the heavy financial and staff support from a national organization, in this case the Police Foundation, and for the flexibility with which these projects were administered and jointly evaluated by the departments and the foundation. Both experiments have produced findings that will have a marked impact upon the development of police service in this country.

LEAA's National Institute of Law Enforcement and Criminal Justice (NILECJ) has the potential for financing similar experiments, but its efforts to date appear to have been seriously constrained by pressures to spread limited funds thinly among many programs in the broad spectrum of criminal justice; by a desire to complete projects and thereby produce specific results in a short time; and, perhaps most significantly, by the absence of a sufficiently large community of researchers with the interest, the ideas, and the competence to carry out promising work. An exception to the commitment to short-term projects is NILECJ's sponsorship of the response-time analysis study now under way in Kansas City, Missouri. That the institute is uniquely equipped to perform continuing functions of great value to policing by virtue of its being a central agency serving the needs of the police and other agencies in the criminal justice system is demonstrated by the testing it has conducted in technological areas; by its identification of exemplary projects and the procedures it has established to disseminate the results of these projects; and by the arrangements it has made to serve as a clearinghouse for published materials on crime and the criminal justice system.

The major action projects directly financed by LEAA, as distinguished from the research program, have had a somewhat schizoid character to them. Attention has focused on some areas, only to shift abruptly to others, and then again, with equal speed, to still others. Critics of both government spending and police reform are constantly pointing to the waste inherent in some programs as they urge support for others. This continuous change of focus results from several factors: the unusually keen competition among long-neglected needs, the sense of urgency in meeting these needs, and the gradual accumulation of experience in how best to satisfy them. It also reflects the frequent change in administration of LEAA, uncertainty as to ultimate goals, and disagreement on how the investment of limited financial resources and human talent might do the greatest amount of good. And in part the frequent change in direction is attributable to political judgments that were rather naively intended to produce quick dramatic results (e.g., a reduction in the crime rate), but more often produced only the embarrassing realization that the expectations were unrealistic.

The heaviest criticism of LEAA has been directed at the proportion of their resources devoted to technological improvements—the actual purchase of communication devices, vehicles, helicopters, weaponry, computers, records systems, and the like. The initial emphasis upon technology is understandable. Many of the leaders in the police field and those who defined its needs had, for years prior to the creation of LEAA, viewed technology as the answer to the problems they considered of greatest importance. The gadgetry of technological improvements holds a certain fascination and dramatic appeal for large segments of the public; it feeds the "Dick Tracy" concept of what policing is all about. Investment in technological improvements has been used by some police agencies and by state planning agencies as a way of avoiding more difficult problems.

The evaluation of federally sponsored programs and constant reassessment of priorities are crucially important tasks. But in trying to meet criticism and set priorities, some have concluded that if a program does not deserve top billing, it deserves no support whatsoever. The simple truth is that progress is needed in all areas; that, as the preceding chapters should have made explicit, they are inextricably interrelated and interdependent. It is grossly unfair to test the value of any single proposal, whether it be a computer application, a training program, or the recommendation that the police undertake to formulate policy, without relating it to other developments. The great need is to balance change in one area with changes in others so that they harmoniously lead toward the common goal of improving police services; so that they are proportional to one another and mutually supportive.

The Courts

Conflicts over hiring practices, personnel policies, and police responses to political protest have been drawing the judiciary more and more frequently into the consideration of basic issues that arise in the running of a police agency. At the same time a noticeable change has taken place in the attitude of appellate courts in recent years when called upon to review the propriety of police performance. Judges are increasingly inclined to acknowledge the realities of police work: the varied uses made of arrest, the impossibility of enforcing all laws, the conflict between different aspects of the police function, and the endless variety of circumstances and unpredictable conditions under which the police must act. With this growing awareness of the complexity of police operations, courts are becoming reluctant to condemn police practices without offering alternative approaches; but they seem equally unwilling to prescribe rules that they fear may be too narrow and thus unworkable. They can judge one way or the other on the factual situation before them, but they are not sufficiently familiar with the intricacies of police work—nor do they have the expertise available to them—to reach into police operations in order to correct the practices or policies that give rise to a particular problem.

As discussed in chapters 5 and 7, some courts have met this situation by encouraging and sometimes requiring the police—who are most familiar with the circumstances—to come up with workable solutions for the problems that the courts identify. (The recent *Rizzo* decision, of course, places major restrictions on the use to be made of the federal Civil Rights Act for this purpose.) Rather than speak to the police indirectly or impose restrictions that are unworkable, the courts seem to be expressing a preference for encouraging the police to undertake themselves to develop a solution for a problem or an alternative for a practice that the courts have determined to be illegal or improper. This trend holds the potential for making judicial review a much more effective vehicle for improving police operations.

It would be helpful if the same concept were implemented at the trial-court level in the routine processing of criminal cases. The trial courts continue to speak indirectly to the police by excluding evidence when, in their judgment, it has been illegally obtained. But they do so repeatedly in many jurisdictions without any indication that the message is heard or, indeed, without any real expectation of changing police practice. Thus, as has often been pointed out, the use of the exclusionary rule as a means of correcting police practice is nullified. Current frustrations could be avoided and police functioning could be sharpened if the trial courts, on examining into a motion to suppress, requested police agencies to produce the policies upon which their questionable action in the given case was based. This would, of course, require that judges in jurisdictions having more than one trial court establish a procedure for agreeing among themselves on the policies submitted for review so that the police would not be faced with conflicting judicial opinions.[23]

ORGANIZATIONS OUTSIDE OF GOVERNMENT

Given the large number of individuals involved in policing and the importance of the police function, the number of organizations—aside from the associations of police employees and government agencies—that have had a continuing interest in the police and their problems is surprisingly small.

By far the largest and most important group is the International Association of Chiefs of Police (IACP). Founded in 1871, the association devoted most of its efforts, through the 1950s, to promoting contact among police chiefs, primarily by means of a secretariat, annual conferences, and a monthly publication. It played a major role in establishing a national clearinghouse for fingerprint identification and the Uniform Crime Reporting System, both of which were subsequently turned over to the FBI. And it created, in conjunction with Northwestern University, a program to promote research, publications, and training related to the police role in traffic safety.

In 1960 the staff of IACP, under new direction, was substantially expanded, and the association began to provide a wide range of services to its members. It became heavily involved in conducting management studies, developing training materials, sponsoring training programs, and collecting data on various aspects of police operations. The association also began to advocate new programs and reforms—mostly in the area of police management. But in all its activities the IACP has been severely limited in the degree to which it can be openly critical of the current state of policing, because such criticism would be viewed as directed at its own membership. This is illustrated by the fact that when the IACP is requested, by municipal officials, to conduct a study of a police agency, it will not take on the job without the agreement of the police chief whose agency is to be studied. Despite this limitation, however, the association has contributed a great deal toward upgrading the efficiency of police agencies throughout the country.

The IACP made the greatest contribution toward directly influencing the quality of policing in the late 1960s when urban rioting became the primary concern of police administrators. The association's staff took the initiative in responding to this crisis by sponsoring a series of intensive training programs designed to provide police administrators and their key assistants with insight into the nature of urban unrest and with the best available thinking on how to reduce community tensions and to control conflict once it erupted. Those who participated in these sessions and who subsequently observed the agencies that were represented, as they handled incidents in their communities, were convinced that the sessions had a dramatic impact upon the quality of the police response. In a very real sense the IACP in that period became a major instrument for effecting change in the approach of police agencies to the problem of large-scale conflict.

In 1972 the Board of Officers of the IACP joined with the American Bar Association in endorsing the standards for policing set out in *The Urban Police Function*, which had been developed through a joint effort of the two organizations.[24] This was of great significance since the standards call for a major restyling of police agencies to increase their ability to provide a higher quality of service in a way that supports and extends democratic values. The IACP continues to espouse the implementation of these standards.

In recent years that portion of IACP's membership representing small communities has assumed greater control of the organization, substantially reducing the likelihood that the organization will address the most critical issues of the field and accounting for a noticeable retreat to a position more defensive of the status quo.[25] The organization will no doubt continue to make a significant contribution by promoting the exchange of information, by furnishing the services it is currently providing, and by supporting advances in the more technical aspects of policing. But the fact that the membership of IACP is determined by those filling the top positions in police agencies, rather than by those who share a commitment to a specific concept for improving policing, makes it unlikely that the IACP can be a strong force in resolving the fundamental problems in policing that are discussed in this book.

Occasional efforts have been made, on both the local and national levels, to organize individuals having a strong commitment to improving policing, regardless of their position or rank, but such efforts have not progressed to the point that any of these groups has become an effective force for change.[26]

In 1970 the Ford Foundation allocated $30 million for the development of a new organization—the Police Foundation—that it hoped would become "a force for constructive change in the police function and an important instrument for reconciling the claims of order and justice in an increasingly complex society."[27] Administered by a board of directors, this newly established organization defined its central aim as developing promising programs of innovation and improvement by supporting police leaders who were ready to experiment.

The Police Foundation has made a unique contribution in the choice of projects it has funded and the emphasis it has placed upon project evaluation. The independent status of the foundation has made it possible for its board of directors—on a highly selective basis—to match their interests and their concept of areas in need of exploration with police agencies that have defined their interests and concerns in a similar manner. As a consequence, although the foundation's annual expenditures are relatively small compared to the federal programs and the operating budgets of police agencies, it has served as a catalyst in drawing attention to areas in need of development and has been in the forefront in exploring new concepts and ideas. The commitment to experimentation has made it possible for the foundation to invest in developing evaluation techniques, carrying out complex evaluations, and giving broad distribution to the results of these studies—thereby promoting discussion, debate, and some replication of its projects. The type of projects the foundation has sponsored and the questions it has been asking have predictably stirred some controversy. The frequent references in this book to the pioneering work that was done under Police Foundation sponsorship in Kansas City, in Cincinnati, in San Diego, in Rochester, and in other communities attest to the fact that the foundation, in its short life, has come to occupy an important position in matters of police reform. And while the direction of its future efforts is not at all clear, it has demonstrated that an organization with independent status can indeed become a force for constructive change in the field.

THE PROSPECTS FOR CHANGE

Considering how arduous it has been to achieve relatively simple and often purely mechanical changes in police operations, is it realistic to expect to make more fundamental changes in policing designed to improve the quality of police service? Are the various forces that have been described likely to press for needed change? Or are they more likely to resist such change or simply remain passive?

Viewed from the perspective of the police administrator who is committed to improving the police, the likelihood of achieving significant change seems remote. The conditions of immediate concern to the police—especially in the large urban areas—continue to grow more acute, with the result that the police are under constant and intense pressure to deal with serious problems: to curb violence; to solve specific crimes and apprehend the offenders; to protect those who have been repeatedly victimized; to end senseless vandalism; to cope with racial conflicts; and to meet insistent demands for more protection on the streets, in the parks, and on public transit.

Reflecting the mood of the central cities, tensions have been building up within police agencies as well. Relationships between white, black, and other minority police officers have become strained as police practices have been attacked by minority groups, as minority groups themselves have become more outspoken about police practices, and as blacks and other minorities have succeeded in having courts confirm their claims to a higher percentage of police jobs and to a greater proportion of the promotional opportunities. The rapid emergence of the unions—with their demands on management and their occasional job actions and strikes—has radically altered the relationship between the rank and file and those supervisory personnel who are considered a part of management. Job tenure, which has been recognized since the Depression as one of the great attractions of police work, has suddenly become less secure—especially for those newly hired—as municipalities have been required to reduce their budgets. And the outlook for future adjustments in salaries and fringe benefits is clouded for all police personnel.

In an atmosphere of tensions and crises, both in the community and within the agency, planning for the future is extremely difficult and, at times, even seems irrelevant. The need for change may be readily recognized, but as a somewhat idealistic notion to which the agency might hopefully turn its attention at some future time when the current pressures abate. Since the problems do not diminish, but actually grow both in number and in severity, what is characterized as a temporary attitude toward change tends to become the permanent posture of the agency.

In the end, however, it is not the attitude of the police administrator and his agency, nor of the legislature or other government agencies, that will determine the nature and rate of change in the police. The position of these forces and the degree to which they succeed in achieving their objectives will be determined by the interest and support of the community.

Within police circles the feeling is strong that the majority of citizens, concerned with their personal safety in an environment they consider threatening, want short-term solutions for the problems at their doorsteps and are therefore not likely to support complex proposals that hold the potential for producing results only after a series of interrelated changes can be executed over an extended period of time. It is assumed, moreover, that the vast majority of citizens will not support changes that are intended, at least in part, to protect minorities and to achieve fairness, due process, and legality in police operations—especially if these changes are viewed as reducing police effectiveness.

In a limited study conducted in Florida, Richard Chackerian found that citizens placed a negative value on professional policing because they apparently do not share the concern that it implies for restraint and fairness.[28] If the police view and Chackerian's findings accurately reflect the attitude of the community, as periodic samplings of public opinion seem to confirm, what chance, if any, is there of making a greater concern for democratic values a major objective of improved policing?

Several factors suggest that the outlook may be brighter than initially appears to be the case, though the rate of progress may continue to be agonizingly slow. First, communities vary a great deal in their makeup. While it is true that present conditions may make it extremely unlikely that there will be community support for needed change in some cities, the attitude will differ radically in others. And to the degree that some progress is realized in these communities, it may stimulate change elsewhere.

Second, conflicts and tension, though taxing on the police, nevertheless produce change. More progress was realized in policing in the last decade, when the police were operating under great pressures, than in any other period in the history of policing in this country. Community tensions forced some agencies to modify their concept of their function; to experiment with alternatives to the criminal justice process; and to implement more effective means for controlling police conduct. Further increases in the crime rate, while hard on the police and society, may well lead a community to face up to the limitations of the police and to explore various alternative approaches to the problem of crime. Likewise, the conflicts caused by racial integration within police agencies will, in all probability, become more intense and more troublesome. But the agency that itself goes through a turbulent period of integration may emerge from the experience better equipped to help the community as a whole to work its way through the same painful process.

Third, community attitudes are heavily influenced by the police. It is not surprising that many people see policing in simplistic terms and fail to support needed change when those in policing continue to mislead the public about their capabilities and insist that theirs is a simple task easily achievable if only they could be relieved of some of the current constraints upon them. By being more open, change-oriented police have it within their capacity to alter the positions that the community as a whole takes on matters affecting the police.

Those in the community who support the status quo should be shown that they are deluding themselves in their assessment of police capabilities; that in fact many of the police operations in which they take comfort are extremely limited in value. Citizens should also be shown how limitations on government expenditures are going to make it impossible to maintain—let alone expand—the present form of policing. New ways will have to be found to deal with complex problems that have previously been handled, albeit temporarily and often quite ineffectively, with the mere assignment of additional manpower. Currently the public is afforded the luxury of reacting impulsively and somewhat emotionally to problems in policing because they are not equipped to respond rationally—the consequences of adopting one alternative over another are not made clear. The greater visibility that the police themselves can provide of both their capacity and their current policies should increase the degree of responsibility with which the public reacts to proposals involving the police.

This emphasis on the extent to which improved policing, in the end, depends on the community will remind some of the old saw that a community receives the quality of policing it deserves. But for this axiom to have meaning today, when our society is so complex, requires that citizens be sufficiently aware of the intricacies of police functioning to know what they can demand and how different demands will affect the quality of police service. That is why more widespread understanding and discussion of the fundamental issues in policing, to which this book is intended to contribute, constitutes one of the great hopes for the future.

NOTES

1. Among the relatively few works dealing directly with the process of organizational change in police agencies are Hans Toch, J. Douglas Grant, and Raymond T. Galvin, *Agents of Change* (New York: John Wiley and Sons, 1975); Robert B. Duncan, "Organizational Climate and Climate for Change in Three Police Departments," *Urban Affairs Quarterly* 8 (1972): 205–245; and Victor Cizanckas and Fritzi Feist, "A Community's Response to Police Change," *Journal of Police Science and Administration* 3 (1975): 284–291. See also the papers collected in *Changing Police Organizations: Four Readings* (Washington, D.C.: National League of Cities and the United States Conference of Mayors, 1973); and the monograph prepared for police leaders, Patrick V. Murphy and David S. Brown, *The Police Leader Looks at the Changing Nature of Police Organization* (Washington, D.C.: Leadership Resources, Inc., 1973).

2. Clarence M. Kelley, "Receptiveness to Change," *Police Chief*, December, 1973, p. 33.

3. By union, I refer to any employee organization that bargains collectively for its members on matters pertaining to salaries, hours, and other conditions of employment.

4. These and other factors are explored in Hervey A. Juris and Peter Feuille, *Police Unionism* (Lexington, Mass.: Lexington Books, D. C. Heath, 1973), pp. 19–23.

5. According to a tabulation compiled in 1972 by the IACP, sixteen states require local subdivisions to engage in collective bargaining with their police employees; six states permit such bargaining; and in three states the parties are required to meet and confer. "Division of Public Employee Labor Relations Comparative Study of State Labor Laws," *Public Safety Labor Reporter*, reference vol. 1 (1972): 1–1 through 1–19 of the Comparative Labor Data section. In 1973 the International City Management Association conducted a survey of all cities of 50,000 population and over. Of 409 cities surveyed, 309 responded. From among those who responded, 234 reported that they engage in collective bargaining—149 on a formal basis and 85 on an informal basis. International City Management Association, *The Municipal Yearbook, 1974* (Washington, D.C.: ICMA 1974), pp. 222–226.

6. One of the strongest statements of the threat posed by the militancy and political activism of police officers and their associations is set forth by Jerome H. Skolnick in *The Politics of Protest* (New York: Ballantine Books, 1969), pp. 268–288.

7. See, generally, Juris and Feuille, *Police Unionism*, pp. 103–163; and Richard M. Ayres, "Police Unions: A Step Toward Professionalism," *Journal of Police Science and Administration* 3 (1975): 400–404. For an interesting example of the position of a former police administrator, see William P. McCarthy, "Key Issues in Police Unionism: Another Viewpoint," in *Guidelines and Papers from the National Symposium on Police Labor Relations* (Washington, D.C.: Police Foundation, 1974), p. 74. For a discussion of a series of recommendations for promoting harmonious relationships between police management and the unions, see John H. Burpo, "Improving Police Agency and Employee Performance Through Collective Bargaining," *Police Chief*, February 1974, pp. 36–38.

8. For an interesting case study of a union's massive resistance to the efforts of a change-oriented police administrator, see Rory Judd Albert, "A Time for Reform: A Case Study of the Interaction Between the Commissioner of the Boston Police Department and the Boston Police Patrolmen's Association," Technical Report No. 11–75, MIT Operations Research Center, mimeographed (Cambridge, Mass., 1975).

9. Juris and Feuille, *Police Unionism*, pp. 119–150.

10. Ibid., p. 184.

11. Juris and Feuille, in assessing the union's role in influencing department policies, concluded that "the union was essentially a conservative, reactionary force." Ibid., p. 184. And as to some of the leadership and personnel issues, they concluded that there was support for those critics who have said that the unions systematically interfere with management's quest for professional status for police officers. "The actions of most of the unions in our sample regarding lateral transfer, education, master-patrolman status, and recruitment and standards have been essentially negative and, from management's point of view, clearly counterproductive." Ibid., p. 117.

12. Stephen C. Halpern, *Police-Association and Department Leaders* (Lexington, Mass.: Lexington Books, D. C. Heath, 1974), p. 90.

13. McCarthy, "Key Issues in Police Unionism," pp. 72–74.

14. Report of Board of Collective Bargaining Impasse Panel, Patrolmen's Benevolent Association of the City of New York and the City of New York, Docket No. I-115-74, mimeographed (30 April 1975), p. 21.

15. The commissioner of police at the time, Patrick V. Murphy, has said "there would have been no Knapp Commission without Burnham's reporting." Patrick V. Murphy, *A Decade of Urban Police Problems*, Sixteenth Annual Wherrett Lecture on Local Government (Pittsburgh: Institute for Urban Policy and Administration, Graduate School of Public and International Affairs, University of Pittsburgh, 1974), p. 10.

16. Statement of the Los Angeles Board of Police Commissioners, "The Public Disorder Intelligence Function of the Los Angeles Police Department," mimeographed (10 April 1975).

17. The extent of state government involvement in matters relating to local

law enforcement as of 1966 was reported as part of an overall survey made by the President's Commission on Law Enforcement and Administration of Justice of efforts to coordinate and consolidate police services. See President's Commission on Law Enforcement and Administration of Justice, *Task Force Report: The Police* (Washington, D.C.: Government Printing Office, 1967), pp. 68–112.

18. 42 *U.S.C.* §3723 1973).

19. See Richard Harris, *Justice: The Crisis of Law, Order and Freedom in America* (New York: Avon Books, 1969), pp. 35–39, 128–131.

20. See chapter 1, note 5.

21. For an interesting account of the development of the federal government's role in relation to local law enforcement in the critical period of the early sixties, see Gerald M. Caplan, "Reflections on the Nationalization of Crime, 1964–1968," *Law and the Social Order* 1973: 583–635.

22. 42 *U.S.C.* §3701 (1973).

23. This problem and some alternatives for dealing with it are discussed in Herman Goldstein, "Trial Judges and the Police," *Crime and Delinquency* 14 (1968): 14–25.

24. American Bar Association, *The Urban Police Function*, Approved Draft (Chicago: American Bar Association, 1973), p. 22 of the Supplement.

25. This is reflected in the formal resolutions adopted by the IACP, reported in the annual *Police Yearbook*, and in the positions taken by its officers in the monthly editorial appearing in the organization's magazine, *Police Chief.*

26. The latest such organization is the American Academy of Professional Law Enforcement, established in 1974 with the merger of two smaller organizations. The academy now has a membership of approximately 500 in twenty states and places an emphasis, in its objectives, on the development of ethical standards in policing and on professionalization through education and training.

27. Ford Foundation, *A More Effective Arm* (New York: Ford Foundation, 1970), p. 2.

28. Richard Chackerian, "Police Professionalism and Citizen Evaluations: A Preliminary Look," *Public Administration Review* 34 (1974): 141–148.

Bibliography

WORKS OF GENERAL INTEREST

Ahern, James F. *Police in Trouble: Our Frightening Crisis in Law Enforcement.* New York: Hawthorn Books, 1972.

Alderson, J. C., and Stead, Philip J., eds. *The Police We Deserve.* London: Wolfe Publishing, 1973.

American Bar Association. *The Urban Police Function.* Approved Draft. Chicago: American Bar Association, 1973.

Berkley, George E. *The Democratic Policeman.* Boston: Beacon Press, 1969.

Bittner, Egon. *The Functions of the Police in Modern Society: A Review of Background Factors, Current Practices, and Possible Role Models.* Chevy Chase, Md.: National Institute of Mental Health, 1970.

Bordua, David J., ed. *The Police: Six Sociological Essays.* New York: John Wiley and Sons, 1967.

National Advisory Commission on Criminal Justice Standards and Goals. *Police.* Washington, D.C.: Government Printing Office, 1973.

National Commission on the Causes and Prevention of Violence, Task Force on Law and Law Enforcement. *Law and Order Reconsidered.* Washington, D.C.: Government Printing Office, 1969.

Niederhoffer, Arthur, *Behind the Shield: The Police in Urban Society.* Garden City, N.J.: Doubleday, 1967.

Niederhoffer, Arthur, and Blumberg, Abraham S. *The Ambivalent Force: Perspectives on the Police.* Waltham, Mass.: Ginn and Co., 1970.

President's Commission on Law Enforcement and Administration of Justice. *The Challenge of Crime in a Free Society.* Washington, D.C.: Government Printing Office, 1967.

———. *Task Force Report: The Police.* Washington, D.C.: Government Printing Office, 1967.

Reiss, Albert J., Jr. *The Police and the Public*. New Haven, Conn.: Yale University Press, 1971.

Rubinstein, Jonathan. *City Police*. New York: Farrar, Straus and Giroux, 1973.

Skolnick, Jerome H. *Justice Without Trial: Law Enforcement in Democratic Society*. New York: John Wiley and Sons, 1966.

Smith, Bruce. *Police Systems in the United States*. 2d rev. ed. New York: Harper & Row, 1960.

Snibbe, John R., and Snibbe, Homa M., eds. *The Urban Policeman in Transition: A Psychological and Sociological Review*. Springfield, Ill.: Charles C. Thomas, 1973.

Westley, William A. *Violence and the Police: A Sociological Study of Law, Custom, and Morality*. Cambridge, Mass.: MIT Press, 1970.

Wilson, James Q. *Varieties of Police Behavior: The Management of Law and Order in Eight Communities*. Cambridge, Mass.: Harvard University Press, 1968.

Wilson, O. W., and McLaren, Roy C. *Police Administration*. 3rd ed. New York: McGraw-Hill, 1972.

CHAPTER 1: THE BASIC PROBLEMS

Bacon, Selden D. "The Early Development of American Municipal Police." Ph.D. thesis, Yale University, 1939.

Bent, Alan E. *Politics of Law Enforcement: Conflict and Power in Urban Communities*. Lexington, Mass.: Lexington Books, D. C. Heath, 1974.

Chackerian, Richard. "Police Professionalism and Citizen Evaluations: A Preliminary Look." *Public Administration Review* 34 (1974): 141–148.

Chapman, Samuel G. *The Police Heritage in England and America*. East Lansing, Mich.: Institute for Community Development and Services, Michigan State University, 1962.

Fosdick, Raymond B. *European Police Systems*. 1915. Reprint. Montclair, N.J.: Patterson Smith, 1969.

———. *American Police Systems*. 1920. Reprint. Montclair, N.J.: Patterson Smith, 1969.

Fuld, Leonhard F. *Police Administration: A Critical Study of Police Organizations in the United States and Abroad*. 1909. Reprint. Montclair, N.J.: Patterson Smith, 1971.

Hahn, Harlan. "A Profile of Urban Police." *Law and Contemporary Problems* 36 (1971): 449–466.

Haller, Mark H. "Police Reform in Chicago 1905–1935." *American Behavioral Scientist* 13 (1970): 649–666.

———. Introduction to *History of the Chicago Police*, by John J. Flinn. Montclair, N.J.: Patterson Smith, 1972.

Hopkins, Ernest J. *Our Lawless Police: A Study of the Unlawful Enforcement of the Law*. New York: Viking Press, 1931.

Lane, Roger. *Policing the City: Boston 1822–1885*. Cambridge, Mass.: Harvard University Press, 1967.

"Law Enforcement Assistance Administration: A Symposium on Its Operation and Impact." *Columbia Human Rights Law Review* 5 (1973): 1–214.

Lohman, Joseph D. "On Law Enforcement and the Police: A Commentary." In *Criminology in Action, Inventory of Contemporary Criminology, Its Principal Fields of Application*, edited by Denis Szabo, pp. 173–217. Montreal: University of Montreal Press, 1968.

Murphy, Patrick V. *A Decade of Urban Police Problems*. Sixteenth Annual Wherrett Lecture on Local Government. Pittsburgh: Institute for Urban Policy and Administration, Graduate School of Public and International Affairs, University of Pittsburgh, 1974.

National Advisory Commission on Civil Disorders. *Report of the National Advisory Commission on Civil Disorders*. Washington, D.C.: Government Printing Office, 1968.

National Commission on Law Observance and Enforcement. *Report on Lawlessness in Law Enforcement*. Washington, D.C.: Government Printing Office, 1931. Reprint. Montclair, N.J.: Patterson Smith, 1968.

National Commission on Law Observance and Enforcement. *Report on Police*. Washington, D.C.: Government Printing Office, 1931. Reprint. Montclair, N.J.: Patterson Smith, 1968.

President's Commission on Campus Unrest. *The Report of the President's Commission on Campus Unrest*. Washington, D.C.: Government Printing Office, 1970.

Reith, Charles. *British Police and the Democratic Ideal*. London: Oxford University Press, 1943.

————. *The Blind Eye of History*. London: Faber and Faber, 1952.

————. *A New Study of Police History*. Edinburgh: Oliver and Boyd, 1956.

Richardson, James F. *The New York Police: Colonial Times to 1901*. New York: Oxford University Press, 1970.

————. *Urban Police in the United States*. Port Washington, N.Y.: National University Publications, Kennikat Press, 1974.

Sherman, Lawrence W. "The Sociology and the Social Reform of the American Police: 1950–1973." *Journal of Police Science and Administration* 2 (1974): 255–262.

Turner, William W. *The Police Establishment*. New York: Putnam, 1968.

Vollmer, August. *The Police and Modern Society*. 1936. Reprint. Montclair, N.J.: Patterson Smith, 1971.

Whitaker, Ben. *The Police*. London: Eyre and Spottiswoode, 1964.

Woods, Arthur. *Policeman and Public*. 1919. Reprint. New York: Arno Press, 1971.

CHAPTER 2: THE POLICE FUNCTION

Allen, Francis. "The Borderland of the Criminal Law: Problems of 'Socializing' Criminal Justice." *Social Service Review* 32 (1958): 107–119.

Arnold, Thurman W. "Law Enforcement: An Attempt at Social Dissection." *Yale Law Journal* 42 (1932): 1–24.

Astor, Gerald. *The New York Cops: An Informal History*. New York: Charles Scribner's Sons, 1971.

Banton, Michael. *The Policeman in the Community*. New York: Basic Books, 1964.

Bercal, Thomas E. "Calls for Police Assistance." *American Behavioral Scientist* 13 (1970): 681–692.

Bittner, Egon. "Florence Nightingale in Pursuit of Willie Sutton: A Theory of the Police." In *The Potential for Reform of Criminal Justice*, edited by Herbert Jacob, pp. 17–45. Beverly Hills, Calif.: Sage Publications, 1974.

————. "The Police on Skid-Row: A Study of Peace Keeping." *American Sociological Review* 32 (1967): 699–715.

California Commission on Peace Officer Standards and Training. *Project Star: Police Officer Role Training Program*. Santa Cruz, Calif.: Davis Publishing Co., 1974.

Cumming, Elaine; Cumming, Ian; and Edell, Laura. "Policeman as Philosopher, Guide and Friend." *Social Problems* 12 (1965): 276–286.

Derbyshire, Robert L. "The Social Control Role of the Police in Changing Urban Communities." *Excerpta criminologica* 6 (1966): 315–321.

Edwards, George. *The Police on the Urban Frontier*. Pamphlet. Institute of Human Relations Press, Pamphlet Series No. 9, 1968.

Feld, Barry C. "Police Violence and Protest." *Minnesota Law Review* 55 (1971): 731–778.

Friedman, Bruce Jay. "Lessons of the Street." *Harper's Magazine*, September 1971, pp. 86–95.

Gardiner, John A. *Traffic and the Police: Variations in Law-Enforcement Policy*. Cambridge, Mass.: Harvard University Press, 1969.

Garmire, Bernard L. "The Police Role in an Urban Society." In *The Police and the Community*, edited by Robert F. Steadman, pp. 4–5. Baltimore: Johns Hopkins University Press, 1972.

Germann, A. C. "What is the Developing Mission and Role of the American Police?" *Journal of California Law Enforcement* 4 (1970): 184–189.

Hall, Jerome. "Police and Law in a Democratic Society." *Indiana Law Journal* 28 (1953): 133–177.

LaFave, Wayne R. *Arrest: The Decision to Take a Suspect into Custody*. Edited by Frank J. Remington. Boston: Little, Brown, 1965.

Liberman, Robert. "Police as a Community Mental Health Resource." *Community Mental Health Journal* 5 (1969): 111–120.

Livermore, Joseph M. "Policing." *Minnesota Law Review* 55 (1971): 649–729.

McIntyre, Donald M., Jr., ed. *Law Enforcement in the Metropolis: A Working Paper on the Criminal Law System in Detroit*. Chicago: American Bar Foundation, 1967.

Matthews, Arthur R. "Observations on Police Policy and Procedures for Emergency Detention of the Mentally Ill." *Journal of Criminal Law, Criminology and Police Science* 6 (1970): 283–295.

Misner, Gordon E. "Enforcement: Illusion of Security." *Nation*, 21 April 1969, pp. 488–490.

Misner, Gordon E., and Hoffman, Richard B. "Police Resource Allocation." Working paper #73. Berkeley: Center for Planning and Development, University of California, n.d.

Murphy, Patrick V. "The Role of the Police in Our Modern Society." *The Record of the Association of the Bar of the City of New York* 26 (1971): 292–300.

Myren, Richard A. "The Role of the Police." Paper submitted to the President's Commission on Law Enforcement and Administration of Justice, 1967.

Packer, Herbert L. *The Limits of the Criminal Sanction*. Palo Alto, Calif.: Stanford University Press, 1968.

———. "Two Models of the Criminal Process." *University of Pennsylvania Law Review* 113 (1964): 1–68.

Parnas, Raymond I. "The Police Response to the Domestic Disturbance." *Wisconsin Law Review* 1967: 914–960.

Petersen, David M. "Police Disposition of the Petty Offender." *Sociology and Social Research* 3 (1972): 320–330.

Pfiffner, John M. "The Function of the Police in a Democratic Society." Paper. Los Angeles: University of Southern California Center for Training and Career Development, 1967.

Remington, Frank J. "The Role of the Police in a Democratic Society." *Journal of Criminal Law, Criminology and Police Science* 56 (1965): 361–365.

Skolnick, Jerome H. *The Police and the Urban Ghetto*. Chicago: American Bar Foundation, 1968.

———. "Professional Police in a Free Society." Pamphlet. New York: National Conference of Christians and Jews, n.d.

Sterling, James W. *Changes in Role Concept of Police Officers*. Gaithersburg, Md.: International Association of Chiefs of Police, 1972.

Terris, Bruce J. "The Role of the Police." *The Annals of the American Academy of Political and Social Science* 374 (1967): 58–69.

Van Maanen, John. "Working the Street: A Developmental View of Police Behavior." In *The Potential for Reform of Criminal Justice*, edited by Herbert Jacob, pp. 83–130. Beverly Hills, Calif.: Sage Publications, 1974.

Webster, John A. *The Realities of Police Work*. Dubuque, Ia.: Hunt Publishing Co., 1973.

———. "Police Task and Time Study." *Journal of Criminal Law, Criminology and Police Science* 61 (1970): 94–100.

Wilson, James Q. "The Police and Their Problems: A Theory." *Public Policy* 12 (1963): 189–216.

CHAPTER 3: THE POLICE AND SERIOUS CRIME

Bloch, Peter B., and Specht, David. *Neighborhood Team Policing*. Washington, D.C.: Government Printing Office, 1973.

Boydstun, John E., et al. *San Diego Field Interrogation: Final Report*. Washington, D.C.: Police Foundation, 1975.

Chaiken, Jan M. *The Impact of Police Activity on Crime: Robberies on the New York City Subway System*. New York: Rand Institute, 1974.

Chamber of Commerce of the United States. *Marshaling Citizen Power Against Crime*. Washington, D.C.: Government Printing Office, 1970.

Clark, Ramsey. *Crime in America: Observations on Its Nature, Causes, Prevention, and Control*. New York: Simon and Schuster, 1970.

Dahmann, Judith S. *High Impact Anti-Crime Program: A Review of Six Research Studies on the Relationship Between Police Patrol Activity and Crime*. Washington, D.C.: The Mitre Corporation, 1974.

Feeney, Floyd, and Weir, Adrianne, eds. *The Prevention and Control of Robbery*. 5 volumes and summary. Davis, Calif.: University of California Center on Administration of Criminal Justice, 1974.

Furstenberg, Frank F., Jr. "Public Reaction to Crime in the Streets." *The American Scholar* 40 (1971): 601–610.

Gray, B. M. *Crime Specific Planning: An Overview*. Springfield, Va.: National Technical Information Service, 1973.

Halper, Andrew, and Ku, Richard. *New York City Police Department: Street Crime Unit*. Washington, D.C.: Government Printing Office, 1975.

Harris, Richard. *The Fear of Crime*. New York: Frederick A. Praeger, 1968.

Jeffrey, C. Ray. *Crime Prevention Through Environmental Design*. Beverly Hills, Calif.: Sage Publications, 1971.

Kelling, George L.; Pate, Tony; Dieckman, Duane; and Brown, Charles E. *The Kansas City Preventive Patrol Experiment: A Summary Report*. Washington, D.C.: Police Foundation, 1974.

―――. *The Kansas City Preventive Patrol Experiment: A Technical Report*. Washington, D.C.: Police Foundation, 1974.

Krantz, Sheldon, and Kramer, William D. "The Urban Crisis and Crime." *Boston University Law Review* 50 (1970): 343–359.

Kupersmith, G. *High Impact Anti-Crime Program: Sample Impact Project Evaluation Components*. Washington, D.C.: Government Printing Office, 1974.

Larson, Richard C. *Urban Police Patrol Analysis*. Cambridge, Mass.: MIT Press, 1972.

Law Enforcement Assistance Administration. *Police Crime Analysis Unit Handbook*. Washington, D.C.: Government Printing Office, 1973.

Marx, Gary T., and Archer, Dane. *Community Police Patrols: An Explanatory Inquiry*. Springfield, Va.: National Technical Information Service, 1972.

Morris, Norval, and Hawkins, Gordon. *The Honest Politician's Guide to Crime Control*. Chicago: University of Chicago Press, 1969.

Murphy, Patrick V., and Bloch, Peter B. "The Beat Commander." *Police Chief*, May 1970, pp. 16–19.

National Advisory Commission on Criminal Justice Standards and Goals. *Community Crime Prevention*. Washington, D.C.: Government Printing Office, 1973.

―――. *A National Strategy to Reduce Crime*. Washington, D.C.: Government Printing Office, 1973.

National Commission on the Causes and Prevention of Violence. *Commission Statement on Violent Crime, Homicide, Assault, Rape, Robbery*. Washington, D.C.: Government Printing Office, 1969.

O'Connor, George W., and Vanderbosch, Charles G. *The Patrol Operation*. Washington, D.C.: International Association of Chiefs of Police, 1967.

President's Commission on Law Enforcement and Administration of Justice. *Task Force Report: Crime and Its Impact—An Assessment*. Washington, D.C.: Government Printing Office, 1967.

Press, James S. *Some Effects of an Increase in Police Manpower in the 20th Precinct of New York City*. New York: Rand Institute, 1971.

Reppetto, Thomas A. *Residential Crime*. Cambridge, Mass.: Ballinger Publishing Co., 1974.

Scarr, Harry A. *Patterns of Burglary*. 2d ed. Washington, D.C.: Government Printing Office, 1973.

Schwartz, Alfred I., and Clarren, Sumner N. "Evaluation of Cincinnati's Community Sector Team Policing Program: A Progress Report—After One Year." Mimeographed. Washington, D.C.: The Urban Institute, 1975.

Sherman, Lawrence W.; Milton, Catherine H.; and Kelly, Thomas V. *Team Policing: Seven Case Studies*. Washington, D.C.: Police Foundation, 1973.

Sweeney, Thomas J., and Ellingsworth, William, eds. *Issues in Police Patrol: A Book of Readings*. Kansas City, Mo.: Kansas City Police Department, 1973.

Ward, Richard H.; Ward, Thomas J.; and Feeley, Jayne. *Police Robbery Control Manual*. Washington, D.C.: Government Printing Office, 1975.

Wilson, James Q. *Thinking About Crime*. New York: Basic Books, 1975.

Zimring, Franklin E. *Perspectives on Deterrence*. Washington, D.C.: National Institute of Mental Health, 1971.

CHAPTER 4: DEVELOPING ALTERNATIVES TO THE CRIMINAL JUSTICE SYSTEM

Bard, Morton. *Training Police as Specialists in Family Crisis Intervention*. Washington, D.C.: Government Printing Office, 1970.

———. "Alternatives to Traditional Law Enforcement." *Police*, November/December 1970, pp. 20–23.

———. *Family Crisis Intervention: From Concept to Implementation*. Washington, D.C.: Government Printing Office, 1974.

Bard, Morton; Zacker, Joseph; and Rutter, Elliot. "Police Family Crisis Intervention and Conflict Management: An Action Research Analysis." Mimeographed. Prepared for the Department of Justice, LEAA, 1972.

Dayton Police Department. *Conflict Management Program*. Pamphlet. Dayton, Ohio: Police Department, 1971.

Force, Robert. "Decriminalization of Breach of the Peace Statutes: A Nonpenal Approach to Order Maintenance." *Tulane Law Review* 46 (1972): 367–493.

Liberman, Robert. "Police as a Community Mental Health Resource." *Community Mental Health Journal* 5 (1969): 111–120.

Matthews, Arthur R. "Observations on Police Policy and Procedures for Emergency Detention of the Mentally Ill." *Journal of Criminal Law, Criminology and Police Science* 61 (1970): 283–295.

Mehlman, Mark F. "Police Initiated Emergency Psychiatric Detention in Michigan." *Journal of Law Reform* 5 (1972): 581–598.

Milton, Catherine H. "Role of Police in Drug Diversion Programs." Mimeographed. Washington, D.C.: Police Foundation, 1972.

Moody, Linda A. "Landlords and Tenants: Oakland's Landlord/Tenant Intervention Unit." *Police Chief*, March 1972, pp. 32–34.

National Institute of Law Enforcement and Criminal Justice. *Citizen Dispute Settlement: The Night Prosecutor Program of Columbus, Ohio.* Washington, D.C.: Government Printing Office, 1974.

Nimmer, Raymond T. *Two Million Unnecessary Arrests: Removing a Social Service Concern from the Criminal Justice System.* Chicago: American Bar Foundation, 1971.

———. *Diversion: The Search for Alternative Forms of Prosecution.* Chicago: American Bar Foundation, 1974.

Palmer, John W. "Pre-Arrest Diversion: Victim Confrontation." *Federal Probation*, September 1974, pp. 12–17.

Parnas, Raymond I. "The Response of Some Relevant Community Resources to Intra-family Violence." *Indiana Law Journal* 44 (1969): 159–181.

———. "Police Discretion and Diversion of Incidents of Intra-Family Violence." *Law and Contemporary Problems* 36 (1971): 539–565.

Piliavin, Irving, and Briar, Scott. "Police Encounters with Juveniles." *American Journal of Sociology* 70 (1964): 206–214.

President's Commission on Law Enforcement and Administration of Justice. *Task Force Report: Drunkenness.* Washington, D.C.: Government Printing Office, 1967.

———. *Task Force Report: Juvenile Delinquency and Youth Crime.* Washington, D.C.: Government Printing Office, 1967.

Simi Valley Police Department. *Simi Valley: Crisis Intervention and the Police.* Pamphlet. Simi Valley, Calif.: Police Department, 1974.

Skoler, Daniel. "Protecting the Rights of Defendants in Pretrial Intervention Programs." *Criminal Law Bulletin* 10 (1974): 473–492.

Stratton, John. "Crisis Intervention Counseling and Police Diversion from the Juvenile Justice System: A Review of the Literature." *Juvenile Justice* 25 (1974): 44–53.

Treger, Harvey; Thomson, Douglas; Collier, James H.; Michaels, Rhoda A.; Quinn, Patricia; and Cousins, James A. *The Police-Social Work Team: A New Model for Interprofessional Cooperation: A University Demonstration Project in Manpower Training and Development.* Springfield, Ill.: Charles C. Thomas, 1975.

Vera Institute of Justice. *The Manhattan Bowery Project: In Lieu of Arrest, Treatment for Homeless Alcoholics.* New York: Vera Institute of Justice, 1970.

Wald, Michael A. "May Day Revisited: Parts I and II." *Criminal Law Bulletin* 10 (1974): 377–435 and 516–543.

Weis, Charles W. *Diversion of the Public Inebriate from the Criminal Justice System.* Washington, D.C.: National Institute of Law Enforcement and Criminal Justice, 1973.

CHAPTER 5: CATEGORIZING AND STRUCTURING DISCRETION

American Law Institute. *A Model Code of Pre-Arraignment Procedure*. Proposed Official Draft. Philadelphia: The American Law Institute, 1975.

Amsterdam, Anthony G. "The Supreme Court and the Rights of Suspects in Criminal Cases." *New York University Law Review* 45 (1970): 785–815.

Arizona State University Project on Law Enforcement Policy and Rulemaking. *Eyewitness Identification. Search Warrant Execution. Stop and Frisk. Searches, Seizures and Inventories of Motor Vehicles. Release of Arrest and Conviction Records. Warrantless Searches of Persons and Places*. Model Rules for Law Enforcement Series. Washington, D.C.: Police Foundation, 1974.

Bittner, Egon. "Police Discretion in Emergency Apprehension of Mentally Ill Persons." *Social Problems* 14 (1967): 278–292.

Breitel, Charles D. "Controls in Criminal Law Enforcement." *University of Chicago Law Review* 27 (1960): 427–435.

Caplan, Gerald M. "The Case for Rulemaking by Law Enforcement Agencies." *Law and Contemporary Problems* 36 (1971): 500–514.

"Contemporary Studies Project: Administrative Control of Police Discretion." *Iowa Law Review* 58 (1973): 893–973.

Cooley, J. W. "Police Discretion." *Abstracts on Police Science* 2 (1974): 131–137.

Council of Judges. *Model Rules of Court on Police Action from Arrest to Arraignment*. New York: National Council on Crime and Delinquency, 1969.

"Criminal Law: The Controlled Use of Police Discretion to Avert Civil Disorder." *Wisconsin Law Review* 1970: 907–914.

Davis, Kenneth Culp. *Discretionary Justice: A Preliminary Inquiry*. Baton Rouge, La.: Louisiana State University Press, 1969.

———. "An Approach to Legal Control of the Police." *Texas Law Review* 52 (1974): 703–725.

———. *Police Discretion*. St. Paul, Minn.: West Publishing Co., 1975.

Dix, George E. "Undercover Investigations and Police Rulemaking." *Texas Law Review* 53 (1975): 203–294.

"Equal Protection as a Defense to Selective Law Enforcement by Police Officials." *Journal of Public Law* 14 (1965): 223–231.

Fisk, James G. *The Police Officer's Exercise of Discretion in the Decision to Arrest: Relationship to Organizational Goals and Societal Values*. Los Angeles: Institute of Government and Public Affairs—University of California at Los Angeles, 1974.

Givelber, Daniel J. "The Application of Equal Protection Principles to Selective Enforcement of the Criminal Law." *University of Illinois Law Forum* 1973: 88–124.

Goldman, Nathan. *The Differential Selection of Juvenile Offenders for Court Appearance*. New York: National Council on Crime and Delinquency, 1963.

Goldstein, Herman. "Police Discretion: The Ideal Versus the Real." *Public Administration Review* 23 (1963): 140–148.

———. "Police Policy Formulation: A Proposal for Improving Police Performance." *Michigan Law Review* 65 (1967): 1123–1146.

Goldstein, Joseph. "Police Discretion Not to Invoke the Criminal Process: Low-Visibility Decisions in the Administration of Justice." *Yale Law Journal* 69 (1960): 543–594.

Greenberg, Reuben M. "Police Discretion v. Discriminatory Law Enforcement." *Police Chief*, July 1974, p. 18.

Igleburger, Robert M., and Schubert, Frank A. "Policy Making for the Police." *American Bar Association Journal* 58 (1972): 307–310.

Logue, John, and Bock, Edwin A. *The Demotion of Deputy Chief Inspector Goldberg*. University, Ala.: University of Alabama Press, 1963.

Lumbard, J. Edward. "Criminal Justice and the Rule-Making Power." *West Virginia Law Review* 70 (1968): 143–154.

McGowan, Carl. "Rule-Making and the Police." *Michigan Law Review* 70 (1972): 656–694.

"Police Discretion and the Judgment that a Crime Has Been Committed—Rape in Philadelphia." *University of Pennsylvania Law Review* 117 (1968): 277–322.

Remington, Frank J., and Rosenblum, Victor G. "The Criminal Law and the Legislative Process." *University of Illinois Law Forum* 1960: 481–499.

Schmidt, Wayne W. "A Proposal for a Statewide Law Enforcement Administrative Law Council." *Journal of Police Science and Administration* 2 (1974): 330–338.

Siegel, Howard L. "Procedural Due Process in the Context of Informal Administrative Action: The Requirement for Notice, Hearing and Prospective Standards Relating to Police Selective Enforcement Practice." *Boston University Law Review* 53 (1973): 1038–1070.

Stinchcombe, Arthur. "Institutions of Privacy in the Determination of Police Administrative Practice." *American Journal of Sociology* 69 (1963): 150–160.

Texas Criminal Justice Council. *Model Rules for Law Enforcement Officers: A Manual on Police Discretion*. Gaithersburg, Md.: International Association of Chiefs of Police, 1974.

Whitlock, Brand. *On the Enforcement of Law in Cities*. 1913. Reprint. Montclair, N.J.: Patterson Smith, 1967.

Williams, D. G. T. "The Police and Law Enforcement." *The Criminal Law Review* 1968: 351–362.

CHAPTER 6: DIRECTING POLICE AGENCIES THROUGH THE POLITICAL PROCESS

Blawie, James L., and Blawie, Marilyn J. "The Other Cease Fires: Wind Down of the Domestic Wars; Cause for Concern About the Relationship Between Crime Control and Local Government Structures." *Journal of Urban Law* 50 (1973): 545–629.

Control of the Baltimore Police, Collected Reports. New York: Arno Press, 1971.

Eidenberg, Eugene, and Rigert, Joe. "The Police and Politics." In *Police in Urban Society*, edited by Harlan Hahn, pp. 291–306. Beverly Hills, Calif.: Sage Publications, 1970.

Flynn, Matthew. "Police Accountability in Wisconsin." *Wisconsin Law Review* 1974: 1131–1166.

Freund, Jeffrey R. "Neighborhood Police Districts: A Constitutional Analysis." *California Law Review* 57 (1969): 907–947.

Furstenberg, Frank F., and Wellford, Charles F. "Calling the Police: The Evaluation of Police Service." *Law and Society Review* 7 (1973): 393–406.

Germann, A. C. "Community Policing: An Assessment." *Journal of Criminal Law, Criminology and Police Science* 60 (1969): 89–96.

Goldstein, Herman. "Trial Judges and the Police." *Crime and Delinquency* 14 (1968): 14–25.

——. "Who's in Charge Here?" *Public Management* 50 (1968): 304–307.

——. "Governmental Setting for Police Work." In *Municipal Police Administration*, edited by George D. Eastman, pp. 2a/1–2a/16. 1969. Reprint. Washington, D.C.: International City Management Association, 1971.

Marshall, Geoffrey. *Police and Government: The Status and Accountability of the English Constable*. London: Methven and Co., 1965.

Myren, Richard A. "Decentralization and Citizen Participation in Criminal Justice Systems." *Public Administration Review* 32 (1972): 718–738.

Ostrom, Elinor; Baugh, William H.; Guarasci, Richard; Parks, Roger B.; and Whitaker, Gordon P. *Community Organization and the Provision of Police Services*. Beverly Hills, Calif.: Sage Publications, 1973.

Ostrom, Elinor; Parks, Roger B.; and Whitaker, Gordon P. "Do We Really Want to Consolidate Urban Police Forces? A Reappraisal of Some Old Assertions." *Public Administration Review* 33 (1973): 423–432.

Ostrom, Elinor, and Whitaker, Gordon P. "Does Local Community Control of Police Make a Difference? Some Preliminary Findings." *American Journal of Political Science* 17 (1973): 48–76.

Royal Commission on the Police 1962. *Final Report*. London: Her Majesty's Stationery Office, 1962.

Ruchelman, Leonard, ed. *Who Rules the Police?* New York: New York University Press, 1973.

Ruchelman, Leonard. *Police Politics: A Comparative Study of Three Cities*. Cambridge, Mass.: Ballinger Publishing Co., 1974.

Sherwood, Frank P. *A City Manager Tries to Fire His Police Chief*. University, Ala.: University of Alabama Press, 1963.

Skolnick, Jerome H. *The Politics of Protest*. New York: Ballantine Books, 1969.

——. "Neighborhood Police." *Nation*, 22 March 1971, pp. 372–373.

Viteritti, Joseph P. *Police, Politics, and Pluralism in New York City: A Comparative Case Study*. Beverly Hills, Calif.: Sage Publications, 1973.

Waskow, Arthur I. "Community Control of the Police." *Trans-Action* 7 (1967): 4–7.

———. *Running Riot: A Journey Through the Official Disasters and Creative Disorder in American Society.* New York: Herder and Herder, 1970.

Wisconsin State Committee, United States Commission on Civil Rights. *Police Isolation and Community Needs.* Washington, D.C.: Government Printing Office, 1972.

CHAPTER 7: CONTROLLING AND REVIEWING POLICE-CITIZEN CONTACTS

Abbott, David W.; Gold, Louis H.; and Rogowsky, Edward T. *Police, Politics and Race: the New York City Referendum on Civilian Review.* New York: American Jewish Committee, 1969.

American Civil Liberties Union of Southern California. *Law Enforcement: The Matter of Redress.* Los Angeles: Institute of Modern Legal Thought, 1969.

Anderson, Stanley V., and Moore, John C. *Establishing Ombudsman Offices: Recent Experience in the United States.* Berkeley, Calif.: Institute of Governmental Studies, 1972.

Bayley, David H., and Mendelsohn, Harold. *Minorities and the Police: Confrontation in America.* New York: Free Press, 1969.

Beral, Harold, and Sisk, Marcus. "The Administration of Complaints by Civilians Against the Police." *Harvard Law Review* 77 (1964): 499–519.

Berger, Mark. "Law Enforcement Control: Checks and Balances for the Police System." *Connecticut Law Review* 4 (1971/72): 467–507.

Black, Algernon D. *The People and the Police.* New York: McGraw-Hill, 1968.

Blalock, Joyce. *Civil Liability of Law Enforcement Officers.* Springfield, Ill.: Charles C. Thomas, 1974.

Bliss, George; George, Emmett; Zeckman, Pamela; and Mullen, William. *Police Brutality.* Booklet. Chicago: Chicago Tribune, 1973.

Broadaway, Fred M. "Police Misconduct: Positive Alternatives." *Journal of Police Science and Administration* 2 (1974): 210–218.

Burger, Warren E. "Who Will Watch the Watchman?" *American University Law Review* 14 (1964): 1–23.

Chevigny, Paul. *Police Power: Police Abuses in New York City.* New York: Vintage Books, 1969.

Cohen, Bernard. *The Police Internal Administration of Justice.* New York: Rand Institute, 1970.

"Federal Injunction as a Remedy for Unconstitutional Police Conduct." *Yale Law Journal* 78 (1968): 143–155.

Foote, Caleb. "Tort Remedies for Police Violations of Individual Rights." *Minnesota Law Review* 39 (1955): 493–516.

Gellhorn, Walter. *Ombudsmen and Others: Citizens' Protectors in Nine Countries.* Cambridge, Mass.: Harvard University Press, 1966.

———. *When Americans Complain: Governmental Grievance Procedures.* Cambridge, Mass.: Harvard University Press, 1966.

Goldstein, Herman. "Administrative Problems in Controlling the Exercise of

Police Authority." *Journal of Criminal Law, Criminology and Police Science* 58 (1967): 160–172.

"Grievance Response Mechanisms for Police Conduct." *Virginia Law Review* 55 (1969): 909–951.

Hudson, James R. "Police Review Boards and Police Accountability." *Law and Contemporary Problems* 36 (1971): 515–538.

———. "Organizational Aspects of Internal and External Review of the Police." *Journal of Criminal Law, Criminology and Police Science* 63 (1972): 427–433.

Hurwitz, Stephan. "Denmark's Ombudsmand: The Parliamentary Commissioner for Civil and Military Government Administration." *Wisconsin Law Review* 1961: 169–199.

"Injunctive Relief for Violations of Constitutional Rights by the Police." *University of Colorado Law Review* 45 (1973): 91–129.

LaFave, Wayne R. "Improving Police Performance Through the Exclusionary Rule." *Missouri Law Review* 30 (1965): 391–458, 566–610.

LaFave, Wayne R., and Remington, Frank J. "Controlling the Police: The Judge's Role in Making and Reviewing Law Enforcement Decisions." *Michigan Law Review* 63 (1965): 987–1012.

Oaks, Dallin H. "Studying the Exclusionary Rule in Search and Seizure." *University of Chicago Law Review* 37 (1970): 665–757.

Packer, Herbert L. "Policing the Police: Nine Men Are Not Enough." *New Republic*, 4 September 1965, pp. 17–21.

Pate, Tony; McCullough, Jack; Bowers, Robert; and Ferrara, Amy. *Kansas City Peer Review Panel: An Evaluation Report*. Washington, D.C.: Police Foundation, 1976.

Reiss, Albert J., Jr. "Police Brutality: Answers to Key Questions." *Trans-Action*, July/August 1968, pp. 10–19.

Rowat, Donald C., ed. *The Ombudsman: Citizen's Defender*. 2d ed. Toronto: University of Toronto Press, 1968.

Schmidt, Wayne W. *Survey of Police Misconduct Litigation 1967–1971*. Evanston, Ill.: Americans for Effective Law Enforcement, Inc., 1974.

Schwartz, Louis B. "Complaints Against the Police: Experience of the Community Rights Division of the Philadelphia District Attorney's Office." *University of Pennsylvania Law Review* 118 (1970): 1023–1035.

Siedel, George J., III. "Injunctive Relief for Police Misconduct in the United States." *Journal of Urban Law* 50 (1973): 681–699.

Stoddard, Ellwyn R. "The Informal 'Code' of Police Deviancy: A Group Approach to Blue-Coat Crime." *Journal of Criminal Law, Criminology and Police Science* 59 (1968): 201–213.

Toch, Hans. "Change Through Participation (And Vice Versa)." *Journal of Research in Crime and Delinquency* 7 (1970): 198–206.

Westley, William A. "Secrecy and the Police." *Social Forces* 34 (1956): 254–257.

Wilson, Jerry V., and Alprin, Geoffrey M. "Controlling Police Conduct: Alternatives to the Exclusionary Rule." *Law and Contemporary Problems* 36 (1971): 488–499.

CHAPTER 8: THE CORRUPTION PROBLEM

Beigel, Herbert. "The Investigation and Prosecution of Police Corruption." *Journal of Criminal Law and Criminology* 65 (1974): 135–156.

Brown, William P. *A Study of the New York City Police Department Anti-Corruption Campaign, October 1970-August 1972.* Albany: New York State University at Albany, 1972.

————. "Police Corruption: The System Is the Problem." *Nation*, April 1973, pp. 456–459.

Burnham, David. "How Corruption Is Built into the System and a Few Ideas for What to Do About It." *New York Magazine*, 21 September 1970, p. 30.

Cook, Fred J. *The Corrupted Land: The Social Morality of Modern America.* New York: Macmillan, 1966.

————. "The Pusher-Cop: The Institutionalizing of Police Corruption." *New York Magazine*, 16 August 1971, pp. 22–30.

Deutsch, Albert. *The Trouble With Cops.* New York: Crown Publishers, 1955.

Dorman, Michael. *Payoff.* New York: McKay, 1972.

Droge, Edward F. *In the Highest Tradition.* New York: Atheneum, 1974.

Ehrlich, Isaac. "Participation in Illegitimate Activities: A Theoretical and Empirical Investigation." *Journal of Political Economy* 81 (1973): 531–565.

Gardiner, John A. *The Politics of Corruption: Organized Crime in an American City.* New York: Russell Sage Foundation, 1970.

Gardiner, John A., and Olson, David J., eds. *Theft of the City: Readings on Corruption in Urban America.* Bloomington: Indiana University Press, 1974.

Hayes, Fredrick O'R. "Patrick Murphy—On Police Corruption." *New York Affairs* 2 (1974): 88–111.

Ingersoll, John E. "The Police Scandal Syndrome." *Crime and Delinquency* 10 (1964): 269–275.

Kohn, Aaron, ed. *The Kohn Report.* Chicago: Independent Voters of Illinois, 1953.

Lumbard, Eliot H. *Encouraging Integrity in Office.* Booklet. New York: Citizens Union Research Foundation, 1964.

Maas, Peter. *Serpico.* New York: Viking Press, 1973.

New York City Commission to Investigate Allegations of Police Corruption and the City's Anti-Corruption Procedures. *The Knapp Commission Report on Police Corruption.* New York: George Braziller, 1972.

Parsons, James C. "A Candid Analysis of Police Corruption." *Police Chief*, March 1973, pp. 20–22.

Pennsylvania Crime Commission. *Report on Police Corruption and the Quality of Law Enforcement in Philadelphia.* Saint Davids, Pa.: Pennsylvania Crime Commission, 1974.

"Police Corruption: Psychological and Organizational Factors." Symposium. *Police Journal* 48 (1975): 21–54.

Price, Barbara R. "Police Corruption: An Analysis." *Criminology* 10 (1972): 161–176.

Roebuck, Julian B., and Barker, Thomas. "A Typology of Police Corruption." *Social Problems* 21 (1974): 423–437.

Shecter, Leonard, and Phillips, William. *On the Pad: The Underworld and Its Corrupt Police, Confessions of a Cop on the Take.* New York: G. P. Putnam's Sons, 1973.

Sherman, Lawrence W., ed. *Police Corruption: A Sociological Perspective.* Garden City, N.Y.: Anchor Press, 1974.

Skogan, Wesley G. "Policy-making and Police Taking: Controlling Behavior on the Beat." *Urban Affairs Quarterly* 9 (1974): 520–528.

Smith, Ralph L. *The Tarnished Badge.* New York: Thomas Y. Crowell, 1965.

Steffens, Lincoln. *The Shame of the Cities.* New York: McClure-Phillips, 1904.

Stern, Mort. "What Makes a Policeman Go Wrong?" *Journal of Criminal Law, Criminology and Police Science* 53 (1962): 97–101.

CHAPTER 9: DEVELOPING CRITICALLY NEEDED LEADERSHIP

Bordua, David J., and Reiss, Albert J., Jr. "Command, Control and Charisma: Reflections on Police Bureaucracy." *American Journal of Sociology* 72 (1966): 68–76.

Calvert, Geoffrey N. *Portable Police Pensions—Improving Inter-Agency Transfers.* Washington, D.C.: Government Printing Office, 1971.

Chapman, Samuel G. "Developing Personnel Leadership." *Police Chief*, March 1966, pp. 24–35.

Garmire, Bernard L. "Appointment of Outside Police Chiefs." *Public Management*, August 1966, pp. 170–175.

Kelly, Michael J. *Police Chief Selection: A Handbook for Local Government.* Washington, D.C.: Police Foundation, 1975.

Kohlan, Richard G. "Police Promotional Procedures in Fifteen Jurisdictions." *Public Personnel Management*, May/June 1973, pp. 167–170.

Myren, Richard A. "A Crisis in Police Management." *Journal of Criminal Law, Criminology and Police Science* 50 (1960): 600–604.

Police Chief Executive Committee of the International Association of Chiefs of Police. *The Police Chief Executive Report.* Washington, D.C.: Government Printing Office, 1976.

Selznick, Philip. *Leadership in Administration.* New York: Row, Peterson and Co., 1957.

Thompson, Wayne E. "The Police as Community Leaders." In *Police and Community Relations: A Sourcebook*, edited by A. F. Brandstatter and Louis A. Radelet, pp. 247–252. Beverly Hills, Calif.: Glencoe Press, 1968.

CHAPTER 10: UPGRADING POLICE PERSONNEL

Alex, Nicholas, *Black in Blue: A Study of the Negro Policeman.* New York: Appleton-Century-Crofts, 1969.

Baehr, Melany E.; Furcon, John E.; and Froemel, Ernest C. *Psychological Assessment of Patrolman Qualifications in Relation to Field Performance.* Washington, D.C.: Government Printing Office, 1968.

Bouza, A. V. "The Policeman's Character Investigation: Lowered Standards or Changing Times?" *Journal of Criminal Law, Criminology and Police Science* 63 (1972): 120–124.

Chaiken, Jan M., and Cohen, Bernard. *Police Civil Service Selection Procedures in New York City: Comparison of Ethnic Groups.* New York: Rand Institute, 1973.

Cohen, Bernard, and Chaiken, Jan M. *Police Background Characteristics and Performance.* New York: Rand Institute, 1972.

Eisenberg, Terry; Kent, Deborah Ann; and Wall, Charles R. *Police Personnel Practices in State and Local Governments.* Washington, D.C.: Police Foundation, 1973.

"First Amendment and Public Employees: An Emerging Constitutional Right to Be a Policeman?" *George Washington Law Review* 37 (1969): 409–424.

Gray, Thomas C. "Selecting for a Police Subculture." In *Police in America*, edited by Jerome H. Skolnick and Thomas C. Gray, pp. 46–56. Boston: Educational Associates, Little, Brown and Co., 1975.

Harris, Richard N. *The Police Academy: An Inside View.* New York: John Wiley and Sons, 1973.

Kent, Deborah A., and Eisenberg, Terry. "The Selection and Promotion of Police Officers: A Selected Review of Recent Literature." *Police Chief*, February 1972, pp. 20–29.

Knoohuizen, Ralph, and Bailey, William. *The Selection and Hiring of Chicago Policemen.* Evanston, Ill.: Chicago Law Enforcement Study Group, 1973.

Law Enforcement Assistance Administration. *Career Development for Law Enforcement.* Washington, D.C.: Government Printing Office, 1973.

Levy, Ruth J. "Predicting Police Failures." *Journal of Criminal Law, Criminology and Police Science* 58 (1967): 265–276.

Piliavin, Irving. *Police-Community Alienation: Its Structural Roots and a Proposed Remedy.* Warner Modular Publication #14. New York: M.S.S. Publications, 1973.

"Policeman: Must He Be a Second-Class Citizen with Regard to His First Amendment Rights?" *New York University Law Review* 46 (1971): 536–559.

Public Safety Labor Relations Center. *Public Safety Labor Relations.* Periodical. Gaithersburg, Md.: International Association of Chiefs of Police, 1971–1975.

Reiss, Albert J., Jr. "Professionalization of the Police." In *Police and Community Relations: A Sourcebook*, edited by A. F. Brandstatter and Louis A. Radelet, pp. 215–229. Beverly Hills, Calif.: Glencoe Press, 1968.

Saunders, Charles B., Jr. *Upgrading the American Police: Education and Training for Better Law Enforcement.* Washington, D.C.: The Brookings Institution, 1970.

Stahl, O. Glenn, and Staufenberger, Richard A., eds. *Police Personnel Administration.* Washington, D.C.: Police Foundation, 1974.

Sterling, James W. "The College Level Entry Requirement: A Real or Imagined Cure-All." *Police Chief*, August 1974, pp. 28–31.

CHAPTER 11: HIGHER EDUCATION AND
THE POLICE

Brown, Lee P. "The Police and Higher Education: The Challenge of the Times." *Criminology* 12 (1974): 114–124.

Comptroller General of the United States. *Problems in Administering Programs to Improve Law Enforcement Education: Law Enforcement Assistance Administration*. Report to the Congress. Washington, D.C.: General Accounting Office, 1975.

Duncan, Robert B.; Juris, Hervey A.; Burnetti, George; and Wilson, Zane. "An Evaluation of the Impact of Education Pay Incentive Plans and the Effect of Education on Officer Attitudes in 22 Illinois Law Enforcement Agencies." Mimeographed. Chicago: Graduate School of Management, Northwestern University, 1974.

Eastman, George D., and McCain, James A. "Police Managers and Their Perceptions of Higher Education." *Journal of Criminal Justice* 1 (1973): 113–124.

Eisenberg, Terry, ed. *Collaboration Between Law Enforcement Executives and Social Scientists: Report of Proceedings of an April 1975 Conference for Law Enforcement Executives and Social Science Practitioners*. San Jose, Calif.: National Conference of Christians and Jews, Inc., 1975.

Ford, Robert E.; Meeker, James; and Zeller, Richard. "Police, Students, and Racial Hostilities." *Journal of Police Science and Administration* 3 (1975): 9–14.

Germann, A. C. "Education and Professional Law Enforcement." *Journal of Criminal Law, Criminology and Police Science* 58 (1967): 603–609.

Gross, Solomon. "Higher Education and Police: Is There a Need for a Closer Look?" *Journal of Police Science and Administration* 1 (1973): 477–483.

Guller, Irving B. "Higher Education and Policemen: Attitudinal Differences Between Freshmen and Senior Police College Students." *Journal of Criminal Law, Criminology and Police Science* 63 (1972): 396–401.

Lankes, George A. "How Should We Educate the Police?" *Journal of Criminal Law, Criminology and Police Science* 61 (1970): 587–592.

Law Enforcement and Criminal Justice Education: Directory 1975–76. Gaithersburg, Md.: International Association of Chiefs of Police, 1975.

Lejins, Peter P. *Introducing a Law Enforcement Curriculum at a State University*. Washington, D.C.: Government Printing Office, 1970.

Myren, Richard A. *Crime Related Programs in Higher Educational Institutions in California: 1969-1970*. Sacramento: California Coordinating Council on Higher Education, 1970.

National Conference on Law Enforcement Education. *Selected Presentations from the 1970 National Conference on Law Enforcement Education (1970)*. Washington, D.C.: Government Printing Office, 1970.

Saunders, Charles B., Jr. *Upgrading the American Police: Education and Training for Better Law Enforcement*. Washington, D.C.: The Brookings Institution, 1970.

Sheehan, Robert. "A Commitment to Change." *Journal of Criminal Law, Criminology and Police Science* 60 (1969): 381–386.

Smith, Alexander B.; Locke, Bernard; and Fenster, Abe. "Authoritarianism in Policemen Who Are College Graduates and Non-College Police." *Journal of Criminal Law, Criminology and Police Science* 61 (1970): 313–315.

Smith, Alexander B.; Locke, Bernard; and Walker, William F. "Authoritarianism in College and Non-College Oriented Police." *Journal of Criminal Law, Criminology and Police Science* 58 (1967): 128–132.

———. "Authoritarianism in Police College Students and Non-College Students." *Journal of Criminal Law, Criminology and Police Science* 59 (1968): 440–443.

Smith, Dennis C., and Ostrom, Elinor. "The Effects of Training and Education on Police Performance: A Preliminary Analysis." In *The Potential for Reform of Criminal Justice*, edited by Herbert Jacob, pp. 45–81. Beverly Hills, Calif.: Sage Publications, 1974.

Sterling, James W. "The College Level Entry Requirement: A Real or Imagined Cure-All?" *Police Chief*, August 1974, pp. 28–31.

Tenney, Charles. *Higher Education Programs in Law Enforcement and Criminal Justice*. Washington, D.C.: Government Printing Office, 1971.

Weiner, Norman L. "The Effect of Education on Police Attitudes." *Journal of Criminal Justice* 2 (1974): 317–328.

CHAPTER 12: EFFECTING CHANGE: AN OVERVIEW

Advisory Commission on Intergovernmental Relations. *For a More Perfect Union: Police Reform*. Washington, D.C.: Government Printing Office, 1971.

Burpo, John H. "Improving Police Agency and Employee Performance Through Collective Bargaining." *Police Chief*, February 1974, pp. 36–38.

Caplan, Gerald M. "The Police Legal Advisor." *Journal of Criminal Law, Criminology and Police Science* 58 (1967): 303–309.

———. "Reflections on the Nationalization of Crime, 1964–1968." *Law and the Social Order* 1973: 583–635.

Changing Police Organizations: Four Readings. Washington, D.C.: National League of Cities and the United States Conference of Mayors, 1973.

Cizanckas, Victor, and Feist, Fritzi. "A Community's Response to Police Change." *Journal of Police Science and Administration* 3 (1975): 284–291.

Danzig, Richard, and Abel, Richard L. *Innovation in a Police Department: A Case Study of the NYPD*. New Haven, Conn.: Yale Law School, 1971.

Doig, Jameson W. "The Police in a Democratic Society." *Public Administration Review* 28 (1968): 393–406.

Duncan, Robert B. "Organizational Climate and Climate for Change in Three Police Departments." *Urban Affairs Quarterly* 8 (1972): 205–245.

Ford Foundation. *A More Effective Arm: A Report on a Police Development Fund, Newly Established by the Ford Foundation*. New York: Ford Foundation, 1970.

Germann, A. C. "Changing the Police—The Impossible Dream?" *Journal of Criminal Law, Criminology and Police Science* 62 (1971): 416–421.

Guidelines and Papers from the National Symposium on Police Labor Relations. Washington, D.C.: Police Foundation, 1974.

Halpern, Stephen C. *Police-Association and Department Leaders: The Politics of Co-optation.* Lexington, Mass.: Lexington Books, D. C. Heath, 1974.

Juris, Hervey A. "The Implications of Police Unionism." *Law and Society Review* 6 (1971): 231–245.

———. "Police Personnel Problems, Police Unions, and Participatory Management." *Traffic Digest and Review* 19 (1971): 11–14.

Juris, Hervey A., and Feuille, Peter. *Police Unionism: Power and Impact in Public Sector Bargaining.* Lexington, Mass.: Lexington Books, D.C. Heath, 1973.

Kelley, Clarence M. "Receptiveness to Change." *Police Chief*, December 1973, pp. 32–34.

Kelling, George L., and Kliesmet, Robert B. "Resistance to the Professionalization of the Police." *Police Chief*, May 1971, pp. 30–39.

Law Enforcement Assistance Administration: A Symposium on Its Operation and Impact. Columbia Human Rights Law Review 5 (1973): 1–259.

Milton, Catherine H. "Demonstration Projects as a Strategy for Change." In *Innovation in Law Enforcement.* Washington, D.C.: Government Printing Office, 1973.

National Institute of Law Enforcement and Criminal Justice. *Annual Report for 1975.* Washington, D.C.: Government Printing Office, 1976.

Police Foundation. *Experiments in Police Improvement: A Progress Report.* Washington, D.C.: Police Foundation, 1972.

Steinberg, J. Leonard, and McEvoy, Donald W., eds. *The Police and the Behavioral Sciences.* Springfield, Ill.: Charles C. Thomas, 1974.

Toch, Hans; Grant, J. Douglas; and Galvin, Raymond T. *Agents of Change: A Study in Police Reform.* New York: John Wiley and Sons, 1975.

Yaron, Jay N. "A Reexamination of the Law Enforcement Assistance Administration." *Stanford Law Review* 27 (1975): 1303–1324.

Index

Abuses. *See* Wrongdoing

Academics, attitudes of toward police, 300

Accountability: administrative arrangements for, 132–134, 146–147; ambiguity of, 132; defined, 131, 157; distinguished from responsiveness, 143; in England, 141; failure of formal systems to clarify, 143–145; at federal level, 154 n.10; inadequacies of present system of, 134–140; and lateral movement, 154; needs to be clear, 143; needs to include all of police function, 147; and openness, 153; quest for in Evanston, Ill., 137–138; quest for in Madison, Wis., 138–139; requires structuring discretion, 147

Administrative practices: to control corruption, 210; to control other forms of wrongdoing, 167–174

Administrative rule-making: and accountability, 147; community role in, 120–122; defined, 115; as method of structuring discretion, 115–124; need for legislatures to promote, 125; need for openness in, 115–116, 119–122; procedures for, 115–116; promotion of by courts, 124–125; responsibility of municipal chief executive to oversee, 151; support for, 116–117, 124–126

Administrative rules: enforcement of, 122–124; and exclusionary rule, 123; possible subversion of, 125–126; and tort liability, 123; violations of, 122–124

Administrators: as accidents of system, 229–230; and alternatives to criminal justice system, 85–86; and atmosphere in agency, 166; attitudes of toward college graduates, 292; and change, 267–268; 292; 309–311, 315; and citizen complaints, 162–163, 173; and civil service, 250–252, 257; conflicts with municipal chief executives, 153–154; contacts between, 311; and control of police behavior, 167–168, 174–175; and corruption, 8, 191, 200–206, 208–209, 216, 218–219; defensiveness of, 8, 169, 230–231; and forms of municipal government, 134; history of, 133; influence of on objectives of agency, 101; and internal investigations, 265–266; and lateral movement, 154, 237–238; and minorities, 269–270; and morale, 166–167, 204–205; need of to delegate authority, 145–146; need of to experiment, 68; need for independence of, 150; need of to involve officers in developing policies and practices, 266; and openness, 14, 85, 110, 208, 253, 311; and personnel reform, 259; pressures on, 250–253, 328–329; resignations of, 154; responses of in the 1960s, 229; role of in public education, 85, 208, 253, 311; and secrecy, 119; and selection of subordinates, 250; and structuring discretion, 99, 107, 110, 112–113, 115–116, 124; and support within agency, 310; and tenure, 133, 150, 209, 249–250; and unions, 4, 257, 312, 315; Wickersham Commission on, 133. *See also* Leadership

Affirmative-action programs, 268, 269

gram of reform, 125–126; problems in, 111–116; problems of administrators in, 124; public misconceptions about, 141; role of legislatures in, 125, 321; types of questions answered in, 113. *See also* Administrative rule-making

Discrimination (racial) in police agencies, 269–271

Dismissals, of administrators, value of, 153

Disorderly conduct: enforcement of statutes depends on context, 95; intent of legislation on, 30; vagueness of statutes on, 87

Diversion projects: defined, 75; legal problems of, 87–88. *See also* Referrals

Domestic disturbances: appropriateness of police responsibility for, 33; discretion in dealing with, 96–97; expectations of police programs, 82; family-crisis intervention projects, 77, 81, 84; frequency of police calls to handle, 76; need for alternatives to criminal justice system for dealing with, 74; need for marriage counselors, 84; need for specific limited authority, 86; policy-making efforts related to, 117; removal of firearms in, 82–83; training as crucial element of programs, 85

Drugs, wide range of police problems relating to, 87

Drunkenness, public: appropriateness of police responsibility for, 33; arrest for, 76, 80; decriminalization of requires alternative provisions, 32; detoxification programs, 79–81; policy-making efforts related to, 117; questions over new programs, 73; Wisconsin statute for dealing with, 84

Due process: conflict with crime-fighting function of police, 9; in discipline procedures, 265; responsibility of police for assuring, 13, 15

"Due process revolution," 157–158

Duplicity: atmosphere of, complicates control of police conduct, 163–164; atmosphere of, encourages corruption, 200

Dyson, Frank, 308

Eavesdropping, discretion in use of, 99, 103

Edell, Laura, 24

Education, police. *See* College education; Community colleges; In-service training; Recruit training; Universities

Education, public: to control corruption, 208; in crime prevention, 64–65; in needs of community for social services, 85; need for understanding of complexities of policing, 14, 253, 331

Efficiency, as one aspect of leadership, 226–227

Elected officials, traditional influence of on police, 132

Emotional stability, screening for, 271–272

England: accountability of police in, 141; appeals panel suggested in, 177; comparison of police with police in U.S., 168; Judges' Rules in, 114; lateral movement in, 240–241; London Metropolitan Police personnel assessment methods, 246; need to attract college graduates in, 286–287; police college at Bramshill, 239–241; problems in adapting their methods of developing leadership to police in the U.S., 240–241; relationship between national and local police in, 320; role of Home Office in, 320; system for producing police leaders, 239–240; White Paper on leadership, 240

Evanston, Ill.: city council policy-making in, 114; report on accountability for shooting by police, 137–138

Examinations: for admission at Bramshill, 240; attempts to measure performance, 262–263; grading of, 234–235; inadequacies of in promotion process, 232–234; job-relatedness of, 233–234; methods of making subjective techniques fair, 264; problems of objective, 263–264; problems of subjective, 264; validating, 245, 262–263

Exclusionary rule: failure of to change police practices, 31–32, 326; ineffective to review police conduct, 32; intent of, 31–32, 157–158; and violations of administrative rules, 123

Ex-convicts, surveillance of, 67–68

Experiential projects in recruit training, 277–278

Experimentation: commitment of Police Foundation to, 328; need for to cope with serious crime, 68; need for in in-service training, 279; reluctance of field to engage in, 8, 45–46

Expertise: ignored by supervisors, 261; in-service training to exploit, 279; need to document, 117–119; soliciting, 264–265; use of in designing alternatives to the criminal justice system, 82–83

External investigations of corruption, 215–217

Extortion, 200

Fabbri, John, 308

Family-crisis intervention. *See* Domestic disturbances

Family Crisis Intervention Project in New York City, 77, 81, 84

Fear of crime, 3, 47–48

✳

About the Author

Herman Goldstein is Professor of Criminal Justice Administration at the Law School, University of Wisconsin—Madison. His first experiences in working with the police were in Philadelphia as a graduate student in governmental administration at the University of Pennsylvania and, subsequently, as an assistant to the city manager of Portland, Maine. He spent two years observing the on-the-street operations of the police in Wisconsin and Michigan as a researcher with the American Bar Foundation's Survey of the Administration of Criminal Justice, and then participated in the analysis phase of that project. From 1960 to 1964, he was executive assistant to O. W. Wilson when Wilson served as superintendent of the Chicago Police Department. Since joining the Wisconsin faculty, he has published widely on such topics as the police function, police discretion, the political accountability of the police, and the control of police conduct. He is co-author of the American Bar Association's *The Urban Police Function* (1973). Professor Goldstein has been a consultant to numerous national and local groups, including the President's Commission on Law Enforcement and Administration of Justice, the National Advisory Commission on Civil Disorders, the National Institute of Law Enforcement and Criminal Justice, the Police Foundation, and New York City's Knapp Commission.